Date Due		
Jan 4 '51		
Dec 14 '51		
Nov 30 '53		
Jan 6 '54		
Oct 18 '54		
LIBRARY		
Jan 4 '55		
Jan 23 '57		
Apr 2 '57		
LIBRARY		
Apr 27 '57		
Jun 17 '58		
Mar 11 '60		
Mar 2 '62		
Jun 12 '66		

PAUL BECOMES
A LITERARY INFLUENCE

THE UNIVERSITY OF CHICAGO PRESS · CHICAGO

THE BAKER & TAYLOR COMPANY, NEW YORK; THE CAMBRIDGE UNIVERSITY
PRESS, LONDON; THE MARUZEN-KABUSHIKI-KAISHA, TOKYO, OSAKA,
KYOTO, FUKUOKA, SENDAI; THE COMMERCIAL PRESS, LIMITED, SHANGHAI

PAUL BECOMES
A LITERARY INFLUENCE

By

ALBERT E. BARNETT

PROFESSOR OF LITERATURE AND HISTORY OF THE BIBLE
SCARRITT COLLEGE FOR CHRISTIAN WORKERS

THE UNIVERSITY OF CHICAGO PRESS
CHICAGO · ILLINOIS

227
B25 p

19450

May 19 43

TO

THE MANY TEACHERS AND FELLOW-STUDENTS

WHO HAVE ENRICHED MY ACQUAINTANCE WITH THE NEW TESTAMENT

AMONG WHOM

I ACKNOWLEDGE ESPECIAL INDEBTEDNESS

TO

EDGAR JOHNSON GOODSPEED

AND THE LATE

ANDREW SLEDD

FOREWORD

No method in literary study is more objective or more
fruitful than the comparison of one work with another to determine the question of literary indebtedness—which one shows acquaintance with the other, use of it, and dependence upon it.
It is a matter of great importance, for example, that the Synoptic Gospels show no acquaintance with the letters of Paul, while
the Gospel of John shows acquaintance with no less than ten of
them; or that Clement of Rome reflects six Pauline letters in
his Letter to the Romans. But to seek out and collect in Greek
these reflections of Paul's letters in the Christian literature
that followed is a difficult and laborious undertaking, to which
few students of the New Testament are equal.

In my student days we resorted to a little book called
The New Testament in the Apostolic Fathers, which had a limited
usefulness, at least for Paul. It is important to know how far
these early Christian writers knew and used Paul; but, of course,
it is almost as important to know how far his letters were known
to other pre-Catholic writers after these Fathers, and far more
important to know what knowledge other New Testament writers had
of his letters.

These are the things Professor Barnett undertakes to as-
certain for us in his book. With great care and admirable skill
he has gathered the reflections of Paul's letters from the other
books of the New Testament, from the Apostolic Fathers, and the
early Apologists—in short from all that remains of pre-Catholic
Christian literature—and has exhibited these reflections in the
Greek text, so that any scholar can satisfy himself on the question of literary relationship.

The result is a book that is indispensable to any serious
literary study of the New Testament and early Christian literature, and also of the influence of Paul upon early Christian
thought. My own indebtedness to Dr. Barnett's work is consider-

able, as the frequent references to it in my <u>Introduction to the New Testament</u> sufficiently show.

It is good that New Testament study is now to have such a tool, an instrument of research, at its command, and I, for my part, am distinctly grateful to Dr. Barnett for having produced it, for it will set serious New Testament study a definite step forward on its way. For some time I have hoped for and urged its publication, knowing how useful it would be to me and to hundreds of others concerned with New Testament study, and I am now happy to be the first to welcome its appearance in print.

EDGAR J. GOODSPEED

Bel-Air, Los Angeles

PREFACE

Interest in the investigation which the present volume represents was stimulated by the suggestive proposals of Professor Edgar J. Goodspeed regarding the occasion and character of Ephesians.[1] The reluctance of many scholars to grant the plausibility of the proposals and the vigorous opposition of others indicated that a detailed examination of the relevant data was the prerequisite of their sound appraisal.

The primary purpose of the study is to trace the emergence of Paul as a literary influence in the early church. Paul lived the life of an active missionary, and his letters were the by-products of his career as an evangelist. In time, however, he became known to the church generally through his collected letters, and thereafter his influence upon the Christian movement was definitely literary in character. The precise location of the juncture at which Paul became a literary influence is a highly important phase of the story of the development of the New Testament, and it is the major task of the present volume.

The time area covered in the investigation is, roughly, the last decade of the first century and the first half of the second. The writings that were later to achieve canonicity had not attained the status of Scripture, nor had the sectarian controversies brought about the crystallization of a well-defined ecclesiasticism.

The literary sources of information are the Christian writings that originated during the period defined. They are the later books of the New Testament, the collection traditionally known as the Apostolic Fathers, except the Epistle to Diog-

---

[1] New Solutions of New Testament Problems (Chicago: University of Chicago Press, 1927); "The Place of Ephesians in the First Pauline Collection," Anglican Theological Review, XII (1930), 189-212; The Meaning of Ephesians (Chicago: University of Chicago Press, 1933); and An Introduction to the New Testament (Chicago: University of Chicago Press, 1937).

netus, and the writings known as the Early Apologists. These
writings are treated chronologically rather than by their traditional groupings because such a sequence contributes to a
clearer visualization of what took place.

In presenting the data that reflect acquaintance with
Paul's collected letters, the procedure is to quote the Greek
text of the writing under examination and to parallel it with
the passage or passages from the letters that seem to have been
in the writer's mind. Conclusions based on the examination are,
admittedly, somewhat subjective, and no claim is made for their
finality, taken separately. The general story they combine to
create, however, is well substantiated and can be confidently
accepted. The effort has been made to keep the examination of
data as objective as possible and to test conclusions by critical positions that are widely accepted.

The letters "A," "B," and "C" serve as symbols of evalua-
tion, indicating, respectively, the practical certainty, a high
degree of probability, and a reasonable degree of probability of
literary indebtedness on the part of the passages quoted. Resemblances that may possibly reflect literary acquaintance but
that are not so clearly of this character are noted by allusion
or are cited without quoting the text at the conclusion of each
document examined. They appear in the table of results under
the heading "unclassed."

Previous studies of similar character, such as may be
found scattered through commentaries or in the brief investigation of the Oxford Society of Historical Theology,[2] have been
too varied in viewpoint and too limited in extent. It is hoped
that New Testament study will be assisted by assembling the materials in a single volume and evaluating them with reference to
their meaning for the single interest that has been mentioned.

The text of all passages from the New Testament quoted
in this book is that of Westcott and Hort and is used by permission of the publishers, Macmillan and Company, Ltd., London.
Quotations from the Apostolic Fathers are from the edition by

---

[2]Oxford Society of Historical Theology, The New Testament
in the Apostolic Fathers (Oxford: Clarendon Press, 1905).

Kirsopp Lake in the "Loeb Classical Library" and are used with
the permission of the president and Fellows of Harvard College,
the owners of the "Loeb Classical Library." The text of passages from the Apologists is that employed by Professor Edgar
J. Goodspeed[3] and is used by permission of the publishers. Permission to quote the several texts is herewith gratefully acknowledged.

---

[3]_Die ältesten Apologeten_ (Göttingen: Vandenhoeck & Ruprecht, 1914).

TABLE OF CONTENTS

THE PUBLICATION OF PAUL'S LETTERS

The letters of Paul were originally addressed to local churches and dealt with the particular needs and problems of the groups addressed. They were entirely occasional in character. There was no thought on the part of author or recipients that these letters would in time be generally circulated, and certainly no thought that they would be accorded canonical status. The Old Testament in its Greek version was the Bible of the church, and it was regarded as embodying the Christian message when rightly understood.

It is true that in many instances the local groups to whom Paul's letters were addressed valued and preserved them. Appreciation of these letters must have increased after Paul's death; and it is not unlikely that there developed a practice of publicly reading a given letter on the anniversary of his death and on other special occasions. There is no evidence, however, that any of these letters circulated singly outside the immediate situation that originally received it.

The publication of Luke-Acts apparently aroused the church generally to a sense of indebtedness to Paul's missionary activity, and out of this grew a desire on the part of at least one discerning leader to let Paul speak to the church at large through his own letters. It is an impressive and significant fact that no extant Christian writing earlier than Luke-Acts evidences any acquaintance with Paul's letters, whereas for more than a quarter of a century after Luke-Acts appeared every Christian document involves reminiscences of a definitely literary character of acquaintance with these letters. Christian literature later than Luke-Acts is significantly different from that of an earlier day in that it so generally shows awareness of the circulation of Paul's letters as a collection.

Ephesians

The New Testament letter that bears the title ΠΡΟΣ
ΕΦΕΣΙΟΥΣ is more significantly a part of the story of the collection and publication of Paul's letters than Luke-Acts. It was a
member of the collection itself from its first appearance,[1] and
yet it was not written by Paul. Its inclusion in the first corpus of the letters can mean only that it represents the earliest
literary testimony to the origin and existence of the collection.

The encyclical character of Ephesians has always made it
difficult to identify the situation that occasioned it.[2] It is
unimaginable, however, that such a document could have been written without definite purpose and with no motive more urgent than
the personal satisfaction of its author.[3] The encyclical character of Ephesians, together with its distinctive emphases, places
it outside the area of Paul's career and makes it equally unsat-
isfactory to attribute it to a hypothetical Paulinist writing in
the eighties.[4]

The understanding of the available data that leaves the
fewest questions unanswered and that clothes Ephesians with in-
telligibility is that the publication of Luke-Acts occasioned the
collection of Paul's letters and that Ephesians was written as a
sort of preface for the published corpus.[5] This view of the origin of Ephesians explains its encyclical character. An encyclical would be a normal way of bringing the collected letters of
Paul to the attention of Christians everywhere, however artificial

---

[1] B. H. Streeter, The Four Gospels[5] (London: Macmillan &
Co., Ltd., 1936).

[2] "Eine klare Vorstellung ueber die Situation, in der ein
Paulus redivivus den Eph. verfasst hat, ist bisher nicht beschaffen
worden" (A. Juelicher, Einleitung in das Neue Testament [5] u. [6]
[Tübingen, 1906], p. 127).

[3] E. F. Scott, The Epistles of Paul to the Colossians, to
Philemon, and to the Ephesians (New York: Richard R. Smith, Inc.,
1930), p. 123.

[4] James Moffatt, An Introduction to the Literature of the
New Testament[4] (New York: Charles Scribner's Sons, 1927), p. 395.

[5] E. J. Goodspeed, The Meaning of Ephesians (Chicago: University of Chicago Press, 1933).

it would have been for Paul himself or for a Paulinist in the eighties writing before Paul had become known to the church pre-eminently as a writer of letters.

Furthermore, such a view of Ephesians provides an adequate occasion for the letter. It places Ephesians in the last decade of the first century and thus makes intelligible its agreement in mood and outlook with Hebrews, the Apocalypse of John, and I Peter. It serves also to accentuate and illustrate the interest in unity that is so prominent in the letter.

The literary indebtedness of Ephesians to Paul's letters is impressive. Its author seems to have been saturated with the ideas and language of the letters. The distinctive positions assumed and the outlook reflected are not attributable to Paul, and yet they are largely expressed in Pauline terminology. The most extensive indebtedness is to Colossians, but the use made of the other letters is hardly less striking. Goodspeed understates the case when he says that the author of Ephesians "does little more than pay his respects to the other letters of Paul."[6]

The author's method in the use of his sources is illustrated by his allusions to the Old Testament. He makes use of materials from the Old Testament in sixteen instances, all of which are brief and some of which consist of a single phrase. They are not formally introduced but are woven into the author's own statements with no suggestion of conscious literary indebtedness. A formula of citation is used in two instances[7]—in the one case to introduce a quotation from Ps. 68:18 and in the other to quote a stanza from what may have been a Christian hymn. The formula in the two instances is διὸ λέγει.

There are no direct quotations of Paul's letters in Ephesians. There is, however, a rather clear reference to Paul as a writer of letters in Eph. 3:3. There is also a plea that Paul's message be heard, presumably as embodied in his collected letters, in Eph. 6:18-20.

It is the plan of this book to abbreviate discussion in

---

[6]"The Place of Ephesians in the First Pauline Collection," _Anglican Theological Review_, XII (1930), 193.

[7]Eph. 4:8 and 5:14.

the interest of a more elaborate display of the literary data.
How well the critical conclusions that have been briefly sketched
are supported by evidence may be judged from the following con-
spectus:

Eph. 1:1,2   Colossians B

Παῦλος ἀπόστολος Χριστοῦ Ιησοῦ διὰ θελήματος Θεοῦ τοῖς
ἁγίοις τοῖς οὖσιν καὶ πιστοῖς ἐν Χριστῷ Ιησοῦ· Χάρις ὑμῖν καὶ
εἰρήνη ἀπὸ Θεοῦ πατρὸς ἡμῶν καὶ κυρίου Ιησοῦ Χριστοῦ.

Col. 1:1, 2. Παῦλος ἀπόστολος Χριστοῦ 'Ιησοῦ διὰ θελήματος
Θεοῦ . . . . τοῖς ἐν Κολοσσαῖς ἁγίοις καὶ πιστοῖς ἀδελφοῖς ἐν
Χριστῷ· Χάρις ὑμῖν καὶ εἰρήνη ἀπὸ Θεοῦ πατρὸς ἡμῶν.

The resemblance to Colossians is sufficiently close to
make dependence probable. Colossians has ἐν Χριστῷ instead of ἐν
Χριστῷ 'Ιησοῦ and lacks καὶ κυρίου 'Ιησοῦ Χριστοῦ. In the addition of this latter phrase Ephesians agrees with Rom. 1:7, I Cor.
1:3, II Cor. 1:2, Gal. 1:3, Phil. 1:2, and Philem. 3, so that in
no instance can dependence on the part of Ephesians be predicated.

The verbatim agreement in the first line of II Cor. 1:1
with that of Eph. 1:1 and the τοῖς ἁγίοις · · · · τοῖς οὖσιν
makes the influence of II Corinthians a possibility.

Eph. 1:3   II Corinthians B

Εὐλογητὸς ὁ Θεὸς καὶ πατὴρ τοῦ κυρίου ἡμῶν 'Ιησοῦ Χριστοῦ,
ὁ εὐλογήσας ἡμᾶς ἐν πάσῃ εὐλογίᾳ πνευματικῇ.

II Cor. 1:3. Εὐλογητὸς ὁ Θεὸς καὶ πατὴρ τοῦ κυρίου ἡμῶν
'Ιησοῦ Χριστοῦ, ὁ πατὴρ τῶν οἰκτιρμῶν καὶ Θεὸς πάσης παρακλήσεως
(cf. Rom. 1:8; I Cor. 1:4).

The opening sentences of Ephesians and II Corinthians are
the same, and the succeeding clauses embody equivalent ideas.
This close resemblance warrants the statement of H. J. Holtzman:
"Namentlich ist es der Eingang des zweiten Korintherbriefes,
welcher ihm von Anfang an vorschwebt."[8]

_____

[8]**Kritik der Epheser und Kolosserbrief** (Leipzig: W. Engle-
man, 1872), p. 133.

Eph. 1:4   Colossians B

Εἶναι ἡμᾶς ἁγίους καὶ ἀμώμους κατενώπιον αὐτοῦ ἐν ἀγάπῃ
(5:27. Ἵνα ᾖ ἁγία καὶ ἄμωμος).

Col. 1:22. Παραστῆσαι ὑμᾶς ἁγίους καὶ ἀμώμους καὶ ἀνεγ-
κλήτους κατενώπιον αὐτοῦ.

The verbal agreement of the descriptive phrases makes
literary dependence highly probable.   Only in Ephesians and Colossians in the New Testament are ἅγιος and ἄμωμος used together in
a phrase.

Eph. 1:5   Romans A

Προορίσας ἡμᾶς εἰς υἱοθεσίαν διὰ Ἰησοῦ Χριστοῦ εἰς αὐτόν.

Rom. 8:29. Ὅτι οὓς προέγνω, καὶ προώρισεν συμμόρφους τῆς
εἰκόνος τοῦ υἱοῦ αὐτοῦ. . . . . 15. Ἀλλὰ ἐλάβετε πνεῦμα υἱοθεσίας.
. . . . 23. Υἱοθεσίαν ἀπεκδεχόμενοι. . . . . 9:4. Ὧν ἡ υἱοθεσία
(cf. Gal. 4:5).

The use of υἱοθεσία in the New Testament is confined to
the passages cited.   The comparative frequency of its occurrence
in Romans and its use in connection with προορίζω makes dependence
on Romans a matter of practical certainty.   The possible influence
of Gal. 4:5 is admitted but cannot be pressed.   There is no parallel in Colossians.

Eph. 1:7   Colossians A

Εν τῷ ἠγαπημένῳ, ἐν ᾧ ἔχομεν τὴν ἀπολύτρωσιν διὰ τοῦ
αἵματος αὐτοῦ, τὴν ἄφεσιν τῶν παραπτωμάτων.

Col. 1:14. Τοῦ υἱοῦ τῆς ἀγάπης αὐτοῦ, ἐν ᾧ ἔχομεν τὴν
ἀπολύτρωσιν, τὴν ἄφεσιν τῶν ἁμαρτιῶν·

The phrase ἐν τῷ ἠγαπημένῳ of Ephesians is not used elsewhere of Christ in the New Testament (cf. Hos. 2:25), but it has
an equivalent in τοῦ υἱοῦ τῆς ἀγάπης αὐτοῦ of Colossians.   Except
for the variation in these phrases, the addition of διὰ τοῦ
αἵματος αὐτοῦ, and the use of παραπτωμάτων instead of ἁμαρτιῶν,
Ephesians follows Colossians exactly.

The use of ἀπολύτρωσις in close connection with the idea
of sacrifice for sin may show acquaintance with Rom. 3:24, 25;
11:26, 27.

Eph. 1:8   Colossians C
Ἐν πάσῃ σοφίᾳ καὶ φρονήσει.
Col. 1:9. Ἐν πάσῃ σοφίᾳ καὶ συνέσει πνευματικῇ.

The contexts of these phrases increase the probability of
literary dependence.

Eph. 1:9   Colossians C
Γνωρίσας ἡμῖν τὸ μυστήριον τοῦ θελήματος αὐτοῦ.
Col. 1:26, 27. Τὸ μυστήριον τὸ ἀποκεκρυμμένον ἀπὸ τῶν
αἰώνιν . . . . ἠθέλησεν ὁ·Θεὸς γνωρίσαι τί τὸ πλοῦτος τῆς δόξης
τοῦ μυστηρίου τούτου. . . . . 2:2. Εἰς ἐπίγνωσιν τοῦ μυστηρίου
τοῦ Θεοῦ.

Eph. 1:10   Romans C
Ἣν προέθετο ἐν αὐτῷ.
Rom. 8:28. Τοῖς κατὰ πρόθεσιν κλητοῖς οὖσιν . . . . 9:11.
Ἵνα ἡ κατ᾽ ἐκλογὴν πρόθεσις τοῦ Θεοῦ μένῃ (cf. II Tim. 1:9 for only
occurrence of the usage outside of Romans and Ephesians).

The idea of πρόθεσις in 1:10 (cf. 1:11, 3:11) agrees so
closely with that of Rom. 8:28 and 9:11 as to suggest dependence.

Eph. 1:10   Colossians B   Romans C
Ἀνακεφαλιώσασθαι τὰ πάντα ἐν τῷ Χριστῷ, τὰ ἐπὶ τοῖς
οὐρανοῖς καὶ τὰ ἐπὶ τῆς γῆς·
Col. 1:20. Καὶ δι᾽ αὐτοῦ ἀποκαταλλάξαι τὰ πάντα εἰς
αὐτόν, εἰρηνοποιήσας διὰ τοῦ αἵματος τοῦ σταυροῦ αὐτοῦ, [δι᾽
αὐτοῦ] εἴτε τὰ ἐπὶ τῆς γῆς εἴτε τὰ ἐν τοῖς οὐρανοῖς·
Rom. 13:9. Ἐν ⌜τῷ λόγῳ τούτῳ⌝ ἀνακεφαλαιοῦται.

The verb ἀνακεφαλαιόομαι is used in the New Testament only
in Rom. 13:9 and Eph. 1:10. It is not a LXX word. The basic dependence of Eph. 1:10 is clearly on Colossians.

Eph. 1:11   Romans C
Ἐν αὐτῷ, ἐν ᾧ καὶ ἐκληρώθημεν προορισθέντες κατὰ πρόθεσιν
τοῦ τὰ πάντα ἐνεργοῦντος κατὰ τὴν βουλὴν τοῦ θελήματος αὐτοῦ
Rom. 8:28-30. Τοῖς κατὰ πρόθεσιν κλητοῖς οὖσιν. ὅτι οὓς
προέγνω, καὶ προώρισεν συμμόρφους τῆς εἰκόνος τοῦ υἱοῦ αὐτοῦ,
εἰς τὸ εἶναι αὐτὸν πρωτότοκον ἐν πολλοῖς ἀδελφοῖς· οὓς δὲ προώρισεν, ·τούους καὶ ἐκάλεσεν·

Eph. 1:13   Colossians C

Τὸν λόγον τῆς ἀληθείας.

Col. 1:5. Εν τῷ λόγῳ τῆς ἀληθείας   (cf. II Cor. 6:7;
Jas. 1:18).

Eph. 1:13, 14   II Corinthians B   Galatians C

Ἐν ᾧ καὶ πιστεύσαντες ἐσφραγίσθητε τῷ πνεύματι τῆς ἐπαγγελίας τῷ ἁγίῳ, ὅ ἐστιν ἀρραβὼν τῆς κληρονομίας ἡμῶν, εἰς ἀπολύτρωσιν τῆς περιποιήσεως.

Gal. 3:14. Ἵνα τὴν ἐπαγγελίαν τοῦ πνεύματος λάβωμεν διὰ
τῆς πίστεως

II Cor. 1:20. Ὅσαι γὰρ ἐπαγγελίαι Θεοῦ. . . . . 1:22.
Ὁ καὶ σφραγισάμενος ἡμᾶς καὶ δοὺς τὸν ἀρραβῶνα τοῦ πνεύματος ἐν
ταῖς καρδίαις ἡμῶν. 5:5. Ὁ δοὺς ἡμῖν τὸν ἀρραβῶνα τοῦ πνεύματος (cf. Acts 2:33).

The use of ἐπαγγελία in the New Testament is confined to
the Pauline letters, Luke-Acts, and the writings that are later
than Luke-Acts (e.g., Ephesians four times, Hebrews fourteen
times, I Timothy once, II Timothy once, II Peter twice, and I
John once). The word occurs six times in the LXX. Its use in
connection with the Spirit is restricted in the New Testament to
Luke-Acts, the Pauline letters, and Ephesians. The possibility
of the influence of Acts on Eph. 1:13, 14 is admitted, but more
probably the indebtedness is to Galatians and II Corinthians.
Ἀρραβών is used in the New Testament only in II Cor. 1:22, 5:5,
and Eph. 1:14. The use of II Corinthians by Ephesians is somewhat clearer than of Galatians, but both of the Pauline passages
were probably known to the later writer. The thought of the passage resembles that of Rom. 8:22, but there are no indications of
literary dependence in that direction.

Eph. 1:15-17   Colossians B   Philemon B

Διὰ τοῦτο κἀγω, ἀκούσας τὴν καθ' ὑμᾶς πίστιν ἐν τῷ κυρίῳ
Ἰησοῦ καὶ τὴν εἰς πάντας τοὺς ἁγίους, οὐ παύομαι εὐχαριστῶν ὑπερ
ὑμῶν μνείαν ποιούμενος ἐπὶ τῶν προσευχῶν μου, ἵνα ὁ Θεὸς τοῦ κυρίου
ἡμῶν Ἰησοῦ Χριστοῦ, ὁ πατὴρ τῆς δόξης, δῴη ὑμῖν πνεῦμα σοφίας
καὶ ἀποκαλύψεως ἐν ἐπιγνώσει αὐτοῦ.

Col. 1:3, 4, 9. Εὐχαριστοῦμεν τῷ Θεῷ πατρὶ τοῦ κυρίου

ἡμῶν Ἰησοῦ [Χριστοῦ] πάντοτε περὶ ὑμῶν προσευχόμενοι, ἀκούσαντες τὴν πίστιν ὑμῶν ἐν Χριστῷ Ἰησοῦ καὶ τὴν ἀγάπην [ἣν ἔχετε] εἰς πάντας τοὺς ἁγίους. . . . . Διὰ τοῦτο καὶ ἡμεῖς, ἀφ' ἧς ἡμέρας ἠκούσαμεν, οὐ παυόμεθα ὑπὲρ ὑμῶν προσευχόμενοι καὶ αἰτούμενοι ἵνα πληρωθῆτε τὴν ἐπίγνωσιν τοῦ θελήματος αὐτοῦ ἐν πάσῃ σοφίᾳ καὶ συνέσει πνευματικῇ.

Philem. 4, 5. Εὐχαριστῶ τῷ Θεῷ μου πάντοτε μνείαν σου ποιούμενος ἐπὶ τῶν πρρσευχῶν μου, ἀκούων σου τὴν ἀγάπην καὶ τὴν πίστιν ἣν ἔχεις εἰς τὸν κύριον Ἰησοῦν καὶ εἰς πάντας τοὺς ἁγίους.

In Eph. 1:15 ℵ^{c} D G ω Syr hl Gothic Chr Theod-Mops 1 at Victorin Ambst read ἀγάπην after καὶ τήν. ℵ* A B P 33 boh Orig Cyr Hier Aug omit ἀγάπην. The evidence clearly favors the omission.

If ἀγάπην is retained in the text, Eph. 1:15 finds its best parallel in Col. 1:3, 4, 9. If it is omitted in accordance with the best textual evidence, the verse becomes an exhortation to mutual confidence with πίστιν understood after καὶ τήν. In the latter case Philem. 4, 5 becomes the closer parallel and a probable source of influence.

In Eph. 1:16, 17 the thought and language correspond closely with that of Col. 1:3, 9. There is also a marked resemblance of verse 16 to Phil. 1:3, 4; but the content of the verse is sufficiently accounted for from other sources, so that there is little reason for the predication of dependence on Philippians here.

The designation of God as ὁ πατὴρ τῆς δόξης in Eph. 1:17 has an analogy in πατὴρ τῶν οἰκτιρμῶν in II Cor. 1:3 (cf. Jas. 2:1. ὁ Χριστὸς τῆς δόξης), but the case does not involve any necessary literary indebtedness.

Eph. 1:18   II Corinthians B
Πεφωτισμένους τοὺς ὀφθαλμούς τῆς καρδίας [ὑμῶν].

II Cor. 4:4, 6. Ἐν οἷς ὁ Θεὸς τοῦ αἰῶνας τούτου ἐτύφλωσεν τὰ νοήματα τῶν ἀπίστων εἰς τὸ μὴ αὐγάσαι τὸν φωτισμὸν τοῦ εὐαγγελίου . . . . ὅτι ὁ Θεὸς ὁ εἰπών Ἐκ σκότους φῶς λάμψει, ὃς ἔλαμψεν ἐν ταῖς καρδίαις ἡμῶν πρὸς φωτισμὸν τῆς γνώσεως τῆς δόξης τοῦ Θεοῦ ἐν προσώπῳ Χριστοῦ (cf. Rom. 1:21).

Φωτίζω is used in the New Testament in Luke 11:36; John 1:9; I Cor. 4:5; Eph. 1:18, 3:9; Heb. 6:4; II Tim. 1:10; and Apoc. 18:1,

21:23, 22:5. Of these, the usage in John 1:9 most closely resembles that of Ephesians, but such literary indebtedness as might
be predicated in this case would be on the part of John.

The noun φωτισμός is used in the New Testament in II Cor.
4:4, 6, and these verses furnish a thought parallel so close as to
create a high degree of probability of their direct influence on
Eph. 1:18.

Eph. 1:18   Colossians C

Εἰς τὸ εἰδέναι ὑμᾶς τίς ἐστιν ἡ ἐλπὶς τῆς κλήσεως αὐτοῦ, τίς
ὁ πλοῦτος τῆς δόξης τῆς κληρονομίας αὐτοῦ ἐν τοῖς ἁγίοις.

Col. 1:27. Νῦν δὲ ἐφανερώθη τοῖς ἁγίοις αὐτοῦ, οἷς ἠθέλησεν ὁ θεὸς γνωρίσαι τί τὸ πλοῦτος τῆς δόξης τοῦ μυστηρίου τούτου
ἐν τοῖς ἔθνεσιν, ὅ ἐστιν Χριστὸς ἐν ὑμῖν, ἡ ἐλπὶς τῆς δόξης.

Eph. 1:18 seems to be a re-working of the material of Col.
1:27 for the development of a somewhat different idea. The central theme of both passages seems to be ἡ ἐλπίς, defined, on the
one hand, as ἡ ἐλπὶς τῆς κλήσεως αὐτοῦ and, on the other, as ὅ
ἐστιν Χριστὸς ἐν ὑμῖν. In each instance that which is made known
is God's intention for "the saints." In Ephesians, however, the
"inheritance" is described as God's, and the community of believers
is the sphere of this κληρονομία. In Colossians the "saints" possess Christ inwardly, and this possession is the basis of their
confidence. There is a close verbal parallel in the phrases τίς
ὁ πλοῦτος τῆς δόξης and τί τὸ πλοῦτος τῆς δόξης but the conclusions of the phrases diverge in language and idea.

Eph. 1:19, 20   Colossians A   II Corinthians C

Καὶ τί τὸ ὑπερβάλλον μέγεθος τῆς δυνάμεως αὐτοῦ εἰς ἡμᾶς
τοὺς πιστεύοντας κατὰ τὴν ἐνέργειαν τοῦ κράτους τῆς ἰσχύος αὐτοῦ
ἣν ⌜ἐνήργηκεν⌝ ἐν τῷ Χριστῷ ἐγείρας αὐτὸν ἐκ νεκρῶν.

Col. 2:12. Ἐν ᾧ καὶ συνηγέρθητε διὰ τῆς πίστεως τῆς ἐνερ-
γείας τοῦ θεοῦ τοῦ ἐγείραντος αὐτὸν ἐκ νεκρῶν· (cf. Phil. 3:10, 21).

II Cor. 3:10. Εἵνεκεν τῆς ὑπερβαλλούσης δόξης· . . . . .
9:14. Διὰ τὴν ὑπερβάλλουσαν χάριν τοῦ θεοῦ ἐφ' ὑμῖν.

The ideas of Eph. 1:19, 20, and Col. 2:12 are the same,
namely, the greatness of God's power as demonstrated in the raising of Jesus and the availability of that same power for the

raising of men who exercise faith.   The wording and phrasing of
the passages are quite similar.

There is also a general resemblance of Eph. 1:19, 20 to
Phil. 3:10, 21.   The latter, however, presents no element that
might not have been drawn from Colossians.

The use of ὑπερβάλλω is confined in the New Testament to
II Corinthians and Ephesians.   The instances of its occurrence
are II Cor. 3:10, 9:14, and Eph 1:19, 2:7, 3:19.   The author of
Ephesians knew II Corinthians and his use of this verb is a probable reminiscence of that acquaintance.

Eph. 1:20-23   Colossians B   Philippians C   I Corinthians C

Καὶ καθίσας ἐν δεξιᾷ αὐτοῦ ἐν τοῖς ἐπουρανίοις ὑπεράνω
πάσης ἀρχῆς καὶ ἐξουσίας καὶ δυνάμεως καὶ κυριότητος καὶ παντὸς
ὀνόματος ὀνομαζομένου οὐ μόνον ἐν τῷ αἰῶνι τούτῳ ἀλλὰ καὶ ἐν τῷ
μέλλοντι· καὶ πάντα ὑπέταξεν ὑπὸ τοὺς πόδας αὐτοῦ, καὶ αὐτὸν
ἔδωκεν κεφαλὴν ὑπὲρ πάντα τῇ ἐκκλησίᾳ, ἥτις ἐστιν τὸ σῶμα αὐτοῦ,
τὸ πλήρωμα τοῦ τὰ ράντα ἐν πᾶσιν πληρουμένου.

The exalted place and creative function of the pre-existent
Christ is the theme of Col. 1:16-19 (cf. Col. 3:1), whereas in
Eph. 1:20-23 the thought is of the exaltation of Christ after the
Resurrection.   Nevertheless, the author of Ephesians has very
clearly used material from Colossians as the following parallels
show:

Ephesians	Colossians
21. Ὑπεράνω πάσης ἀρχῆς καὶ ἐξουσίας καὶ δυνάμεως καὶ κυριότητος	16. Εἴτε κυριότητες εἴτε ἀρχαὶ εἴτε ἐξουσίαι
22, 23. Καὶ αὐτὸν ἔδωκεν κεφαλὴν ὑπὲρ πάντα τῇ ἐκ- κλησίᾳ ἥτις ἐστιν τὸ σῶμα αὐτοῦ, τὸ πλήρωμα τοῦ τὰ πάντα ἐν πᾶσιν πληρουμένου	18, 19. Καὶ αὐτός ἐστιν ἡ κεφαλὴ τοῦ σώματος, τῆς ἐκκλησίας . . . . ὅτι ἐν αὐτῷ εὐδόκησεν πᾶν τὸ᾽ πλήρωμα κατοικῆσαι

The only occurrences of κυριότης in the New Testament are
Col. 1:16, Eph. 1:21, II Pet. 2:10, and Jude 8, so that Ephesians
would naturally have drawn the term from Colossians.   It is not a
LXX word.

Eph. 1:20 and Col. 3:1 both employ the conceptions of Ps.
110:1 in indicating Christ's present position in heaven. Ephesians
and Phil. 2:9 resemble in general theme—the exaltation of the
risen Christ. The likelihood of indebtedness to Philippians on
the part of Ephesians is increased by the following parallel:

Ephesians	Philippians
20. Ὑπεράνω . . . . παντὸς ὀνόματος ὀνομαζομένου	9. Καὶ ἐχαρίσατο αὐτῷ τὸ ὄνομα τὸ ὄνομα τὸ ὑπὲρ πᾶν ὄνομα

There is a similar resemblance in theme with I Cor. 15:20-
29. But beyond this general point of contact there are the following specific parallels:

Ephesians	I Corinthians
20. Ὑπεράνω πάσης ἀρχῆς καὶ ἐξουσίας καὶ δυνάμεως	24. Ὅταν καταργήσῃ πᾶσαν ἀρχὴν καὶ πᾶσαν ἐξουσίαν καὶ δύναμιν
22. Καὶ πάντα ὑπέταξεν ὑπὸ τοὺς πόδας αὐτοῦ	27. Πάντα γὰρ ὑπέταξεν ὑπὸ τοὺς πόδας αὐτοῦ
23. Τὰ πάντα ἐν πᾶσιν	28. Ἵνα ᾖ· ὁ Θεὸς πάντα ἐν πᾶσιν

The second parallel of this series of three comes ultimately from
Ps. 8:6, and Ephesians was not necessarily indebted to I Corinthians for it. The quotation is similarly used also in Heb. 2:8,
but if Ephesians depends on any secondary source all the probabilities would favor I Corinthians. The agreement in the idea of the
resurrection of Jesus, the reference to the supernatural beings,
the thought of the universal subjection of everything under Christ's
feet, and the concluding emphasis represented in τὰ πάντα ἐν πᾶσιν,
when taken together, carry the strong probability of dependence on
I Corinthians.

Eph. 2:2, 3   Colossians B
'Ἐν αἷς ποτὲ περιεπατήσατε . . . . ἐν οἷς καὶ ἡμεῖς
πάντες ἀνεστράφημέν ποτε.
        Col. 3:7. Ἐν οἷς καὶ ὑμεῖς περιεπατήσατέ ποτε ὅτε ἐζῆτε
ἐν τούτοις·

Eph. 2:2   II Thessalonians B
Κατὰ τὸν αἰῶνα τοῦ κόσμου τούτου, κατὰ τὸν αρχοντα τῆς

ἐξουσίας τοῦ ἀέρος, τοῦ πνεύματος τοῦ νῦν ἐνεργοῦντος ἐν τοῖς
υἱοῖς τῆς ἀπειθίας·

II Thess. 2:3. ῞Οτι ἐὰν μὴ ἔλθη ἡ ἀποστασία πρῶτον καὶ
ἀποκαλυφθῇ ὁ ἄνθρωπος τῆς ἀνομίας, ... 7. Τὸ γὰρ μυστήριον
ἤδη ἐνεργεῖται τῆς ἀνομίας· μόνον ὁ κατέχων ἄρτι ἕως ἐκ μέσου
γένηται. καὶ τότε ἀποκαλυφθήσεται ὁ ἄνομος.

Ephesians may reflect merely a general acquaintance with
Pauline demonology (cf. Rom. 8:35-39; Phil. 2:9; Col. 1:16, 2:10).
The allusion to "the master-spirit of the air, who is still at
work among the disobedient" finds, however, a strikingly clear
parallel in II Thess. 2:3-10.

| Eph. 2:5, 6 | Colossians A |

Καὶ ὄντας ἡμᾶς νεκροὺς τοῖς παραπτώμασιν συνεζωοποίησεν
τῷ Χριστῷ . . . . καὶ συνήγειρεν.

Col. 2:13. Καὶ ὑμᾶς νεκροὺς ὄντας τοῖς παραπτώμασιν . . . .
συνεζωοποίησεν ὑμᾶς σὺν αὐτῷ. . . . 2 12. ᾽Εν ᾧ καὶ συνηγέρθητε.

| Eph. 2:6 | Romans C |

Καὶ συνήγειρεν καὶ συνεκάθισεν ἐν τοῖς ἐπουρανίοις ἐν
Χριστῷ ᾽Ιησοῦ.

Rom. 6:5. Εἰ γὰρ σύμφυτοι γεγόναμεν τῷ ὁμοιώματι τοῦ
θανάτου αὐτοῦ, ἀλλὰ καὶ τῆς ἀναστάσεως ἐσόμεθα. . . . . 8. Εἰ
δὲ ἀπεθάνομεν σὺν Χριστῷ, πιστεύομεν ὅτι καὶ συνζήσομεν αὐτῷ.
. . . . 11. Ζῶντας δὲ τῷ θεῷ ἐν Χριστῷ ᾽Ιησοῦ (cf. Phil. 3:20).

Eph. 2:6 and Rom. 6:5-11 (cf. Rom. 8:10, 11) both express
the expectation of salvation through union with Christ. The author of Ephesians would naturally be indebted to the Pauline letters for this conception, and he would in all probability owe his
use of it to some such statement as Rom. 6:5-11 supplies. The ἐν
τοῖς ἐπουρανίοις may be an echo of the related conception of Phil.
3:20 (cf. II Cor. 5:1).

| Eph. 2:7 | Romans C |

Τὸ ὑπερβάλλον πλοῦτος τῆς χάριτος αὐτοῦ ἐν χρηστότητι ἐφ᾽
ἡμᾶς ἐν Χριστῷ ᾽Ιησοῦ.

Rom. 2:4. ῾Η τοῦ πλούτου τῆς χρηστότητος αὐτοῦ . . . .
καταφρονεῖς.·

The use of χρηστότης in the New Testament is confined to the letters of the Pauline and secondary-Pauline groups. Its use in Rom. 2:4 in association with πλοῦτος is closely parallel in Eph. 2:7. The term is used seventeen times in the LXX.

Eph. 2:8   Romans C

Τῇ γὰρ χάριτί ἐστε σεσωμένοι διὰ πίστεως.
Rom. 4:16. Διὰ τοῦτο ἐκ πίστεως, ἵνα κατὰ χάριν.

Only in these two passages in the New Testament are πίστις and χάρις used together to express the present thought. The phrase διὰ πίστεως is distinctively Pauline and most of its occurrences are in Romans.

Eph. 2:8   Romans B

Τῇ γὰρ χάριτί ἐστε σεσωμένοι . . . . καὶ τοῦτο οὐκ ἐξ ὑμῶν, Θεοῦ τὸ δῶρον·

Rom. 3:24. Δικαιούμενοι δωρεὰν τῇ αὐτοῦ χάριτι
9:16 ἄρα οὖν οὐ τοῦ θέλοντος οὐδὲ τοῦ τρέχοντος, ἀλλὰ τοῦ ἐλεῶντος Θεοῦ (cf. Gal. 2:16).

Only in Eph. 2:8 in the New Testament is δῶρον used of the divine gift of salvation to men. The adverbial use of δωρεάν in Rom. 3:24 carries a meaning that is substantially the same as that of Eph. 2:8, and the term is used in this sense only in Romans in the New Testament (cf. Apoc. 21:17). Because of the similarity of thought and the close association of δῶρον(or δωρεάν) with χάρις it is probable that Rom. 3:24 influenced Ephesians.

Eph. 2:9   I Corinthians B

Ουκ ἐξ ἔργων, ἵνα μή τις καυχήσηται.

I Cor. 1:29. ῞Οπως μὴ καυχήσηται πᾶσα σάρξ ἐνώπιον τοῦ Θεοῦ.

The verb καυχάομαι is used forty-one times in the New Testament. Two of its occurrences are in James (1:9, 4:16), one is in Ephesians (2:9), and the remaining thirty-eight are in the nine Pauline letters. The similarity of the contexts in I Cor. 1:29 and Eph. 2:9 makes literary dependence of the latter on the former highly probable. The verb occurs thirty-three times in the LXX.

Eph. 2:10   II Corinthians B   Colossians C

Αὐτοῦ γάρ ἐσμεν ποίημα, κτισθέντες ἐν Χριστῷ Ἰησοῦ ἐπὶ ἔργοις ἀγαθοῖς . . . . ἵνα εν αὐτοῖς περιπατήσωμεν.

II Cor. 5:17. Ὥστε εἴ τις ἐν Χριστῷ, καινὴ κτίσις (cf. Gal. 6:15).

Col. 1:10. Περιπατῆσαι ἀξίως τοῦ κυρίου . . . . ἐν παντὶ ἔργῳ ἀγαθῷ.

The creative significance of being ἐν Χριστῷ represents an emphasis which Ephesians very probably drew from II Corinthians. The περιπατήσωμεν, referring as it does to ἐπὶ ἔργοις ἀγαθοῖς, probably represents a reminiscence of Col. 1:10.

Eph. 2:11   Colossians B   Romans B

Διὸ μνημονεύετε ὅτι ποτὲ ὑμεῖς τὰ ἔθνη ἐν σαρκί, οἱ λεγόμενοι ἀκροβυστία ὑπὸ τῆς λεγομένης περιτομῆς ἐν σαρκὶ χειρο-ποιήτου.

Col. 2:11. Ἐν ᾧ καὶ περιετμήθητε περιτομῇ ἀχειροποιήτῳ ἐν τῇ ἀπεκδύσει τοῦ σώματος τῆς σαρκός, ἐν τῇ περιτομῇ τοῦ Χριστοῦ

Rom. 2:26-29. Ἐὰν οὖν ἡ ἀκροβυστία τὰ δικαιώματα τοῦ νόμου φυλάσσῃ, οὐχ ἡ ἀκροβυστία αὐτοῦ εἰς περιτομὴν λογισθήσεται; καὶ κρινεῖ ἡ ἐκ φύσεως ἀκροβυστία τὸν νόμον τελοῦσα σὲ τὸν διὰ γράμματος καὶ περιτομῆς παραβάτην νόμου. οὐ γὰρ ὁ ἐν τῷ φανερῷ Ἰουδαῖός ἐστιν, οὐδὲ ἡ ἐν τῷ φανερῷ ἐν σαρκὶ περιτομή· ἀλλ' ὁ ἐν τῷ κρυπτῷ Ἰουδαῖος, καὶ περιτομὴ καρδίας ἐν πνεύματι οὐ γράμματι (cf. I Cor. 12:2 and Phil. 3:3).

The same essential contrast of physical with spiritual circumcision is involved in all the passages; but the terms employed make it clear that the indebtedness of Ephesians is to Colossians and Romans, with the possibility that there is a reminiscence of I Cor. 12:2.

The term ἀχειροποίητος is used three times in the New Testament (Mark 14:58, II Cor. 5:1, and Col. 2:11), but only in Colossians does it describe circumcision. Χειροποίητος is used six times (Mark 14:58, Acts 7:48, 17:24, Eph. 2:11, Heb. 9:11, 24) but only in Eph. 2:11 does it apply to circumcision.

Ακροβυστία is used in the New Testament twenty times as follows: Acts 11:3, Eph. 2:11, and the remaining eighteen times in the nine generally recognized letters of Paul. The phrase οἱ λεγόμενοι ἀκροβυστία is not found in Paul's letters, but it may easily have been suggested by οὐχ ἡ ἀκροβυστία αὐτοῦ εἰς περιτομὴν λογισθήσεται.

Eph. 2:12   Colossians B   Romans C

ὍΟτι ἦτε τῷ καιρῷ ἐκείνῳ χωρὶς Χριστοῦ, ἀπηλλοτριωμένοι τῆς πολιτείας τοῦ Ἰσραήλ καὶ ξένοι τῶν διαθηκῶν τῆς ἐπαγγελίας

Col. 1:21. Καὶ ὑμᾶς ποτὲ ὄντας ἀπηλλοτριωμένους

Rom. 9:4. Οἵτινες εἰσιν Ἰσραηλεῖται, ὧν . . . . αἱ διαθῆκαι . . . . καὶ αἱ ἐπαλλελίαι

The verb ἀπαλλοτριόομαι is used in the New Testament only three times (Col. 1:21 and Eph. 2:12, 4:18). It is highly probable that its use in Ephesians is directly due to its use in Colossians. The verb occurs eleven times in the LXX.

The similarity of the connection in which διαθήκη and ἐπαγγελία are used in Ephesians and Romans suggests the probability of literary dependence.

Eph. 2:14   Romans C

Αὐτὸς γάρ ἐστιν ἡ εἰρήνη (cf. 2:17).

Rom. 5:1,2. Εἰρήνην ἔχωμεν πρὸς τὸν Θεὸν διὰ τοῦ κυρίου ἡμῶν Ἰησοῦ Χριστοῦ, δι' οὖ καὶ τὴν προσαγωγὴν ἐσχήκαμεν [τῇ πίστει] εἰς τὴν χάριν ταύτην ἐν ᾗ ἐστήκαμεν (cf. Isa. 57:19).

Although the thought of Ephesians is primarily of the union of Jew and Gentile, the basic idea of peace with God through Christ is very probably present also.

Eph. 2:14, 15   Galatians C

Ὁ ποιήσας τὰ ἀμφότερα ἓν καὶ τὸ μεσότοιχον τοῦ φραγμοῦ λύσας.

Gal. 3:28. Οὐκ ἔνι Ἰουδαῖος οὐδὲ Ἕλλην, οὐκ ἔνι δοῦλος οὐδὲ ἐλεύθερος, οὐκ ἔνι ἄρσεν καὶ θῆλυ· πάντες γὰρ ὑμεῖς εἷς ἐστὲ ἐν Χριστῷ Ἰησοῦ.

The unity of Jew and Gentile in Christ is the theme common to the passages. The ὁ ποιήσας τὰ ἀμφότερα ἕν of Ephesians was probably suggested by πάντες γὰρ ὑμεῖς εἷς ἐστὲ ἐν Χρ:στῷ Ἰησοῦ.

Eph. 2:15-16   Colossians A

Τὴν ἔχθραν ἐν τῇ σαρκὶ αὐτοῦ, τὸν νόμον τῶν ἐντολῶν ἐν δόγμασιν, καταργήσας, ἵνα τοὺς δύο κτίσῃ ἐν αὐτῷ εἰς ἕνα καινὸν ἄνθρωπον ποιῶν εἰρήνην, καὶ ἀποκαταλλάξῃ τοὺς ἀμφοτέρους ἐν ἑνὶ σώματι τῷ θεῷ διὰ τοῦ σταυροῦ ἀποκτείνας τὴν ἔχθραν ἐν αὐτῷ· Col. 2:14. Ἐξαλείψας τὸ καθ' ἡμῶν χειρόγραφον τοῖς δόγμασιν ὃ ἦν ὑπεναντίον ἡμῖν. . . . . 1:20, 22. Καὶ δι' αὐτοῦ ἀποκαταλλάξαι τὰ πάντα εἰς αὐτόν, εἰρηνοποιήσας διὰ τοῦ αἵματος τοῦ σταυροῦ αὐτοῦ . . . . καὶ ἐχθροὺς . . . . νυνὶ δὲ ⌐ἀποκατήλλαξεν⌐ ἐν τῷ σώματι τῆς σαρκὸς αὐτοῦ διὰ τοῦ θανάτου.

Eph. 2:17   Romans A

Καὶ ἐλθὼν εὐηγγελίσατο εἰρήνη ὑμῖν τοῖς μακρὰν καὶ εἰρήνην τοῖς ἐγγύς. Ὅτι δι' αὐτοῦ ἔχομεν τὴν προσαγωγὴν οἱ ἀμφότεροι ἐν ἑνὶ πνεύματι πρὸς τὸν πατέρα.

Rom. 5:1, 2. See the text in the note on Eph. 2:14 (cf. Phil. 1:27).

The combination of the ideas of Christ as the giver of peace and the guarantor of access to God makes the indebtedness of Ephesians to Romans rather clear. Ὅτι δι' αὐτοῦ ἔχομεν τὴν προσαγωγήν . . . . πρὸς τὸν πατέρα is almost certainly an echo of δι' οὗ καὶ τὴν προσαγωγὴν ἐσχήκαμεν of Romans. The only occurrences of προσαγωγή in the New Testament are Rom. 5:2 and Eph. 2:18, 3:12. The word does not occur in the LXX.

Eph. 2:20-22   I Corinthians B

Ἐποικοδομηθέντες ἐπὶ τῷ θεμελίῳ τῶν ἀποστόλων καὶ προφητῶν, ὄντος ἀκρογωνιαίου αὐτοῦ Χριστοῦ Ἰησοῦ, ἐν ᾧ πᾶσα οἰκοδομὴ συναρμολογουμένη αὔξει εἰς ναὸν ἅγιον ἐν κυρίῳ, ἐν ᾧ καὶ ὑμεῖς συνοικοδομεῖσθε εἰς κατοικητήριον τοῦ Θεοῦ ἐν πνεύματι (cf. Col. 2:7).

I Cor. 3:9-12. Θεοῦ οἰκοδομή ἐστε. Κατὰ τὴν χάριν τοῦ Θεοῦ τὴν δοθεῖσάν μοι ὡς σοφὸς ἀρχιτέκτων θεμέλιον ἔθηκα, ἄλλος δὲ ἐποικοδομεῖ. ἕκαστος δὲ βλεπέτω πῶς ἐποικοδομεῖ· θεμέλιον γὰρ ἄλλον οὐδεὶς δύναται θεῖναι παρὰ τὸν κείμενον ὅς ἐστιν Ἰησοῦς Χριστός· εἰ δέ τις ἐποικοδομεῖ ἐπὶ τὸν θεμέλιον . . . . 16, 17. Οὐκ οἴδατε ὅτι ναὸς Θεοῦ ἐστὲ καὶ τὸ πνεῦμα τοῦ Θεοῦ ἐν ὑμῖν οἰκεῖ; εἴ τις τὸν ναὸν τοῦ Θεοῦ φθείρει, φθερεῖ τοῦτον ὁ Θεός· ὁ γὰρ ναὸς τοῦ Θεοῦ ἅγιος ἐστιν, οἵτινες ἐστε ὑμεῖς (cf. 6:19 and II Cor. 6:16).

The use of θεμέλιος in the New Testament is limited to
Luke-Acts, Romans, I Corinthians, Eph. 2:20, and the writings that
show the influence of the Pauline letter collection (Hebrews, the
Apocalypse of John, and I and II Timothy). The verb ἐποικοδομέω
is used in the New Testament only in I Cor. 2:10, 12, 14; Eph. 2:
20; Col. 2:7; I Pet. 2:5; and Jude 20. Its use in I Peter resembles its use in I Corinthians and Ephesians, but I Peter is
later than both and so is ruled out as a source of possible influence. The possibility of the influence of Colossians is admitted because of the large use of that writing in Ephesians. In
so far as the literary dependence of Eph. 2:20-22 can be traced,
it seems to be on I Cor. 3:9-12, where the figures of foundation
and building are used, and on I Cor. 3:16, 17 (cf. 6:19 and II
Cor. 2:16), where the Christian group is designated as ὁ ναὸς
ἅγιος.

Eph. 3:1   Colossians C   Philemon B
    Τούτου χάριν ἐγὼ Παῦλος ὁ δέσμιος τοῦ Χριστοῦ 'Ιησοῦ
ὑπὲρ ὑμῶν τῶν ἐθνῶν (cf. 3:13. 'Εν ταῖς θλίψεσίν μου ὑπὲρ ὑμῶν).
    Col. 1:24. Νῦν χαίρω ἐν τοῖς παθήμασιν ὑπὲρ ὑμῶν, καὶ
ἀνταναπληρῶ τὰ ὑστερήματα τῶν θλίψεων τοῦ Χριστοῦ.
    Philem. 1. Παῦλος δέσμιος Χριστοῦ 'Ιησοῦ. . . . .
9. Παῦλος . . . . δέσμιος Χριστοῦ 'Ιησοῦ.

The ὑπὲρ ὑμῶν τῶν ἐθνῶν suggests the influence of Col. 1:
24. A clear indication of literary indebtedness is contained in
Παῦλος ὁ δέσμιος τοῦ Χριστοῦ 'Ιησοῦ, which points rather definitely to acquaintance with Philemon. Acts closes with Paul in prison, and it speaks of him as ὁ δέσμιος; but only in Philemon and
Ephesians is Paul designated as ὁ δέσμιος τοῦ Χριστοῦ 'Ιησοῦ (cf.
II Tim. 1:8).

Eph. 3:2, 3, 5   Colossians A   I Corinthians C
    .There is a parallelism of thought and language between
Eph. 3:2, 3, 5 and Col. 1:25, 26 that clearly indicated the dependence of the one on the other:

Ephesians	Colossians
2. Τὴν οἰκονομιαν τῆς χάριτος τοῦ Θεοῦ τῆς δοθείσης μοι εἰς ὑμᾶς	25. Κατὰ τὴν οἰκονομίαν τοῦ Θεοῦ τὴν δοθεῖσαν μοι εἰς ὑμᾶς

3, 5. Κατὰ ἀποκάλυψιν ἐγνωρίσθη   26. Τὸ μυστήριον τὸ
μοι τὸ μυστήριον . . . . ὃ ἑτέραις   ἀποκεκρυμμένον ἀπὸ τῶν αἰώνων
γενεαῖς οὐκ ἐγνωρίσθη . . . . ὡς   καὶ ἀπὸ τῶν γενεῶν,—νῦν δὲ
νῦν ἀπεκαλύφθη τοῖς ἁγίοις   ἐφανερώθη τοῖς ἁγίοις αὐτοῦ
ἀποστόλοις αὐτοῦ

A similarly impressive parallelism between Ephesians and
I Corinthians exists. In I Cor. 2:1 Paul describes his message as
τὸ μυστήριον τοῦ θεοῦ. In 2:7 he further describes it as θεοῦ
σοφίαν . . . . τὴν ἀποκεκρυμμένην, which he preaches only ἐν
μυστηρίῳ. In 2:9, ἡμῖν γὰρ ἀπεκάλυψεν ὁ θεὸς διὰ τοῦ πνεύματος
supplies a close parallel for ὡς νῦν ἀπεκαλύφθη . . . . ἐν
πνεύματι. It is worthy of note that Ephesians agrees with I
Corinthians against Colossians in the use of ἀποκαλύπτω and that
ἐν πνεύματι, which has no parallel in Colossians, is paralleled
in I Corinthians by διὰ τοῦ πνεύματος.

Eph. 3:3, 4   Galatians B
Κατὰ ἀποκάλυψιν ἐγνωρίσθη μοι τὸ μυστήριον, καθὼς προέγραψα ἐν ὀλίγῳ, πρὸς ὃ δύνασθε ἀναγινώσκοντες νοῆσαι τὴν σύνεσίν
μου ἐν τῷ μυστηρίῳ τοῦ Χριστοῦ.

Gal. 1:12. Οὐδὲ ἐγὼ παρὰ ἀνθρώπου παρέλαβον αὐτό . . . .
ἀλλὰ δι' ἀποκαλύψεως Ἰησοῦ Χριστοῦ. 16. Ἀποκαλύψαι τὸν υἱὸν
αὐτοῦ ἐν ἐμοὶ ἵνα εὐαγγελίζωμαι αὐτὸν ἐν τοῖς ἔθνεσιν. . . . .
2:2. Ἀνέβην δὲ κατὰ ἀποκάλυψιν. . . . . 7, 8. Ὅτι πεπίστευμαι
τὸ εὐαγγέλιον τῆς ἀκροβυστίας . . . . καὶ ἐμοὶ εἰς τὰ ἔθνη (cf.
II Cor. 11:16).

The καθὼς προέγραψα ἐν ὀλίγῳ is an allusion to Paul as a
letter-writer and to some definite discussion that may be found
in his letters. The allusion is not satisfied by any statement
that has been made in Ephesians. Ἀναγινώσκοντες refers to something they are going to read rather than to what they have read
hitherto. This reference is best satisfied if taken as an allusion to Gal. 1:12, 16 and 2:2.7.8.

The "mystery" made known by revelation is for the author
of Ephesians that "through union with Christ Jesus the heathen are
fellow-heirs with the Jews." This is approximately what Paul says
in Galatians that he received by revelation.

Eph. 3:6   Galatians B   Romans B

Εἶναι τὰ ἔθνη συνκληρονόμα καὶ σύνσωμα καὶ συνμέτοχα τῆς ἐπαγγελίας ἐν Χριστῷ Ἰησοῦ διὰ·τοῦ εὐαγγελίου.

Gal. 3:28, 29. Πάντες γὰρ ὑμεῖς εἷς ἐστὲ ἐν Χριστῷ Ἰησοῦ. εἰ δὲ ὑμεῖς Χριστοῦ, ἄρα τοῦ Ἀβραὰμ σπέρμα ἐστέ, κατ' ἐπαγγελίαν κληρονόμοι.

Rom. 4:13-16. Οὐ γὰρ διὰ νόμου ἡ ἐπαγγελία τῷ Ἀβραὰμ ἢ τῷ σπέρματι αὐτοῦ, τὸ κληρονόμον αὐτὸν εἶναι κόσμου, ἀλλὰ διὰ δικαιοσύνης πίστεως· εἰ γὰρ οἱ ἐκ νόμου κληρονόμοι, κεκένωται ἡ πίστις καὶ κατήργηται ἡ ἐπαγγελία·. . . . . Διὰ τοῦτο ἐκ πίστεως, ἵνα κατὰ χάριν, εἰς τὸ εἶναι βεβαίαν τὴν ἐπαγγελίαν παντὶ τῷ σπέρματι, οὐ τῷ ἐκ τοῦ νόμου μόνον ἀλλὰ καὶ τῷ ἐκ πίστεως Ἀβραάμ, ὅς ἐστιν πατὴρ ·πάντων ἡμῶν. 8:17. Κληρονόμοι μέν Θεοῦ συνκληρονόμοι δὲ Χριστοῦ.

The use of ἐπαγγελία in the New Testament is confined to Luke-Acts, the Pauline letters, and the letters written under the influence of the Pauline corpus (Ephesians, I and II Timothy, Hebrews, II Peter, and I John). Συνκληρονόμος is used in Rom. 8:17, Eph. 3:6, Heb. 11:9, and I Pet. 3:7. Κληρονόμος is used in the sense of the passage cited in Romans, Galatians, Titus, Hebrews, and James. Σύνσωμος and συνμέτοχος are peculiar to Ephesians, but the conceptions they represent are distinctively Pauline.

Eph. 3:7   Colossians A

Οὗ ἐγενήθην διάκονος κατὰ τὴν δωρεὰν τῆς χάριτος τοῦ Θεοῦ τῆς δοθείσης μοι κατὰ τὴν ἐνέργειαν τῆς δυνάμεως αὐτοῦ.

Col. 1:23. Οὗ ἐγενόμην ἐγὼ Παῦλος διάκονος. . . . . 25. Κατὰ τὴν οἰκονομίαν τοῦ Θεοῦ τὴν δοθεῖσάν μοι. . . . . 29. Κατὰ τὴν ἐνέργειαν αὐτοῦ τὴν ἐνεργουμένην ἐν ἐμοὶ ἐν δυνάμει.

The indebtedness of Ephesians to Colossians is clear. There is a similar association of χάρις and διδόναι in Rom. 12:3, 6 (cf. I Cor. 1:4, 3:10; II Cor. 8:1; Gal. 2:9) and this, taken together with the close association of χάρις and δωρεά in Romans 3:24 and 5:15 (cf. II Cor. 9:15) suggests a bare possibility of indebtedness to Romans also.

Eph. 3:8   I Corinthians B   Romans C

Ἐμοὶ τῷ ἐλαχιστοτέρῳ πάντων ἁγίων ἐδόθη ἡ χάρις αὕτητοῖς ἔθνεσιν εὐαγγελίσασθαι τὸ ἀνεξιχνίαστον πλοῦτος τοῦ Χριστοῦ.

I Cor. 15:9. Ἐγὼ γάρ εἰμι ὁ ἐλάχιστος τῶν ἀποστόλων (cf. Gal. 1:16).

Rom. 11:33. Ὦ βάθος πλούτου καὶ σοφίας καὶ γνώσεως Θεοῦ· ὡς . . . . ἀνεξιχνίαστοι αἱ ὁδοὶ αὐτοῦ.

(Cf. Col. 1:27. Οἷς ἠθέλησεν ὁ Θεὸς γνωρίσαι τί τὸ πλοῦτος τῆς δόξης τοῦ μυστηρίου τούτου ἐν τοῖς ἔθνεσιν.)

The use of ἐλάχιστος in the self-description of Paul in I Cor. 15:9 must have suggested its very similar use in Eph. 3:8. The term is so used only in these passages.

The second half of the statement looks toward acquaintance with Galatians in its use of εὐαγγελίζομαι and toward Rom. 11:33 in its use of πλοῦτος. The use of πλοῦτος in connection with ἀνεξιχνίαστον increases the likelihood of dependence on Romans, since the latter term is used in the New Testament only in Rom. 11:33 and Eph. 3:8.

Eph. 3:9   Colossians A   I Corinthians C

Καὶ φωτίσαι τίς ἡ οἰκονομία τοῦ μυστηρίου τοῦ ἀποκεκρυμμένου ἀπὸ τῶν αἰώνων.

Col. 1:25, 26. Κατὰ τὴν οἰκονομίαν τοῦ Θεοῦ . . . . πληρῶσαι τὸν λόγον τοῦ Θεοῦ, τὸ μυστήριον τὸ ἀποκεκρυμμένον ἀπὸ τῶν αἰώνων.

I Cor. 2:7. Ἀλλὰ λαλοῦμεν Θεοῦ σοφίαν ἐν μυστηρίῳ, τὴν ἀποκεκρυμμένην.

Ἀποκρύπτω is used in the following four instances in the New Testament: Luke 10:21, I Cor. 2:7, Eph. 3:9, and Col. 1:26. The use in the last three instances is identical, referring in each to a divine μυστήριον, long hidden but now revealed. The point of contact with I Corinthians is adequately satisfied from Colossians, and yet the resemblance is such as to allow for the probability of acquaintance.

Eph. 3:10   I Corinthians C   Romans C

Ἵνα γνωρισθῇ νῦν ταῖς ἀρχαῖς καὶ ταῖς ἐξουσίαις ἐν τοῖς ἐπουρανίοις διὰ τῆς ἐκκλησίας ἡ πολυποίκιλος σοφία τοῦ Θεοῦ, κατὰ πρόθεσιν τῶν αἰώνων ἣν ἐποίησεν ἐν τῷ Χριστῷ Ἰησοῦ τῷ κυρίῳ ἡμῶν.

I Cor. 4:9. Ὅτι θέατρον ἐγενήθημεν τῷ κόσμῳ καὶ ἀγγέλοις
καὶ ἀνθρώποις. 1:24. Χριστὸν Θεοῦ . . . . σοφίαν. . . . . 30. Ἐξ
αὐτοῦ δὲ ὑμεῖς ἐστε ἐν Χριστῷ Ἰησοῦ, ὅς ἐγενήθη σοφία ἡμῖν ἀπὸ
Θεοῦ.

The rather unusual idea of I Cor. 4:9 that the apostles
were made "a spectacle to the whole universe, angels as well as
men" probably suggested to the author of Ephesians the equally
distinctive idea that through the church the many-sided wisdom of
God was made known "to the rulers and authorities in heaven."

In Eph. 1:11 the influence of κατὰ πρόθεσιν of Rom. 8:28
is probably felt. That passage in all likelihood was also influential in 3:10. This use of πρόθεσις occurs in the New Testament earlier than Ephesians only in Rom. 8:28, 9:11. The term occurs in the LXX but never in this sense.

Eph. 3:12   Romans A   II Corinthians A
Ἐν ᾧ ἔχομεν τὴν παρρησίαν καὶ προσαγωγὴν ἐν πεποιθήσει
διὰ τῆς πίστεως αὐτοῦ.

Rom. 5:2. Δι' οὗ καὶ τὴν προσαγωγὴν ἐσχήκαμεν τῇ πίστει
εἰς τὴν χάριν ταύτην ἐν ᾗ ἐστήκαμεν.

II Cor. 3:4. Πεποίθησιν δὲ τοιαύτην ἔχομεν διὰ τοῦ Χριστοῦ
πρὸς τὸν Θεόν (see the notes on Eph. 2:14 and 2:17 for the influence of Rom. 5:2 on Ephesians).

The influence of II Corinthians is equally clear.
Πεποίθησις is used in the New Testament in II Cor. 1:15, 3:4, 8:
22, 10:2; Eph. 3:12; and Phil. 3:4. In Philippians the allusion
is to reliance on "physical advantages," so that the correspondence
of usage is with II Corinthians.

Eph. 3:13   II Cor. B
Διὸ αἰτοῦμαι μὴ ἐνκακεῖν ἐν ταῖς θλίψεσίν μου ὑπὲρ ὑμῶν.

II Cor. 4:1. Καθὼς ἠλεήθημεν οὐκ ἐγκακοῦμεν. . . . . 16.
Διὸ οὐκ ἐγκακοῦμεν. . . . . 7:4. Ὑπερπερισσεύομαι τῇ χαρᾷ ἐπὶ
πάσῃ τῇ θλίψει ἡμῶν. . . . . 11:7, 8. Ἢ ἁμαρτίαν ἐποίησα ἐμαυτον
ταπεινῶν ἵνα ὑμεῖς ὑψωθῆτε, ὅτι δωρεὰν τὸ τοῦ Θεοῦ εὐαγγέλιον
εὐηγγελισάμην ὑμῖν; ἄλλας ἐκκλησίας ἐσύλησα λαβὼν ὀψώνιον πρὸς
τὴν ὑμῶν διακονίαν (cf. Col. 2:1).

Ἐνκακέω is used in the New Testament in Luke 18:1, II Cor.

4:1, 16, Gal. 6:9, Eph. 3:13, and II Thess. 3:13.   In both instances
in II Corinthians and in Eph. 3:13 it refers to Paul himself.

The ὑπὲρ ὑμῶν indicates the possibility that Col. 2:1 might
have influenced Eph. 3:13.   However, II Cor. 11 is the most impressive description of Paul's hardships in the New Testament, and
verses 7 and 8 of this chapter clearly indicate that they were endured for the sake of his gentile mission and converts.   Dependence on II Corinthians is probable.

Eph. 3:17   Colossians C

'Ερριζωμένοι καὶ τεθεμελιωμένοι (cf. 2:20).

Col. 2:7. 'Ερριζωμένοι καὶ ἐποικοδομούμενσι ἐν αὐτῷ.
1:23. Εἴ γε ἐπιμένετε τῇ πίστει. τεθεμελιωμένοι.

'Ριζόομαι is used in the New Testament only in Col. 2:7
and Eph. 3:17.   It is used four times in the LXX. Θεμελιόω is used
in the New Testament in Matt. 7:25, Luke 6:48, Col. 1:23, Eph. 3:
17, Heb. 1:10, and I Pet. 5:10.   Its use in Colossians is more
nearly identical with that of Ephesians than is true of its other
instances.

Eph. 3:19   Colossians B

"Ινα ⌐πληρωθῆτε εἰς¬ πᾶν τὸ πλήρωμα τοῦ Θεοῦ.

Col. 2:9. "Οτι ἐν αὐτῷ κατοικεῖ πᾶν τὸ πλήρωμα τῆς Θεότητος
σωματικῶς, καὶ ἐστὲ ἐν αὐτῷ πεπληρωμένοι.

This idea of being filled with "the very fulness of God"
was probably borrowed from Colossians.

Eph. 3:20   Colossians A

Κατὰ τὴν δύναμιν τὴν ἐνεργουμένην ἐν ἡμῖν.

Col. 1:29. Κατὰ τὴν ἐνέργειαν αὐτοῦ τὴν ἐνεργουμένην ἐν
ἐμοὶ ἐν δυνάμει.

Eph. 3:21, 4:1   Romans B

3:21. Αὐτῷ ἡ δόξα . . . . εἰς πάσας τὰς γενεὰς τοῦ αἰῶνος
τῶν αἰωνων· ἀμήν. 4:1. Παρακαλῶ οὖν ὑμᾶς. . . . .

Rom. 11:36. Αὐτῷ ἡ δόξα εἰς τοὺς αἰῶνας· ἀμήν. 12:1.
Παρακαλῶ οὖν ὑμᾶς. . . . .

The correspondence in each instance marks the close of
the doctrinal and the beginning of the paranetic section. Romans
probably served as a model for Ephesians.

Eph. 4:1   Philemon B
Ἐγὼ ὁ δέσμιος ἐν κυρίῳ (see the note on Eph. 3:1).

Eph. 4:1   I Thessalonians B
Ἀξίως περιπατῆσαι τῆς κλήσεως ἧς ἐκλήθητε.
I Thess. 2:12. Εἰς τὸ περιπατεῖν ὑμᾶς ἀξίως τοῦ Θεοῦ τοῦ
⌜καλοῦντος⌝ ὑμᾶς (cf. Rom. 1:7, I Cor. 1:2, and Col. 1:10).

I Thessalonians so nearly satisfies all elements in Eph.
4:1 as to create the probability of influence.

Eph. 4:2   Colossians A
Μετὰ πάσης ταπεινοφροσύνης καὶ πραΰτητος μετὰ μακροθυμίας,
ἀνεχόμενοι ἀλλήλων ἐν ἀγάπῃ.
Col. 3:12. Ἐνδύσασθε οὖν . . . . ταπεινοφροσύνην, πραΰτητα
μακροθυμίαν, ἀνεχόμενοι ἀλλήλων (cf. Phil. 2:3).

Eph. 4:3-7   I Corinthians B Romans A Colossians C
Ἀνεχόμενοι ἀλλήλων ἐν ἀγάπῃ, σπουδάζοντες τηρεῖν τὴν
ἑνότητα τοῦ πνεύματος ἐν τῷ συνδέσμῳ τῆς εἰρήνης· ἐν σῶμα καὶ ἓν
πνεῦμα, καθὼς [καὶ] ἐκλήθητε ἐν μιᾷ ἐλπίδι τῆς κλήσεως ὑμῶν· εἷς
κύριος, μία πίστις, ἓν βάπτισμα· εἷς Θεὸς καὶ πατὴρ πάντων, ὁ ἐπὶ
πάντων καὶ διὰ πάντων καὶ ἐν πᾶσιν. Ἑνὶ δὲ ἑκάστῳ ἡμῶν ἐδόθη[ἡ]
χάρις κατὰ τὸ μέτρον τῆς δωρεᾶς τοῦ Χριστοῦ.
Col. 3:14-15. Ἐπὶ πᾶσι δὲ τούτοις τὴν ἀγάπην, ὅ ἐστιν
σύνδεσμος τῆς τελειότητος. καὶ ἡ εἰρήνη τοῦ Χριστοῦ βραβε υέτω
ἐν ταῖς καρδίαις ὑμῶν, εἰς ἣν καὶ ἐκλήθητε ἐν ἑνὶ σώματι·

The exhortation to harmony and unity in Phil. 2:2 is note-
worthy as a possible model for Ephesians. The emphasis on love,
the similar use of σύνδεσμος, the plea for peace within the body,
and the parallel use of καλέω establish the probability of indebtedness to Colossians. It is significant that I Corinthians
and Romans supply the elements for this whole section of Ephesians:
    1. Eph. 4:3. Ἀνεχόμενοι ἀλλήλων ἐν ἀγάπῃ.
    Rom. 13:10. Ἡ ἀγάπη τῷ πλησίον κακὸν οὐκ ἐργάζεται.

. . . . 8. Εἰ μὴ τὸ ἀλλήλους ἀγαπᾶν (cf. I Thess. 4:9. Εἰς τὸ ἀγαπᾶν ἀλλήλους).

2. Eph. 4:4. ῍Εν σῶμα καὶ ἓν πνεῦμα.

I Cor. 10:17. ῍Εν σῶμα οἱ πολλοί ἐσμεν. . . . . 12:4. Τὸ δὲ αὐτὸ πνεῦμα. . . . . 13. ᾽Εν ἑνὶ πνεῦμα ἡμεῖς πάντες εἰς ἓν σῶμα ἐβαπτίσθημεν . . . . καὶ πάντες ἓν πνεῦμα ἐπιτίσθημεν.

Rom. 12:4, 5. Καθάπερ γὰρ ἐν ἑνὶ σώματι πολλὰ μέλη ἔχομεν . . . . οὕτως οἱ πολλοὶ ἓν σῶμά ἐσμεν ἐν Χριστῷ.

3. Eph. 4:4. Καθὼς καὶ ἐκλήθητε ἐν μιᾷ ἐλπίδι τῆς κλήσεως ὑμῶν.

The noun ἐλπίς is used in the New Testament in Luke-Acts, the Pauline letters, and the later literature that was influenced by those letters. Κλῆσις is used only in the Pauline letters and the later New Testament epistles. In I Cor. 7:20 it occurs in connection with καλέω (ἕκαστος ἐν τῇ κλήσει ᾗ ἐκλήθη). The conception of the Christian as a "called" person permeates Paul's letters.

4. Eph. 4:5-6. Εἷς κύριος, μία πίστις, ἓν βάπτισμα· εἷς Θεὸς καὶ πατὴρ πάντων, ὁ ἐπὶ πάντων καὶ διὰ πάντων καὶ ἐν πᾶσιν.

I. Cor. 8:6. ῾Ημῖν εἷς Θεὸς ὁ πατήρ, ἐξ οὗ τὰ πάντα καὶ ἡμεῖς εἰς αὐτόν, καὶ εἷς κύριος. . . . . 12:5, 6. ῾Ο αὐτὸς κύριος . . . . καὶ ὁ αὐτὸς Θεός, ὁ ἐνεργῶν τὰ πάντα ἐν πᾶσιν.

Rom. 3:30. Εἴπερ εἷς ὁ Θεός.

The reference to "one baptism" may easily reflect the influence of I Cor. 1:15. ῞Ινα μή τις εἴπῃ ὅτι εἰς τὸ ἐμὸν ὄνομα ἐβαπτίσθητε, and of 12:13. ᾽Εν ἑνὶ πνεύμα ἡμεῖς πάντες εἰς ἓν σῶμα ἐβαπτίσθημεν.

5. Eph. 4:7. ῾Ενὶ δὲ ἑκάστῳ ἡμῶν ἐδόθη ἡ χάρις κατὰ τὸ μέτρον τῆς δωρεᾶς τοῦ Χριστοῦ.

Rom. 12:3-6. Λέγω γὰρ διὰ τῆς χάριτος τῆς δοθείσης μοι . . . . . ἑκάστῳ ὡς ὁ Θεὸς ἐμέρισεν μέτρον πίστεως. . . . . ῎Εχοντες δὲ χαρίσματα κατὰ τὴν χάριν τὴν δοθεῖσαν ἡμῖν διάφορα κτλ.

I. Cor. 12:7-11. Ἑκάστῳ δὲ δίδοται ἡ φανέρωσις τοῦ
πνεύματος πρὸς τὸ συμφέρον. . . . . πάντα δὲ ταῦτα
ἐνεργεῖ τὸ ἓν καὶ τὸ αὐτὸ πνεῦμα, διαιροῦν ἰδίᾳ
ἑκάστῳ καθὼς βούλεται.

Eph. 4:11-13   I Corinthians C

Καὶ αὐτὸς ἔδωκεν τοὺς μὲν ἀποστόλους, τοὺς δὲ προφήτας,
τοὺς δὲ εὐαγγελιστάς, τοὺς δὲ ποιμένας καὶ διδασκάλους πρὸς τὸν
καταρτισμὸν τῶν ἁγίων εἰς ἔργον διακονίας, εἰς οἰκοδομὴν τοῦ
σώματος τοῦ Χριστοῦ.

I Cor. 12:28. Καὶ οὓς μὲν ἔθετο ὁ Θεὸς ἐν τῇ ἐκκλησίᾳ
πρῶτον ἀποστόλους, δεύτερον προφήτας, τρίτον διδασκάλους (cf. II
Cor. 12:19).

The account of the orders in the church as given in Ephesians probably reflects the acquaintance of the author with I
Corinthians. The addition of εὐαγγελιστής (cf. Acts 21:8 and II
Tim. 4:5) and of ποιμήν (cf. John 10:12 and I Pet. 5:2) reflects
the development that belonged to the close of the century.

The use of οἰκοδομή and καταρισμός may reflect acquaintance
with II Corinthians. Καταρισμός is used in the New Testament only
in Eph. 4:12, and its equivalent κατάρτισις is used only in II
Cor. 13:9.

Eph. 4:13   Philemon C

Εἰς τὴν ἑνότητα τῆς πίστεως καὶ τῆς ἐπιγνώσεως τοῦ υἱοῦ
τοῦ Θεοῦ· (cf. 1:17. Ἐν ἐπιγνώσει αὐτοῦ).

Philem. 6. Ὅπως ἡ κοινωνία τῆς πίστεώς σου ἐνεργὴς γένηται ἐν ἐπιγνώσει παντὸς ἀγαθοῦ τοῦ ἐν ἡμῖν εἰς Χριστόν·

The use of ἐπίγνωσις is confined to the Pauline and post-
Pauline letters. Its use in Eph. 4:13 occurs in a context whose
wording resembles that of Philem. 6 sufficiently to suggest literary reminiscence.

Eph. 4:13, 14   Colossians C   I Corinthians C

Εἰς ἄνδρα τέλειον, εἰς μέτρον ἡλικίας τοῦ πληρώματος τοῦ
Χριστοῦ, ἵνα υηκέτι ὦμεν νήπιοι.

Col. 1:28. Ἵνα παραστήσωμεν πάντα ἄνθρωπον τέλειον ἐν
Χριστῷ. 2:9. Ὅτι ἐν αὐτῷ κατοικεῖ πᾶν τὸ πλήρωμα τῆς Θεότητος

. . . . καὶ ἐστὲ ἐν αὐτῷ πεπληρωμένοι.

I Cor. 2:6. Σοφίαν δὲ λαλοῦμεν ἐν τοῖς τελείοις. . . . .
3:1. Ὡς νηπίοις ἐν Χριστῷ. . . . . 14:20. Τῇ κακίᾳ νηπιάζετε,
ταῖς δὲ φρεσὶν τέλειοι γίνεσθε.

The contrast of τέλειος and νήπιος probably reflects acquaintance with I Corinthians.

Eph. 4:14   Colossians C

Κλυδωνιζόμενοι καὶ περιφερόμενοι παντὶ ἀνέμῳ τῆς διδασκαλίας ἐν τῇ κυβίᾳ τῶν ἀνθρώπων ἐν πανουργίᾳ πρὸς τὴν μεθοδίαν τῆς
πλάνης.

Col. 2:8. Βλέπετε μή τις ⌈ὑμᾶς ἔσται⌉ ὁ συλαγωγῶν διὰ τῆς
φιλοσοφίας καὶ κενῆς ἀπάτης κατὰ τὴν παράδοσιν τῶν ἀνθρώπων, κατὰ
τὰ στοιχεῖα τοῦ κόσμου καὶ οὐ κατὰ Χριστόν·

Eph. 4:15, 16   Colossians A

Αὐξήσωμεν εἰς αὐτὸν τὰ πάντα, ὅς ἐστιν ἡ κεφαλή, Χριστός,
ἐξ οὗ πᾶν τὸ σῶμα συναρμολογούμενον καὶ συνβιβαζόμενον διὰ πάσης
ἀφῆς τῆς ἐπιχορηγίας κατ' ἐνέργειαν ἐν μέτρῳ ἑνὸς ἑκάστου ⌈μέρους⌉
τὴν αὔξησιν τοῦ σώματος ποιεῖται εἰς οἰκοδομὴν ἑαυτοῦ ἐν ἀγάπῃ.

Col. 2:19. Τὴν κεφαλήν, ἐξ οὗ πᾶν τὸ σῶμα διὰ τῶν ἀφῶν καὶ
συνδέσμων ἐπιχορηγούμενον καὶ συνβιβαζόμενον αὔξει τὴν αὔξησιν τοῦ
Θεοῦ (cf. Rom. 12:4, 5 and I Cor. 12:12).

Eph. 4:17-19   Romans A   Colossians B

Τοῦτο οὖν λέγω καὶ μαρτύρομαι ἐν κυρίῳ, μηκέτι ὑμᾶς
περιπατεῖν καθὼς καὶ τὰ ἔθνη περιπατεῖ ἐν ματαιότητι τοῦ νοὸς
αὐτῶν, ἐσκοτωμένοι τῇ διανοίᾳ ὄντες, ἀπηλλοτριωμένοι τῆς ζωῆς
τοῦ Θεοῦ, διὰ τὴν ἄγνοιαν τὴν οὖσαν ἐν αὐτοῖς, διὰ τὴν πώρωσιν
τῆς καρδίας αὐτῶν, οἵτινες ἀπηλγηκότες ἑαυτοὺς παρέδωκαν τῇ
ἀσελγείᾳ εἰς ἐργασίαν ἀκαθαρσίας πάσης ἐν πλεονεξίᾳ.

The following table of parallels indicates the indebtedness of Ephesians to Romans and Colossians:

Ephesians

17. Τοῦτο οὖν λέγω	Col. 2:4. Τοῦτο λέγω
ἐν ματαιότητι τοῦ νοὸς αὐτῶν	Rom. 1:21. 'Αλλὰ ἐματαιώθησαν ἐν
	τοῖς διαλογισμοῖς αὐτῶν . . . .
	8:20. Τῇ γὰρ ματαιότητι ἡ κτί-
	οις ὑπετάγη
18. 'Εσκοτωμένοι τῇ διανοίᾳ	Rom. 1:21. Καὶ ἐσκοτίσθη ἡ ἀσύνε-
ὄντες	τος αὐτῶν καρδία
ἀπηλλοτριωμένοι τῆς ζωῆς	Col. 1:21. ″Οντας ἀπηλλοτριω-
τοῦ θεοῦ	μένους. 3:3. 'Η ζωὴ ὑμῶν κέκρυπ
	ται σὺν Χριστῷ ἐν τῷ θεῷ
19. Διὰ τὴν ἄγνοιαν τὴν	Rom. 1:22. Φάσκοντες εἶναι σοφοὶ
οὖσαν ἐν αὐτοῖς, διὰ τὴν	ἐμωράνθησαν
πώρωσιν τῆς καρδίας αὐτῶν	
ἑαυτοὺς παρέδωκαν τῇ ἀσελ-	Rom. 1:24. Παρέδωκεν αὐτοὺς ὁ
γείᾳ εἰς ἐργασίαν ἀκαθαρσίας	Θεὸς . . . . εἰς ἀκαθαρσίαν
πάσης ἐν πλεονεξίᾳ	Col. 3:5. 'Ακαθαρσίαν . ′. . . . καὶ
	τὴν πλεονεξίαν (cf. Gal. 5:19).

The use of ἀπαλλοτριόομαι in Eph. 4:18 points to dependence on Col. 1:21. The verb is used in the New Testament in Col. 1:21 and Eph. 2:12, 4:18. It occurs eleven times in the LXX. The τῆς ζωῆς τοῦ θεοῦ used with ἀπαλλοτριόομαι is a vivid contrast to the picture of Col. 3:3 and probably shows the influence of that picture. The point of resemblance to the vice list of Col. 3:5 is not sufficient to indicate literary dependence (cf. Gal. 5:19. 'Ακαθαρσία, ἀσέλγεια).

The resemblance to Rom. 1:18-32 is so strong as to make literary dependence a matter of practical certainty. The description in Ephesians of the way the heathen live sounds like a summary of the more elaborate description in Romans.

Eph. 4:20, 21   Colossians C
'Υμεῖς δὲ οὐχ οὕτως ἐμάθετε τὸν Χριστόν, εἴ γε αὐτὸν ἠκούσατε καὶ ἐν αὐτῷ ἐδιδάχθητε.

Col. 2:6, 7. ῾Ως οὖν παρελάβετε τὸν Χριστὸν Ἰησοῦν τὸν κύριον ἐν αὐτῷ περιπατεῖτε . . . . καθὼς ἐδιδάχθητε (cf. Rom. 10:14).

Eph. 4:22-25, 29, 31   Colossians A   Romans C

The following table of parallels indicates the literary indebtedness of Ephesians. The basic dependence is clearly on Colossians. The influence of Romans is probable, particularly in verses 23 and 24 (cf. Rom. 12:2).

Ephesians

22. Ἀποθέσθαι ὑμᾶς κατὰ τὴν προτέραν ἀναστροφὴν τὸν παλαιὸν ἄνθρωπον τὸν φειρόμενον κατὰ τὰς ἐπιθυμίας τῆς ἀπάτης

Col. 3:8. Νυνὶ δὲ ἀπόθεσθε καὶ ὑμεῖς τὰ πάντα . . . . 9. Ἀπεκδυσάμενοι τὸν παλαιὸν ἄνθρωπον σὺν ταῖς πράξεσιν αὐτοῦ
Rom. 6:6. Ὁ παλαιὸς ἡμῶν ἄνθρωπος. (Only in these instances in the New Testament is παλαίος used in this connection.)

23, 24. Ἀνανεοῦσθαι δὲ τῷ πνεύματι τοῦ νοὸς ὑμῶν καὶ ἐνδύσασθαι τὸν καινὸν ἄνθρωπον κτισθέντα ἐν δικαιοσύνη

Col. 3:10. Καὶ ἐνδυσάμενοι τὸν νέον τὸν ἀνακαινούμενον εἰς ἐπίγνωσιν κατ᾿ εἰκόνα τοῦ κτίσαντος αὐτόν
Rom. 12:2. Μεταμορφοῦσθε τῇ ἀνακαινώσει τοῦ νοός (νοῦς is used in the New Testament once in Luke, sixteen times in Paul's letters, and seven times in later writings)

25. Διὸ ἀποθέμενοι τὸ ψεῦδος λαλεῖτε ἀλήθειαν ἕκαστος μετὰ τὸν πλησίον αὐτοῦ.

Col. 3:9. Μὴ ψεύδεσθε εἰς ἀλλήλους

31. Πᾶσα πικρία καὶ θυμὸς καὶ ὀργὴ καὶ κραυγὴ καὶ βλασφημία ἀρθήτω ἀφ᾿ ὑμῶν σὺν πάσῃ κακίᾳ

Col. 3:8. Ἀπόθεσθε . . . . ὀργήν, θυμόν, κακίαν, βλασφημίαν
Rom. 2:8 Ὀργὴ καὶ θυμός

Eph. 4:25   Romans B
Ὅτι ἐσμὲν ἀλλήλων μέλη

Rom. 12:5. Οὕτως οἱ πολλοὶ ἕν σῶμα ἐσμεν ἐν Χριστῷ, τὸ
δὲ καθ' εἷς ἀλλήλων μέλη (cf. I Cor. 12:25).

Μέλος occurs in Christian literature prior to Ephesians
only in Matt. 5:29, 30. It occurs twenty-seven times in the nine
recognized Pauline letters and three times in James. Its use in
Eph. 5:25 probably reflects the influence of Rom. 12:5.

Eph. 4:28   I Thessalonians C
Μᾶλλον δὲ κοπιάτω ἐργαζόμενος ταῖς χερσὶν τὸ ἀγαθόν,
ἵνα ἔχῃ μεταδιδόναι τῷ χρείαν ἔχοντι.
I Thess. 4:11, 12. Παρακαλοῦμεν δὲ ὑμᾶς . . . . ἐργάζεσθαι
ταῖς χερσὶν ὑμῶν . . . . καὶ μηδενὸς χρείαν ἔχητε (cf. I Cor.
4:12).

The statement in I Cor. 4:12 is in the nature of an auto-
biographical note, but it is possible that the author of Ephesians
had Paul's example in mind in his exhortation. It is more probable that he had the direct and fuller exhortation of I Thessalonians in mind, however, and this is strengthened by the association of "work" and the relief of need.

Eph. 4:30   I Thessalonians B   II Corinthians B
Μὴ λυπεῖτε τὸ πνεῦμα τὸ ἅγιον τοῦ Θεοῦ, ἐν ᾧ ἐσφραισθητε
εἰς ἡμέραν ἀπολυτρώσεως.
I Thess. 4:8. Τοιγαροῦν ὁ ἀθετῶν οὐκ ἄνθρωπον ἀθετεῖ
ἀλλὰ τὸν Θεὸν τὸν διδόντα τὸ πνεῦμα αὐτοῦ τὸ ἅγιον εἰς ὑμᾶς (cf.
Ezek. 37:14). 5:19. Τὸ πνεῦμα μὴ σβέννυτε.
II. Cor. 1:22. Καὶ σφραγισάμενος ἡμᾶς καὶ δοὺς τὸν ἀρραβῶνα τοῦ πνεύματος ἐν ταῖς καρδίαις ἡμῶν. 6:2. Ἰδοὺ νῦν ἡμέρα
σωτηρίας (cf. Isa. 49:8).

For a discussion of the indebtedness of Ephesians to II
Corinthians see the note on Eph. 1:13, 14.

Eph. 4:32   Colossians C
Γίνεσθε δὲ εἰς ἀλλήλους χρηστοί, εὔσπλαγχνοι, χαριζόμενοι
ἑαυτοῖς καθὼς καὶ ὁ Θεὸς ἐν Χριστῷ ἐχαρίσατο ⌜ὑμῖν.⌝ γίνεσθε οὖν
μιμηταὶ τοῦ Θεοῦ, ὡς τέκνα ἀγαπητά.
Col. 3:12, 13. Ἐνδύσασθε . . . . σπλάγχνα . . . . χρηστό-
τητα . . . . χαριζόμενοι ἑαυτοῖς . . . . καθὼς καὶ ὁ ⌜κύριος⌝
ἐχαρίσατο ὑμῖν οὕτως καὶ ὑμεῖς·

Eph. 5:2   Romans C
Καὶ περιπατεῖτε ἐν ἀγάπῃ.
Rom. 14:15. Εἰ γὰρ διὰ βρῶμα ὁ ἀδελφός σου λυπεῖται,
οὐκέτι κατὰ ἀγάπην περιπατεῖς.

These are the only instances in the New Testament in which
the figure of "walking in love" is used.

Eph. 5:3-6   Colossians B   I and II Corinthians C
Πορνεία δὲ καὶ ἀκαθαρσία πᾶσα ἢ πλεονεξία μηδὲ ὀνομαζέσθω
ἐν ὑμῖν, καθὼς πρέπει ἁγίοις, καὶ αἰσχρότης καὶ μωρολογία ἢ εὐτρα-
πελία, ἃ οὐκ ἀνῆκεν, ἀλλὰ μᾶλλον εὐχαριστία. τοῦτο γὰρ ἴστε γινώσκοντες ὅτι
πᾶς πόρνος ἢ ἀκάθαρτος ἢ πλεονέκτης, ὅ ἐστιν εἰδωλολάτρης, οὐκ
ἔχει κληρονομίαν ἐν τῇ βασιλείᾳ τοῦ Χριστοῦ καὶ Θεοῦ. Μηδεὶς
ὑμᾶς ἀπατάτω κενοῖς λόγοις, διὰ ταῦτα γὰρ ἔρχεται ἡ ὀργὴ τοῦ Θεοῦ
ἐπὶ τοὺς υἱοὺς τῆς ἀπειθίας.

These verses in Ephesians have a number of points of contact with Col. 3:5, 8. Their indebtedness is not limited to
Colossians, however, but looks in the direction of several other
letters. The following is a display of the parallels that indicate the several sources of literary influence:

Ephesians

3. Πορνεία δὲ καὶ ἀκαθαρσία   Col. 3:5. Πορνείαν ἀκαθαρσίαν
πᾶσα ἢ πλεονεξία, μηδὲ ὀνομα-   . . . . καὶ τὴν πλεονεξίαν. . . . .
ζέσθω ἐν ὑμῖν   I Cor. 5:11. Ἐάν τις ἀδελφὸς
                                 ὀνομαζόμενος ἢ πόρνος ἢ
                                 πλεονέκτης. . . . . (The use of
                                 ὀνομάζω is rather a definite
                                 trace of literary relationship.)

4. Καὶ αἰσχρότης καὶ μωρο-   Col. 3:8. Ἀπόθεσθε . . . . αἰσχρολογία   λογίαν ἐκ τοῦ στόματος ὑμῶν.

Αἰσχρότης and αἰσχρολογία are used only in these instances
in the New Testament.

4. Ἃ οὐκ ἀνῆκεν   Rom. 1:28. Τὰ μὴ καθήκοντα

In Col. 3:18 and Philemon ἀνήκω is used, but there are no
indications of dependence. The statement of Ephesians is the
equivalent of the statement of Rom. 1:28 and in both cases serves

to close the vice list.

4. 'Αλλὰ μᾶλλον εὐχαριστία   I Thess. 5:18. 'Εν παντὶ
                                     εὐχαριστεῖτε

5. Γινώσκοντες ὅτι πᾶς πόρνος   Col. 3:5. Πορνείαν, ἀκαθαρσίαν
ἢ ἀκάρθαρτος ἢ πλεονέκτης, ὅ   . . . . καὶ τὴν πλεονεξίαν ἥτις
ἐστιν εἰδωλολάτρης, οὐκ ἔχει   ἐστὶν εἰδωλολατρία
κληρονομίαν ἐν τῇ βασιλείᾳ τοῦ   I Cor. 5:10, 11. Οὐ πάντως τοῖς
Χριστοῦ καὶ Θεοῦ   πόρνοις . . . . ἢ τοῖς πλεονέκταις
                                     . . . . ἢ εἰδωλολάτραις . . . .
                                     ἐάν τις ἀδελφὸς ὀνομαζόμενος ᾖ
                                     πόρνος ἢ πλεονέκτης ἢ εἰδωλολάτ-
                                     ρης. . . . . 6:9, 10. Οὔτε
                                     πόρνοι οὔτε εἰδωλολάτραι . . . .
                                     οὔτε πλεονέκται . . . . βασιλείαν
                                     Θεοῦ κληρονομήσουσιν (cf. Gal.
                                     5:19-21).

In I Corinthians, πλεονέκτης is associated with εἰδωλολάτρης after πορνεία. The modifying phrase in Colossians more closely resembles Ephesians, however, and is a more probable source of influence. The added statement about exclusion from the Kingdom points to I Corinthians and Galatians, where it follows a similar list of vices.

It is possible that this whole section in Ephesians should be understood as a utilization of early Christian paranesis instead of in terms of specific literary indebtedness.

6. Μηδεὶς ὑμᾶς ἀπατάτω κενοῖς   Col. 2:4. "Ινα μηδεὶς ὑμᾶς
λόγοις, διὰ ταῦτα γὰρ ἔρχεται   παραλογίζηται ἐν πιθανολογίᾳ
ἡ ὀργὴ τοῦ Θεοῦ ἐπὶ τοὺς υἱοὺς   8. Βλέπετε μή τις ὑμᾶς ἔσται
τῆς ἀπειθίας   ὁ συλαγωγῶν διὰ τῆς φιλοσοφίας
                                     καὶ κενῆς ἀπάτης . . . .
                                     3:6. Δι' ἃ ἔρχεται ἡ ὀργὴ τοῦ
                                     Θεοῦ (cf. Rom. 1:18).

Dependence of Ephesians on Colossians here seems highly probable on the basis of the cumulative character of the evidence. Dependence on I and II Corinthians is reasonably probable, and on Romans and Galatians, possible.

Eph. 5:7, 8   II Corinthians C

Μὴ οὖν γίνεσθε συμμέτοχοι αὐτῶν· ἦτε γάρ ποτε σκότος, νῦν δὲ φῶς ἐν κυρίῳ.

II Cor. 6:14. Μὴ γίνεσθε ἑτεροζυγοῦντες ἀπίστοις· τίς γὰρ μετοχὴ δικαιοσύνῃ καὶ ἀνομίᾳ, ἢ τίς κοινωνία φωτὶ πρὸς σκότος (cf. Rom. 13:12 and I Thess. 5:5).

Μετοχή is used in the New Testament in II Cor. 4:14, and συνμέτοχος is used only in Eph. 3:6 and 5:7. Μέτοχος is used in Luke 5:7 and five times in Hebrews.

The employment of the term in question in connection with a very similar negative exhortation and the same essential metaphors makes literary dependence probable.

Eph. 5:15, 16   Colossians A

Βλέπετε οὖν ἀκριβῶς πῶς περιπατεῖτε, μὴ ὡς ἄσοφοι ἀλλ' ὡς σοφοί, ἐξαγοραζόμενοι τὸν καιρόν.

Col. 4:5. Ἐν σοφίᾳ περιπατεῖτε πρὸς τοὺς ἔξω, τὸν καιρὸν ἐξαγοραζόμενοι

Ἐξαγοράζω is used in the New Testament only in Gal. 3:13, 4:5 and Col. 4:5 and Eph. 5:16. The use of the term in Colossians and Ephesians is the same.

Eph. 5:19-21   Colossians A

Λαλοῦντες ἑαυτοῖς ψαλμοῖς καὶ ὕμνοις καὶ ᾠδαῖς πνευματικαῖς, ᾄδοντες καὶ ψάλλοντες τῇ καρδίᾳ ὑμῶν τῷ κυρίῳ, εὐχαριστοῦντες πάντοτε ὑπὲρ πάντων ἐν ὀνόματι τοῦ κυρίου ἡμῶν Ἰησοῦ Χριστοῦ τῷ Θεῷ καὶ πατρί, ὑποτασσόμενοι ἀλλήλοις ἐν φόβῳ Χριστοῦ.

Col. 3:16, 17. Διδάσκοντες καὶ νουθετοῦντες ἑαυτοὺς ψαλμοῖς, ὕμνοις, ᾠδαῖς πνευματικαῖς ἐν χάριτι, ᾄδοντες ἐν ταῖς καρδίαις ὑμῶν τῷ Θεῷ· καὶ πᾶν ὅτι ἐὰν ποιῆτε ἐν λόγῳ ἢ ἐν ἔργῳ, πάντα ἐν ὀνόματι κυρίου Ἰησοῦ, εὐχαριστοῦντες τῷ Θεῷ πατρὶ δι' αὐτοῦ (cf. I Thess. 5:18).

The closing clause is not paralleled in Colossians and may have been suggested by the διὰ τῆς ἀγάπης δουλεύετε ἀλλήλοις of Gal. 5:13.

Eph. 5:22-24   Colossians A   I Corinthians B

Αἱ γυναῖκες τοῖς ἰδίοις ἀνδράσιν ὡς τῷ κυρίῳ, ὅτι ἀνήρ
ἐστιν κεφαλὴ τῆς γυναικὸς ὡς καὶ ὁ Χριστὸς κεφαλὴ τῆς ἐκκλησίας,
αὐτὸς σωτὴρ τοῦ σώματος. ἀλλὰ ὡς ἡ ἐκκλησία ὑποτάσσεται τῷ
Χριστῷ, οὕτως καὶ αἱ γυναῖκες τοῖς ἀνδράσιν ἐν παντί.

Col. 3:18. Αἱ γυναῖκες, ὑποτάσσεσθε τοῖς ἀνδράσιν, ὡς
ἀνῆκεν ἐν κυρίῳ.

I Cor. 11:3. Παντὸς ἀνδρὸς ἡ κεφαλὴ ὁ Χριστός ἐστιν,
κεφαλὴ δὲ γυναικὸς ὁ ἀνήρ.

The emphasis of Colossians is specifically social, while
that of Ephesians is ecclesiastical. Here, as elsewhere, the author of Ephesians has used material from Colossians, but in illustration of a distinctive interest of his own. He amplifies the
statement of Colossians with material from I Corinthians, which
latter material may have suggested the new ideas embodied in his
amplification of the statement of Colossians. The idea of Christ
as "the head of every man" may have suggested his headship of the
church.

The term σωτήρ occurs frequently in the New Testament
writings that follow the publication of the Pauline corpus. Its
only occurrences in the Pauline letter collection are Phil. 3:20
and Eph. 5:23. It also occurs twice in Luke and twice in Acts.
No literary dependence on Philippians is required, but it is interesting to note the literary area in which the term occurs.

Eph. 5:25-27   Colossians A II Corinthians B Galatians C

Οἱ ἄνδρες, ἀγαπᾶτε τὰς γυναῖκας, καθὼς καὶ ὁ Χριστὸς
ἠγάπησεν τὴν ἐκκλησίαν καὶ ἑαυτὸν παρέδωκεν ὑπὲρ αὐτῆς, ἵνα αὐτὴν
ἁγιάσῃ καθαρίσας τῷ λουτρῷ τοῦ ὕδατος ἐν ῥήματι, ἵνα παραστήσῃ
αὐτὸς ἑαυτῷ ἔνδοξον τὴν ἐκκλησίαν, μὴ ἔχουσαν σπίλον ἢ ῥυτίδα ἢ
τι τῶν τοιούτων, ἀλλ' ἵνα ᾖ ἁγία καὶ ἄμωμος.

Col. 3:19. Οἱ ἄνδρες ἀγαπᾶτε τὰς γυναῖκας. 1:22. Παραστῆσαι ὑμᾶς ἁγίους καὶ ἀμώμους . . . . κατενώπιον αὐτοῦ.

Gal. 2:20. Τοῦ ἀγαπήσαντος με καὶ παραδόντος ἑαυτὸν ὑπὲρ
ἐμοῦ.

II Cor. 11:2. Ζηλῶ γὰρ ὑμᾶς Θεοῦ ζήλῳ, ἡρμοσάμην γὰρ ὑμᾶς
ἑνὶ ἀνδρὶ παρθένον ἁγνὴν παραστῆσαι τῷ Χριστῷ (cf. Rom. 10:9).

In Eph. 5:25-27 the author takes his starting-point from
Col. 3:19, which he quotes verbatim. He builds up an allegory on
the basis of Colossians, however, which is not involved in Colossians at all and the suggestion for which, together with the language used, probably was supplied from Galatians, Romans, and II
Corinthians.

The starting-point of Ephesians is evidently Col. 3:19.
Then the conception which in Gal. 2:20 Paul applies to himself is
applied to the church. The emphasis indicated in the phrase ἐν
ῥήματι suggests acquaintance with Rom. 10:9. 'Ρῆμα was a technical
word for "confession," and Rom. 10:9 is a statement of the content
of this "confession." The allegorizing of the relation of husbands
and wives was almost certainly suggested by II Cor. 11:2. The
language of Col. 1:22 seems to be employed in completing the figure.

Eph. 5:28, 29   Colossians A

Οὕτως ὀφείλουσιν [καὶ] οἱ ἄνδρες ἀγαπᾶν τας ἑαυτῶν γυναῖκας ὡς τὰ ἑαυτῶν σώματα· ὁ ἀγαπῶν τὴν ἑαυτοῦ γυναῖκα ἑαυτὸν
ἀγαπᾷ, οὐδεὶς γάρ ποτε τὴν ἑαυτοῦ σάρκα ἐμίσεν, ἀλλὰ ἐκτρέφει καὶ
θάλπει αὐτήν.

Col. 3:19. See the text in the note on Eph. 5:25-27 and
cf. I Thess. 2:8.

After the elaborate development of his figure of the church
as the bride of Christ in Eph. 25-27, there is a return in verses
28 and 29 to the thought of Col. 3:19. Θάλπειν is used in the New
Testament only in I Thess. 2:7 and Eph. 5:29. It is barely possible that the one instance of its use suggested the other. The
verb occurs four times in the LXX.

Eph. 6:1-9   Colossians A

Τὰ τέκνα, ὑπακούετε τοῖς γονεῦσιν ὑμῶν [ἐν κυρίῳ], τοῦτο
γάρ ἐστιν δίκαιον· τίμα τὸν πατέρα σου καὶ τὴν μητέρα, ἥτις
ἐστὶν ἐντολὴ ⌐πρώτη ἐν ἐπαγγελίᾳ, ἵνα⌐ εὖ σοι γένηται καὶ ἔσῃ
μακροχρόνιος ἐπὶ τῆς γῆς. Καὶ οἱ πατέρες, μὴ παροργίζετε τὰ
τέκνα ὑμῶν, ἀλλὰ ἐκτρέφετε αὐτὰ ἐν παιδείᾳ καὶ νουθεσίᾳ κυρίου.
Οἱ δοῦλοι, ὑπακούετε τοῖς κατὰ σάρκα κυρίοις μετὰ φόβου καὶ τρόμου
ἐν ἁπλότητι τῆς καρδίας ὑμῶν ὡς τῷ Χριστῷ, μὴ κατ' ὀφθαλμοδουλίαν
ὡς ἀνθρωπάρεσκοι ἀλλ' ὡς δοῦλοι Χριστοῦ ποιοῦντες τὸ θέλημα τοῦ

Θεοῦ, ἐκ ψυχῆς μετ' εὐνοίας δουλεύοντες, ὡς τῷ κυρίῳ καὶ οὐκ ἀνθρώποις, εἰδότες ὅτι ἕκαστος, ἐάν τι ποιήσῃ ἀγαθόν, τοῦτο κομίσεται
παρὰ κυρίου, εἴτε δοῦλος εἴτε ἐλεύθερος. Καὶ οἱ κύριοι, τὰ αὐτὰ
ποιεῖτε πρὸς αὐτούς, ἀνιέντες τὴν ἀπειλήν, εἰδότες ὅτι καὶ αὐτῶν
καὶ ὑμῶν ὁ κύριός ἐστιν ἐν οὐρανοῖς, καὶ προσωπολημψία οὐκ ἔστιν
παρ' αὐτῷ.

        Col. 3:20—4:1. Τὰ τέκνα, ὑπακούετε τοῖς γονεῦσιν κατὰ
πάντα, τοῦτο γὰρ εὐάρεστον ἐστιν ἐν κυρίῳ. Οἱ πατέρες μὴ ἐρεθίζετε
τὰ τέκνα ὑμῶν, ... Οἱ δοῦλοι, ὑπακούετε κατὰ πάντα τοῖς κατὰ
σάρκα κυρίοις, μὴ ἐν ⌈ὀφθαλμοδουλίαις⌉, ὡς ἀνθρωπάρεσκοι, ἀλλ'
ἐν ἁπλότητι καρδίας, φοβούμενοι τὸν κύριον. ὃ ἐὰν ποιῆτε, ἐκ
ψυχῆς ἐργάζεσθε, ὡς τῷ κυρίῳ καὶ οὐκ ἀνθρώποις, ... τῷ κυρίῳ
Χριστῷ δουλεύετε· . . . . καὶ οὐκ ἔστιν προσωπολημψία. Οἱ κύριοι,
τὸ δίκαιον καὶ τὴν ἰσότητα τοῖς δούλοις παρέχεσθε, εἰδότες ὅτι καὶ
ὑμεῖς ἔχετε κύριον ἐν οὐρανῷ (cf. I Cor. 7:21-23).

        The order of the domestic relations considered in Ephe-
sians and Colossians is the same, and the advice given in each
case is in close agreement, both in substance and in expression.
Ephesians is more fully elaborated and gives the impression of
being less concrete and immediate than Colossians. The possibility of independent incorporation of a "Haustafel" by Colossians
and Ephesians is admitted.

            Eph. 6:10-17   I Thessalonians B
        Τοῦ λοιποῦ ⌈ἐνδυναμοῦσθε⌉ ἐν κυρίῳ καὶ ἐν τῷ κράτει τῆς
ἰσχύος αὐτοῦ. ἐνδύσασθε τὴν πανοπλίαν τοῦ Θεοῦ πρὸς τὸ δύνασθαι
ὑμᾶς στῆναι πρὸς τὰς μεθοδίας τοῦ διαβόλου. ὅτι οὐκ ἔστιν ἡμῖν
ἡ πάλη πρὸς αἷμα καὶ σάρκα, ἀλλὰ πρὸς τὰς ἀρχάς, πρὸς τὰς ἐξουσίας,
πρὸς τοὺς κοσμοκράτορας τοῦ σκότους τούτου πρὸς τὰ πνευματικὰ τῆς πονηρίας ἐν τοῖς ἐπουρανίοις. διὰ τοῦτο ἀναλάβετε τὴν πανοπλίαν τοῦ
Θεοῦ, ἵνα δυνηθῆτε ἀντιστῆναι, ἐν τῇ ἡμέρᾳ τῇ πονηρᾷ καὶ ἅπαντα
κατεργασάμενοι στῆναι. στῆτε οὖν περιζωσάμενοι τὴν ὀσφὺν ὑμῶν ἐν
ἀληθείᾳ, καὶ ἐνδυσάμενοι τὸν θώρακα τῆς δικαιοσύνης, καὶ ὑποδησάμε-
νοι τοὺς πόδας ἐν ἑτοιμασίᾳ τοῦ εὐαγγελίου τῆς εἰρήνης, ἐν πᾶσιν
ἀναλαβόντες τὸν θυρεὸν τῆς πίστεως, ἐν ᾧ δυνήσεσθε πάντα τὰ βέλη
τοῦ πονηροῦ τὰ πεπυρωμένα σβέσαι· καὶ τὴν περικεφαλαίαν τοῦ σωτη-
ρίου δέξασθε, καὶ τὴν μάχαιραν τοῦ πνεύματος, ὅ ἐστιν ῥῆμα Θεοῦ.

        I Thess. 5:8. Ἡμεῖς δὲ ἡμέρας ὄντες νήφωμεν, ἐνδυσάμενοι
θώρακα πίστεως καὶ ἀγάπης καὶ περικεφαλαίαν ἐλπίδα σωτηρίας·

(cf. Rom. 13:12. Τὰ ὅπλα τοῦ φωτός. II Cor. 6:7. Διὰ τῶν ὅπλων
τῆς δικαιοσύνης τῶν δεξιῶν καὶ ἀριστερῶν; cf. Isa. 59:17 and Wisd.
of Sol. 5:17-20).

There is no parallel for Eph. 6:10-17 in Colossians. This
section is inserted between Col. 4:1 and 2 by the author of Ephesians. Though not found in Colossians, the figure of "spiritual
armor" does appear in other Pauline letters and is considerably
elaborated in I Thess. 5:8. The specific parallels between Ephesians and I Thessalonians are as follows:

Ephesians	I Thessalonians
Ἐνδυσάμενοι τὸν θώρακα τῆς δικαιοσύνης	Ἐνδυσάμενοι θώρακα πίστεως καὶ ἀγάπης
καὶ τὴν περικεφαλαίαν τοῦ σωτηρίου δέξασθε	καὶ περικεφαλαίαν ἐλπίδα σωτηρίας

It appears that Ephesians is closer to the LXX of Isa. 59:
17 than I Thessalonians is. The likelihood of dependence on the
LXX is increased by the use of terms from Isa. 11:5 and 52:7 which
are not found in I Thessalonians at all, although the figure in
these latter passages is not military. The πανοπλία of Ephesians
finds a parallel in Wisdom but not in Isaiah, and this is also the
case with θυρεός (cf. ἀσπίς) and μάχαιρα (cf. ῥομφαία).

There is no great difficulty in supposing that the author
of Ephesians used Wisdom. The Muratorian Fragment mentions Wisdom
as a New Testament book which indicates its popularity in Christian circles. However, dependence on Wisdom is not required, because πανοπλία is used in Luke 11:22 (its only use in the New Testament except Eph. 6:11, 13) and in a connection descriptive of
the spiritual enemies of men and the latter's need of spiritual
armor. The details are merely an itemizing of πανοπλία such as
would suggest no literary dependence.

There is one important item in which Ephesians agrees with
I Thessalonians against Wisdom. In Wisdom it is God who puts on
his armor, whereas in Ephesians it is man who puts on the divine
armor.

The probabilities are that the fundamental suggestion for
Ephesians came from I Thessalonians and from Luke 11:18-26 and

THE PUBLICATION OF PAUL'S LETTERS

that the picture was amplified by the use of imagery from Isaiah.

Eph. 6:18-20   Colossians A   II Corinthians C

Διὰ πάσης προσευχῆς καὶ δεήσεως προσευχόμενοι ἐν παντὶ
καιρῷ ἐν πνεύματι, καὶ εἰς αὐτὸ ἀγρυπνοῦντες ἐν πάσῃ προσκαρτερή-
σει καὶ δεήσει περὶ πάντων τῶν ἁγίων, καὶ ὑπὲρ ἐμοῦ, ἵνα μοι δοθῇ
λόγος ἐν ἀνοίξει τοῦ στόματός μου, ἐν παρρησίᾳ γνωρίσαι τὸ μυστήριον [τοῦ εὐαγγελίου] ὑπὲρ οὗ πρεσβεύω ἐν ἁλύσει, ἵνα ἐν αὐτῷ
παρρησιάσωμαι ὡς δεῖ με λαλῆσαι.

Col. 4:2-4. Τῇ προσευχῇ προσκαρτερεῖτε, γρηγοροῦντες ἐν
αὐτῇ ἐν εὐχαριστίᾳ, προσευχόμενοι ἅμα καὶ περὶ ἡμῶν, ἵνα ὁ Θεὸς
ἀνοίξῃ ἡμῖν θύραν τοῦ λόγου, λαλῆσαι τὸ μυστήριον τοῦ Χριστοῦ, δι'
ὃ καὶ δέδεμαι, ἵνα φανερώσω αὐτὸ ὡς δεῖ με λαλῆσαι.

Dependence of Eph. 6:18-20 on Col. 4:2-4 is unmistakable.
The request for prayer is more generalized than in Colossians.
These verses in Ephesians are a sort of plea for a hearing for the
message of Paul as it is embodied in his collected letters. They
make a most appropriate closing touch if Ephesians is regarded as
a preface to the Pauline corpus of letters.

The clause ὑπὲρ οὗ πρεσβεύω ἐν ἁλύσει may reflect the recollection of II Cor. 5:20. Ὑπὲρ Χριστοῦ οὖν πρεσβεύομεν and
Philem. 9. Παῦλος πρεσβύτης νυνὶ δὲ καὶ δέσμιος Χριστοῦ Ἰησοῦ
(cf. Acts 28:20. Εἵνεκεν γὰρ τῆς ἐλπίδος τοῦ Ἰσραὴλ τὴν ἅλυσιν
ταύτην περίκειμαι). Πρεσβεύω is used in the New Testament only in
II Cor. 5:20 and Eph. 6:20, and the dependence of Ephesians for
its use is rather clear. The ἐν ἁλύσει, however, indicates dependence on Acts rather than on Philemon. Acts closed with Paul
"in chains," and Ephesians combines the picture of Acts with that
of II Corinthians.

Eph. 6:21, 22   Colossians A

Ἵνα δὲ ⌜εἰδῆτε καὶ ὑμεῖς⌝ τὰ κατ' ἐμέ, τί πράσσω, πάντα
γνωρίσει ὑμῖν Τύχικος ὁ ἀγαπητὸς ἀδελφὸς καὶ πιστὸς διάκονος ἐν
κυρίῳ, ὃν ἔπεμψα πρὸς ὑμᾶς εἰς αὐτὸ τοῦτο ἵνα γνῶτε τὰ περὶ ἡμῶν
καὶ παρακαλέσῃ τὰς καρδίας ὑμῶν.

Col. 4:7, 8. Τὰ κατ' ἐμὲ πάντα γνωρίσει ὑμῖν Τύχικος ὁ
ἀγαπητὸς ἀδελφὸς καὶ πιστὸς διάκονος καὶ σύνδουλος ἐν κυρίῳ, ὃν
ἔπεμψα πρὸς ὑμᾶς εἰς αὐτὸ τοῦτο ἵνα γνῶτε τὰ περὶ ἡμῶν καὶ παρακαλέσῃ τὰς καρδίας ὑμῶν

The story of Acts leaves Paul in prison, and this makes the personal note from Colossians an appropriate closing for Ephesians.

Instances of Possible Literary Reminiscence

Eph. 1:6; cf. Phil. 1:11. Ἔπαινος occurs eleven times in the New Testament, nine of them in the ten letters of the Pauline corpus and two in I Peter. Only in Eph. 1:6 and Phil. 1:11 does the term refer directly to God.

Eph. 1:10; cf. Gal. 4:4. This temporal use of πλήρωμα occurs in the New Testament only in Eph. 1:10 and Gal. 4:4.

Eph. 1:14; cf. Phil. 1:11.

Eph. 2:1, 3; cf. Col. 1:21 and Rom. 11:15.

Eph. 2:3; cf. Gal. 2:15. The use of φύσις in the New Testament is confined to the Pauline corpus and the later letters.

Eph. 29; cf. Phil. 3:20.

Eph. 3:2; cf. Gal. 1:13. The clause εἴ γε ἠκούσατε of Eph. 3:2 may represent a reminiscence of ἠκούσατε γὰρ τὴν ἐμὴν ἀναστροφήν ποτε ἐν τῷ Ἰουδαισμῷ from Gal. 1:13.

Eph. 3:14; cf. Rom. 11:4 and Phil. 2:10. The only instances in the New Testament where κάμπτω is used are the passages cited. In Romans and Philippians the verb occurs in quotations from the LXX.

Eph. 3:15; cf. I Cor. 8:5 and Col. 1:5.

Eph. 3:16; cf. Rom. 9:23 and Col. 1:27.

Eph. 3:16; cf. Rom. 7:22 and II Cor. 4:16. The use of εἰς τὸν ἔσω ἄνθρωπον points to possible indebtedness to Romans and II Corinthians. Only in the three instances cited is ἔσω so used in the New Testament.

Eph. 3:18; cf. Rom. 8:39.

Eph. 3:19; cf. I Cor. 8:2 and II Cor. 9:14. The idea of love that surpasses knowledge may represent the influence of I Corinthians. The use of ὑπερβάλλω may represent a trace of the influence of II Corinthians.

Eph. 3:20; cf. I Thess. 3:10; 5:13. The adverb ὑπερεκπερισσοῦ is used in the New Testament only in I Thess. 3:10 and 5:13 and in Eph. 3:20. Ὑπερεκπερισσῶς is used in I Thess. 5:13. Neither form occurs in the LXX.

Eph. 4:9, 10; cf. Rom. 10:6-8. The idea of the descent
"to the under parts of the earth" may have been suggested by Rom.
10:6-8.

Eph. 4:15; cf. Gal. 4:16. Ἀληθεύω is used in the New
Testament only in Gal. 4:16 and Eph. 4:15.   It occurs five times
in the LXX.

Eph. 4:21; cf. Phil. 1:18 and II Cor. 11:10.

Eph. 4:26; cf. I Cor. 15:34. The quotation of Ps. 4:4 in
Ephesians may have been suggested by I Corinthians.

Eph. 4:27; cf. II Cor. 2:11 and Rom. 12:19.

Eph. 4:28; cf. Rom. 2:21; 13:9.

Eph. 4:29; cf. Col. 4:6.

Eph. 5:1; cf. I Cor. 4:15.   Only in the instances cited
is ἀγαπητός used in the New Testament with τέκνον.   Μιμητής is
also used in the New Testament only in the instances cited and in
Heb. 6:12.

Eph. 5:2; cf. Gal. 2:20.

Eph. 5:2; cf. Phil. 4:18 and II Cor. 2:14, 15.   Paul's description of the gift received through Epaphroditus may have suggested the Ephesian description of Christ's gift of himself.
Εὐωδία is used in the New Testament only in II Cor. 2:15, Phil.
4:18, and Eph. 5:2. Ὀσμή is used only in II Cor. 2:14, Phil. 4:18,
Eph. 5:2, and John 12:3.

Eph. 5:9; cf. I Thess. 5:5.

Eph. 5:9, 10; cf. Gal. 5:22 and Rom. 12:2.   The use of
Ἀγαθωσύνη in connection with καρπός may be significant.

Eph. 5:11; cf. Rom. 13:12 and II Cor. 6:14.

Eph. 5:12, 13; cf. I Cor. 11:6 and 14:35.

Eph. 5:14; cf. Rom. 13:11.

Eph. 5:16; cf. Gal. 1:14.

Eph. 5:18; cf. Rom. 13:13.

Eph. 5:30, 31; cf. I Cor. 6:15, 17.

Eph. 6:10; cf. I Cor. 16:13.

Eph. 6:12; cf. Rom. 8:38, 39.

TABLE OF RESULTS

	A	B	C	Unclassed
Romans............	5	5	12	18
I Corinthians......	..	5	8	14
II Corinthians.....	1	7	5	11
Galatians..........	..	2	3	12
Philippians........	..	..	1	13
Colossians.........	19	11	12	6
I Thessalonians....	..	3	1	4
II Thessalonians...	..	1	..	....
Philemon...........	..	3	1	....

II

THE POPULARITY OF THE PUBLISHED LETTERS

Any publication ordinarily enjoys its maximum of popularity immediately following its appearance. Paul's published letters at once aroused widespread interest among Christians. Leaders throughout the church seem to have read them and been profoundly affected by them. A burst of literary activity extending over a quarter of a century or more was apparently inaugurated by this venture in publication.

The Apocalypse of John

The Apocalypse of John is illustrative of this popular response and stands as the first witness to the existence of the published corpus. The author of the Muratorian Canon sensed a relationship of some kind between the Pauline letter collection and the corpus of letters with which the Apocalypse is introduced, for he notes that "the blessed Apostle Paul himself, following the order of his predecessor John, writes only by name to seven churches. . . . ." If this sequence is reversed and the Apocalypse is seen as having been written under the shadow of the published letters of Paul, then this introduction of an Apocalypse with a corpus of seven letters prefaced by a cover letter (Apoc. 1:20) becomes intelligible. The Pauline letter collection is the unmistakable precedent, containing, as it does, letters to seven churches prefaced by an encyclical.

Prior to the year A.D. 90 there are no letters of instruction from Christian leaders except the letters of Paul. These letters were apparently collected and published as a result of the revival of interest in Paul aroused by the publication of Luke-Acts. The introductory letter corpus of the Apocalypse of John is a certain witness to the existence of Paul's published letters.

There are other general features of the Apocalypse that

point to acquaintance with the collected letters of Paul, as, for
instance, the distinctively Pauline salutation χάρις ὑμῖν καὶ
εἰρήνη of 1:4. This phrase is used here and in nine letters of
the Pauline corpus and is apparently not earlier than those letters.[1]

The liturgical interest which is common to Ephesians and
the Apocalypse may reflect the influence of the one on the other.
Acquaintance with Ephesians on the part of the Apocalypse is rather
certain, and this implies acquaintance with Paul's collected letters since it is an assured fact that Ephesians was a member of
the original Pauline collection.

The author of the Apocalypse makes frequent use of Old
Testament material. He drew mostly from the prophets and Psalms
but shows acquaintance with all the groups of writings in the Old
Testament and with such apocryphal books as the Testaments, I Enoch,
the Assumption of Moses, and probably II Enoch and the Psalms of
Solomon. His method of using his sources is that of the incorporation of phrases and clauses rather than of definite quotation.[2]

         Apoc. 1:5   Colossians B
ʽΟ πρωτότοκος τῶν νεκρῶν.
Col. 1:18. ῝Ος ἐστιν . . . πρωτότοκος ἐκ τῶν νεκρῶν.

The phrase common to the two passages occurs nowhere else
in the New Testament (cf. I Cor. 15:20, ἐγήγερται ἐκ νεκρῶν ἀπαρχὴ
τῶν κεκοιμημένων).

         Apoc. 1:5   Ephesians C
Τῷ ἀγαπῶντι ἡμᾶς καὶ λύσαντι ἡμᾶς ἐκ τῶν ἁμαρτιῶν [ἡμῶν]
ἐν τῷ αἵματι αὐτοῦ.
Eph. 5:2. Ο Χριστὸς ἠγάπησεν ὑμᾶς καὶ παρέδωκεν ἑαυτὸν
ὑπὲρ ⌐ὑμῶν¬ . . . 1:7. ᾽Εν ᾧ ἔχομεν τὴν ἀπολύτρωσιν διὰ τοῦ
αἵματος αὐτοῦ, τὴν ἄφεσιν τῶν παραπτωμάτων (cf. Gal. 2:20).

_____

[1]R. H. Charles, The Revelation of St. John (New York:
Charles Scribner's Sons, 1920), I, lxxxiii, 9, and 13.

[2]E. Lohmeyer, Die Offenbarung des Johannes (Tübingen:
J. C. B. Mohr, 1926), p. 191.

The stress on the efficacy of Jesus' blood in connection
with redemption and the forgiveness of sins makes literary dependence on Ephesians probable.

Apoc. 1:9   Philippians C   II Thessalonians C
Ἐγὼ Ἰωάνης, ὁ ἀδελφὸς ὑμῶν καὶ συνκοινωνὸς ἐν τῇ θλίψει
καὶ βασιλείᾳ καὶ ὑπομονῇ ἐν Ἰησοῦ.
Phil. 4:14. Συνκοινωνήσαντές μου τῇ θλίψει. . . . . 3:10.
κοινωνίαν παθημάτων αὐτοῦ.
II Thess. 3:5. Εἰς τὴν ὑπομονὴν τοῦ Χριστοῦ.

The verb συνκοινωνέω occurs in the New Testament only in
Phil. 4:14, Eph. 5:11, and Apoc. 18:4. In Phil. 4:14 it is used
in connection with θλίψις.
Συνκοινωνός occurs in the New Testament in Rom. 11:17,
I Cor. 9:23, Phil. 1:7, and Apoc. 1:9. Its use in the last instance in connection with θλίψις suggests dependence on Philippians.
Ὑπομονή occurs in the New Testament in Luke 8:15 and 21:
19, the Pauline letters, and the later New Testament writings.
Its use in Apoc. 1:9 in connection with the phrase ἐν Ἰησοῦ suggests the influence of II Thess. 3:5.

Apoc. 2:2   I Thessalonians C
Οἶδα τὰ ἔργα σου, καὶ τὸν κόπον καὶ τὴν ὑπομονήν.
I Thess. 1:2. Μνημονεύοντες ὑμῶν τοῦ ἔργου τῆς πίστεως
καὶ τοῦ κόπου τῆς ἀγάπης καὶ τῆς ὑπομονῆς τῆς ἐλπίδος.

The sequence ἔργον . . . . κόπος . . . . ὑπομονή suggests
literary reminiscence. These terms, while not exclusively Pauline,
find their most frequent use in Paul's letters and the later writings influenced by those letters. The sense in which they are
used, as well as the striking sequence in which they fall, corresponds with that of I Thessalonians.

Apoc. 2:9   II Corinthians C
Οἶδα σου . . . . τὴν πτωχείαν, ἀλλὰ πλούσιος εἶ.
II Cor. 6:10. Ὡς πτωχοὶ πολλοὺς δὲ πλουτίζοντες.
8:9. Ὅτι δι' ὑμᾶς ἐπτώχευσεν πλούσιος ὤν, ἵνα ὑμεῖς τῇ ἐκείνου
πτωχείᾳ πλουτήσητε (cf. Jas. 2:5).

The contrast of πτωχείαν and πλούσιος suggests dependence
on II Corinthians. The verb πτωχεύω is found in the New Testament only in II Cor. 8:9, and the noun πτωχεία only in II Cor. 8:2,
9, and Apoc. 2:9. The adjective πτωχός is used in all sections of
the New Testament but only in the passages noted as part of the
contrast involved.

       Apoc. 2:9   Romans C   Galatians C

Οἶδα . . . . τὴν βλασπημίαν ἐκ τῶν λεγόντων ᾽Ιουδαίους
εἶναι ἑαυτούς, καὶ οὐκ εἰσίν.

Rom. 2:28, 29. Οὐ γὰρ ὁ ἐν τῷ φανερῷ ᾽Ιουδαῖός ἐστιν . . . . ἀλλ᾽
ὁ ἐν τῷ κρυπτῷ ᾽Ιουδαῖος, καὶ περιτομὴ καρδίας ἐν πνεύματι οὐ
γράμματι, οὗ ὁ ἔπαινος οὐκ ἐξ ἀνθρώπων ἀλλ᾽ ἐκ τοῦ Θεοῦ.

Gal. 3:29. Εἰ δὲ ὑμεῖς Χριστοῦ, ἄρα τοῦ ᾽Αβραὰμ σπέρμα
ἐστέ. 6:15, 16. Οὔτε γὰρ περιτομή τι ἔστιν οὔτε ἀκροβυστία, ἀλλὰ
καινὴ κτίσις. καὶ ὅσοι τῷ κανόνι τούτῳ στοιχήσουσιν, εἰρήνη ἐπ᾽
αὐτοὺς καὶ ἔλεος, καὶ ἐπὶ τὸν ᾽Ισραὴλ τοῦ Θεοῦ (cf. II Cor. 11:14 f.).

The three passages contrast Jews who are Jews in race only
and who lack true spirituality with those who embody the highest
spiritual heritage of Israel. It is probable that the author of
the Apocalypse used the Pauline position to good effect in a persecution situation in which Jews probably played an aggravating
part.

       Apoc. 3:9   Romans C   Galatians C

Τῶν λεγόντων ἑαυτοὺς ᾽Ιουδαίους εἶναι.
See the note on Apoc. 2:9.

       Apoc. 3:12   Galatians C

῾Ο νικῶν ποιήσω αὐτὸν στύλον ἐν τῷ ναῷ τοῦ Θεοῦ μου.
Gal. 2:9. Οἱ δοκοῦντες στύλοι εἶναι.

The metaphorical use of στύλος was common in rabbinic literature, but in the New Testament it occurs only in Gal. 2:9;
Apoc. 3:12, 10:1; and I Tim. 3:15. The figure is a natural one
and does not require literary dependence for its explanation. The
sense in which it is used in 3:12 so closely resembles its use in
Galatians, however, as to make literary reminiscence a probable
explanation.

Apoc. 3:14   Colossians C
Καὶ τῷ ἀγγέλῳ ⌜τῆς⌝ ἐν Λαοδικίᾳ ἐκκλησίας.

Laodicea is mentioned in the New Testament only in Col.
2:1, 4:13, 15, 16 and Apoc. 1:11, 3:14.

Apoc. 3:14   Colossians B
Ἡ ἀρχὴ τῆς κτίσεως τοῦ Θεοῦ.
Col. 1:15. Ὅς ἐστιν . . . . πρωτότοκος πάσης κτίσεως.
. . . . 18. Ὅς ἐστιν [ἡ] ἀρχή.

There can be little doubt of the influence of Colossians
in the description of Christ in Apoc. 3:14. A letter to Laodicea
is mentioned in Col. 4:16, which adds weight to the likelihood of
the influence of Colossians in the address to the Laodicean church
in the Apocalypse.

Apoc. 3:17   II Corinthians C
Ὅτι λέγεις ὅτι Πλούσιός εἰμι καὶ πεπλούτηκα καὶ οὐδὲν
χρείαν ἔχω, καὶ οὐκ οἶδας ὅτι σὺ εἶ ὁ ταλαίπωρος καὶ ἐλεινὸς καὶ
πτωχὸς καὶ τυφλὸς καὶ γυμνός.

See the note on Apoc. 2:9 for the reflection of the influence of II Cor. 6:10 in the contrast of πλούσιος and πτωχός.

Apoc. 7:3   Ephesians C
Ἄχρι σφραγίσωμεν τοὺς δούλους τοῦ Θεοῦ.
Eph. 4:30. Ἐν ᾧ ἐσφραγίσθητε εἰς ἡμέραν ἀπολυτρώσεως.

The connotation of σφραγίζω in the two passages is very
similar. In the one it denotes a "sign" on believers which would
immunize them to the harmful influences of spiritual enemies, and
in the other it constitutes a guaranty of spiritual preservation.

Apoc. 10:7   Ephesians B
Χρόνος οὐκέτι ἔσται ἀλλ' ἐν ταῖς ἡμέραις τῆς φωνῆς τοῦ
ἑβδόμου ἀγγέλου, ὅταν μέλλῃ σαλπίζειν, καὶ ἐτελέσθη τὸ μυστήριον
τοῦ Θεοῦ, ὡς εὐηγγέλισεν τοὺς ἑαυτοῦ δούλους τοὺς προφήτας.
Eph. 3:4, 5. Δύνασθε ἀναγινώσκοντες νοῆσαι τὴν σύνεσίν
μου ἐν τῷ μυστηρίῳ τοῦ Χριστοῦ, ὃ ἑτέραις γενεαῖς οὐκ ἐγνωρίσθη
τοῖς υἱαῖς τῶν ἀνθρώπων ὡς νῦν ἀπεκαλύφθη τοῖς ἁγίοις ἀποστόλοις

αὐτοῦ καὶ προφήταις ἐν πνεύματι (cf. II Thess. 2:6-8 and Amos 3:7).

     In each of the two passages a definite time is indicated prior to which a divine μυστήριον was concealed, which was then revealed to the prophets. The use of ἀπεκαλύφθη in Ephesians (cf. Eph. 1:17, πνεῦμα ἀποκαλύψεως, and Apoc. 19:10, πνεῦμα τῆς προφητείας) corresponds with the idea of Apoc. 10:7. Τοῖς ἁγίοις ἀποστόλοις αὐτοῦ καὶ προφήταις of Ephesians is very probably echoed in the τοῖς δούλοις σου τοῖς προφήταις καὶ τοῖς ἁγίοις of Apoc. 11:18. The ἐν πνεύματι of Ephesians is a common conception in the Apocalypse for describing the state of mind in which revelation takes place. The emphasis on the Apostles in Eph. 2:20 and 3:5 is matched in Apoc. 21:14. It is highly probable that the Apocalypse reflects acquaintance with Ephesians, and the present passage is an instance in which this acquaintance is rather clearly visible.

     There may be an echo of I Cor. 15:51, 52 in the ὅταν μέλλῃ σαλπίζειν, καὶ ἐτελέσθη τὸ μυστήριον τοῦ Θεοῦ.

Apoc. 11:18   Ephesians B

Τοῖς δούλοις σου τοῖς προφήταις καὶ τοῖς ἁγίοις.

     See the text of Eph. 3:5 and a discussion of its influence on the Apocalypse in the note on Apoc. 10:7. The allusion is evidently to Christian prophets, so that the πρὸς τοὺς δούλους αὐτοῦ τοὺς προφήτας is at best a verbal parallel and gives no equivalent for τοῖς ἁγίοις.

Apoc. 14:13   I Thessalonians C

Οἱ νεκροὶ οἱ ἐν κυρίῳ ἀποθνήσκοντες
I Thess. 4:16. Οἱ νεκροὶ ἐν Χριστῷ (cf. I Cor. 15:18).

     The phrase that is common to I Thessalonians and the Apocalypse occurs only in these instances, although the same idea is present in I Cor. 15:18.

Apoc. 18:4   Ephesians B

Ἵνα μὴ συνκοινωνήσητε ταῖς ἁμαρτίαις αὐτῆς.
Eph. 5:11. Μὴ συνκοινωνεῖτε τοῖς ἔργοις τοῖς ἀκάρποις τοῦ σκότους (cf. II Cor. 6:14-16).

The verb συνκοινωνέω occurs in the New Testament only in
Eph. 5:11, Phil. 4:14, and Apoc. 18:4.   Its use in Ephesians and
the Apocalypse is so nearly identical as to make literary dependence highly probable.

                Apoc. 19:7, 8   Ephesians B
      ῞Οτι ἦλθεν ὁ γάμος τοῦ ἀρνίου, καὶ ἡ γυνὴ αὐτοῦ ἡτοίμασεν
ἑαυτήν, καὶ ἐδόθη αὐτῇ ἵνα περιβάληται βύσσινον λαμπρον καθαρόν,
τὸ γὰρ βύσσινον τὰ δικαιώματα τῶν ἁγίων ἐστίν.
      Eph. 5:25-27, 29, 32.   Καθὼς καὶ ὁ Χριστὸς ἠγάπησεν τὴν
ἐκκλησίαν καὶ ἑαυτὸν παρέδωκεν ὑπὲρ αὐτῆς, ἵνα αὐτὴν ἁγιάσῃ καθαρίσας τῷ λουτρῷ τοῦ ὕδατος ἐν ῥήματι, ἵνα παραστήσῃ αὐτὸς ἑαυτῷ
ἔνδοξον τὴν ἐκκλησίαν, μὴ ἔχουσαν σπίλον ἢ ῥυτίδα ἤ τι τῶν τοιούτων, ἀλλ' ἵνα ᾖ ἁγία καὶ ἄμωμος. . . . . ἀλλὰ ἐκτρέφει καὶ θάλπει
αὐτήν, καθὼς καὶ ὁ Χριστὸς τὴν ἐκκλησίαν . . . . τὸ μυστήριον τοῦτο μέγα ἐστίν, ἐγὼ δὲ λέγω εἰς Χριστὸν καὶ [εἰς] τὴν ἐκκλησίαν.

      The nearest approach to the employment of the figure of
Christ and the church as bridegroom and bride in the genuine letters of Paul is found in II Cor. 11:2.   In Ephesians and the Apocalypse, however, Christ is much more specifically identified as
the bridegroom and the church as the bride.   A common emphasis on
the purification of the bride tends further to relate the Apocalypse to Ephesians.

                Apoc. 21:2   Ephesians B
      ῾Ητοιμασμένην ὡς νύμφην κεκοσμημένην τῷ ἀνδρὶ αὐτῆς.

      For the influence of Eph. 5:25 ff. and the possible in-
fluence of II Cor. 11:2 on the Apocalypse see the note on Apoc.
19:7, 8.

                Apoc. 21:9   Ephesians B
      Δείξω σοι τὴν νύμφην τὴν γυναῖκα τοῦ ἀρνίου.
      See the note on Apoc. 19:7, 8.

                Apoc. 21:14, 22   Ephesians B
      Καὶ τὸ τεῖχος τῆς πόλεως ἔχων θεμελίους δώδεκα, καὶ ἐπ'
αὐτῶν δώδεκα ὀνόματα τῶν δώδεκα ἀποστόλων τοῦ ἀρνίου . . . . καὶ
ναὸν οὐκ εἶδον ἐν αὐτῇ, ὁ γὰρ κύριος, ὁ θεός . . . . ναὸς αὐτῆς ἐστίν.
      Eph. 2:20-22. ᾿Εποικοδομηθέντες ἐπὶ τῷ θεμελίῳ τῶν ἀποστόλων

καὶ προφητῶν, ὄντος ἀκρογωνιαίου αὐτοῦ Χριστοῦ Ἰησοῦ, ἐν ᾧ πᾶσα οἰκοδομὴ συναρμολογουμένη αὔξει εἰς ναὸν ἅγιον ἐν κυρίῳ, ἐν ᾧ καὶ ὑμεῖς συνοικοδομεῖσθε εἰς κατοικητήριον τοῦ Θεοῦ ἐν πνεύματι.

This idea of the church as founded on the apostles is peculiar in the New Testament to Ephesians and the Apocalypse. The latter very probably derived it from the former. The close association of the idea of a spiritual temple in both contexts strengthens the probability of literary relationship.

Apoc. 22:13 Colossians B

Ἐγὼ τὸ Ἄλφα καὶ τὸ Ὦ, ⌜ὁ πρῶτος καὶ ὁ⌝ ἔσχατος, ἡ ἀρχὴ καὶ τὸ τέλος (cf. Isa. 44:6 and 48:12).

Col. 1:18. Ὅς ἐστιν [ἡ] ἀρχή.

The Christology of the two passages is similar and is expressed in a way that suggests the probability of literary relationship.

Apoc. 22:17 Ephesians B

Καὶ ⌜τὸ πνεῦμα καὶ ἡ⌝ νύμφη λέγουσιν Ἔρχου· καὶ ὁ ἀκούων εἰπάτω Ἔρχου.

The idea of the church as the bride reflects the influence of Ephesians (see the note on Apoc. 19:7, 8). The Ἔρχου may reflect the influence of Μαρὰν ἀθά in I Cor. 16:22 (cf. Did. 10:6).

Instances of possible literary reminiscence.—Apoc. 1:3; cf. Rom. 13:11. Ὁ γὰρ καιρὸς ἐγγύς possibly reflects acquaintance with Rom. 13:11; cf. Matt. 26:18.

Apoc. 1:6; cf. Rom. 16:27.

Apoc. 1:7; cf. II Cor. 1:20. This use of the Greek and Hebrew affirmative expressions to supplement each other may reflect the influence of II Corinthians. The influence of II Corinthians is clearer in Apoc. 3:14, where ὁ Ἀμην designates Christ as the divine "Amen" expressed in terms of personality.

Apoc. 1:8; cf. II Cor. 6:18. The designation of God as ὁ παντοκράτωρ occurs frequently in the Apocalypse. Aside from its occurrence there, it is found in the New Testament only in II Cor. 6:18.

Apoc. 1:10; cf. Eph. 3:5 and II Cor. 1:2-4. All Christians were regarded as ἐν πνεύματι in contrast with unbelievers,

who were ἐν σαρκί (Rom. 8:9). The phrase in Apoc. 1:10 and Eph.
3:5, however, denotes the state of mind·in which supernatural revelation is received.

Apoc. 1:10; cf. I Cor. 11:20. Κυριακός occurs in the New
Testament only in I Cor. 11:20 and Apoc. 1:10 (cf. I Cor. 10:21,
ποτήριον κυρίου and τράπεζα κυρίου).

Apoc. 1:18; cf. II Cor. 6:9.

Apoc. 1:20; cf. Eph. 5:32. The association of μυστήριον
and ἐκκλησία may indicate literary acquaintance.

Apoc. 2:2; cf. II Cor. 11:13. In Paul's address to the
Ephesian elders at Miletus, there is a warning against "savage
wolves" who might "teach perversions of the truth." This passage
in Apoc. 2:2 breathes the atmosphere of Acts 20:29-31 and probably
reflects its influence, although the language reminds one of II
Cor. 11:13.

Apoc. 2:3; cf. Eph. 6:10-13. The two passages center about
the similar ideas of conflict and victory.

Apoc. 2:11; cf. I Cor. 9:25. The figure is a popular one
with Paul. The most direct parallel for Apoc. 2:11 in the Pauline
letters is I Cor. 9:25. Charles thinks the Apocalypse depends on
James.[3]

Apoc. 2:15, 16; cf. I Cor. 8:7-13 and 10:20, 30. The
meaning of the phrase φαγεῖν εἰδωλόθυτα is obscure and may refer
to meat bought in a public shop which had been consecrated to an
idol or to sacramental participation in pagan meals. The term
εἰδωλόθυτος occurs in the New Testament in Acts 15:29, 21:25;
I Cor. 8:4, 7, 10, 10:19; and Apoc. 2:14, 20.

Apoc. 2:24; cf. I Cor. 2:10.

Apoc. 3:2; cf. Eph. 5:14 and II Cor. 6:9.

Apoc. 3:3; cf. I Thess. 5:2.

Apoc. 3:5; cf. Phil. 4:3.

Apoc. 3:11; cf. I Cor. 9:25.

Apoc. 3:12; cf. Gal. 4:26.

Apoc. 3:15; cf. II Cor. 1:20.

Apoc. 3:18; cf. Eph. 1:17.

Apoc. 3:21; cf. Col. 2:1 and Eph. 1:20.

----

[3] Op. cit., I, lxxxiii and lxxxiv.

Apoc. 4:11; cf. Eph. 3:9.

Apoc. 5:6; cf. I Cor. 5:8.

Apoc. 5:9; cf. I Cor. 6:20 and Eph. 2:13. The use of ἀγοράζω may reflect acquaintance with I Corinthians. It is used in the sense of this passage only in I Cor. 6:20, 7:23; Apoc. 5:9; and II Pet. 2:1.

The union of Jew and Greek ἐν τῷ αἵματι τοῦ Χριστοῦ in Eph. 2:13 may have suggested the fundamental thought of Apoc. 5:9.

Apoc. 7:14; cf. I Cor. 6:11. Πλύνω is used in the New Testament only in Luke 5:2 and Apoc. 7:14 and 22:14. Ἀπολούω is used only in I Cor. 6:11 and Acts 22:16.

Apoc. 11:18; cf. Rom. 2:5 and I Thess. 1:10.

Apoc. 12:17; cf. Gal. 4:26.

Apoc. 13:2; cf. Rom. 13:1-6. The position of the Apocalypse with reference to the state contradicts that of Romans. This may be an intentional contradiction. The likelihood of its having been conscious is strengthened by the probability that I Peter proposed to counteract the vindictiveness of the Apocalypse by advocating the Pauline insistence on patience and love.

Apoc. 13:8; cf. Phil. 4:3.

Apoc. 14:3, 5; cf. Eph. 1:4.

Apoc. 16:15; cf. I Thess. 5:2, 4, 6.

Apoc. 18:20; cf. Eph. 3:5.

Apoc. 19:10; cf. Eph. 1:17.

Apoc. 20:4; cf. I Cor. 6:2 and I Thess. 4:17.

Apoc. 20:12; cf. Phil. 4:3.

Apoc. 21:2; cf. Gal. 4:26.

Apoc. 21:3-7; cf. II Cor. 5:17 and 6:16, 18.

Apoc. 21:11; cf. Phil. 2:15. Φωστήρ occurs in the New Testament only in these two passages. It is used in both instances in substantially the same sense.

Apoc. 21:16; cf. Eph. 3:18. The only occurrences of μῆκος and πλάτος in the New Testament are in these two passages. Ὕψος occurs in Luke, Ephesians, James, and the Apocalypse. The sequence of these terms creates the possibility of literary dependence, although both writers might have been familiar with them in some Gnostic context.

Apoc. 22:21; cf. Eph. 6:24.

Charles says that the author of the Apocalypse "appears to have used . . . . I Thessalonians, I and II Corinthians, Colossians, Ephesians and possibly Galatians."[4] The present study finds the evidence for Romans, Philippians, and I Thessalonians stronger than for I Corinthians and raises Galatians from the category of the merely possible to that of the probable. Traces of nine of the letters of the Pauline corpus are found. Philemon, the one letter of which no trace is found, may have been known to the author of the Apocalypse as Laodiceans[5] (cf. Col. 4:16), and his severe attitude toward that church (3:14-19) may account for the absence of any reminiscence of the letter addressed to it.

TABLE OF RESULTS

	A	B	C	Unclassed
Romans..............	.	.	2	4
I Corinthians.......	.	.	.	11
II Corinthians......	.	.	2	7
Galatians..........	.	.	3	4
Ephesians..........	.	8	2	13
Philippians........	.	.	1	4
Colossians.........	.	3	1	1
I Thessalonians.....	.	.	2	3
II Thessalonians....	.	.	1	1
Philemon...........	.	.	.	....

The First Epistle of Peter

The First Epistle of Peter is an equally impressive witness with the Apocalypse to the existence and influence of Paul's letters as a published collection. The point at which I Peter falls most naturally in the development of early Christian literature is just following the Apocalypse. It may even represent an answer to the vindictiveness of the Apocalypse, in which case it is to be re-

---

[4] Ibid., p. lxxxiii.

[5] E. J. Goodspeed, New Solutions of New Testament Problems (Chicago: University of Chicago Press, 1927), pp. 51-57.

garded as a conscious assertion of the Pauline attitude as against
that of the Apocalypse toward civil authority.

First Peter evidences acquaintance not simply with Pauline
ideas but with those ideas as they are expressed in Paul's letters. The writer was not a Paulinist in the sense of being completely controlled by Paul's distinctive emphases. He seems
rather to have read his letters selectively and used with freedom
those ideas that suited his practical purposes. The encyclical
character of the letter is an almost certain indication of the influence of Ephesians.

The character of the author's method in the use of sources
is illuminated by his use of the Old Testament. The data here are
abundant, since he uses the Old Testament in twenty-nine instances.
He does not hesitate to combine allusions and short quotations from
different books and from separate contexts. His method is more
frequently that of allusion than that of direct quotation. Where
he employs formal quotation he does so sometimes with no introductory formula, as in 3:10 ff., where he quotes Ps. 34:12-16.
In other instances formulas are used, as 1:16, διότι γέγραπται;
1:18, εἰδότες ὅτι; 1:24, διότι; 2:6, διότι περιέχει ἐν γραφῇ;
5:5, ὅτι. The quotations are generally brief and are woven in with
the author's own thought with no indication of conscious literary
indebtedness.

I Pet. 1:1   Ephesians B

Πέτρος ἀπόστολος ᾽Ιησοῦ Χριστοῦ ἐκλεκτοῖς παρεπιδήμοις
διασπορᾶς Πόντου, Γαλατίας, Καππαδοκίας, ᾽Ασίας, καὶ Βιθυνίας.

Eph. 1:1. Παῦλος ἀπόστολος Χριστοῦ ᾽Ιησοῦ διὰ θελήματος
Θεοῦ τοῖς ἁγίοις τοῖς οὖσιν . . . . καὶ πιστοῖς ἐν Χριστῷ ᾽Ιησοῦ·

The writer's description of himself is typically Pauline.
The catholic character of the address furnishes a strong hint of
literary acquaintance with Ephesians. Both letters are addressed
to Christians everywhere, and the precedent furnished by Ephesians
probably suggested the plan of I Peter to its author. The description of those addressed as ἐκλεκτοῖς corresponds with that
of Eph. 1:4, καθὼς ἐξελέξατο ἡμᾶς (cf. Col. 3:12, ὡς ἐκλεκτοὶ τοῦ
Θεοῦ).

I Pet. 1:2   Romans A II Thessalonians C Ephesians C

Κατὰ πρόγνωσιν θεοῦ πατρός, ἐν ἁγιασμῷ πνεύματος, εἰς
ὑπακοὴν καὶ ῥαντισμὸν αἵματος Ἰησοῦ Χριστοῦ· Χάρις ὑμῖν καὶ
εἰρήνη πληθυνθείη.

I Pet. 1:2 is made up almost entirely of ideas and expressions that seem to be taken directly from Pauline letters. The
connection with Romans is clearest, but Ephesians and II Thessalonians seem also to have supplied ideas and phrases. (1) The
basis of "election" as expressed in the first clause corresponds
with that of Rom. 8:28-30. Οἴδαμεν δὲ ὅτι τοῖς ἀγαπῶσι τὸν θεὸν
πάντα συνεργεῖ [ὁ θεὸς] εἰς ἀγαθόν, τοῖς κατὰ πρόθεσιν κλητοῖς
οὖσιν. ὅτι οὓς προέγνω, καὶ προώρισεν συμμόρφους τῆς εἰκόνος
τοῦ υἱοῦ αὐτοῦ, εἰς τὸ εἶναι αὐτὸν πρωτότοκον ἐν πολλοῖς ἀδελφοῖς·
οὓς δὲ προώρισεν, τούτους καὶ ἐκάλεσεν· Προγινώσκω is used in the
New Testament in Acts 26:5; Rom. 8:29, 11:2; I Pet. 1:20; and II
Pet. 3:17. Πρόγνωσις is used in Acts 2:23 and I Pet. 1:2. The
thought accords closely also with that of Eph. 1:5 (προορίσας
ἡμᾶς). The latter, however, seems to have rested on Rom. 8:28-30
(προορίζω occurs in the New Testament in Acts 4:28; Rom. 8:29, 30;
I Cor. 2:7; Eph. 1:5, 11), so that Romans is here the adequate explanation of I Peter. (2) The phrase ἐν ἁγιασμῷ πνεύματος occurs
in the New Testament in I Pet. 1:2 and in II Thess. 2:13. Ἁγιασμός
occurs only in the Pauline letters and the later writings that
were influenced by them (Heb. 12:14, I Pet. 1:2, and I Tim. 2:15).
(3) Εἰς ὑπακοήν is a phrase that occurs in Rom. 1:5, 6:16, 15:18,
16:26, and II Cor. 10:5. The noun is found in the New Testament
only in the Pauline letters and in Hebrews and I Peter. (4) Εἰς
. . . . ῥαντισμὸν αἵματος Ἰησοῦ Χριστοῦ may reflect the influence
of Heb. 12:24 (ῥαντισμός occurs in the New Testament only in Heb.
12:24 and I Pet. 1:2). Ῥαντίζω is used in Mark 7:4; Heb. 9:13,
19, 21, 10:22; and Apoc. 19:13, but it may also reflect acquaintance with Eph. 1:5, 7, εἰς υἱοθεσίαν διὰ Ἰησοῦ Χριστοῦ . . . .
ἐν ᾧ ἔχομεν τὴν ἀπολύτρωσιν διὰ τοῦ αἵματος αὐτοῦ. (5) Χάρις
ὑμῖν καὶ εἰρήνη is the salutation in Rom. 1:7, I Cor. 1:3, II Cor.
1:2, Gal. 1:3, Eph. 1:2, Phil. 1:2, Col. 1:2, I Thess. 1:1, II
Thess. 1:2, and Philem. 3. Paul's regular use of this salutation
almost certainly reflects itself in I Peter. It is not the ordi-

nary Greek usage but was apparently Paul's own coinage. In combination
with πληθύνω the salutation occurs in I and II Peter (cf. Jude 2).

I Pet. 1:3-13   Ephesians A

Εὐλογητὸς ὁ Θεὸς καὶ πατὴρ τοῦ κυρίου ἡμῶν Ἰησοῦ Χριστοῦ,
ὁ κατὰ τὸ πολὺ αὐτοῦ ἔλεος ἀναγεννήσας ἡμᾶς εἰς ἐλπίδα ζῶσαν δι'
ἀναστάσεως Ἰησοῦ Χριστοῦ ἐκ νεκρῶν, εἰς κληρονομίαν ἄφθαρτον καὶ
ἀμίαντον καὶ ἀμάραντον, τετηρημένην ἐν οὐρανοῖς εἰς ὑμᾶς τοὺς ἐν δυνάμει Θεοῦ
φρουρουμένους διὰ πίστεως εἰς σωτηρίαν ἑτοίμην ἀποκαλυφθῆναι ἐν
καιρῷ ἐσχάτῳ.   ἐν ᾧ ἀγαλλιᾶσθε, ὀλίγον ἄρτι εἰ δέον λυπηθέντες
. . . . ἵνα τὸ δοκίμιον ὑμῶν τῆς πίστεως . . . . εὑρεθῇ εἰς ἔπαινον καὶ δόξαν
καὶ τιμὴν ἐν ἀποκαλύψει Ἰησοῦ Χριστοῦ.   ὃν οὐκ ἰδόντες ἀγαπᾶτε,
εἰς ὃν ἄρτι μὴ ὁρῶντες πιστεύοντες δὲ ἀγαλλιᾶτε χαρᾷ ἀνεκλαλήτῳ
καὶ δεδοξασμένῃ, κομιζόμενοι τὸ τέλος τῆς πίστεως σωτηρίαν ψυχῶν.
Περὶ ἧς σωτηρίας ἐξεζήτησαν . . . . προφῆται . . . . . οἷς ἀπεκαλύφθη
ὅτι οὐχ ἑαυτοῖς ὑμῖν δὲ διηκόνουν αὐτά, ἃ νῦν ἀνηγγέλη ὑμῖν διὰ τῶν
εὐαγγελισαμένων ὑμᾶς πνεύματι ἁγίῳ ἀποσταλέντι ἀπ' οὐρανοῦ, εἰς ἃ
ἐπιθυμοῦσιν ἄγγελοι παρακύψαι.

Eph. 1:3-20.   Εὐλογητὸς ὁ Θεὸς καὶ πατὴρ τοῦ κυρίου ἡμῶν
Ἰησοῦ Χριστοῦ, ὁ εὐλογήσας ἡμᾶς ἐν πάσῃ εὐλογίᾳ πνευματικῇ ἐν τοῖς ἐπουρανίοις ἐν Χριστῷ, καθὼς ἐξελέξατο ἡμᾶς ἐν αὐτῷ πρὸ καταβολῆς κόσμου
. . . . προορίσας ἡμᾶς εἰς υἱοθεσίαν διὰ Ἰησοῦ Χριστοῦ . . . .
εἰς ἔπαινον δόξης τῆς χάριτος αὐτοῦ ἧς ἐχαρίτωσεν ἡμᾶς ἐν τῷ ἠγαπημένῳ, ἐν ᾧ
ἔχομεν τὴν ἀπολύτρωσιν διὰ τοῦ αἵματος αὐτοῦ, ... εἰς τὸ εἶναι
ἡμᾶς εἰς ἔπαινον δόξης αὐτοῦ . . . . ἐν τῷ Χριστῷ· ἐν ᾧ καὶ ὑμεῖς
ἀκούσαντες τὸν λόγον τῆς ἀληθείας, τὸ εὐαγγέλιον τῆς σωτηρίας ὑμῶν,
ἐν ᾧ καὶ πιστεύσαντες ἐσφραγίσθητε τῷ πνεύματι τῆς ἐπαγγελίας τῷ
ἁγίῳ, ὅ ἐστιν ἀρραβὼν τῆς κληρονομίας ἡμῶν, ... εἰς ἔπαινον
τῆς δόξης αὐτοῦ. . . . . εἰς τὸ εἰδέναι ὑμᾶς τίς ἐστιν ἡ ἐλπὶς τῆς
κλήσεως αὐτοῦ, τίς ὁ πλοῦτος τῆς δόξης τῆς κληρονομίας αὐτοῦ ἐν
ταῖς ἁγίαις, καὶ τί τὸ ὑπερβάλλον μέγεθος τῆς δυνάμεως αὐτοῦ . . . .
καὶ καθίσας ἐν δεξιᾷ αὐτοῦ ἐν τοῖς ἐπουρανίοις ὑπεράνω πάσης ἀρχῆς
καὶ ἐξουσίας καὶ δυνάμεως καὶ κυριότητος καὶ παντὸς ὀνόματος ὀνομαζομένου οὐ μόνον ἐν τῷ αἰῶνι τούτῳ ἀλλὰ καὶ ἐν τῷ μέλλοντι·.

There is an unmistakable resemblance in the elevated tone
and liturgical quality of these two passages. Specific agreements
in idea and expression when taken with this striking resemblance
in tone make literary relationship a matter of practical certainty.

I Pet. 1:4, 5   Galatians C

Εἰς κληρονομίαν ἄφθαρτον καὶ ἀμίαντον καὶ ἀμάραντον, τετηρ-
μένην ἐν οὐρανοῖς εἰς ὑμᾶς τοὺς ἐν δυνάμει Θεοῦ φρουρουμένους διὰ
πίστεως εἰς σωτηρίαν ἑτοίμην ἀποκαλυφθῆναι ἐν καιρῷ ἐσχάτῳ.

Gal. 3:18. Εἰ γὰρ ἐκ νόμου ἡ κληρονομία. . . . . 23. Πρὸ
τοῦ δὲ ἐλθεῖν τὴν πίστιν ὑπὸ νόμον ἐφρουρούμεθα συνκλειόμενοι εἰς
τὴν μέλλουσαν πίστιν ἀποκαλυφθῆναι. 4:7. Ὥστε οὐκέτι εἶ δοῦλος
ἀλλὰ υἱός· εἰ δὲ υἱός, καὶ κληρονόμος διὰ Θεοῦ (cf. Rom. 8:16-18,
κληρονόμοι μὲν Θεοῦ; cf. also Col. 1:4, 5).

The ideas of Galatians and I Peter differ, but the language of the one very probably influenced that of the other.
Φρουρέω occurs in the New Testament in II Cor. 11:32, Gal. 3:23,
Phil. 4:7, and I Pet. 1:5. Its use in Galatians and I Peter in
connection with πίστις argues for literary dependence. The very
similar employment of ἀποκαλυφθῆναι and κληρονομία in these contexts strengthens the likelihood of literary acquaintance. Similarly, the influence of Col. 1:5 may be reflected in εἰς κληρονομίαν . . . . τετηρημένην ἐν οὐρανοῖς εἰς ὑμᾶς.

I Pet. 1:6, 7   Romans C

Ἐν ᾧ ἀγαλλιᾶσθε, ὀλίγον ἄρτι εἰ δέον λυπηθέντες ἐν ποικίλοις πειρασμοῖς, ἵνα τὸ δοκίμιον ὑμῶν τῆς πίστεως πολυτιμότερον
χρυσίου τοῦ ἀπολλυμένου διὰ πυρὸς δὲ δοκιμαζομένου εὑρεθῇ εἰς
ἔπαινον καὶ δόξαν καὶ τιμὴν ἐν ἀποκαλύψει Ἰησοῦ Χριστοῦ.

Rom. 5:3, 4. Καὶ καυχώμεθα ἐπ᾽ ἐλπίδι τῆς δόξης τοῦ Θεοῦ·
οὐ μόνον δέ, ἀλλὰ καὶ ⌜καυχώμεθα⌝ ἐν ταῖς θλίψεσιν, εἰδότες ὅτι ἡ
θλῖψις ὑπομονὴν κατεργάζεται, ἡ δὲ ὑπομονὴ δοκιμήν, ἡ δὲ δοκιμὴ
ἐλπίδα, ἡ δὲ ἐλπὶς οὐ καταισχύνει.

The attitude toward trial in I Peter is very similar to
that expressed in Romans (cf. II Cor. 4:17) and is probably a conscious assertion of the Pauline position as against that expressed
in the Apocalypse. The use of δοκίμιον in I Peter corresponds
with the use of δοκιμή in Romans and strengthens the case for literary influence. Δοκιμή occurs only in Romans, II Corinthians,
and Philippians; and δοκίμιον only in James and I Peter.

. I Pet. 1:12   Ephesians B

Προφῆται . . . . οἷς ἀπεκαλύφθη ὅτι οὐχ ἑαυταῖς ὑμῖν δὲ
διηκόνουν ⌜αὐτά, ἃ⌝ νῦν ἀνηγγέλη ὑμῖν διὰ τῶν εὐαγγελισαμένων
ὑμᾶς πνεύματι ἁγίῳ ἀποσταλέντι ἀπ' οὐρανοῦ, εἰς ἃ ἐπιθυμοῦσιν
ἄγγελοι παρακύψαι.

Eph. 3:5. Ὃ ἑτέραις γενεαῖς οὐκ ἐγνωρίσθη τοῖς υἱοῖς
τῶν ἀνθρώπων ὡς νῦν ἀπεκαλύφθη τοῖς ἁγίοις ἀποστόλοις αὐτοῦ καὶ
προφήταις ἐν πνεύματι . . . . 10. Ἵνα γνωρισθῇ νῦν ταῖς ἀρχαῖς
καὶ ταῖς ἐξουσίαις ἐν τοῖς ἐπουρανίοις διὰ τῆς ἐκκλησίας ἡ πολυποίκιλος σοφία τοῦ θεοῦ.

The conception of prophecy and its fulfilment is strikingly similar in both writings. Christian prophets, led by the Spirit, have received by revelation an insight not granted the prophets
of the old order. The interest of angels in redemption is an additional point of contact between the passages and strengthens
the probability of literary indebtedness.

I Pet. 1:13   Ephesians C

Διὸ ἀναζωσάμενοι τὰς ὀσφύας τῆς διανοίας ὑμῶν.

Eph. 6:14. Στῆτε οὖν περιζωσάμενοι τὴν ὀσφὺν ὑμῶν ἐν
ἀληθείᾳ (cf. Isa. 11:5, καὶ ἔσται δικαιοσύνη ἐζωσμένος τὴν ὀσφὺν
αὐτοῦ, καὶ ἀληθείᾳ εἰλημένος τὰς πλευράς).

The figure of the "girded loin" occurs in the New Testament only in Luke 12:35, Eph. 6:14, and I Pet. 1:13. The symbolism in Ephesians and I Peter creates the probability of indebtedness on the part of the latter, although the possibility of
dependence on the LXX is recognized.

I Pet. 1:14, 15   Romans B   Ephesians B

Ὡς τέκνα ὑπακοῆς, μὴ συνσχηματιζόμενοι ταῖς πρότερον ἐν
τῇ ἀγνοίᾳ ὑμῶν ἐπιθυμίαις, ἀλλὰ κατὰ τὸν καλέσαντα ὑμᾶς ἅγιον καὶ
αὐτοὶ ἅγιοι ἐν πάσῃ ἀναστροφῇ γενήθητε.

Rom. 12:2. Καὶ μὴ συνσχηματίζεσθε τῷ αἰῶνι τούτῳ

Eph. 2:2, 3 . . . Ἐν τοῖς υἱοῖς τῆς ἀπειθείας, ἐν οἷς
καὶ ἡμεῖς πάντες ἀνεστράφημέν ποτε ἐν ταῖς ἐπιθυμίαις τῆς σαρκὸς
ἡμῶν, ποιοῦντες τὰ θελήματα τῆς σαρκὸς καὶ τῶν διανοιῶν, καὶ ἤμεθα
τέκνα φύσει ὀργῆς ὡς καὶ οἱ λοιποί. 4:17, 18. Τοῦτο οὖν λέγω καὶ

μαρτύρομαι ἐν κυρίῳ, μηκέτι ὑμᾶς περιπατεῖν καθὼς καὶ τὰ ἔθνη
περιπατεῖ ἐν ματαιότητι τοῦ νοὸς αὐτῶν, ἐσκοτωμένοι τῇ διανοίᾳ
ὄντες, ἀπηλλοτριωμένοι τῆς ζωῆς τοῦ Θεοῦ, διὰ τὴν ἄγνοιαν τὴν
οὖσαν ἐν αὐτοῖς.

Moffatt takes I Pet. 1:14 to be an "obvious reminiscence
of the thought" of Rom. 12:2.[6] In addition to this evident resemblance in thought, which of itself would not require the predication of literary dependence, there is the use of συνσχηματίζομαι
—a verb that occurs in the New Testament only in Rom. 12:2 and
I Pet. 1:14 and which is not used in the LXX. The phrase ὡς
τέκνα ὑπακοῆς may represent conscious contrast with ἐν τοῖς υἱοῖς
τῆς ἀπειθείας in Eph. 2:2, although it more probably reflects acquaintance with the conception of the faith-approved life as it is
described in Romans. For the use of ὑπακοή in the New Testament
see the note on I Pet. 1:2.

The very similar references to former modes of living in
I Peter and Ephesians suggest acquaintance, and this is strengthened by their employment of ἄγνοια and μάταιος (cf. ἐν ματαιότητι
in Eph. 4:17) to describe the pre-conversion condition of these
Christians. ῎Αγνοια is used in the New Testament only in Acts,
Ephesians, and I Peter; and only in Eph. 4:18 and I Pet. 1:14 is
it applied to Christians as a description of their former condition, although in Acts 17:30 it does describe to the unconverted
their existing condition.

I Pet. 1:19, 20   Ephesians C
᾽Αλλὰ . . . . αἵματι . . . . Χριστοῦ, προεγνωσμένου μὲν
πρὸ καταβολῆς κόσμου.
Eph. 1:4. Καθὼς ἐξελέξατο ἡμᾶς ἐν αὐτῷ πρὸ καταβολῆς κοσ-
μοῦ. . . . 7. ᾽Εν ᾧ ἔχομεν τὴν ἀπολύτρωσιν διὰ τοῦ αἵματος αὐτοῦ.

The phrase πρὸ καταβολῆς κόσμου occurs in the New Testament
in John 17:24, Eph. 1:4, and I Pet. 1:20. Coupled with the ideas
of predestination and of ransom through the blood of Christ as it
is in I Peter, it probably indicates acquaintance with Ephesians.

---

[6]James Moffatt, An Introduction to the Literature of the
New Testament (New York: Charles Scribner's Sons, 1927), p. 330.

I Pet. 1:20, 21   Ephesians C   Romans C

Χριστοῦ, προεγνωσμένου μὲν πρὸ καταβολῆς κόσμου φανερωθέντος δὲ ἐπ' ἐσχάτου τῶν χρόνων δι' ὑμᾶς τοὺς δι' αὐτοῦ πιστοὺς εἰς
Θεὸν τὸν ἐγείραντα αὐτὸν ἐκ νεκρῶν καὶ δόξαν αὐτῷ δόντα.

Eph. 3:9, 10. Καὶ φωτίσαι τίς ἡ οἰκονομία τοῦ μυστηρίου
τοῦ ἀποκεκρυμμένου ἀπὸ τῶν αἰώνων ἐν τῷ Θεῷ τῷ τὰ πάντα κτίσαντι,
ἵνα γνωρισθῇ νῦν ταῖς ἀρχαῖς καὶ ταῖς ἐξουσίαις ἐν τοῖς ἐπουρανίοις
διὰ τῆς ἐκκλησίας ἡ πολυποίκιλος σοφία τοῦ Θεοῦ (cf. Col. 1:27).

Rom. 4:24. Ταῖς πιστεύουσιν ἐπὶ τὸν ἐγείραντα 'Ιησοῦν
τὸν κύριον ἡμῶν ἐκ νεκρῶν.

The conception of redemption through Christ as predestined
and foreknown and yet as lately disclosed to and through Christians
probably represents the influence of Eph. 3:9, 10. The probable
influence of Romans is found in the clause δι' ὑμᾶς τοὺς δι'
αὐτοῦ πιστοὺς εἰς Θεὸν τὸν ἐγείραντα αὐτὸν ἐκ νεκρῶν in I Pet.
1:21.

I Pet. 1:22   Romans C

Τὰς ψυχὰς ὑμῶν ἡγνικότες ἐν τῇ ὑπακοῇ τῆς ἀληθείας εἰς
φιλαδελφίαν ἀνυπόκριτον ἐκ καρδίας ἀλλήλους ἀγαπήσατε ἐκτενῶς.

Rom. 12:9, 10. Ἡ ἀγάπη ἀνυπόκριτος . . . . τῇ φιλαδελφίᾳ
εἰς ἀλλήλους φιλόστοργοι.

The emphasis on sincerity and love for the "brotherhood"
may indicate acquaintance with Romans. Φιλαδελφία is used in the
New Testament only in Rom. 12:10, I Thess. 4:9, Heb. 13:1, I Pet.
1:22, and II Pet. 1:7. The use of ὑπακοή strengthens the probability of dependence on Romans.

I Pet. 2:1, 2   Ephesians C   Romans C

'Αποθέμενοι οὖν πᾶσαν κακίαν καὶ πάντα δόλον καὶ ⌜ὑπόκρι-
σιν⌝ καὶ φθόνους καὶ πάσας καταλαλιάς, ὡς ἀρτιγέννητα βρέφη τὸ
λογικὸν ἄδολον γάλα ἐπιποθήσατε.

Eph. 4:22, 23. 'Αποθέσθαι ὑμᾶς κατὰ τὴν προτέραν ἀναστροφὴν τὸν παλαιὸν ἄνθρωπον τὸν φθειρόμενον κατὰ τὰς ἐπιθυμίας τῆς
ἀπάτης, ἀνανεοῦσθαι δὲ τῷ πνεύματι τοῦ νοὸς ὑμῶν, καὶ ἐνδύσασθαι
τὸν καινὸν ἄνθρωπον.

Rom. 12:1. Παρακαλῶ . . . . παραστῆσαι τὰ σώματα ὑμῶν
θυσίαν ζῶσαν ἁγίαν ⌜τῷ Θεῷ εὐάρεστον⌝ ,τὴν λογικὴν λατρείαν ὑμῶν·

13:12, 13. 'Αποθώμεθα οὖν τὰ ἔργα τοῦ σκότους, ἐνδυσώμεθα [δὲ]
τὰ ὅπλα τοῦ φωτός. ὡς ἐν ἡμέρᾳ εὐσχημόνως περιπατήσωμεν, μὴ
κώμοις καὶ μέθαις, μὴ κοίταις καὶ ἀσελγείαις, μὴ ⌐ἔριδι καὶ ζήλῳ⌐
(cf. I Cor. 3:2).

There are ideas and terms in I Pet. 2:1, 2 that seem to
indicate acquaintance with Eph. 4:22-24 and Rom. 12:1 and 13:12 f.
and that may involve indebtedness to I Cor. 3:2. ''Αποτίθεμαι
used in the sense of putting aside an evil mode of life as preliminary to the espousal of a good mode of life occurs in Rom. 13:12;
Eph. 4:22, 25; Col. 3:8; James 1:21; and I Pet. 2:1 (cf. Heb. 12:1,
where the figure is somewhat different). Acquaintance with Romans
is made more likely by the use of λογικός. In Rom. 12:1 the conduct of Christians is described as λογικὴ λατρεία, involving the
presentation of themselves as θυσία ζῶσα. In I Peter the craving
of Christians is for τὸ λογικὸν ἄδολον γάλα, and such people offer to God (2:5) πνευματικὰς θυσίας. Λογικός occurs in the New
Testament only in Rom. 12:1 and I Pet. 2:2. Γάλα is used in I Cor.
3:2, 9:7; Heb. 5:12, 13; and I Pet. 2:2. It is used figuratively
in these instances with the exception of I Cor. 9:7. The figurative use in I Peter is different from that of I Cor. 3:2 and Heb.
5:12, 13, and all probably represent merely the natural uses of a
popular metaphor.

I Pet. 2:3-6   Ephesians C   Romans C
"Ινα ἐν αὐτῷ αὐξηθῆτε εἰς σωτηρίαν, ... πρὸς ὃν προσερ-
χόμενοι, λίθον ζῶντα, ὑπὸ ἀνθρώπων μὲν ἀποδεδοκιμασμένον παρὰ δὲ
Θεῷ ἐκλεκτὸν ἔντιμον καὶ αὐτοὶ ὡς λίθοι ζῶντες οἰκοδομεῖσθε οἶκος
πνευματικὸς εἰς ἱεράτευμα ἅγιον . . . . διότι περιέχει ἐν γραφῇ
'Ιδοὺ τίθημι ἐν Σιὼν λίθον ἐκλεκτὸν ἀκρογωνιαῖον ἔντιμον, καὶ ὁ
πιστεύων αὐτῷ οὐ μὴ καταισχυνθῇ.
     Eph. 2:18-22. "Οτι δι' αὐτοῦ ἔχομεν τὴν προσαγωγὴν . . . .
ἐν ἑνὶ πνεύματι πρὸς τὸν πατέρα. . . . . ἐστὲ . . . . οἰκεῖοι τοῦ
Θεοῦ, ἐποικοδομηθέντες . . . . ὄντος ἀκρογωνιαίου αὐτοῦ Χριστοῦ
'Ιησοῦ, ἐν ᾧ πᾶσα οἰκοδομὴ συναρμολογουμένη αὔξει εἰς ναὸν ἅγιον
ἐν κυρίῳ, ἐν ᾧ καὶ ὑμεῖς συνοικοδομεῖσθε εἰς κατοικητήριον τοῦ
Θεοῦ ἐν πνεύματι.
     Rom. 9:32, 33. 'Αλλ' ὡς ἐξ ⌐ἔργων⌐. προσέκοψαν τῷ λίθῳ
τοῦ προσκόμματος, καθὼς γέγραπται 'Ιδοὺ τίθημι ἐν Σιὼν λίθον προσ-

κόμματος καὶ πέτραν σκανδάλου, καὶ ὁ πιστεύων ἐπ' αὐτῷ οὐ καταισχυνθήσεται (cf. Isa. 28:16).

The idea of the religious man or group as ναὸς θεοῦ is found in the Corinthian letters. It is elaborated in Ephesians under the probable influence of I Cor. 3:16 and II Cor. 6:16. It is the elaborated figure of Ephesians that seems to have influenced I Peter (cf. Hermas Vis. III, Sim. IX). The use of αὐξάνω in the clause ἵνα ἐν αὐτῷ αὐξηθῆτε εἰς σωτηρίαν is remarkably similar to its use in Eph. 2:21. It is to be borne in mind, however, that the allegory may, in part at least, have been suggested by such LXX passages as Ex. 19:6, Ps. 117:22, and Isa. 28:16, the last passage being specifically quoted in verse 6 (cf. Rom. 9:33). The idea of the οἶκος πνευματικός is best explained by the influence of Ephesians (cf. Heb. 3:6 and 10:21).

The Old Testament allusions in I Peter suggest the influence of Romans. I Pet. 2:6 fuses Isa. 28:16 and 8:14 just as Rom. 9:32, 33 does, and in the immediately succeeding context (I Pet. 2:10 and Rom. 9:25) both quote Hos. 2:23 to illustrate their former status as heathen as compared with their existing status as Christians. It is worthy of particular note that in the use of Isa. 28:16, I Peter agrees with Romans against the LXX in the opening clause 'Ιδοὺ τίθημι ἐν Σιὼν λίθον, and also in the addition of ἐπ' αὐτῷ after ὁ πιστεύων. These differences from the LXX may be explained in terms of textual variation, because ἐπ' αὐτῷ is the reading of א A Q. The context, however, makes dependence on Romans the more probable explanation.[7]

I Pet. 2:5   Romans C

'Ανενέγκαι πνευματικὰς θυσίας εὐπροσδέκτους θεῷ.

Rom. 12:1. Παραστῆσαι . . . . θυσίαν ζῶσαν ἁγίαν ⌜τῷ θεῷ εὐάρεστον⌝.

I Pet. 2:9   Ephesians C

Λαὸς εἰς περιποίησιν, ὅπως τὰς ἀρετὰς ἐξαγγείλητε τοῦ ἐκ σκότους ὑμᾶς καλέσαντος εἰς τὸ θαυμαστὸν αὐτοῦ φῶς·

Eph. 1:14. Εἰς ἀπολύτρωσιν τῆς περιποιήσεως, εἰς ἔπαινον

---

[7]Ibid.

τῆς δόξης αὐτοῦ. 5:8. Ἦτε γάρ ποτε σκότος, νῦν δὲ φῶς ἐν κυρίῳ·
ὡς τέκνα φωτὸς περιπατεῖτε.

The noun περιποίησις occurs in the New Testament in Eph.
1:14, I Thess. 5:9, II Thess. 2:14, Heb. 10:39, and I Pet. 2:9.
Its connotation in Ephesians and I Peter is distinctly passive as
against the clearly active connotation in I and II Thessalonians.
This, coupled with the similarly figurative use of φῶς and σκότος
makes dependence on Ephesians probable.

I Pet. 2:10-   Romans C

Οἵ ποτε οὐ λαὸς νῦν δὲ λαὸς θεοῦ, οἱ οὐκ ἠλεημένοι νῦν δὲ
ἐλεηθέντες.

Rom. 9:25, 26. Ὡς καὶ ἐν τῷ Ὡσηὲ λέγει Καλέσω τὸν οὐ
λαόν μου λαόν μου καὶ τὴν οὐκ ἠγαπημένην ἠγαπημένην· καὶ ἔσται
ἐν τῷ τόπῳ οὗ ἐρρέθη [αὐτοῖς] Οὐ λαός μου ὑμεῖς, ἐκεῖ κληθήσονται
υἱοὶ θεοῦ ζῶντος.

Both writings refer to Hos. 2:23; see the note on I Pet.
2:3-6.

I Pet. 2:11   Romans C   Galatians C

Ἀγαπητοί, παρακαλῶ ὡς παροίκους καὶ παρεπιδήμους ἀπέχεσθαι
τῶν σαρκικῶν ἐπιθυμιῶν, αἵτινες στρατεύονται κατὰ τῆς ψυχῆς·

Rom. 7:23. Βλέπω δὲ ἔτερον νόμον ἐν τοῖς μέλεσίν μου ἀντι-
στρατευόμενον τῷ νόμῳ τοῦ νοός μου καὶ αἰχμαλωτίζοντά με [ἐν] τῷ
νόμῳ τῆς ἁμαρτίας τῷ ὄντι ἐν τοῖς μέλεσίν μου.

Gal. 5:16, 17. Λέγω δέ, πνεύματι περιπατεῖτε καὶ ἐπιθυμίαν σαρκὸς οὐ μὴ τελέσητε. ἡ γὰρ σὰρξ ἐπιθυμεῖ κατὰ τοῦ πνεύματος,
τὸ δὲ πνεῦμα κατὰ τῆς σαρκός, ταῦτα γὰρ ἀλλήλοις ἀντίκειται.

The verb στρατεύομαι is used figuratively in II Cor. 10:
13, Jas. 4:1, and I Pet. 2:11. James and I Peter were both probably influenced by the picture of inner warfare in Rom. 7:23—a
picture even more strikingly drawn in Gal. 5:16, 17.

I Pet. 2:13-17   Romans B   Galatians C

Ὑποτάγητε πάσῃ ἀνθρωπίνῃ κτίσει διὰ τὸν κύριον· εἴτε
βασιλεῖ ὡς ὑπερέχοντι, εἴτε ἡγεμόσιν ὡς δι' αὐτοῦ πεμπομένοις εἰς
ἐκδίκησιν κακοποιῶν ἔπαινον δὲ ἀγαθοποιῶν· (ὅτι οὕτως ἐστὶν τὸ

θέλημα τοῦ θεοῦ, ἀγαθοποιοῦντας φιμοῖν τὴν τῶν ἀφρόνων ἀνθρώπων
ἀγνωσίαν·) ὡς ἐλεύθεροι, καὶ μὴ ὡς ἐπικάλυμμα ἔχοντες τῆς κακίας
τὴν ἐλευθερίαν, ἀλλ' ὡς θεοῦ δοῦλοι. πάντας τιμήσατε, τὴν ἀδελφό-
τητα ἀγαπᾶτε, τὸν θεὸν φοβεῖσθε, τὸν βασιλέα τιμᾶτε.

The attitude in I Peter toward governmental authority is
notably like that expressed by Paul in Rom. 13:1-7. That Rom.
13:1-7 was in the mind of the author of I Peter is highly probable. The theme, the arrangement of thought, the resemblances in
language, support this probability. Submission to rulers is the
theme of both. The exhortation in each instance rests on the
hypothesis that the authority they exercise is delegated by God.
Only wrongdoers need fear the officials, and the truly righteous
will establish their righteousness by living lovingly and obedi-
ently. The verb ὑποτάσσω is the key word of both passages. It is
used with reference to civil authorities only in Rom. 13:1, 5;
I Pet. 2:13; and Titus 3:1. The exhortation πάντας τιμήσατε
. . . . τὸν βασιλέα τιμᾶτε very probably looks back to ἀπόδοτε
πᾶσι τὰς ὀφειλάς . . . . τῷ τὴν τιμὴν τὴν τιμήν of Romans.

In 2:16 the ὡς ἐλεύθεροι, καὶ μὴ ὡς ἐπικάλυμμα ἔχοντες
τῆς κακίας τὴν ἐλευθερίαν κτλ. is a probable echo of Gal. 5:13,
ὑμεῖς γὰρ ἐπ' ἐλευθερίᾳ ἐκλήθητε . . . . μόνον μὴ τὴν ἐλευθερίαν
εἰς ἀφορμὴν τῇ σαρκί κτλ.

      I Pet. 2:19   Romans C
      Διὰ συνείδησιν.
      Rom. 13:5.   Διὰ τὴν συνείδησιν.

Συνείδησις is used in the New Testament with διὰ in Rom.
13:5; I Cor. 10:25, 27, 28; and I Pet. 2:19.

      I Pet. 2:21-24   II Corinthians C   Romans C
Ὅτι καὶ Χριστὸς ἔπαθεν ὑπὲρ ὑμῶν . . . . ὃς ἁμαρτίαν οὐκ
ἐποίησεν . . . . ὃς τὰς ἁμαρτίας ἡμῶν αὐτὸς ἀνήνεγκεν ἐν τῷ σώματι
αὐτοῦ ἐπὶ τὸ ξύλον, ἵνα ταῖς ἁμαρτίαις ἀπογενόμενοι τῇ δικαιοσύνῃ
ζήσωμεν.
      II Cor. 5:21. Τὸν μὴ γνόντα ἁμαρτίαν ὑπὲρ ἡμῶν ἁμαρτίαν
ἐποίησεν, ἵνα ἡμεῖς γενώμεθα δικαιοσύνη θεοῦ ἐν αὐτῷ.
      Rom. 6:2. Οἵτινες ἀπεθάνομεν τῇ ἁμαρτίᾳ, πῶς ἔτι ζήσομεν
ἐν αὐτῇ; . . . . . 8. Εἰ δὲ ἀπεθάνομεν σὺν Χριστῷ, πιστεύομεν ὅτι

καὶ συνζήσομεν αὐτῷ· . . . . 18. Ἐλευθερωθέντες δὲ ἀπὸ τῆς
ἁμαρτίας ἐδουλώθητε τῇ δικαιοσύνῃ.

The emphasis on Christ as sinless and yet bearing the sins
of others is best explained in terms of dependence on II Cor.
5:21. The purpose clause in that passage parallels the similar
clause in I Peter. The figures of dying to sin and living for
uprightness were probably drawn from Romans.

        I Pet. 3:6   Galatians C
ᵀΗς ἐγενήθητε τέκνα ἀγαθοποιοῦσαι καὶ μὴ φοβούμεναι μηδεμίαν πτόησιν.

        Gal. 4:24, 26. Αὗται γάρ εἰσιν δύο διαθῆκαι . . . . ἡ δὲ
ἄνω Ἰερουσαλὴμ ἐλευθέρα ἐστίν, ἥτις ἐστὶν μήτηρ ἡμῶν·

The conception of Christians as the ideal children of Sara
(cf. Heb. 11:11) occurs in the New Testament only in Gal. 4:26 and
I Pet. 3:6.

        I Pet. 3:8   Ephesians C
Εὔσπλαγχνοι.
Eph. 4:32. Εὔσπλαγχνοι.

This term occurs in the New Testament only in the instances
cited. In each case it appears as an item in a list of Christian
virtues. It is not a LXX word.

        I Pet. 3:9   Romans C
Μὴ ἀποδιδόντες κακὸν ἀντὶ κακοῦ.
        Rom. 12:17. Μηδενὶ κακὸν ἀντὶ κακοῦ ἀποδιδόντες (cf. I
Thess. 5:15, Prov. 17:13, and II Enoch 50:4).

There can be no unqualified predication of literary relationship as the explanation of resemblances in such paranetic material. There are, however, numerous evidences of acquaintance
with Romans on the part of I Peter, and these lend probability to
that explanation of similarity in the present instance.

        I Pet. 3:13   Romans C
 Καὶ τίς ὁ κακώσων ὑμᾶς ἐὰν τοῦ ἀγαθοῦ ζηλωταὶ γένησθε;
ἀλλ' εἰ καὶ πάσχοιτε διὰ δικαιοσύνην, μακάριοι.

Rom. 13:3. Οἱ γὰρ ἄρχοντες οὐκ εἰσὶν φόβος τῷ ἀγαθῷ ἔργῳ ἀλλὰ τῷ κακῷ. Θέλεις δὲ μὴ φοβεῖσθαι τὴν ἐξουσίαν; τὸ ἀγαθὸν ποίει, καὶ ἕξεις ἔπαινον ἐξ αὐτῆς·

Both passages deal with the attitude of Christians toward governmental authority.

I Pet. 3:18   Romans B

῞Οτι καὶ Χριστὸς ἅπαξ περὶ ἁμαρτιῶν ⌐ἀπέθανεν⌐, δίκαιος ὑπὲρ ἀδίκων, ἵνα ὑμᾶς προσαγάγῃ τῷ θεῷ, θανατωθεὶς μὲν σαρκὶ ζωοποιηθεὶς δὲ πνεύματι·

Rom. 5:6. Εἴ γε Χριστὸς ὄντων ἡμῶν ἀσθενῶν ἔτι κατὰ καιρὸν ὑπὲρ ἀσεβῶν ἀπέθανεν . . . . συνίστησιν δὲ τὴν ἑαυτοῦ ἀγάπην εἰς ἡμᾶς ὁ θεὸς ὅτι ἔτι ἁμαρτωλῶν ὄντων ἡμῶν Χριστὸς ὑπὲρ ἡμῶν ἀπέθανεν. 2. Διὰ τοῦ κυρίου ἡμῶν ᾿Ιησοῦ Χριστοῦ δι᾿ οὗ καὶ τὴν προσαγωγὴν ἐσχήκαμεν. . . . (cf. Eph. 2:18 and 3:12).

The two ideas in I Pet. 3:18 of Christ's death for sinful men and of the resulting access to God can both be accounted for from Romans. The contrast involved and the language used also relate the passage to Romans. The use of προσαγωγή in the New Testament is confined to Rom. 5:2 and Eph. 2:18 and 3:12, and its meaning is the equivalent of προσάγω in I Peter. Ζωοποιέω occurs in the New Testament only in Paul's letters and in the writings clearly influenced by his letters. The use of this verb in I Pet. 3:18 is an additional bit of evidence pointing to dependence on Romans.

I Pet. 3:21, 22   Ephesians C

Δι᾿ ἀναστάσεως ᾿Ιησοῦ Χριστοῦ, ὅς ἐστιν ἐν δεξιᾷ θεοῦ πορευθεὶς εἰς οὐρανὸν ὑποταγέντων αὐτῷ ἀγγέλων καὶ ἐξουσιῶν καὶ δυνάμεων.

Eph. 1:19-22. Κατὰ τὴν ἐνέργειαν τοῦ κράτους τῆς ἰσχύος αὐτοῦ ἣν ⌐ἐνήργηκεν⌐ ἐν τῷ Χριστῷ ἐγείρας αὐτὸν ἐκ νεκρῶν, καὶ καθίσας ἐν δεξιᾷ αὐτοῦ ἐν τοῖς ἐπουρανίοις ὑπεράνω πάσης ἀρχῆς καὶ ἐξουσίας καὶ δυνάμεως . . . . · καὶ πάντα ὑπέταξεν ὑπὸ τοὺς πόδας αὐτοῦ.

I Pet. 4:1   Romans C

Χριστοῦ οὖν παθόντος σαρκὶ καὶ ὑμεῖς τὴν αὐτὴν ἔννοιαν ὁπλίσασθε, ὅτι ὁ παθὼν σαρκὶ πέπαυται ⌐ἁμαρτίαις⌐.

Rom. 6:6-8. Τοῦτο γινώσκοντες ὅτι ὁ παλαιὸς ἡμῶν ἄνθρωπος συνεσταυρώθη, ἵνα καταργηθῇ τὸ σῶμα· τῆς ἁμαρτίας, τοῦ μηκέτι δουλεύειν ἡμᾶς τῇ ἁμαρτίᾳ, ὁ γὰρ ἀποθανὼν δεδικαίωται ἀπὸ τῆς ἁμαρτίας. εἰ δὲ ἀπεθάνομεν σὺν Χριστῷ, πιστεύομεν ὅτι καὶ συνζήσομεν αὐτῷ·

I Pet. 4:2, 3	Ephesians C

Εἰς τὸ μηκέτι ἀνθρώπων ἐπιθυμίαις ἀλλὰ θελήματι Θεοῦ τὸν ἐπίλοιπον ἐν σαρκὶ βιῶσαι χρόνον. ἀρκετὸς γὰρ ὁ παρεληλυθὼς χρόνος τὸ βούλημα τῶν ἐθνῶν κατειργάσθαι.

Eph. 2:3. Ἐν οἷς καὶ ἡμεῖς πάντες ἀνεστράφημέν ποτε ἐν ταῖς ἐπιθυμίαις τῆς σαρκὸς ἡμῶν, ποιοῦντες τὰ θελήματα τῆς σαρκὸς καὶ τῶν διανοιῶν, καὶ ἤμεθα τέκνα φύσει ὀργῆς ὡς καὶ· οἱ λοιποί·

I Pet. 4:7-11	Romans A
7. Πάντων δὲ τὸ τέλος ἤγγικεν	13:11, 12. Καὶ τοῦτο εἰδότες τὸν καιρόν, ... νῦν γὰρ ἐγγύτερον ἡμῶν ἡ σωτηρία ἤ ὅτε ἐπιστεύσαμεν. ἡ νὺξ προέκοψεν, ἡ δὲ ἡμέρα ἤγγικεν
Σωφρονήσατε οὖν καὶ νήψατε εἰς προσευχάς·	12:13. Τῇ προσευχῇ προσκαρτεροῦντες
8. Πρὸ πάντων τὴν εἰς ἑαυτοὺς ἀγάπην ἐκτενῆ ἔχοντες	9. Ἡ ἀγάπη ἀνυπόκριτος . . . . τῇ φιλαδελφίᾳ εἰς ἀλλήλους φιλόστοργοι
9. Φιλόξενοι εἰς ἀλλήλους ἄνευ γογγυσμοῦ	13. Τὴν φιλοξενίαν διώκοντες
10, 11. Ἕκαστος καθὼς ἔλαβεν χάρισμα, εἰς ἑαυτοὺς αὐτὸ διακονοῦντες ὡς καλοὶ οἰκονόμοι ποικίλης χάριτος Θεοῦ· εἴ τις λαλεῖ, ὡς λόγια Θεοῦ· εἴ τις διακονεῖ, ὡς ἐξ ἰσχύος ἧς χορηγεῖ ὁ Θεός·	3. Λέγω γὰρ διὰ τῆς χάριτος τῆς δοθείσης μοι παντὶ τῷ ὄντι ἐν ὑμῖν . . . . φρονεῖν εἰς τὸ σωφρονεῖν, ἑκάστῳ ὡς ὁ Θεὸς ἐμέρισεν μέτρον πίστεως. . . . . 6. Ἔχοντες δὲ χαρίσματα κατὰ τὴν χάριν τὴν δοθεῖσαν ἡμῖν διάφορα, εἴτε προφητείαν κατὰ τὴν ἀναλογίαν τῆς πίστεως, εἴτε διακονίαν ἐν τῇ διακονίᾳ

A series of such close agreements in narrowly limited contexts has cumulative significance. It points rather clearly to literary dependence.

I Pet. 4:10   Ephesians C

Ὡς καλοὶ οἰκονόμοι ποικίλης χάριτος Θεοῦ·

Eph. 3:2. Εἴ γε ἠκούσατε τὴν οἰκονομίαν τῆς χάριτος τοῦ Θεοῦ τῆς δοθείσης μοι εἰς ὑμᾶς (cf. Col. 1:25).

The use of οἰκονόμος and οἰκονομία is confined to Luke, the Pauline letters, the Pastorals, and I Peter. Only in Eph. 3:2 and I Pet. 4:10 are these terms used in connection with ἡ χάρις τοῦ Θεοῦ.

I Pet. 4:13, 14   Romans B

Ἀλλὰ καθὸ κοινωνεῖτε τοῖς τοῦ Χριστοῦ παθήμασιν χαίρετε, ἵνα καὶ ἐν τῇ ἀποκαλύψει τῆς δόξης αὐτοῦ χαρῆτε ἀγαλλιώμενοι. εἰ ὀνειδίζεσθε ἐν ὀνόματι Χριστοῦ, μακάριοι, ὅτι τὸ τῆς δόξης καὶ τὸ τοῦ Θεοῦ πνεῦμα ἐφ' ὑμᾶς ἀναπαύεται.

Rom. 8:17, 18. Αὐτὸ τὸ πνεῦμα συνμαρτυρεῖ τῷ πνεύματι ἡμῶν ὅτι ἐσμὲν τέκνα Θεοῦ. . . . . εἴπερ συνπάσχομεν ἵνα καὶ συνδοξασθῶμεν. Λογίζομαι γὰρ ὅτι οὐκ ἄξια τὰ παθήματα τοῦ νῦν καιροῦ πρὸς τὴν μέλλουσαν δόξαν ἀποκαλυφθῆναι εἰς ἡμᾶς.

The combination of the ideas of sharing the sufferings of Christ in the expectation of a future sharing of his glory and of being sustained and assured by the present possession of the Spirit argues strongly for familiarity with Rom. 8:17, 18.

I Pet. 5:1   Romans B

Πρεσβυτέρους οὖν ἐν ὑμῖν παρακαλῶ ὁ συνπρεσβύτερος καὶ μάρτυς τῶν τοῦ Χριστοῦ παθημάτων, ὁ καὶ τῆς μελλούσης ἀποκαλύπτεσθαι δόξης κοινωνός.

The ideas in 5:1 are the same as those noted in 4:13, 14, and the probability of dependence on Rom. 8:17, 18 is equally strong.

I Pet. 5:3   II Corinthians C

Μηδ' ὡς κατακυριεύοντες τῶν κλήρων.

II Cor. 1:24. Οὐχ ὅτι κυριεύομεν ὑμῶν τῆς πίστεως.

Κυριεύω is used in the New Testament in Luke, Romans, II Corinthians, and I Timothy. Its use in Luke 22:25 and II Cor. 1:24 is similar but not identical. The thought of I Peter is closest to that of II Corinthians.

Instances of possible literary reminiscence.—I Pet. 1:3; cf. II Cor. 1:3. The influence of II Cor. 1:3 seems to have reached I Peter at this point through Ephesians. However, the influence of II Corinthians is not precluded.

I Pet. 1:8; cf. Eph. 6:24 and II Cor. 5:7.

I Pet. 1:9; cf. Rom. 6:22.

I Pet. 1:13; cf. I Cor. 1:7. 'Αποκάλυψις is used in the New Testament in Luke, the Pauline letters, I Peter, and the Apocalypse. Its use in connection with Jesus Christ occurs in I Cor. 1:7; II Cor. 12:1; Gal. 1:1; II Thess. 1:7; I Pet. 1:7, 13; and Apoc. 1:1. The instances in which the emphasis in the phrase most clearly resembles that of I Pet. 1:13 are I Cor. 1:7 and II Thess. 1:7. The context favors I Corinthians above II Thessalonians as a source of influence.

I Pet. 1:17; cf. Rom. 2:11. 'Απροσωπολήμπτως is used in the New Testament only in I Pet. 1:17. Προσωπολημψία is used in the New Testament in Rom. 2:11, Eph. 6:9, Col. 3:25, and Jas. 2:1. In Romans, Ephesians, and Colossians the reference is to divine judgment.

I Pet. 2:18; cf. Eph. 6:5. The language of the passage does not relate it very closely to Ephesians or Colossians, and the frequence with which similar exhortations occur in early Christian literature (cf. Did. 4:11; Barn. 19:7) would seem to indicate that it is an element in a generally recognized standard of Christian conduct.[8]

I Pet. 3:1, 7; cf. Eph. 5:22.

I Pet. 3:4; cf. Rom. 2:16 and I Cor. 14:25. Only in Paul's letters and in I Peter in the New Testament does κρυπτός refer to the inner life of man.

I Pet. 3:19; cf. Eph. 4:9. The reference in Ephesians seems to be to the descent of Christ into Hades. If this is the

---

[8] K. Weidinger, Die Haustafeln: Ein Stück urchristlicher Paränese (Leipzig: J. C. Hinrichs, 1928).

idea in I Peter also, the case for literary influence would be
strong. However, the allusion in I Peter is very probably to
Enoch instead of to Christ. Rendel Harris[9] conjectures that the
true text of 3:19 is 'Ενώχ instead of ἐν ᾧ καί. This rendering
of the text fits in with the allusion to Noah that follows, with
the theme of the early chapters of the book of Enoch, and with the
fact that the early Fathers do not quote I Pet. 3:19 in referring
to the descent of Christ into the nether world.

I Pet. 4:4; cf. Eph. 5:18.   'Ασωτία occurs in the New Testament in Eph. 5:18, I Pet. 4:4, and Titus 1:6.   In Ephesians and
I Peter it appears in an exhortation against unworthy living.

I Pet. 4:6; cf. Eph. 4:9.

I Pet. 4:19; cf. I Thess. 5:24.

I Pet. 5:4; cf. I Cor. 9:25.

I Pet. 5:7; cf. I Thess. 5:6.   The use of νήφω with
γρηγορέω suggests literary dependence.   However, there may be a
common use of a familiar apocalyptic formula.

I Pet. 5:8; cf. Eph. 6:11, 13.

I Pet. 5:12; cf. Rom. 5:2.

Goodspeed finds evidence for acquaintance with Romans and
Ephesians "unmistakable" and suggests the strong likelihood of
familiarity with II Corinthians.[10]   Moffatt finds the influence
of Romans and Galatians clearest, but he regards as "indubitable"
also the author's acquaintance with I Corinthians and Colossians.[11]
The present study finds traces of acquaintance clearest for Romans,
Ephesians, Galatians, and II Corinthians, but with the likelihood
of acquaintance with several other letters of the corpus.

---

[9]Alexander Souter, Novum Testamentum Graece (Oxford:
Clarendon Press, 1910); see note on I Pet. 3:19.

[10]Op. cit., p. 32.   [11]Op. cit., p. 330.

TABLE OF RESULTS

	A	B	C	Unclassed
Romans..............	2	5	13	4
I Corinthians.......	..	..	..	4
II Corinthians......	..	..	2	2
Galatians...........	..	..	4	....
Ephesians...........	1	3	11	8
Philippians.........	..	..	..	....
Colossians..........	..	..	..	1
I Thessalonians.....	..	..	..	3
II Thessalonians....	..	..	1	....
Philemon............	..	..	..	....

The Epistle to the Hebrews

The writing of Hebrews followed closely upon the publication of the Pauline letter collection. The adoption by its author of the letter form for a nonepistolary message probably reflects the influence of the impressive demonstration which the Pauline corpus made of the effectiveness of the letter as a literary medium for religious instruction.

The content, language, and structure of Hebrews are so distinctively individual as to make its ascription to Paul impossible, and yet the influence of Paul is sufficiently evident to lend some color to such an ascription. This evident Pauline influence in the document was probably the basic reason for its acceptance as Pauline in Alexandria and later by the church in general.

Scott thinks that such coincidences in expression and idea as occur between Hebrews and Paul's letters have no significance and are due to the acceptance by both leaders of certain broad assumptions that were quite generally shared.[12] It is true, as he says, that Hebrews "makes no quotations from Paul";[13] but he

---

[12] E. F. Scott, The Epistle to the Hebrews (Edinburgh: T. & T. Clark, 1923), pp. 48 f.

[13] Ibid.

goes too far in asserting that our author "does not allude, even indirectly, to the Epistles or their author."[14] In Heb. 13:7, Paul is almost certainly in the author's mind (cf. I Clem. 5:4, 5), and there are numerous allusions that are more easily than otherwise explicable in terms of literary dependence.

Although his general conclusions are more traditional than Scott's, George Salmon more clearly discerned the alternatives which the data involve in his statement that "if the writer is not Paul, he must have read some of Paul's epistles,—in particular those to the Romans and Corinthians."[15]

Pauline influence on Hebrews is clear, and it is literary rather than personal. This influence differs in character and extent from that observed in Ephesians, but it is sufficiently pronounced to be well-nigh indubitable.[16]

The author of Hebrews makes extensive use of the Old Testament. As a rule he quotes with exactness, and his deviations from the LXX text are probably due in the main to textual variations. Only in 4:7 (ἐν Δαυεὶδ λέγων) does he refer his quotations to a definite source. It would seem from Heb. 1:6, 8 that he regarded God as the speaker in all Scripture (cf. 1:5, 13; 4:3; 5:5, 6; 7:17; 8:5, 8), and yet he refers to the Holy Spirit (3:7 and 10:15), Christ (12:12 and 10:5), and even human beings (2:6 and 7:21) as speaking.

The familiar formula ὡς γέγραπται does not appear in Hebrews, and yet most of the quotations are formally introduced. Illustrative of the formulas of citation are the following: 1:6, λέγει; 3:7, καθὼς λέγει τὸ πνεῦμα τὸ ἅγιον; 4:7, σήμερον ἐν Δαυεὶδ λέγων; 5:6, καθὼς καὶ ἐν ἑτέρῳ λέγει; 6:14, ὤμοσεν καθ᾽ ἑαυτοῦ λέγων; 8:9, κἀγὼ ἠμέλησα αὐτῶν λέγει Κύριος; 10:5, διὸ εἰσερχόμενος εἰς τὸν κόσμον λέγει.

---

[14] Ibid.

[15] A Historical Introduction to the Study of the Books of the New Testament6, (London: John Murrey, 1892), p. 423.

[16] E. Jacquier, Histoire des livres du Nouveau Testament (Paris: V. Lecoffre, 1903), I, 482.

Heb. 1:2   Colossians C

Δι' οὗ καὶ ἐποίησεν τοὺς αἰῶνας·

Col. 1:16, 17. Ἐν αὐτῷ ἐκτίσθη τὰ πάντα . . . . τὰ πάντα δι' αὐτοῦ καὶ εἰς αὐτὸν ἔκτισται (cf. I Cor. 8:6 and 11:3).

Moffatt remarks that "this passing allusion to the function of Christ in relation to the universe probably originated, as in the case of Paul, in the religious conception of redemption."[17] Not only is there resemblance of conception but a probable indebtedness for the idea to Paul's representation. Colossians is regarded as the more probable source because of the fuller development of the idea in 3:15-17.

Heb. 1:3   Colossians C

Ὃς ὢν ἀπαύγασμα τῆς δόξης καὶ χαρακτὴρ τῆς ὑποστάσεως αὐτοῦ, φέρων τε τὰ πάντα τῷ ῥήματι τῆς δυνάμεως αὐτοῦ.

Col. 1:15. Ὅς ἐστιν εἰκὼν τοῦ Θεοῦ τοῦ ἀοράτου. . . . . 17. Καὶ τὰ πάντα ἐν αὐτῷ συνέστηκεν (cf. II Cor. 4:4-6).

The association of ideas common to Hebrews and Colossians makes the dependence of one on the other probable, although the ideas are expressed in terms drawn from the LXX (cf. Wisd. of Sol. 7:26, Ἀπαύγασμα γάρ ἐστιν φωτὸς αἰδίου). The use of αὐγάζω in II Cor. 4:4 (its only occurrence in the New Testament) carries a strongly similar implication, and the whole elaboration of the idea there would have formed a very suggestive basis for the conception as it is expressed in Hebrews.

Heb. 1:3, 4   Ephesians C

Ἐκάθισεν ἐν δεξιᾷ τῆς μεγαλωσύνης ἐν ὑψηλοῖς, τοσούτῳ κρείττων γενόμενος τῶν ἀγγέλων ὅσῳ διαφορώτερον παρ' αὐτοὺς κεκληρονόμηκεν ὄνομα.

Eph. 1:20, 21. Καὶ καθίσας ἐν δεξιᾷ αὐτοῦ ἐν τοῖς ἐπουρανίοις ὑπεράνω πάσης ἀρχῆς καὶ ἐξουσίας καὶ δυνάμεως καὶ κυριότητος καὶ παντὸς ὀνόματος ὀνομαζομένου οὐ μόνον ἐν τῷ αἰῶνι τούτῳ ἀλλὰ καὶ ἐν τῷ μέλλοντι· (cf. Phil. 2:9, 10, and Ps. 110:1).

---

[17]James Moffatt, A Critical and Exegetical Commentary on the Epistle to the Hebrews (New York: Charles Scribner's Sons, 1924), p. 5.

Ps. 110:1 was popular among the writers of early Christianity. It is formally quoted in Heb. 1:13 (cf. Mark 12:36).
It is the association of ideas and not simply this quotation that
points to literary dependence on Ephesians. The emphasis on the
exaltation of Christ in heaven and on his having a name that is
above every name and the similar employment of the Psalm to substantiate the position taken look strongly in the direction of
literary dependence, even though Moffatt feels that they show
nothing more than "a common atmosphere of religious feeling and
phraseology."[18] Both Eph. 1:20 f. and Heb. 1:3, 4 may be based
on Phil. 2:9, 10, although the indebtedness of Hebrews to Ephesians is more evident than to Philippians.

Heb. 1:6   Colossians C
Ὅταν δὲ πάλιν εἰσαγάγῃ τὸν πρωτότοκον εἰς τὴν οἰκουμένην·
Col. 1:15. Ὅς ἔστιν . . . . πρωτότοκος πάσης κτίσεως
(cf. Rom. 8:29).

Although the sense in which πρωτότοκος is used in Colossians and Hebrews is not identical, it is more nearly so than in
the case of Romans. In the former it emphasizes Christ's superiority to all angelic beings, whereas in Romans it refers to his
relation to men by virtue of his victory over death.

Heb. 2:4   I and II Corinthians C
Συνεπιμαρτυροῦντος τοῦ Θεοῦ σημείοις τε καὶ τέρασιν καὶ
ποικίλαις δυνάμεσιν καὶ πνεύματος ἁγίου μερισμοῖς κατὰ τὴν αὐτοῦ
θέλησιν;
II Cor. 12:12. Τὰ μὲν σημεῖα τοῦ ἀποστόλου κατειργάσθη
εν ὑμῖν ἐν πάσῃ ὑπομονῇ, σημείοις [τε] καὶ τέρασιν καὶ δυνάμεσιν
(cf. Acts 2:22. Ἄνδρα ἀποδεδειγμένον ἀπὸ Θεοῦ εἰς ὑμᾶς δυνάμεσι
καὶ τέρασι καὶ σημείοις).
I Cor. 12:11. Διαιροῦν ἰδίᾳ ἑκάστῳ καθὼς βούλεται (cf.
Gal. 3:5).

In II Cor. 12:12, σημεῖον, τέρας, and δύναμις describe the
miracles that attended the work of the true apostle. The order
in the enumeration is in exact agreement with that of Hebrews, and

_____
[18]Introduction, p. 385.

the sense is the same. In Acts 2:22 these terms are used in the reverse order to describe the manifestations that attended the ministry of Jesus (cf. Philo, Vit. Mos. i. 16, ᾽ατε δὴ τοῦ θεοῦ τρανοτέραις χρησμῶν ἀποδείξεσι ταῖς διὰ σημείων καὶ τεράτων τὸ βούλημα δεδηλωκότος).

In I Corinthians, chapters 12-14, there is an elaborate description of the manifestations of the activity of the Spirit which accompanied the preaching of Christian missionaries. The distribution of the endowments of the Spirit mentioned in I Cor. 12:11 may have suggested the similar description in Heb. 2:4. Gal. 3:5 indicates more specifically the content of such endowments and may also have been in the mind of the author of Hebrews.

Heb. 2:8   I Corinthians C

Πάντα ὑπέταξας ὑποκάτω τῶν ποδῶν αὐτοῦ· ἐν τῷ γὰρ ὑποτάξαι [αὐτῷ] τὰ πάντα οὐδὲν ἀφῆκεν αὐτῷ ἀνυπότακτον. νῦν δὲ οὔπω῾ὁρῶμεν αὐτῷ τὰ πάντα ὑποτεταγμένα·

I Cor. 15:24-28. ῞Οταν καταργήσῃ πᾶσαν ἀρχὴν καὶ πᾶσαν ἐξουσίαν καὶ δύναμιν, δεῖ γὰρ αὐτὸν βασιλεύειν ἄχρι οὗ θῇ πάντας τοὺς ἐχθροὺς ὑπὸ τοὺς πόδας αὐτοῦ. ἔσχατος ἐχθρὸς καταργεῖται ὁ θάνατος, πάντα γὰρ ὑπέταξεν ὑπὸ τοὺς πόδας αὐτοῦ. ὅταν δὲ εἴπῃ ὅτι πάντα ὑποτέτακται, δῆλον ὅτι ἐκτὸς τοῦ ὑποτάξαντος αὐτῷ τὰ πάντα. ὅταν δὲ ὑποταγῇ αὐτῷ τὰ πάντα, τότε [καὶ] αὐτὸς ὁ υἱὸς ὑποταγήσεται τῷ ὑποτάξαντι αὐτῷ τὰ πάντα, ἵνα ᾖ ὁ θεὸς πάντα ἐν πᾶσιν.

In I Cor. 15:24-28, Paul rings the changes on ὑποτάσσω, and the whole section consists of his comment on Ps. 8:6. This same passage is the basis of the thought of Heb. 2:8, and there is a similar play on ὑποτάσσω.

Heb. 2:9-10   Philippians C

Τὸν δὲ βραχύ τι παρ᾽ ἀγγέλους ἠγαττωμένον βλέπομεν ᾽Ιησοῦν διὰ τὸ πάθημα τοῦ θανάτου δόξῃ καὶ τιμῇ ἐστεφανωμένον ὅπως χάριτι θεοῦ ὑπὲρ παντὸς γεύσηται θανάτου. ῎Επρεπεν γὰρ αὐτῷ δι᾽ ὃν τὰ πάντα καὶ δι᾽ οὗ τὰ πάντα, πολλοὺς υἱοὺς εἰς δόξαν ἀγαγόντα τὸν ἀρχηγὸν τῆς σωτηρίας αὐτῶν διὰ παθημάτων τελειῶσαι.

Phil. 2:6-9. ῝Ος ἐν μορφῇ θεοῦ ὑπάρχων οὐχ ἁρπαγμὸν ἡγήσατο τὸ εἶναι ἴσα θεῷ, ἀλλὰ ἑαυτὸν ἐκένωσεν μορφὴν δούλου λαβών, ἐν ὁμοιώματι ἀνθρώπων γενόμενος· καὶ σχήματι εὑρεθεὶς ὡς ἄνθρωπος ἐταπε νωσεν ἑαυτὸν γενόμενος ὑπήκοος μέχρι θανάτου, θανάτου δὲ σταυροῦ· διὸ καὶ ὁ θεὸς αὐτὸν ὑπερύψωσεν.

The author of Hebrews interprets βραχύ τι as "temporarily" and uses it to assert that, though Jesus was temporarily put lower than the angels, his experience was the pathway to saviorhood. This is very similar to Paul's representation of Christ's humiliation and exaltation in Philippians.

Heb. 2:10   Romans C

῎Επρεπεν γὰρ αὐτῷ, δι᾿ ὅν τὰ πάντα καὶ δι᾿ οὗ τὰ πάντα πολλοὺς υἱοὺς εἰς δόξαν ἀγαγόντα.

Rom. 11:36. ᾿Εξ αὐτοῦ καὶ δι᾿ αὐτοῦ καὶ εἰς᾿ αὐτὸν τὰ πάντα. 8:29. Εἰς τὸ εἶναι αὐτὸν πρωτότοκον ἐν πολλοῖς ἀδελφοῖς (cf. I Cor. 8:6).

The description of God in Hebrews corresponds closely with Paul's description in Rom. 11:36. Also, πολλοί is in antithesis to ἀρχηγός, just as in Rom. 8:29 it contrasts with προτότομον.

Heb. 2:14   I Corinthians B

῎Ινα διὰ τοῦ θανάτου καταργήσῃ τὸν τὸ κράτος ἔχοντα τοῦ θανάτου (cf. Wisd. of Sol. 2:23, 24).

I Cor. 15:26. ῎Εσχατος ἐχθρὸς καταργεῖται ὁ θάνατος.

Καταργέω is used in the New Testament twenty-eight times, of which twenty-four are in Paul's letters. The four instances of its occurrence outside Paul's letters are Luke 13:7, Eph. 2:15, II Tim. 1:10, and Heb. 2:14. In I Cor. 15:26, Heb. 2:14, and II Tim. 1:10 it refers to θάνατος. Dependence in the two latter instances is probably on I Corinthians.

Heb. 3:6   Ephesians C   Romans C

Οὗ οἶκος ἐσμεν ἡμεῖς, ἐὰν τὴν παρρησίαν καὶ τὸ καύχημα τῆς ἐλπίδος [μέχρι τέλους βεβαίαν] κατάσχωμεν.

Eph. 2:19. ῎Αρα οὖν οὐκέτι ἐστὲ ξένοι καὶ πάροικοι, ἀλλὰ ἐστὲ . . . . οἰκεῖοι τοῦ Θεοῦ (cf. Gal. 6:10. Μάλιστα δὲ πρὸς τοὺς οἰκείους τῆς πίστεως).

Rom. 5:2. Δι᾿ οὗ καὶ τὴν προσαγωγὴν ἐσχήκαμεν [τῇ πίστει] εἰς τὴν χάριν ταύτην ἐν ᾗ ἐστήκαμεν, καὶ καυχώμεθα ἐπ᾿ ἐλπίδι τῆς δόξης τοῦ Θεοῦ· 15:4. ῎Ινα διὰ τῆς ὑπομονῆς καὶ διὰ τῆς παρακλήσεως τῶν γραφῶν τὴν ἐλπίδα ἔχωμεν.

The use of πάροικοι and οἰκεῖοι τοῦ Θεοῦ in Ephesians

strongly resembles the use of οἶκος in Hebrews and very probably
influenced the latter. This is not to overlook the fact pointed
out by Moffatt that the figure "was a commonplace of ancient
thought."[19] The context and the sense in which ἐλπίς is used in
Hebrews probably reflects the influence of Romans. The thought
of the two passages is exactly the same (cf. Ps. 5:12).

Heb. 3:16—4:2   I Corinthians B

Τίνες γὰρ ἀκούσαντες παρεπίκραναν; ἀλλ' οὐ πάντες οἱ ἐξελ-
θόντες ἐξ Αἰγύπτου διὰ Μωυσέως; τίσιν δὲ προσώχθισεν τεσσεράκοντα
ἔτη; οὐχὶ τοῖς ἁμαρτήσασιν, ὧν τὰ κῶλα ἔπεσεν ἐν τῇ ἐρήμῳ; τίσιν
δὲ ὤμοσεν μὴ εἰσελεύσεσθαι εἰς τὴν κατάπαυσιν αὐτοῦ εἰ μὴ τοῖς
ἀπειθήσασιν; καὶ βλέπομεν ὅτι οὐκ ἠδυνήθησαν εἰσελθεῖν δι' ἀπιστίαν.
φοβηθῶμεν οὖν μή ποτε καταλειπομένης ἐπαγγελίας εἰσελθεῖν εἰς τὴν
κατάπαυσιν αὐτοῦ δοκῇ τις ἐξ ὑμῶν ὑστερηκέναι· καὶ γὰρ ἐσμεν εὐηγ-
γελισμένοι καθάπερ κἀκεῖνοι, ἀλλ' οὐκ ὠφέλησεν ὁ λόγος τῆς ἀκοῆς
ἐκείνους, ⌜μὴ ⌜συνκεκερασμένους τῇ πίστει τοῖς ἀκούσασιν.⌝

Hebrews is rather clearly influenced here by I Cor. 10:1-
11. The passages are based on the same historical allusion and
sound the same warning.

Heb. 4:16   Ephesians B

Προσερχώμεθα οὖν μετὰ παρρησίας τῷ θρονῷ τῆς χάριτος.

Eph. 3:11, 12. Κατὰ πρόθεσιν τῶν αἰώνων ἣν ἐποίησεν ἐν
τῷ Χριστῷ Ἰησοῦ τῷ κυρίῳ ἡμῶν, ἐν ᾧ ἔχομεν τὴν παρρησίαν καὶ
προσαγωγὴν ἐν πεποιθήσει (cf. Rom. 5:2).

This exhortation to "confidence" clearly looks back to
the statement regarding Christ in verses 14 and 15. He is the
warrant for this "confidence." This is exactly the thought of
Ephesians, and the use of παρρησία in both passages points rather
clearly to literary dependence. Except for its use in this sense
in I John, where dependence on Ephesians is highly probable,
παρρησία is used of approach to God only in Heb. 4:16 and Eph.
3:11, 12.

---

[19]*A Critical and Exegetical Commentary on the Epistle to
the Hebrews*, p. 42.

Heb. 5:8, 9   Philippians C

Καίπερ ὢν υἱός, ἔμαθεν ἀφ' ὧν ἔπαθεν τὴν ὑπακοήν, καὶ· τελειωθεὶς ἐγένετο πᾶσιν τοῖς ὑπακούουσιν αὐτῷ αἴτιος σωτηρίας αἰωνίου.

Phil. 2:7-11. Καὶ σχήματι εὑρεθεὶς ὡς ἄνθρωπος ἐταπείνωσεν ἑαυτὸν γενόμενος ὑπήκοος μέχρι θανάτου . . . . διὸ καὶ ὁ θεὸς αὐτὸν ὑπερύψωσεν, καὶ ἐχαρίσατο αὐτῷ τὸ ὄνομα τὸ ὑπὲρ πᾶν ὄνομα, ἵνα ἐν τῷ ὀνόματι 'Ινσοῦ πᾶν γόνυ κάμψῃ . . . . καὶ πᾶσα γλῶσσα ἐξομολογήσηται ὅτι κύριος 'Ιησοῦς Χριστός. . . . .

The idea that Jesus "learned obedience" through his earthly experience is different from the conception of Philippians, and yet the one passage suggests the other, and the one may have been influenced by the other. The fact that verse 9 deals with the exaltation of Christ at the appointment of God, paralleling Phil. 2:9-11, creates the probability of such influence.

Heb. 5:12-14   I Corinthians B

Καὶ γὰρ ὀφείλοντες εἶναι διδάσκαλοι διὰ· τὸν χρόνον, πάλιν χρείαν ἔχετε τοῦ διδάσκειν ὑμᾶς τινὰ τὰ στοιχεῖα τῆς ἀρχῆς τῶν λογίων τοῦ θεοῦ, καὶ γεγόνατε χρείαν ἔχοντες γάλακτος, οὐ στερεᾶς τροφῆς. πᾶς γὰρ ὁ μετέχων γάλακτος ἄπειρος λόγου δικαιοσύνης, νήπιος γάρ ἐστιν· τελείων δέ ἐστιν ἡ στερεὰ τροφή, τῶν διὰ τὴν ἕξιν τὰ· αἰσθητήρια γεγυμνασμένα ἐχόντων πρὸς διάκρισιν καλοῦ· τε καὶ κακοῦ.

I Cor. 3:1, 2. Κἀγώ, ἀδελφοί, οὐκ ἠδυνήθην λαλῆσαι ὑμῖν ὡς πνευματικοῖς ἀλλ' ὡς σαρκίνοις, ὡς νηπίοις ἐν Χριστῷ. γάλα ὑμᾶς ἐπότισα, οὐ βρῶμα, οὔπω γὰρ ἐδύνασθε. 2:6. Σοφίαν δὲ λαλοῦμεν ἐν τοῖς τελείοις (cf. Eph. 4:14. ῞Ινα μηκέτι ὦμεν νήπιοι).

The author of Hebrews employs the same comparison of milk and solid food and draws the same contrast between νήπιοι and τέλειοι that Paul does in I Corinthians. The probabilities favor his indebtedness to I Corinthians for these figures, although it must be admitted that he might have drawn them from current Hellenistic usage (cf. Epictetus ii. 16.39: Οὐ θέλεις ἤδη ὡς τὰ παιδία ἀπογαλακτισθῆναι καὶ ἄπτεσθαι τροφῆς στερεωτέρας. iii. 24.9: Οὐκ ἀπογαλακτίσομεν ἤδη ποθ' ἑαυτούς. Philo, De agric. 2: 'Επεὶ δὲ νηπίοις μὲν ἐστι γάλα τροφή, τελείοις δὲ τὰ ἐκ πυρῶν πέμματα, καὶ ψυχῆς γαλακτώδεις μὲν ἂν εἶεν τροφαὶ κατὰ τὴν παιδικὴν ἡλικίαν τὰ τῆς ἐγκυκλίου μουσικῆς προπαιδεύματα, τέλειαι δὲ καὶ ἀνδράσιν ἐμπρεπεῖς αἱ διὰ φρονήσεως καὶ σωφροσύνης καὶ ἁπάσης ἀρετῆς ὑφηγήσεις).

Heb. 6:4   Ephesians C   II Corinthians C

Φωτισθέντας (cf. 10:32).

Eph. 1:18. Πεφωτισμένους τοὺς ὀφθαλμοὺς τῆς καρδίας.

II Cor. 4:6. "Οτι ὁ Θεὸς ὁ εἰπών 'Εκ σκότους φῶς λάμψει, ὃς ἔλαμψεν ἐν ταῖς καρδίαις ἡμῶν πρὸς φωτισμὸν τῆς γνώσεως τῆς δόξης τοῦ Θεοῦ ἐν προσώπῳ Χριστοῦ.

Φωτίζω is used in Luke 11:36 to describe spiritual illumination but not the initial Christian experience. Aside from this Lukan use it occurs in the New Testament only in I Cor. 4:5 and Eph. 1:18, 3:9 and in the later writings that were influenced by Paul's collected letters (John, Hebrews, the Apocalypse, and II Timothy). Although the verb is not used in II Corinthians, the noun φωτισμός is used in 4:4, 6, and it is used nowhere else.

Heb. 6:6   Galatians C

'Ανασταυροῦντας ἑαυτοῖς τὸν υἱὸν τοῦ Θεοῦ καὶ παραδειγματίζοντας.

Gal. 3:1. Ὦ ἀνόητοι Γαλάται, τίς ὑμᾶς ἐβάσκανεν, οἷς κατ' ὀφθαλμοὺς 'Ιησοῦς Χριστὸς προεγράφη ἐσταυρωμένος;

The implications of both passages are the same. Both deal with the problem of those who abandon or are tempted to abandon their Christian faith or some aspect of it. The significance of the Crucifixion is made a basis of appeal and warning in both instances.

Heb. 6:12   Romans C

"Ινα μὴ νωθροὶ γένησθε, μιμηταὶ δὲ τῶν διὰ πίστεως καὶ μακροθυμίας κληρονομούντων τὰς ἐπαγγελίας.

Rom. 4:13. Οὐ γὰρ διὰ νόμου ἡ ἐπαγγελία τῷ 'Αβραὰμ ἢ τῷ σπέρματι αὐτοῦ, τὸ κληρονόμον αὐτὸν εἶναι κόσμου, ἀλλὰ διὰ δικαιοσύνης πίστεως. 20. Εἰς δὲ τὴν ἐπαγγελίαν τοῦ Θεοῦ οὐ διεκρίθη τῇ ἀπιστίᾳ ἀλλὰ ἐνεδυναμώθη τῇ πίστει, δοὺς δόξαν τῷ Θεῷ καὶ πληροφορηθεὶς ὅτι ὃ ἐπήγγελται δυνατός ἐστιν καὶ ποιῆσαι.

The use of ἐπαγγελία is limited in the New Testament to Luke-Acts, the Pauline letters, and the later writings that were

influenced by Paul's collected letters. Its use in Hebrews in
connection with κληρονομέω and διὰ πίστεως points rather strongly
to familiarity with Romans.

Heb. 7:18, 19   Romans C   Ephesians C
᾽Αθέτησις μὲν γὰρ γίνεται προαγούσης ἐντολῆς διὰ τὸ αὐτῆς
ἀσθενὲς καὶ ἀνωφελές, οὐδὲν γὰρ ἐτελείωσεν ὁ νόμος, ἐπεισαγωγὴ δὲ
κρείττονος ἐλπίδος, δι' ἧς ἐγγίζομεν τῷ θεῷ.
Rom. 8:3. Τὸ γὰρ ἀδύνατον τοῦ νόμου, ἐν ᾧ ἠσθένει.
Eph. 2:13. ᾽Ελπίδα μὴ ἔχοντες . . . . νυνὶ δὲ ἐν Χριστῷ
᾽Ιησοῦ ὑμεῖς οἵ ποτε ὄντες μακρὰν ἐγενήθητε ἐγγύς.

The description of the Law as ἀσθενής is an indication of
probable acquaintance with Rom. 8:3. The "better hope" and the
"drawing near to God" look in the direction of dependence on Eph.
2:13.

Heb. 7:25   Romans B
Πάντοτε ζῶν εἰς τὸ ἐντυγχάνειν ὑπὲρ αὐτῶν.
Rom. 8:34. ῞Ος καὶ ἐντυγχάνει ὑπὲρ ἡμῶν.

The idea of the passages is the same. ᾽Εντυγχάνω is used
in the New Testament only in Acts 25:24; Rom. 8:27, 34; and Heb.
7:25. Its use in the two latter instances is so nearly identical
as to leave little doubt of literary dependence of Hebrews on
Romans.

Heb. 9:12   Ephesians B
Διὰ δὲ τοῦ ἰδίου αἵματος, εἰσῆλθεν ἐφάπαξ εἰς τὰ ἅγια,
αἰωνίαν λύτρωσιν εὑράμενος.
Eph. 1:7. ᾽Εν ᾧ ἔχομεν τὴν ἀπολύτρωσιν διὰ τοῦ αἵματος
αὐτοῦ.

Λύτρωσις is used in the New Testament only in Luke and
Hebrews, and ἀπολύτρωσις in Luke, the letters of the Pauline letter collection, and Hebrews. The use of these terms in connection
with διὰ . . . . αἵματος creates a strong probability of literary
relationship with Ephesians. Only in these two passages in the
New Testament are these expressions and ideas so directly associated (cf. Rom. 3:24).

Heb. 9:14   I Thessalonians C

Καθαριεῖ τὴν συνείδησιν ⌜ἡμῶν⌝ ἀπὸ νεκρῶν ἔργων· εἰς τὸ· λατρεύειν Θεῷ ζῶντι.

I Thess. 1:9. ᾿Επεστρέψατε πρὸς τὸν Θεὸν ἀπὸ τῶν εἰδώλων δουλεύειν Θεῷ ζῶντι.

Both λατρεύειν and δουλεύειν are used in a general sense and are practical equivalents here. The contrasts involved are the same.

Heb. 9:15   Ephesians B.
Εἰς ἀπολύτρωσιν.
Eph. 1:14. Εἰς ἀπολύτρωσιν.

This phrase occurs only in these two instances in the New Testament.

Heb. 9:28   I Thessalonians C
᾿Εκ δευτέρου χωρὶς ἁμαρτίας ὀφθήσεται τοῖς αὐτὸν ἀπεκδεχο- μένοις εἰς σωτηρίαν.

I Thess. 1:10. ᾿Αναμένειν τὸν υἱὸν αὐτοῦ ἐκ τῶν οὐρανὸν. . . . . ᾿Ιησοῦν τὸν ῥυόμενον ἡμᾶς ἐκ τῆς ὀργῆς τῆς ἐρχομένης.

An eschatological expectancy and the emphasis on a future salvation are common to these passages.

Heb. 10:10   Romans B
Διὰ τῆς προσφορᾶς τοῦ σώματος ᾿Ιησοῦ Χριστοῦ ἐφάπαξ.
Rom. 6:10. ῾Ο γὰρ ἀπέθανεν, τῇ ἁμαρτίᾳ ἀπέθανεν ἐφάπαξ.

᾿Εφάπαξ is used in the New Testament in Rom. 6:10, I Cor. 15:6, and in Heb. 8:27, 9:12, and 10:10. Its meaning in Hebrews is in exact agreement with its use in Romans, denoting something that is final in the sense of not being repeated. Its application in 10:10 to the sacrifice of Christ makes dependence on Romans particularly probable.

Heb. 10:25   Romans C
Καὶ τοσούτῳ μᾶλλον ὅσῳ βλέπετε ἐγγίζουσαν τὴν ἡμέραν.
Rom. 13:11, 12. Καὶ τοῦτο εἰδότες τὸν καιρόν . . . . νῦν γὰρ ἐγγύτερον ἡμῶν ἡ σωτηρία ἢ ὅτε ἐπιστεύσαμεν . . . . ἡ δὲ

ἡμέρα ἤγγικεν (cf. I Thess. 5:4 and I Cor. 3:13).

"The Day" in Hebrews and Romans refers to the messianic day of early Christian expectation. Its use in both instances in connection with ἐγγίζω suggests literary relationship.

Heb. 10:30   Romans C
Οἴδαμεν γὰρ τὸν εἰπόντα ᾿Εμοὶ ἐκδίκησις ἐγὼ ἀνταποδώσω· καὶ πάλιν Κρινεῖ κύριος τὸν λαὸν αὐτοῦ.
Rom. 12:19. Γέγραπται γὰρ ᾿Εμοὶ ἐκδίκησις, ἐγὼ ἀνταποδώσω, λέγει Κύριος (cf. Deut. 32:35).

In Rom. 12:19, Paul cites Deut. 32:35 as sanction for his exhortation against revenge. The author of Hebrews quotes it to establish the certainty of punishment for those who desert God. The quotation in Hebrews is in exact agreement with Romans, as against the LXX and the Hebrew. This may have been the result of dependence on Romans, although it may have been the result of common dependence on a current Greek version of the passage in Deuteronomy. The latter possibility is strengthened by the quotation of Deut. 32:36 in Heb. 10:30, which latter passage is not a part of Paul's quotation.

Heb. 10:32, 33   I Corinthians B Ephesians C II Corinthians C
᾿Αναμιμνῄσκεσθε δὲ τὰς πρότερον ἡμέρας, ἐν αἷς φωτισθέντες πολλὴν ἄθλησιν ὑπεμείνατε παθημάτων, τοῦτο μὲν ὀνειδισμοῖς τε καὶ· θλίψεσιν θεατριζόμενοι, τοῦτο δὲ κοινωνοὶ τῶν οὕτως ἀναστρεφομένων γενηθέντες·
I Cor. 4:9. ῞Οτι θέατρον ἐγενήθημεν τῷ κόσμῳ.

Θέατρον is used in the New Testament in Acts 19:29, 31, and in I Cor. 4:9, in the one instance of a place and in the other of a spectacle. Θεατρίζομαι is used in the New Testament only in Heb. 10:33 and in a sense that corresponds with that of I Cor. 4:9.

For the probable dependence on Eph. 1:18 and II Cor. 4:6, which is involved in the phrase ἐν αἷς φωτισθέντες see the note on Heb. 6:4.

Heb. 11   I Corinthians B
῎Εστιν δὲ πίστις ἐλπιζομένων ⌜ὑπόστασις, πραγμάτων⌝ ἔλεγχος

οὐ βλεπομένων· ἐν ταύτη γὰρ ἐμαρτυρήθησαν οἱ πρεσβύτεροι. Πίστει
νοοῦμεν κατηρτίσθαι τοὺς αἰῶνας ῥήματι Θεοῦ, ... Πίστει
πλείονα θυσίαν "Αβελ. . . . . Πίστει 'Ενὸχ μετετέθη τοῦ μὴ ἰδεῖν
θάνατον. . . . . Πίστει χρηματισθεὶς Νῶε περὶ τῶν μηδέπω βλεπομέ-
νων εὐλαβηθείς. . . . . Πίστει καλούμενος 'Αβραὰμ ὑπήκουσεν ἐξελ-
θεῖν εἰς τόπον ὃν ἤμελλεν λαμβάνειν εἰς κληρονομίαν, ...
Πίστει παρῴκησεν εἰς γῆν τῆς ἐπαγγελίας ὡς ἀλλοτρίαν, ... κτλ.

The central principle of Paul's teaching was faith. It
is this principle that is magnified in Hebrews, chapter 11, although with a connotation that is distinctive. The literary form
of the author's presentation reminds of Paul's glorification of
love in I Corinthians, chapter 13 and was very probably patterned
on it.

Heb. 11:7   Romans C

Καὶ τῆς κατὰ πίστιν δικαιοσύνης ἐγένετο κληρονόμος.

Rom. 4:13. Τὸ κληρονόμον αὐτὸν εἶναι κόσμου, ἀλλὰ διὰ
δικαιοσύνης πίστεως (cf. 3:22, δικαιοσύνη δὲ Θεοῦ διὰ πίστεως. . . .;
9:30, δικαιοσύνην δὲ τὴν ἐκ πίστεως . . . .; 10:6, ἡ δὲ ἐκ πίστεως
δικαιοσύνη; Phil. 3:9, μὴ ἔχων ἐμὴν δικαιοσύνην . . . . ἀλλὰ τὴν
διὰ πίστεως).

Heb. 11:11, 12   Romans C

Πίστει καὶ ⌜αὐτὴ Σάρρα⌝ δύναμιν εἰς καταβολὴν σπέρματος
ἔλαβεν καὶ παρὰ καιρὸν ἡλικίας, ἐπεὶ πιστὸν ἡγήσατο τὸν ἐπαγγειλά-
μενον· διὰ καὶ ἀφ' ἑνὸς ⌜ἐγεννήθησαν⌝, καὶ ταῦτα νενεκρωμένου,
καθὼς τὰ ἄστρα τοῦ οὐρανοῦ τῷ πλήθει καὶ ὡς ἡ ἄμμος ἡ παρὰ τὸ
χεῖλος τῆς θαλάσσης ἡ ἀναρίθμητος.

Rom. 4:19, 20. Καὶ μὴ ἀσθενήσας τῇ πίστει κατενόησεν τὸ
ἑαυτοῦ σῶμα [ἤδη] νενεκρωμένον, ἑκατονταετής που ὑπάρχων, καὶ τὴν
νέκρωσιν τῆς μήτρας Σάρρας, εἰς δὲ τὴν ἐπαγγελίαν τοῦ Θεοῦ οὐ
διεκρίθη τῇ ἀπιστίᾳ ἀλλὰ ἐνεδυναμώθη τῇ πίστει.

Neither the Genesis story nor Paul's use of it in Romans
mentions Sara's faith. Νενεκρωμένου is used in the same sense as
in Rom. 4:19 and may be an indication of literary dependence. The
point of the story in Hebrews is the same as in Romans, although
the one emphasizes the faith of Sara and the other that of

Abraham. Hebrews would not necessarily depend on Romans for this use of the story, but the probabilities are that it did. Νεκρόω is used in the New Testament only in Rom. 4:19, Col. 3:5, and Heb. 11:12, and νέκρωσις is used only in Rom. 4:19 and II Cor. 4:10.

Heb. 11:26   Romans C
Τὸν ὀνειδισμὸν τοῦ Χριστοῦ.
Rom. 15:3. Καθὼς γέγραπται Οἱ ὀνειδισμοὶ τῶν ὀνειδιζόντων σὲ ἐπέπεσαν ἐπ' ἐμέ.

In Romans the words of Ps. 69:10 are applied to Christ. The words of the Psalm are quoted exactly. "The reproach of Christ" in Hebrews may be an adaptation of Ps. 89:50, 51, or it may have been derived by implication from Rom. 15:3. The latter has as much in its favor as the former.

Heb. 12:1   Philippians B   I Corinthians C
Δι' ὑπομονῆς τρέχωμεν τὸν προκείμενον ἡμῖν ἀγῶνα, ἀφορῶν-τες εἰς τὸν. . . . . 'Ιησοῦν.
Phil. 1:30. Τὸν αὐτὸν ἀγῶνα ἔχοντες οἷον εἴδετε ἐν ἐμοί. 3:12-15. Οὐχ ὅτι ἤδη ἔλαβον ἢ ἤδη τετελείωμαι, διώκω δὲ εἰ καὶ καταλάβω, ἐφ' ᾧ καὶ κατελήμφθην ὑπὸ Χριστοῦ ['Ιησοῦ]. 'Αδελφοί, ἐγὼ ἐμαυτὸν ⌜οὔπω⌝ λογίζομαι κατειληφέναι· ἐν δέ, τὰ μὲν ὀπίσω ἐπιλανθανόμενος τοῖς δὲ ἔμπροσθεν ἐπεκτεινόμενος, κατὰ σκοπὸν διώκω εἰς τὸ βραβεῖον τῆς ἄνω κλήσεως τοῦ Θεοῦ ἐν Χριστῷ 'Ιησοῦ. "Οσοι οὖν τέλειοι, τοῦτο φρονῶμεν·
I Cor. 9:24, 25. Οὐκ οἴδατε ὅτι οἱ ἐν σταδίῳ τρέχοντες πάντες μὲν τρέχουσιν, εἷς δὲ λαμβάνει τὸ βραβεῖον; οὕτως τρέχετε ἵνα καταλάβητε. πᾶς δὲ ὁ ἀγωνιζόμενος πάντα ἐγκρατεύεται, ἐκεῖ-νοι μὲν οὖν ἵνα φθαρτὸν στέφανον λάβωσιν, ἡμεῖς δὲ ἄφθαρτον.

The figure that is common to these three passages was a popular one in the literature of the period.[20] The mere fact of its employment in Hebrews does not establish literary dependence in any direction (cf. Epictetus iii.25.1-3; iv.4.31; IV Macc. 17:

---

[20]P. Wendland, Die hellenistisch-römische Kultur: Die urchristlichen Literaturformen[5] (Tübingen, J. C. B. Mohr, 1912), pp. 357 f

11-14), although the probabilities favor such dependence. Ἀγών
is used in the New Testament in the Pauline letters, Hebrews, and
the Pastorals. Ἀγωνίζομαι is used in Luke, John, the Pauline
letters, and the Pastorals. The ideas involved, with the proper
chronological sequence of the various writings in mind, clearly
indicate dependence on Philippians and I Corinthians, if there is
dependence in any direction. The phrase εἰς τὸν . . . . Ἰησοῦν
in Hebrews is used in connection with the figure in question in a
sense that is the equivalent of κατὰ σκοπὸν διώκω εἰς τὸ βραβεῖον
τῆς ἄνω κλήσεως τοῦ Θεοῦ ἐν Χριστῷ Ἰησοῦ. The hortatory character of the statement in Hebrews may reflect the influence of the
τοῦτο φρονῶμεν of Phil. 3:15. The language more closely resembles
that of I Corinthians, but the point of the thought is that of
Philippians.

Heb. 12:2   Philippians B

Ὅς ἀντὶ τῆς προκειμένης αὐτῷ χαρᾶς ὑπέμεινεν σταυρὸν
αἰσχύνης καταφρονήσας, ἐν δεξιᾷ τε τοῦ θρόνου τοῦ Θεοῦ κεκάθικεν.

Phil. 2:7-9. Καὶ σχήματι εὑρεθεὶς ὡς ἄνθρωπος ἐταπείνωσεν
ἑαυτὸν γενόμενος ὑπήκοος μέχρι θανάτου, θανάτου δὲ σταυροῦ· διὸ
καὶ ὁ Θεὸς αὐτὸν ὑπερύψωσεν, καὶ ἐχαρίσατο αὐτῷ τὸ ὄνομα τὸ ὑπὲρ
πᾶν ὄνομα.

Christ's submission to crucifixion and his subsequent and
resultant exaltation at the hands of God are parallel ideas in
these passages. The rather clear dependence of Heb. 12:1 on Phil.
3:12-14 strengthens the probability of dependence here.

Heb. 12:4, 5   Philippians B   I Corinthians C

Οὔπω μέχρις αἵματος ἀντικατέστητε πρὸς τὴν ἁμαρτίαν ἀντα-
γωνιζόμενοι, καὶ ἐκλέλησθε τῆς παρακλήσεως.

The figure of Heb. 12:4, 5 clearly looks back to that of
12:1, where the probabilities favored dependence on Philippians
and I Corinthians.

Heb. 12:14   Romans C

Εἰρήνην διώκετε μετὰ πάντων καὶ τὸν ἁγιασμόν.

Rom. 12:19. Τὸ ἐξ ὑμῶν μετὰ πάντων ἀνθρώπων εἰρηνεύοντες·
14:19. Ἄρα οὖν τὰ τῆς εἰρήνης ⌜διώκωμεν⌝ καὶ τὰ τῆς οἰκοδομῆς
(cf. Ps. 34:15).

Dependence on Romans is as likely as on Psalm 34. Only in Rom. 14:19, Heb. 12:14, and I Pet. 3:11 is διώκω used in connection with εἰρήνη. In I Peter the allusion is clearly to Ps. 34:15, but in Hebrews the case is indecisive.

Heb. 12:22   Galatians C
Ἰερουσαλὴμ ἐπουρανίῳ.
Gal. 4:26. Ἡ ἄνω Ἰερουσαλήμ (cf. Apoc. 3:12).

Paul draws a contrast between Mount Sinai, the earthly Jerusalem, and ἡ ἄνω Ἰερουσαλήμ. Although the author of Hebrews does not name Mount Sinai, he contrasts it, in effect, with Mount Zion, which is Ἰερουσαλὴμ ἐπουράνιος.

Heb. 13:1   Romans B
Ἡ φιλαδελφία μενέτω. Τῆς φιλοξενίας μὴ ἐπιλανθάνεσθε.
Rom. 12:10. Τῇ φιλαδελφίᾳ εἰς ἀλλήλους φιλόστοργοι.
. . . . 13. Τὴν φιλοξενίαν διώκοντες (cf. I Thess. 4:9).

Φιλαδελφία is used in the New Testament in Rom. 12:10, I Thess. 4:9, Heb. 13:1, I Pet. 1:22, and II Pet. 1:7. Φιλοξενία is used only in Rom. 12:13 and Heb. 13:1. Dependence on Romans is very probable, although it is not certain because such paranetic material may have been the expression of common Christian emphasis.

Heb. 13:9   I Corinthians C
Καλὸν γὰρ χάριτι βεβαιοῦσθαι τὴν καρδίαν, οὐ βρώμασιν, ἐν οἷς οὐκ ὠφελήθησαν οἱ ⌐περιπατοῦντες⌐.
I Cor. 8:8. Βρῶμα δὲ ἡμᾶς οὐ παραστήσει τῷ θεῷ· οὔτε ἐὰν μὴ φάγωμεν, ὑστερούμεθα, οὔτε ἐὰν φάγωμεν, περισσεύομεν (cf. Rom. 14:3 f.).

The "strange varieties of teaching" are evidently connected with βρώματα, although the exact connotation of the latter does not appear. The allusion is probably to some such participation in cult festivals as that with which Paul deals in I Corinthians. The immediately succeeding context in Hebrews shows that the writer had in mind a contrast of such rites with the Christian sacrament of the Lord's supper, in which case his warning may have been influenced by I Cor. 10:14-21.

Heb. 13:16   Philippians C

Τῆς δὲ εὐποιίας καὶ κοινωνίας μὴ ἐπιλανθάνεσθε, τοιαύταις
γὰρ θυσίαις εὐαρεστεῖται ὁ Θεός.

Phil. 4:15. Πλὴν καλῶς ἐποιήσατε συνκοινωνήσαντές μου
τῇ θλίψει . . . . ὅτε ἐξῆλθον ἀπὸ Μακεδονίας, οὐδεμία μοι ἐκκλησία
ἐκοινώνησεν εἰς λόγον δόσεως καὶ λήμψεως εἰ μὴ ὑμεῖς μόνοι. . . . .
18. Θυσίαν . . . . εὐάρεστον τῷ Θεῷ (cf. II Cor. 9:11-13).

Κοινωνέω is found in the Pauline letters and in Hebrews,
I Timothy, I Peter, and II John. Κοινωνία is found in Acts 2:42,
the Pauline letters, Hebrews, and I John. Συνκοινωνέω is found
in Eph. 5:11, Phil. 4:14, and Apoc. 18:4. Συνκοινωνός occurs in
the Pauline letters and Apoc. 1:9. The usage in Heb. 13:16 suggests the probable influence of Philippians.

Instances of possible literary reminiscence.—Heb. 1:1, 2;
cf. I Cor. 10:11. The view of the function of Scripture and the
eschatological outlook of both passages are very similar. The context of I Cor. 10:11 accentuates this resemblance: οἱ πατέρες
ἡμῶν in I Cor. 10:1 has the same connotation as τοῖς πατράσιν (cf.
Zech. 1:5). In both instances the reference is to the ancient Hebrew leaders whom Christians as God's "chosen people" claimed and
reverenced as their own.

Heb. 1:2; cf. Gal. 3:16, 18, 29. The relationship between Christ and the Christian heritage as Paul describes it in
Galatians may have suggested to the author of Hebrews the description of Christ as κληρονόμος πάντων.

Heb. 2:2; cf. Gal. 3:19. There is the bare possibility
that Hebrews was indebted to Galatians for this idea of the Law's
having been mediated through angels. The idea might have been derived, however, from Acts 7:53 or the LXX (cf. Deut. 33:2 and Ps.
68:18) or from the influence of Hellenistic Judaism (cf. Josephus
Ant. xv.136).

Heb. 2:5; cf. I Cor. 6:2, 3. The assertion that God has
assigned the dominion of the world to others than angels and the
use of Ps. 8:5-7 to emphasize man's loftier position in the universe suggest the possibility of dependence on I Corinthians.
However, it is not the comparison of men and angels about which
the author's thought centers but the supremacy of the Son.

Heb. 2:11; cf. Rom. 8:15-17 and Gal. 4:4-7. In verse 11 the author of Hebrews makes more explicit the implications of πολλοὺς υἱούς. The unity between the "many sons" and their "leader" is one of nature based on sonship to God. These ideas are substantially the same as those found in Rom. 8:15-17 and Gal. 4:4-7 and may owe their suggestion to these sources. The phrase δι' ἣν αἰτίαν occurs elsewhere in the New Testament in II Tim. 1:6, 12 and Titus 1:13. If there is literary dependence, it is on the part of the Pastorals, however.

Heb. 2:14; cf. Eph. 6:12. The αἷμα καὶ σάρκα of Ephesians may find an echo in αἵματος καὶ σαρκός of Hebrews.

Heb. 2:16; cf. Gal. 3:16. Σπέρμα is used in connection with 'Αβραάμ in Luke-Acts, the Pauline letters, and the later writings that were influenced by Paul's collected letters (twice in John and once in Hebrews). The sense of the phrase in Hebrews agrees exactly with its meaning in Galatians (cf. Rom. 4:13).

Heb. 2:17, 18; cf. Rom. 8:34. Paul never uses the term ἀρχιερεύς, but he clearly employs the conception in Rom. 8:34.

Heb. 3:1; cf. Phil. 3:14.

Heb. 3:12; cf. Col. 2:8.

Heb. 4:2; cf. I Thess. 2:13. 'Ο λόγος τῆς ἀκοῆς occurs only in these two passages in the New Testament.

Heb. 4:14; cf. Rom. 8:34.

Heb. 6:1, 2; cf. I Thess. 1:9, 10 and I Cor. 3:10, 11. The "simple gospel" according to Hebrews corresponds in substance with Paul's similar statement in I Thessalonians. The use of θεμέλιος is limited to Luke-Acts, Romans, I Corinthians, Ephesians, Hebrews, the Apocalypse, and I and II Timothy. Its use in I Cor. 3:10, 11, while not distinctive, is sufficiently striking to suggest its possible influence on Hebrews.

Heb. 6:6; cf. Col. 3:10. Hebrews 6:6 is the only occurrence of ἀνακαινίζω in the New Testament. 'Ανακαινόω occurs, however, in II Cor. 4:16 and Col. 3:10. Its use in the latter instance may have influenced Hebrews.

Heb. 6:10; cf. II Cor. 8:1-4. Both passages describe instances of Christian liberality that has expressed itself in meeting the needs of other Christians. In II Corinthians God inspires this giving, and in Hebrews he is represented as sure to recognize and reward it.

Heb. 6:11; cf. Col. 2:2 and I Thess. 1:5. Πληροφορία is used in the New Testament only in I Thessalonians, Colossians, and Hebrews. It is not found in the LXX, although πληροφορεῖσθαι is found in Eccles. 8:11.

Heb. 6:18; cf. II Cor. 8:12. The possibility of literary relationship is suggested by the common use of πρόκειμαι.

Heb. 6:20; cf. I Cor. 15:23. The use of πρόδρομος resembles the use of ἀπαρχή in that both describe Jesus as having entered upon the enjoyment of eternal blessedness and both relate this fact as a basis of assurance for all who identify themselves with him.

Heb. 7:22; cf. I Cor. 11:25 and II Cor. 3:6. Paul's statements involve a contrast of the new and old "agreements," and this contrast may have suggested the idea of a κρείττων διαθήκη to the author of Hebrews.

Heb. 7:26; cf. Eph. 4:10.

Heb. 8:6; cf. I Cor. 11:25 and II Cor. 3:6.

Heb. 9:15; cf. I Cor. 11:25 and II Cor. 3:6.

Heb. 9:17, 18; cf. Rom. 8:17. In Hebrews, Christ is the "testator" and men are his heirs, and in Romans they are "fellow-heirs" with Christ.

Heb. 10:10; cf. Eph. 5:26.

Heb. 10:38; cf. Rom. 1:17 and Gal. 3:12. The textual evidence for Heb. 10:38 is: א A H* Latin (vt^r vg) Am. Clem. μου ἐκ πίστεως; p^13 D H** W boh. Euthal ^cod· ἐκ πίστεως;   D* Lat. (vt^d) Syr. (vg. hl.) Eus. ἐκ πίστεως μου. This passage has the highest significance for Paul, and he alters it to bear the two-fold sense he wants to convey. The quotation in Hebrews is evidently in agreement with the LXX rather than with Romans, although Paul's use of it may have suggested its use in Hebrews.

Heb. 11:25; cf. II Cor. 4:18. Πρόσκαιρος is used in the New Testament only in Matt. 13:21, Mark 4:17, and the two instances cited.

Heb. 12:11; cf. I Cor. 9:27.

Heb. 12:23; cf. Rom. 8:29 and Phil. 3:20. The distinctly social connotation of πρωτότοκος in Hebrews and Romans may indicate literary relationship. The conception of Christians as "enrolled as citizens in heaven" may be a reminiscence of Phil. 3:20.

Heb. 13:12; cf. Eph. 5:25, 26. The sacrificial suffering of Christ as designed to purify τὸν λαὸν or τὴν ἐκκλησίαν is the idea that both passages set forth and that may indicate dependence of the one on the other.

Heb. 13:18; cf. II Cor. 1:11.

Heb. 13:20, 21; cf. I Thess. 3:11-13.

Heb. 13:24; cf. Phil. 4:21.

TABLE OF RESULTS

	A	B	C	Unclassed
Romans.............	..	3	10	7
I Corinthians......	..	5	5	9
II Corinthians.....	..	..	3	9
Galatians..........	..	..	2	6
Ephesians..........	..	3	5	4
Philippians........	..	3	3	4
Colossians.........	..	..	3	3
I Thessalonians....	..	..	2	5
II Thessalonians...	..	..	..	....
Philemon...........	..	..	..	....

The First Epistle of Clement to the Corinthians

In his letter to the Romans (iii.1) Ignatius praises that church for having instructed others: "You never have envied anyone, you taught others. But I desire that those things may stand fast which you enjoin in your instructions." The author of Hebrews (5:12) had challenged Rome to assume the role of teacher, and there are indications that I Peter and I Clement are illustrations of the effort of Roman leadership to function as they were challenged to do in Hebrews and as they were commended for undertaking by Ignatius. This fact makes it the appropriate sequence for the examination of I Clement to follow that of Hebrews.

The allusions to the Old Testament in I Clement vary in the degree of their exactness. The tendency is in the direction of accuracy in the longer quotations and of looseness in the

shorter.   Formulas of citation for the Old Testament are: I Clem.
3:1, καὶ ἐπετελέσθη τὸ γεγραμμένον; I Clem. 4:1, γέγραπται γὰρ
οὕτως; I Clem. 16:2, καθὼς τὸ πνεῦμα τὸ ἅγιον περὶ αὐτοῦ ἐλάλησεν.

In references to writings that compose our New Testament
the tendency is to freedom of rendering.   These allusions, particularly in the case of the letters of the Pauline corpus, have no
introductory formulas.   Illustrations are: I Clem. 13:1, μεμνημέ-
ναι τῶν λόγων τοῦ κυρίου 'Ιησοῦ, οὓς ἐλάλησεν διδάσκων ἐπιείκειαν
καὶ μακροθυμίαν; I Clem. 47:1, ἀναλάβετε τὴν ἐπιστολὴν τοῦ μακαρίου Παύλου τοῦ ἀποστόλου.

| I Clem. Salutation | I Corinthians C |

Τῇ ἐκκλησίᾳ τοῦ Θεοῦ τῇ παροικούσῃ Κόρινθον, κλητοῖς
ἡγιασμένοις ἐν θελήματι Θεοῦ διὰ τοῦ κυρίου ἡμῶν 'Ιησοῦ Χριστοῦ.
Χάρις ὑμῖν καὶ εἰρήνη ἀπὸ παντοκράτορος Θεοῦ διὰ 'Ιησοῦ Χριστοῦ
πληθυνθείη.

I Cor. 1:2, 3. Τῇ ἐκκλησίᾳ τοῦ Θεοῦ τῇ οὔσῃ ἐν Κορίνθῳ,
ἡγιασμένοις ἐν Χριστῷ 'Ιησοῦ, κλητοῖς ἁγίοις. . . . . Χάρις ὑμῖν
καὶ εἰρήνη ἀπὸ Θεοῦ πατρὸς ἡμῶν καὶ κυρίου 'Ιησοῦ Χριστοῦ.

Clement does not quote Paul's language exactly, but the
wording and ideas of his salutation suggest his acquaintance with
I Cor. 1:2, 3. Χάρις ὑμῖν καὶ εἰρήνη is regularly a part of
Paul's greeting. Clement's use of the phrase probably reflects
this usage of the Pauline letters. With the addition of
πληθυνθείη, however, the greeting occurs in I and II Peter.
Κλητοῖς ἡγιασμένοις may echo I Cor. 1:2 (cf. Rom. 1:7). The term
παντοκράτορος occurs frequently in the LXX and is used six times
in I Clement. Its only use in the New Testament, aside from its
nine occurrences in the Apocalypse, is to be found in II Cor. 6:18,
where Paul has gotten it in a quotation from the LXX of II Sam.
7:8 and Amos. 4:13.

| I Clem. 2:1 | Galatians C |

Καὶ τὰ παθήματα αὐτοῦ ἦν πρὸ ὀφθαλμῶν ὑμῶν.

Gal. 3:1. Οἷς κατ' ὀφθαλμοὺς 'Ιησοῦς Χριστὸς προεγράφη
ἐσταυρωμένος.

There is a fair degree of probability that Clement was influenced by Galatians here. Both passages have in view the suffer-

ings of Christ and the effect which a "placarding" of those sufferings before the eyes of men should have. It is possible that Paul
was influenced by Deut. 26:66 and that Clement was affected by
both Paul and his Old Testament source, but his major dependence
would be on Paul. The Christian tradition of the Crucifixion was
the more likely source of the imagery in Galatians, and Clement's
statement may well have been a recollection of that passage.
Knopf's statement is to this effect: "Die Wendung τὰ παθήματα
κτλ wird wohl Erinnerung an Gal. 3:1 sein."[21]

           I Clem. 5:2   Galatians C
    Διὰ ζῆλον καὶ φθόνον οἱ μέγιστοι καὶ δικαιότατοι στύλοι
ἐδιώχθησαν.
    Gal. 2:9.   Οἱ δοκοῦντες στύλοι εἶναι.

The word στύλοι appears in the Apostolic Fathers only in
I Clem. 5:2. It is used in Dial. Just. 131:3, but in a different
sense. Its earlier Christian usage in the present metaphorical
sense was apparently limited to the two passages under examination. Clement's employment of the term is probably an evidence of
acquaintance with Galatians. Knopf inclines to this view: "Die
Säulen stammen sicher aus Gal 2."[22]

           I Clem. 5:6   II Corinthians B
    Ἑπτάκις δεσμὰ φορέσας, φυγαδευθείς, λιθασθείς, κῆρυξ
γενόμενος ἔν τε τῇ ἀνατολῇ καὶ ἐν τῇ δύσει, τὸ γενναῖον τῆς πίστεως αὐτοῦ κλέος ἔλαβεν.
    II Cor. 11:23-27. Ἐν κόποις περισσοτέρως, ἐν φυλακαῖς
περισσοτέρως, ἐν πληγαῖς ὑπερβαλλόντως ἐν θανάτοις πολλάκις ὑπὸ
Ἰουδαίων πεντάκις τεσσεράκοντα παρὰ μίαν ἔλαβον, τρὶς ἐραβδίσθην,
ἅπαξ ἐλιθάσθην.

A comparison of the details of these two lists of Paul's
sufferings reveals only the following two points of correspondence:

---

[21]R. Knopf, Die Lehre der zwölf Apostel—Die zwei Clemens-
briefe (Tübingen, J. C. B. Mohr, 1920), p. 46.

[22]Ibid., p. 50.

Ἑπτάκις δεσμὰ φορέσας   Ἐν φυλακαῖς περισσοτέρως
Λιθασθείς   Ἅπαξ ἐλιθάσθην

But there is the massive fact of the list itself. The suggestion
of such a list would almost certainly come from a recollection of
the list in II Corinthians.

    I Clem. 13:1   I Corinthians B
  Μὴ καυχάσθω ὁ σοφὸς ἐν τῇ σοφίᾳ αὐτοῦ μηδὲ ὁ ἰσχυρὸς ἐν
τῇ ἰσχύι αὐτοῦ μηδὲ ὁ πλούσιος ἐν τῷ πλούτῳ αὐτοῦ, ἀλλ' ἢ ὁ καυχώμενος ἐν κυρίῳ καυχάσθω.
  I Cor. 1:31. ῞Ινα καθὼς γέγραπται ῾Ο καυχώμενος ἐν Κυρίῳ
καυχάσθω (cf. I Sam. 2:10 and Jer. 9:23, 24).

  Both Paul and Clement seem to have had I Sam. 2:10 and
Jer. 9:23, 24 in mind. Yet in the portion of the LXX quotation
that is common to them there is exact verbal correspondence, and
this wording does not appear in the extant text of the Old Testament. It is possible that both quote from a lost source,[23] but
the suggestion of Lightfoot that "Clement, writing afterwards, unconsciously combines and confuses S. Paul's quotation with the
original text"[24] seems to be a sound one.

    I Clem. 24:1   I Corinthians B
  Κατανοήσωμεν, ἀγαπητοί, πῶς ὁ δεσπότης ἐπιδείκνυται διηνε-
κῶς ἡμῖν τὴν μέλλουσαν ἀνάστασιν ἔσεσθαι ἧς τὴν ἀπαρχὴν ἐποιήσατο
τὸν κύριον ᾽Ιησοῦν Χριστὸν ἐκ νεκρῶν ἀναστήσας.
  I Cor. 15:20, 23. Νυνὶ δὲ Χριστὸς ἐγήγερται ἐκ νεκρῶν,
ἀπαρχὴ τῶν κεκοιμήνων . . . . ἀπαρχὴ Χριστός, ἔπειτα οἱ τοῦ Χριστοῦ.

  The whole context in I Clem., chapter 24, is suggestive of
I Cor. 15:20-23. The word ἀπαρχή, applied as it is to the Resurrection of Jesus and as giving assurance to believers of their own
resurrection, leaves little room for doubt that the Corinthian
passage was in Clement's mind.

---

[23] Ibid., p. 64.

[24] J. B. Lightfoot, The Apostolic Fathers (London: Macmillan
& Co., Ltd., 1890), II, Part I, 51.

I Clem. 24:4, 5   I Corinthians B

Λάβωμεν τοὺς καρπούς. ὁ σπόρος πῶς καὶ τίνα τρόπον γίνεται; ἐξῆλθεν ὁ σπείρων καὶ ἔβαλεν εἰς τὴν γῆν ἕκαστον τῶν σπερμάτων, ἅτινα πεσόντα εἰς τὴν γῆν ξηρὰ καὶ γυμνὰ διαλύεται. εἶτ' ἐκ
τῆς διαλύσεως ἡ μεγαλειότης τῆς προνοίας τοῦ δεσπότου ἀνίστησιν
αὐτά, καὶ ἐκ τοῦ ἑνὸς πλείονα αὔξει καὶ ἐκφέρει καρπόν.

I Cor. 15:36, 37.   Σὺ ὃ σπείρεις οὐ ζωοποιεῖται ἐὰν μὴ
ἀποθάνη. καὶ ὃ σπείρεις, οὐ τὸ σῶμα τὸ γενησόμενον σπείρεις ἀλλὰ
γυμνὸν κόκκον εἰ τύχοι σίτου ἤ τινος τῶν λοιπῶν. ὁ δὲ Θεὸς δίδωσιν αὐτῷ σῶμα καθὼς ἠθέλησεν, καὶ ἑκάστῳ τῶν σπερμάτων ἴδιον σῶμα.

Clement very probably derived this analogy from I Corinthians. The different development which he makes of the figure is
probably due to the fact that he wrote from memory and was more
concerned to make his idea suggestive than to duplicate his model.
With the Pauline figure he has apparently blended reminiscences
of the Parable of the Sower (Mark 4:3, 8).

I Clem. 32:2   Romans C

'Εξ αὐτοῦ γὰρ ἱερεῖς καὶ Λευῖται πάντες οἱ λειτουργοῦντες
τῷ θυσιαστηρίῳ τοῦ Θεοῦ. ἐξ αὐτοῦ ὁ κύριος 'Ιησοῦς τὸ κατὰ σάρκα.

Rom. 9:4. Οἵτινες εἰσιν 'Ισραηλεῖται, ὧν . . . . ἡ λατρεία
. . . . καὶ ἐξ ὧν ὁ Χριστὸς τὸ κατὰ σάρκα.

The context shows that Clement and Paul were not making
the same point in their arguments, and yet these lists of attributes sound remarkably alike. Particularly indicative of literary
relationship are the phrases οἱ λειτουργοῦντες and τὸ κατὰ σάρκα.

I Clem. 33:1   Romans C

Τί οὖν ποιήσωμεν, ἀδελφοί; ἀργήσωμεν ἀπὸ τῆς ἀγαθοποιίας
καὶ ἐγκαταλίπωμεν τὴν ἀγάπην; μηθαμῶς τοῦτο ἐάσαι ὁ δεσπότης ἐφ'
ἡμῖν γε γενηθῆναι.

Rom. 6:1. Τί οὖν ἐροῦμεν; ἐπιμένωμεν τῇ ἁμαρτίᾳ, ἵνα ἡ
χάρις πλεονάσῃ; μὴ γένοιτο.

Clement's argument here follows the form of the Pauline
dialectic. Seven times in Romans (3:5, 4:1, 6:1, 7:7, 8:31, 9:14,
9:30) there is the rhetorical question τί οὖν ἐροῦμεν, and in four
of these instances (3:5, 6:1, 7:7, 9:14) there follows a strong

negative assertion. This is, of course, a characteristic feature
of the diatribe style,[25] and Clement might have employed that
style in independence of Paul.

I Clem. 34:8   I Corinthians B

'Οφθαλμὸς οὐκ εἶδεν, καὶ οὖς οὐκ ἤκουσεν καὶ ἐπὶ καρδίαν
ἀνθρώπου οὐκ ἀνέβη, ὅσα ἡτοίμασεν κύριος τοῖς ὑπομένουσιν αὐτόν.

I Cor. 2:9. 'Αλλὰ καθὼς γέγραπται, ʽΑ ὀφθαλμὸς οὐκ εἶδεν
καὶ οὖς οὐκ ἤκουσεν καὶ ἐπὶ καρδίαν ἀνθρώπου οὐκ ἀνέβη, ὅσα ἡτοίμασεν ὁ Θεὸς τοῖς ἀγαπῶσιν αὐτόν (cf. Isa. 64:4; Apost. Const.
7:32; Clem. Alex. Protrept. 10:49).

Except for minor changes (a relative clause made into a
principal clause and ἀγαπῶσιν replaced by ὑπομένουσιν) Clement's
statement is in verbatim agreement with the quotation in I Cor.
2:9. Textual variations in the manuscripts of I Clement tend to
make the agreement complete: SLC insert ἃ before ὀφθαλμός in
agreement with I Corinthians; SLC read ὁ κύριος as against ὁ Θεός
of I Corinthians; CS read ἀγαπῶσιν instead of ὑπομένουσιν.

The thought of the two passages is not in such close agreement as the wording. Clement refers to the future rewards that
are in store for those who serve God, whereas Paul has in mind
divine mysteries which the Spirit reveals. The futuristic emphasis of Clement is in agreement with that of Isa. 64:4.

Paul's introductory formula indicates that he was quoting
a written and authoritative source. This argues strongly for Isa.
64:4 as his source, because it is difficult to identify any other
writing to which such reference would be made. Although not ac-
cepting Isaiah as Paul's source, Resch emphasizes the significance
of the introductory formula as indicating literary indebtedness
on Paul's part to a written source.[26]

The problem of the source of the quotation is created by
the fact that it occurs a number of times in early apocryphal and

---

[25]R. Bultmann, Der Stil der Paulinischen Predigt und die
kynisch-stoische Diatribe (Göttingen: Vandenhoeck & Ruprecht,
1910).

[26]A. Resch, Agrapha in Texte und Untersuchungen zur
Geschichte der altchristlichen Literatur (Leipzig: J. C. Hinrichs,
1906), XXX, 25.

patristic writings. This furnishes ground for the hypothesis that
a source other than Isaiah was used by Paul and that this source
rather than I Cor. 2:9 was also used by the other writers.

Reference is made to the occurrences of the quotation in
Apost. Const. 7:32 and Clem. Alex. Protrept. 10:49 because, except
for these two instances (see the complete list in Resch, Agrapha[27]),
all the quotations are confined to the limits of the Pauline rendering. These go beyond the confines of I Cor. 2:9. Resch holds
that the εὐαγγελίζεται of Clem. Alex. indicates a Gospel source,
and this character of the source is further borne out by καὶ
χαρήσονται ἐπὶ τῇ βασιλείᾳ τοῦ κυρίου αὐτῶν εἰς τοὺς αἰῶνας. He
draws the following comparison between I Cor. 2:9 and passages in
the canonical Gospels:

I Cor. 2:9	Synoptics
ˆΑ ὀφθαλμὸς οὐκ εἶδεν	Luke 10:23, Matt. 13:16. Μακάριοι
	ὑμῶν οἱ ὀφθαλμοὶ οἱ βλέποντες
	ἃ βλέπετε
Καὶ οὓς οὐκ ἤκουσεν	Καὶ ὑμῶν τὰ ὦτα τὰ ἀκούοντα
	ἃ ἀκούετε
Καὶ ἐπὶ καρδίαν ἀνθρώπου	Luke 24:38. Διὰ τί διαλογιισμοὶ
οὐκ ἀνέβη	ἀναβαίνουσιν ἐν τῇ καρδίᾳ ὑμῶν
ˆΑ ἡτοίμασεν ὁ θεός	Matt. 25:41, D. ˆΟ ἡτοίμασεν ὁ
	πατήρ μου

His conclusion is that all of the quotations are drawn from some
early written record of the sayings of Jesus and that, because they
were the words of Jesus, Paul cited them as though they were Scripture.[28]

The difficulty which Resch leaves untouched and which constitutes a hindrance to the acceptance of his position lies in the
supposition that at the time of Paul there was a Greek record of
the teachings of Jesus in general circulation and that this record
was used in independence of the canonical Gospels in the large
number of instances listed.

Carlyle agrees with Resch that I Cor. 2:9 was not the
source of the latter citations and that Isaiah was not the common

---

[27]Ibid.   [28]Ibid., pp. 28, 29.

source on which they all drew. Instead of a Gospel source, however, he thinks that all the quotations run back to an unknown
pre-Christian source.[29]

Lightfoot, Knopf, and Jacquier agree that, whatever its
ultimate derivation, Clement got the passage from I Corinthians.
Lightfoot thinks the case analogous to I Clem. 13:1, where the
verbal resemblance is to I Cor. 1:30 and the thought dependence on
Jer. 9:23-24. He thinks that Clement mixes the passage as it
stands in the LXX of Isa. 64:4 with Paul's paraphrase of it.[30] On
the authority of Origen, Knopf accepts the Elias Apocalypse as the
origin of Paul's citation, but he thinks that Clement borrowed it
directly from Paul.[31] Jacquier does not attempt to identify the
source used by Paul, but he agrees with Knopf that Clement's source
was Paul.[32]

   I Clem. 35:5, 6   Romans A

'Απορρίψαντες ἀφ' ἑαυτῶν πᾶσαν ἀδικίαν καὶ πονηρίαν, πλεονεξίαν, ἔρεις, κακοηθείας, τε καὶ δόλους, ψιθυρισμούς τε καὶ καταλαλιάς, θεοστυγίαν, ὑπερηφανίαν τε καὶ ἀλαζονείαν, κενοδοξίαν τε
καὶ ἀφιλοξενίαν. ταῦτα γὰρ οἱ πράσσοντες στυγητοὶ τῷ Θεῷ ὑπάρχουσιν. οὐ μόνον δὲ οἱ πράσσοντες αὐτά, ἀλλὰ καὶ οἱ συνευδοκοῦντες
αὐτοῖς.

The occurrence of a vice list in I Clement is not unusual,
as it represents a popular literary device of the time. But the
coincidences between these two lists are remarkable. The list in
Rom. 1:29-32 is longer and more detailed, but the types of vice in
I Clement are inclusive. Clement mentions eleven, and Paul eighteen, vices. Of Clement's eleven, only two fail of a parallel in
Paul's list: κενοδοξίαν and ἀφιλοξενίαν. Each list is introduced
with a general formula, and the resemblance begins with these
formulas. The formula in Romans is πεπληρωμένους πάσῃ ἀδικίᾳ
⌐πονηρίᾳ πλεονεξίᾳ κακίᾳ⌐, and that in I Clement is πᾶσαν ἀδικίαν

---

[29]A. J. Carlyle, "First Clement," in The New Testament in
the Apostolic Fathers (Oxford: Oxford University Press, 1901),
p. 43.

[30]Op. cit., p. 106.   [31]Op. cit., p. 103.

[32]E. Jacquier, Le Nouveau Testament dans l'église chré-
tienne³ (Paris: J. Gabalda & Co., 1911), I, 44.

καὶ πονηρίαν. The sentences with which the catalogues close are equally similar in thought and wording: ῞Οιτινες τὸ δικαίωμα τοῦ Θεοῦ ἐπιγνόντες, ὅτι οἱ τὰ τοιαῦτα πράσσοντες ἄξιοι θανάτου εἰσιν, οὐ μόνον αὐτὰ ποιοῦσιν ἀλλὰ καὶ συνευδοκοῦσιν τοῖς πράσσουσιν, and ταῦτα γὰρ οἱ πράσσοντες στυγητοὶ τῷ Θεῷ ὑπάρχουσιν. οὐ μόνον δὲ οἱ πράσσοντες αὐτά, ἀλλὰ καὶ οἱ συνευδοκοῦντες αὐτοῖς.

I Clem. 36:2 II Corinthians C

Διὰ τούτου ἀτενίζομεν εἰς τὰ ὕψη τῶν οὐρανῶν, διὰ τούτου ἐνοπτριζόμεθα τὴν ἄμωμον καὶ ὑπερτάτηω ὄψιν αὐτοῦ.

II Cor. 3:18. ῾Ημεῖς δὲ πάντες ἀνακεκαλυμμένῳ προσώπῳ τὴν δόξαν κυρίου κατοπτριζόμενοι τὴν αὐτὴν εἰκόνα μεταμορφούμεθα ἀπὸ δόξης εἰς δόξαν ⌜καθάπερ⌝ ἀπὸ κυρίου πνεύματος.

The suggestion of relationship between these passages is contained in the words ἐνοπτριζόμεθα and κατοπτριζόμενοι.

Philo uses a similar phrase in **Legum allegor.**iii.33: μηδὲ κατοπρισαίμην ἐν ἄλλῳ τινὶ τὴν σὴν ἰδέαν ἢ ἐν σοὶ τῷ Θεῷ. Reitzenstein presents an elaborate list of instances from Hellenistic literature which illustrate the widespread use of the imagery employed by Paul and Clement.[33]

I Clem. 37:5 I Corinthians A

Λάβωμεν τὸ σῶμα ἡμῶν. ἡ κεφαλὴ δίχα τῶν ποδῶν οὐδέν ἐστιν, οὕτως οὐδέ οἱ πόδες δίχα τῆς κεφαλῆς. τὰ δὲ ἐλάχιστα μέλη τοῦ σώματος ἡμῶν ἀναγκαῖα καὶ εὔχρηστά εἰσιν ὅλῳ τῷ σώματι. ἀλλὰ πάντα συνπνεῖ καὶ ὑποταγῇ μιᾷ χρῆται εἰς τὸ σώζεσθαι ὅλον τὸ σῶμα.

The metaphorical use of the unity of the body with its members of varying function is a favorite device in the letters of the Pauline corpus (see I Cor. 6:15; Rom. 12:4, 5; Eph. 4:4-6, and 5:30-32) and with Clement (see here and 46:7). In his discussion of I Cor. 12:12, Leitzmann gives an exhibit of the use of the figure in Hellenistic literature which illustrates its general popularity and widespread use.[34]

---

[33]R. Reitzenstein, **Historia monachorum und historia Lausiaca** (Göttingen: Vandenhoeck & Ruprecht, 1916), pp. 244-51.

[34]H. Leitzmann, **An die Korinther I. II**^{2} (Tübingen: J. C. B. Mohr, 1923), p. 63.

Clement's development of the analogy shows the influence
of I Cor. 12:12-26 rather than of this general usage, however.
The correspondence in detail makes this clear.

I Clement	I Corinthians 12
Ἡ κεφαλὴ δίχα τῶν ποδῶν.	21. Ἡ κεφαλὴ τοῖς ποσίν
οἱ πόδες δίχα τῆς κεφαλῆς	
Τὰ δὲ ἐλάχιστα μέλη τοῦ	22. Τὰ δοκοῦντα μέλη τοῦ
σώματος ἡμῶν ἀναγκαῖα	σώματος ἀσθενέστερα ὑπάρχειν
	ἀναγκαῖα ἐστιν
Εὔχοηστα. verse 4: χρῆσις	21. Χρείαν
Ὅλον τὸ σῶμα	17. Ὅλον τὸ σῶμα
Συνπνεῖ	26. Συνπάσχει . . . . συνχάρει

Furthermore, the application of the illustration in 38:1
is distinctly Pauline. The one element in the Pauline picture
which Clement omits is the definitely mystical note sounded in
verse 27.

I Clem. 38:1   Romans C

Σωζέσθω οὖν ἡμῶν ὅλον τὸ σῶμα ἐν Χριστῷ Ἰησοῦ, καὶ ὑποτασ-
σέσθω ἕκαστος τῷ πλησίον αὐτοῦ.

Rom. 12:4, 6. Καθάπερ γὰρ ἐν ἑνὶ σώματι ⌜πολλὰ μέλη⌝ ἔχομεν, τὰ δὲ μέλη πάντα οὐ τὴν αὐτὴν ἔχει πρᾶξιν, οὕτως οἱ πολλοὶ ἕν
σῶμά ἐσμεν ἐν Χριστῷ, τὸ δὲ καθ᾽ εἷς ἀλλήλων μέλη . . . . ἔχοντες
δὲ χαρίσματα κατὰ τὴν χάριν τὴν δοθεῖσαν ἡμῖν διάφορα.

I Clem. 42:4   I Corinthians C

Κατὰ χώρας οὖν καὶ πόλεις κηρύσσοντες καθίστανον τὰς ἀπαρχὰς αὐτῶν . . . . εἰς ἐπισκόπους καὶ διακόνους.

I Cor. 16:15. Οἴδατε τὴν οἰκίαν Στεφανᾶ, ὅτι ἐστὶν ἀπαρχὴ
τῆς Ἀχαίας καὶ εἰς διακονίαν τοῖς ἁγίοις ἔταξαν ἑαυτούς (cf. Rom.
16:5).

The use of τὰς ἀπαρχὰς αὐτῶν in Clement corresponds exactly with the use of ἀπαρχή in Romans and Corinthians. The additional touch in Clement of εἰς . . . . διακόνους may be an additional reminiscence of I Cor. 16:15.

I Clem. 46:6   Ephesians C

Ἡ οὐχὶ ἕνα Θεὸν ἔχομεν καὶ ἕνα Χριστὸν καὶ ἐν πνεῦμα τῆς

χάριτος τὸ ἐκχυθὲν ἐφ' ἡμᾶς; καὶ μία κλῆσις ἐν Χριστῷ;

Eph. 4:4-6. ῾Εν σῶμα καὶ ἓν πνεῦμα, καθὼς [καὶ] ἐκλήθητε
ἐν μιᾷ ἐλπίδι τῆς κλήσεως ὑμῶν. εἷς κύριος, μία πίστις, ἓν βάπτισμα. εἷς Θεὸς καὶ πατὴρ πάντων, ὁ ἐπὶ πάντων καὶ διὰ πάντων
καὶ ἐν πᾶσιν.

This "unity formula" of Eph. 4:4-6 has a background of
cosmological speculation in Hellenistic thought (cf. Marcus
Aurelius Antonin, Meditations, vii.9 [Dibelius, p. 78]) and of
distinctly religious and cult emphasis in the literature of
Diaspora Judaism (cf. Philo De opif. mund. 77 [Dibelius, p. 18],
De confus. ling. 170 [Dibelius, p. 43], De spec. leg. 1.66
[Dibelius, p. 222]; Josephus, Antiq. iv.200; Apion ii.193) and the
conceptions of the mystery cults (A. Dieterich, Die Grabschrift
des Aberikos [1896], thinks that the author of the Aberikos inscription was an Attis devotee).[35]
     The rhythm of the statement in Ephesians gives it almost
the sound of a cultic formula:
          εἷς κύριος, μία πίστις, ἓν βάπτισμα.
          εἷς Θεὸς καὶ πατὴρ πάντων,
          ὁ ἐπὶ πάντων καὶ διὰ πάντων καὶ ἐν πᾶσιν.
     There is a noteworthy similarity in the two lists of re-
ligious ties that create unity in the group. Note Clement's series: ἕνα Θεὸν, ἕνα Χριστὸν, ἓν πνεῦμα τῆς χάριτος, μία κλῆσις
ἐν Χριστῷ. It is probable that Clement depends on Ephesians.
Yet the character of the passage and the fact that aside from
this single instance there is no very clear indication that Clement
used Ephesians considerably decreases the probability of dependence here.

     I Clem. 47:1-3   I Corinthians A
     Ἀναλάβετε τὴν ἐπιστολὴν τοῦ μακαρίου Παύλου τοῦ ἀποστόλου.
τί πρῶτον ὑμῖν ἐν ἀρχῇ τοῦ εὐαγγελίου ἔγραψεν; ἐπ' ἀληθείας πνευματικῶς ἐπέστειλεν ὑμῖν περὶ ἑαυτοῦ τε καὶ Κηφᾶ τε καὶ Ἀπολλώ,
διὰ τὸ καὶ τότε προσκλίσεις ὑμᾶς πεποιῆσθαι.

---

[35]M. Dibelius, "Die Christianisierung einer hellenistischen
Formel," Neue Jahrbücher für das klassische Altertum Geschichte und
deutsche Literatur, XXXV (1915), 224-36.

I Cor. 1:11-13. 'Εδηλώθη γὰρ μοι περὶ ὑμῶν, ἀδελφοί μου,
ὑπὸ τῶν Χλόης ὅτι ἔριδες ἐν ὑμῖν εἰσίν. λέγω δὲ τοῦτο ὅτι ἕκαστος
ὑμῶν λέγει 'Εγὼ μὲν εἰμι Παύλου, 'Εγὼ δὲ 'Απολλώ, 'Εγὼ δὲ Κηφᾶ,
'Εγὼ δὲ Χριστοῦ.

Clement's reference to the partisanship that divided the
church into petty factions, together with his specific injunction,
ἀναλάβετε τὴν ἐπιστολὴν τοῦ μακαρίου Παύλου, make it a matter of
practical certainty that he had I Cor. 1:11-13 in mind.

It is not legitimate to interpret τὴν ἐπιστολὴν . . . .
Παύλου as excluding a knowledge of II Corinthians on the part of
Clement. The allusion was sufficiently clear for the writer to
assume that his readers would know to which letter he referred.

I Clem. 47:2   Philippians C
Τί πρῶτον ὑμῖν ἐν ἀρχῇ τοῦ εὐαγγελίου ἔγραψεν;
Phil. 4:15. Οἴδατε δὲ καὶ ὑμεῖς Φιλιππήσιοι, ὅτι ἐν ἀρχῇ
τοῦ εὐαγγελίου, ὅτε ἐξῆλθον ἀπὸ Μακεδονίας.

The phrase ἐν ἀρχῇ τοῦ εὐαγγελίου occurs in the New Testament only in Phil. 4:15. Its duplication in I Clement carries the
suggestion of literary acquaintance with Philippians. Harnack
thinks that the address of I Corinthians was an addition intended
to give that letter a universalistic appeal as the introductory
letter of the Pauline letter collection.[36] On this hypothesis
the phrase in question would more probably be an allusion to I
Corinthians than to Philippians. Knopf interprets the address
just as Harnack does and finds in this phrase a reference to I
Corinthians as the introductory letter of the Pauline Corpus. He
admits, however, that this is not the necessary meaning.[37] The
weight of argument, however, is that Ephesians rather than I Corinthians stood at the head of the first collection of Paul's letters. This being true, the phrase is probably a reminiscence of
Philippians, which is the possibility suggested by Knopf[38] as an
alternative view.

---

[36]A. Harnack, Die Briefsammlung des Apostles Paulus
(Leipzig: J. C. Hinrichs, 1926), p. 9.

[37]Op. cit., p. 123.   [38]Ibid.

I Clem. 48:5   I Corinthians C

"Ητω τις πιστός, ἤτω δυνατὸς γνῶσιν ἐξειπεῖν, ἤτω σοφὸς
ἐν διακρίσει λόγων, ἤτω ἀγνὸς ἐν ἔργοις.

I Cor. 12:8, 9. ῖΩι μὲν γὰρ διὰ τοῦ πνεύματος δίδοται
λόγος σοφίας, ἄλλῳ δὲ λόγος γνώσεως κατὰ τὸ αὐτὸ πνεῦμα, ἑτέρῳ
πίστις ἐν τῷ αὐτῷ πνεύματι.

Clement and Paul are both giving a list of "spiritual
gifts." Clement's list consists of πίστις, γνῶσις, σοφία, and
ἀγνεία. Parallels for these in Paul's list are πίστις, λόγος
γνώσεως, and λόγος σοφίας. These parallels are not to be too
strongly pressed, and yet they are sufficiently marked to suggest
literary reminiscence. Both writers are dealing with factiousness
by urging humility.

I Clem. 49:5   I Corinthians A

'Αγάπη πάντα ἀνέχεται, πάντα μακροθυμεῖ. οὐδὲν βάναυσον
ἐν ἀγάπῃ οὐδὲν ὑπερήφανον. 'Αγάπη σχίσμα οὐκ ἔχει, ἀγάπη οὐ στα-
σιάζει, ἀγάπη πάντα ποιεῖ ἐν ὁμονοίᾳ.

This panegyric on love as a whole and in the particular
attributes ascribed carries the strong suggestion of dependence
on I Corinthians, chapter 13. Paul's great picture almost certainly served Clement as a pattern. Significant parallels are the
following:

I Clement	I Corinthians 13
Πάντα ἀνέχεται	7. Πάντα στέγει . . . . πάντα ὑπομένει
Πάντα μακροθυμεῖ	4. 'Η ἀγάπη μακροθυμεῖ
Οὐδὲν ὑπερήφανον	5. Οὐ φυσιοῦται

I Clem. 50:6, 7   Romans C

Γέγραπται γάρ. Μακάριοι, ὧν ἀφέθησαν αἱ ἀνομίαι καὶ ὧν
ἐπεκαλύφθησαν αἱ ἁμαρτίαι. μακάριας ἀνήρ, οὗ οὐ μὴ λογίσηται
κύριος ἁμαρτίαν, οὐδέ ἐστιν ἐν τῷ στόματι αὐτοῦ δόλος. οὗτος ὁ
μακαρισμὸς ἐγένετο ἐπὶ τοὺς ἐκλελεγμένους.

Rom. 4:7-9. Μακάριοι ὧν ἀφέθησαν αἱ ἀνομίαι καὶ ὧν ἐπεκαλύφθησαν αἱ ἁμαρτίαι, μακάριος ἀνὴρ ⌐οὗ⌐ οὐ μη λογίσηται κύριος
ἁμαρτίαν. ὁ μακαρισμὸς οὖν οὗτος ἐπὶ τὴν περιτομὴν ἢ καὶ ἐπὶ τὴν
ἀκροβυστίαν (cf. Ps. 31:1, 2).

The formula γέγραπται γάρ shows that Clement was quoting
the Old Testament. Furthermore, he quotes more fully from Psalm
31 than Paul does. The words οὐδέ ἐστιν ἐν τῷ στόματι αὐτοῦ
δόλος do not form a part of Paul's quotation. There is, however,
a rather clear indication that Clement quoted the LXX at the suggestion of the passage in Romans, for after the close of his
quotation he adds ὁ μακαρισμὸς ἐγένετο ἐπὶ τοὺς ἐκλελεγμένους. . . . .

      I Clem. 56:1   Galatians C
Καὶ ἡμεῖς οὖν ἐντύχωμεν περὶ τῶν ἔν τινι παραπτώματι ὑπαρ-
χόντων.
      Gal. 6:1. 'Ἐὰν καὶ προλημφθῇ ἄνθρωπος ἔν τινι παραπτώματι.

There is a probable reminiscence of Galatians in the phrase
ἔν τινι παραπτώματι. The purport of the passage is also similar.
    <u>Instances of possible literary reminiscence.</u>—I Clem. 2:4;
cf. Col. 2:1. The suggestion of relationship between these passages is found in the phrases ἀγὼν . . . . ὑπὲρ πάσης τῆς
ἀδελφότητος and ἡλίκον ἀγῶνα . . . . ὑπὲρ ὑμῶν. This solicitude
for the brotherhood coupled with the similarity of expression that
is evident may represent a reminiscence of Colossians.
    I Clem. 2:5; cf. Phil. 1:10 and 2:15. There is a possible
reminiscence of Phil. 1:10 in the εἰλικρινεῖς καὶ ἀκέραιοι of I
Clem. 2:5.
    I Clem. 2:7; cf. II Cor. 9:8 (Titus 3:1, II Tim. 2:21, and
3:17). The early and wide influence achieved by I Clement is evi-
denced in its use by Polycarp and its inclusion in the Muratorian
canon. The author of the Pastorals may also have used I Clement.
The case is more probably a common use of paranesis. It is possible that the expression in I Clement and the Pastorals harks
back to ἵνα . . . . περισσεύητε εἰς πᾶν ἔργον ἀγαθόν of II Cor.
9:8.
    I Clem. 2:8; cf. Phil. 1:27, 3:20, and Eph. 2:12. The
present possession of Christian virtues which indicate citizenship
in a higher spiritual order is the thought common to these passages. Only in the Philippian and Ephesian passages cited and in
Acts 23:1 are forms of πολιτεία, πολίτευμα, and πολιτεύομαι used
in a distinctly religious sense in the New Testament. Under the

influence of Roman persecution it had come to connote an element
of political group consciousness on the part of Christians that is
not reflected in the letters of Paul.

I Clem. 5:1, 5; cf. I Cor. 9:24 and Phil. 3:14. The term
βραβεῖον occurs in the New Testament only in the passages cited.
The term and the analogies in which it is employed are athletic.
In I Clem. 5:5 it is used in exactly the metaphorical sense of the
Pauline passages (cf. Mart. Polyc. 17:1).

I Clem. 7:1; cf. Phil. 1:30. The phrases ὁ αὐτὸς ἡμῖν
ἀγὼν and τὸν αὐτὸν ἀγῶνα offer a slender basis for the possibility
of literary acquaintance.

I Clem. 10:6; cf. Rom. 4:3 (Gen. 15:5, 6). The dependence
of I Clement is clearly on the LXX of Gen. 15:5, 6. Furthermore,
he illustrates obedience rather than faith in his use of Abraham.
Clement's objective is the cultivation of obedience to the authorities of the church. However, by the omission of καὶ before
ἐπίστευσεν and the insertion of δέ before 'Αβραάμ in the portion
of the quotation which he uses in common with Paul there may be an
indication of the influence of the Romans passage on his quotation
from the LXX.

I Clem. 16:2, 17; cf. Phil. 2:6. This use of the example
of Christ for the purpose of developing humility among believers
bears strong resemblance to Phil. 2:6 ff. and may be an echo of it.
Καίπερ δυνάμενος and ταπεινοφρονῶν may be reminiscences of ἐν μορφῇ
Θεοῦ ὑπάρχων and ἐταπείνωσεν ἑαυτόν.

I Clem. 21:1; cf. Phil. 1:27. Moffatt feels that "it is
fair to admit a trace" of Phil. 1:27 in I Clem. 21:1.[39]

I Clem. 36:2; cf. Rom. 1:21 and Eph. 4:18.

I Clem. 37:3; cf. I Cor. 15:23. The phrase ἐν τῷ ἰδίῳ
τάγματι may represent a reminiscence of I Cor. 15:23.

I Clem. 38:2; cf. I Cor. 16:17. There is a slender basis
for possible literary relationship in the phrase δι' οὗ ἀναπληρωθῇ
αὐτοῦ τὸ ὑστέρημα.

I Clem. 40:1; cf. I Cor. 2:10, Rom. 11:33, Eph. 3:18. As
the context shows, γνῶσις means for Clement a proper understanding
of the Old Testament. The resemblance of his statement to the

---

[39]Introduction, p. 176.

Pauline passages cited is found in the phrase τὰ βάθη τῆς θείας γνώσεως.

I Clem. 41:1; cf. I Cor. 15:23.

I Clem. 46:7; cf. I Cor. 6:15. There is a possible echo of I Cor. 6:15 in the τὰ μέλη τοῦ Χριστοῦ of I Clement.

I Clem. 47:7; cf. Rom. 2:24.

I Clem. 48:6; cf. I Cor. 10:24, 33.

I Clem. 59:3; cf. Eph. 1:18. The metaphor employed and the agreement in meaning where the terms are not the same establish a basis for possible literary relationship. The imagery probably had its origin in the usage of the mystery cults. Its employment there is illustrated from the liturgy of Mithras: εἶτα ἄνοιξον τοὺς ὀφθαλμοὺς καὶ ὄψει ἀνεῳγυίας τὰς θύρας καὶ τὸν κόσμον τῶν θεῶν, ὅς ἐστιν ἐντὸς τῶν θυρῶν, ὥστε ἀπὸ τῆς τοῦ θεάματος ἡδονῆς καὶ τῆς χαρᾶς τὸ πνεῦμά σου συντρέχειν καὶ ἀναβαίνειν.[40] This does not preclude the possibility of Clement's indebtedness to Ephesians.

I Clem. 61:1; cf. Rom. 13:1. The attitude toward the government which Paul and Clement seek to encourage is similar. There is, of course, a political group consciousness among Christians in the time of I Clement and I Peter which did not exist for the contemporaries of Paul.

I Clem. 64:1; cf. Eph. 1:4. There may be a trace of Eph. 1:4 in the phrase καὶ ἡμᾶς δι' αὐτοῦ (cf. I Cor. 8:6).

In view of its Roman origin, its Corinthian destination, and its general purpose, it is to be expected that First Clement would show more numerous traces of Romans and First Corinthians than of other Pauline letters. This turns out to be true on the basis of the present study. Leipoldt thinks these two letters are the only ones of the Pauline corpus of whose use in First Clement there is certainty.[41] The present study indicates that Clement also probably used Second Corinthians, Galatians, Ephesians, and

---

[40]A. Dieterich, Eine Mithrasliturgie[2] (Leipzig: B. G. Teubner, 1910), (10:19).

[41]J. Leipoldt, Geschichte des neutestamentlichen Kanons (Leipzig: J. C. Hinrichs, 1907), I, 188.

Philippians. Leipoldt thinks there is evidence for a probable
use of Titus,[42] but the judgment of this study is that there are
no convincing traces of acquaintance with any of the Pastorals.

TABLE OF RESULTS

	A	B	C	Unclassed
Romans................	1	.	4	5
I Corinthians........	3	4	3	7
II Corinthians.......	.	1	1	1
Galatians............	.	.	3	....
Ephesians............	.	.	1	4
Philippians..........	.	.	1	6
Colossians...........	.	.	.	1
I Thessalonians......	.	.	.	....
II Thessalonians.....	.	.	.	....
Philemon.............	.	.	.	....

The Gospel According to John

The close resemblance of the Gospel According to John to
the Pauline letters is generally admitted. The reader of the Gospel is constantly reminded of Pauline ideas and phrases. The
fundamental conception of Christianity expressed by Paul and the
author of the Gospel is largely the same. Paul differs from the
evangelist in his originality and creativeness, and the genius of
the evangelist seems to be in adaptation and synthesis. The latter's method seems to be to throw Pauline ideas into new combina-
tions, using what he counts valuable and appealing and letting the
rest fall away. Scott feels that "for almost all of his larger
doctrines the evangelist is indebted, more or less immediately,
to Paul."[43]

Bacon raises the question of the directness of John's indebtedness to Paul and suggests that coincidences between the two

[42]Ibid.

[43]E. F. Scott, The Fourth Gospel2 (Edinburgh: T. & T.
Clark, 1923), p. 49.

may be due "in a much larger degree than has hitherto been sus-
pected to a common element of early Hellenistic-Christian mysti-
cism on which Paul and the Ephesian gospel are dependent."[44] At
many points, however, Bacon is convinced of direct indebtedness
to the Pauline letters.[45]

Streeter thinks that the main sources on which the evangelist depended were Mark and the Pauline letters and that "the
ten Epistles of the Apostle must have been the main authority for
the 'essence of Christianity.'"[46] So conservative a critic as
William Sanday was sufficiently impressed by the close parallels
between certain passages in the Gospel and the epistles to con-
clude that "it is not by any means incredible that St. John should
actually have seen the Pauline letters."[47]

The character of the use which the Gospel writer makes of
the letters of Paul is in keeping with his own individuality.
There is no painful copying on his part, although the actual expressions of the letters are occasionally reproduced. More frequently, however, the resemblance is in the realm of the fundamental modes of thought and of controlling ideas.

John's use of Mark is the best analogy for an estimation
of his use of Paul's letters. Of his use of Mark, Streeter says:

The materials he uses have all been fused in the crucible
of his creative imagination, and it is from the image in his
mind's eye, far more vivid than the written page, that he paints
his picture. Accordingly, when he tells a story that occurs in
Mark, not 20% of the words he uses are the same,—but that is pre-
cisely what makes it specially significant that he often repro-
duces some of the more out-of-the-way phrases of Mark.[48]

Exactly this may be said of the use made of the letters of Paul.

The use of the Old Testament in the Gospel is also instructive. There are nineteen instances in which Old Testament material
is employed either by allusion or direct quotation. In two in-

---

[44]B. W. Bacon, "Pauline Elements in the Fourth Gospel,"
Anglican Theological Review, January, 1929, p. 202.

[45]Ibid.   [46]Op. cit., p. 371.

[47]William Sanday, The Criticism of the Fourth Gospel (New
York: Charles Scribner's Sons, 1905), p. 156.

[48]Op. cit., p. 397.

stances (1:51 and 10:16) the use is entirely allusive. In two
other instances (12:27 and 16:22) Old Testament statements are put
into the mouth of Jesus and in one instance into the mouth of the
multitude (12:13). In the remainder of the cases there is an introductory formula. Illustrations of these formulas of citation
are as follows: (1) Where a saying is attributed to a specific
writer (1:23, καθὼς εἶπεν 'Ησαίας ὁ προφήτης; 12:38, ὁ λόγος
'Ησαίου τοῦ προφήτου πληρωθῇ ὃν εἶπεν; 12:39, πάλιν εἶπεν 'Ησαίας);
(2) where citation is made from a section of the Old Testament
(6:45, ἔστιν γεγραμμένον ἐν τοῖς προφήταις; 15:25, ἵνα πληρωθῇ ὁ
λόγος ὁ ἐν τῷ νόμῳ αὐτῶν γεγραμμένος); (3) where the Old Testament
is called ἡ γραφή (7:42, ἡ γραφὴ εἶπεν; 13:18, ἵνα ἡ γραφὴ
πληρωθῇ; see also 19:24 and 19:36; 19:29, ἵνα τελειωθῇ ἡ γραφή;
19:37, πάλιν ἑτέρα γραφὴ λέγει);and (4) the general formula ἐστιν
γεγραμμένον is used in 2:17, 6:31, 6:45, 12:14, and 15:25.

John 1:1   Colossians B
  'Εν ἀρχῇ ἦν ὁ λόγος, καὶ ὁ λόγος ἦν πρὸς τὸν Θεόν, καὶ
Θεὸς ἦν ὁ λόγος.
  Col. 1:15-18. Ὅς ἐστιν εἰκὼν τοῦ Θεοῦ τοῦ ἀοράτου, πρωτότοκος πάσης κτίσεως, ... καὶ αὐτὸς ἔστιν πρὸ πάντων . . . .
ὅς ἐστιν ἡ ἀρχή (cf. Apoc. 19:13 and 22:13; cf. also Phil. 2:6
and I Cor. 15:47).

  The title ὁ λόγος is not applied to Christ in Paul's letters, but the Christology which is implied in John 1:1 is contained
in Colossians and Philippians. In Colossians his pre-existence and
likeness to God are asserted, and he is specifically designated as
ἡ ἀρχή. In Philippians the thought closely parallels the Johannine conception, καὶ Θεὸς ἦν ὁ λόγος.

John 1:3   Colossians B
  Πάντα δι' αὐτοῦ ἐγένετο, καὶ χωρὶς αὐτοῦ ἐγένετο οὐδὲ ἕν.
  Col. 1:16. Ὅτι ἐν αὐτῷ ἐκτίσθη τὰ πάντα ἐν τοῖς ουρανοῖς
καὶ ἐπὶ τῆς γῆς . . . . τὰ πάντα δι' αὐτοῦ καὶ εἰς καὶ εἰς αὐτὸν
ἔκτισται (cf. I Cor. 8:6).

  The πάντα δι' αὐτοῦ of John constitutes an exact verbal
parallel for the τὰ πάντα δι' αὐτοῦ of Colossians.

John 1:9 I and II Corinthians C

Ἦν τὸ φῶς τὸ ἀληθινὸν ὃ φωτίζει πάντα ἄνθρωπον ἐρχόμενον εἰς τὸν κόσμον.

II Cor. 4:6. Ὃς ἔλαμψεν ἐν ταῖς καρδίαις ἡμῶν πρὸς φωτισμὸν τῆς γνώσεως τῆς δόξης τοῦ Θεοῦ ἐν προσώπῳ Χριστοῦ.

I Cor. 4:5. Ὥστε μὴ πρὸ καιροῦ τι κρίνετε, ἕως ἂν ἔλθῃ ὁ κύριος, ὃς καὶ φωτίσει τὰ κρυπτὰ τοῦ σκότους καὶ φανερώσει τὰς βουλὰς τῶν καρδιῶν, καὶ τότε ὁ ἔπαινος γενήσεται ἑκάστῳ ἀπὸ τοῦ Θεοῦ (cf. Eph. 1:18, Heb. 6:4, Test. Levi 14).

The noun φωτισμός occurs in the New Testament in II Corinthians only. The verb φωτίζω occurs in Luke 11:36; I Cor. 4:5; Eph. 1:18, 3:9; Heb. 6:4, 10:32; and Apoc. 18:1, 21:23, 22:5. Although used in a figurative sense in Luke, the figure is different from that of John 1:9. In John it is Christ, who as the "true light," "sheds light on everyone." Paul in I Corinthians indicates that in the Day of Judgment Christ will "light up the darkness that now hides things and show what the motives in people's minds are." In II Corinthians it is God who "gives light." According to Isa. 49:6 (cf. 42:6) the Servant of God was to be εἰς φῶς ἐθνῶν, and the figure as applied in Christian literature may represent a development of that idea. However, the historical probabilities and the similarities in language favor an indebtedness to I and II Corinthians.

John 1:10 Colossians C

Ἐν τῷ κόσμῳ ἦν, καὶ ὁ κόσμος δι' αὐτοῦ ἐγένετο.

Col. 1:17. Καὶ αὐτὸς ἔστιν πρὸ πάντων καὶ τὰ πάντα ἐν αὐτῷ συνέστηκεν.

The Johannine idea of the immanence of the Logos closely parallels the thought in Col. 1:17.

John 1:10 I Corinthians C

Καὶ ὁ κόσμος αὐτὸν οὐκ ἔγνω (cf. 14:7 and 17:25).

I Cor. 1:21. Ἐπειδὴ γὰρ ἐν τῇ σοφίᾳ τοῦ Θεοῦ οὐκ ἔγνω ὁ κόσμος διὰ τῆς σοφίας τὸν Θεόν (cf. Rom. 1:21).

John 1:12, 13 Romans C Galatians C

Ὅσοι δὲ ἔλαβον αὐτόν, ἔδωκεν αὐτοῖς ἐξουσίαν τέκνα Θεοῦ

γενέσθαι, τοῖς πιστεύουσιν εἰς τὸ ὄνομα αὐτοῦ, οἳ οὐκ ἐξ αἱμάτων
οὐδὲ ἐκ θελήματος σαρκὸς οὐδὲ ἐκ θελήματος ἀνδρὸς ἀλλ' ἐκ Θεοῦ
ἐγεννήθησαν.

Rom. 8:14, 15. Ὅσοι γὰρ πνεύματι Θεοῦ ἄγονται, οὗτοι
υἱοὶ Θεοῦ εἰσίν. οὐ γὰρ ἐλάβετε πνεῦμα δουλείας πάλιν εἰς φόβον,
ἀλλὰ ἐλάβετε πνεῦμα υἱοθεσίας, ἐν ᾧ κράζομεν 'Αββά ὁ πατήρ (cf.
II Cor. 3:17).

Gal. 4:5. Ἵνα τὴν υἱοθεσίαν ἀπολάβωμεν. 3:26. Πάντες
γὰρ υἱοὶ Θεοῦ ἐστὲ διὰ τῆς πίστεως ἐν Χριστῷ 'Ιησοῦ (cf. Eph. 1:5,
2:8).

The Johannine idea of sonship as distinctly "adoptionist"
is Pauline.

John 1:14, 16   Colossians B   Ephesians C

Καὶ ὁ λόγος σὰρξ ἐγένετο καὶ ἐσκήνωσεν ἐν ἡμῖν, καὶ ἐθεα-
σάμεθα τὴν δόξαν αὐτοῦ, δόξαν ὡς μονογενοῦς παρὰ πατρός, πλήρης
χάριτος καὶ ἀληθείας· . . . . ὅτι ἐκ τοῦ πληρώματος αὐτοῦ ἡμεῖς
πάντες ἐλάβομεν, καὶ χάριν ἀντὶ χάριτος·

Col. 1:19. 'Εν αὐτῷ εὐδόκησεν πᾶν τὸ πλήρωμα κατοικῆσαι.
2:9. 'Εν αὐτῷ κατοικεῖ πᾶν τὸ πλήρωμα τῆς Θεότητος σωματικῶς, καὶ
ἐστὲ ἐν αὐτῷ πεπληρωμένοι.

Eph. 4:13. Εἰς μέτρον ἡλικίας τοῦ πληρώματος τοῦ Χριστοῦ.

Πλήρωμα is used in the New Testament in Matt. 9:16 and
Mark 2:21, 6:43, 8:21, but not in the sense of its use in John.
The term is used this one time in John and is used elsewhere in
the New Testament only in Col. 1:19 and 2:9 and Eph. 4:12 (cf.
Eph. 1:23 and Rom. 15:29). The likelihood of dependence on Colossians is strengthened by the parallel which ὁ λόγος σὰρξ ἐγένετο
finds in σωματικῶς, the practical agreement in sense of ἐσκήνωσεν
and κατοικεῖ, and the substantial agreement of ἐκ τοῦ πληρώματος
αὐτοῦ ἡμεῖς πάντες ἐλάβομεν and ἐστὲ ἐν αὐτῷ πεπληρωμένοι. There
is a possible trace of Rom. 8:3 in ὁ λόγος σὰρξ ἐγένετο.

John 1:17   Romans A   Ephesians A

Ὅτι ὁ νόμος διὰ Μωυσέως ἐδόθη, ἡ χάρις καὶ ἡ ἀλήθεια διὰ
'Ιησοῦ Χριστοῦ ἐγένετο.

Rom. 4:16. Ἵνα κατὰ χάριν . . . . οὐ τῷ ἐκ τοῦ νόμου.
. . . . 5:20, 21. Νόμος δὲ παρεισῆλθεν ἵνα πλεονάσῃ τὸ παράπτωμα·
οὗ δὲ ἐπλεόνασεν ἡ ἁμαρτία, ὑπερεπερίσσευσεν ἡ χάρις, ἵνα ὥσπερ

ἐβασίλευσεν ἡ ἁμαρτία ἐν τῷ θανάτῳ, οὕτως καὶ ἡ χάρις βασιλεύσῃ
διὰ δικαιοσύνης εἰς ζωὴν αἰώνιον διὰ Ἰησοῦ Χριστοῦ τοῦ κυρίου
ἡμῶν.   6:14.   Οὐ γάρ ἐστε ὑπὸ νόμον ἀλλὰ ὑπὸ χάριν.   10:4-6.
Τέλος γὰρ νόμου Χριστὸς εἰς δικαιοσύνην παντὶ τῷ πιστεύοντι.
Μωυσῆς γὰρ γράφει . . . . ἡ δὲ ἐκ πίστεως δικαιος ύνη οὕτως λέγει
. . . . (cf. Gal. 3:19 f., 5:4).

        Eph. 1:12.   Ἐν τῷ Χριστῷ ἐν ᾧ καὶ ὑμεῖς ἀκούσαντες τὸν
λόγον τῆς ἀληθείας.   4:21.   Καθὼς ἔστιν ἀλήθεια ἐν τῷ Ἰνσοῦ
(cf. Col. 1:7).

        The use of χάρις in the New Testament is restricted to
Luke-Acts, the Pauline letters, and the later writings. Paul uses
it to describe the spiritual status of Christians, represents it
as operative through Christ, and makes it stand for the superiority
of the privilege which the faith-approved enjoy. The whole conception is so characteristically Pauline and is so nearly expressed
in terms of its presentation in Romans as to make literary relationship a matter of practical certainty.

        Christ as the source of "truth" (cf. John 14:6) very prob-
ably represents the influence of Ephesians. The association of
χάρις and ἀλήθεια may also reflect acquaintance with Colossians.

        John 1:29   I Corinthians C
     "Ἴδε ὁ ἀμνὸς τοῦ Θεοῦ ὁ αἴρων τὴν ἁμαρτίαν τοῦ κόσμου.
     I Cor. 5:8.   Καὶ γὰρ τὸ πάσχα ἡμῶν ἐτύθη Χριστός· (cf.
Isa. 53:6, 7).

        The word ἀμνός occurs in the New Testament only in John
1:29, 36, Acts 8:32 (cf. Isa. 53:7) and I Pet. 1:19. Ἀρνίον appears in John 21:15 and twenty-nine times in the Apocalypse, where
it is applied to Christ as paschal lamb (15:3). In John 19:36 f.
and probably in 1:29 there is a similar allusion to Passover symbolism. In I Cor. 5:8, Christ is specifically designated τὸ
πάσχα ἡμῶν.

        The idea of deliverance from sin through the blood of
Christ was fundamental in Paul's letters, but it does not appear
as an important phase of Christ's saving work in the Fourth Gospel.
John 1:29 is hardly more than "a vague concession to the earlier

doctrine,"[49] but it testifies to familiarity with Paul's letters.

John 1:42   I Corinthians C   Galatians C
Σὺ κληθήσῃ Κηφᾶς.

That Simon was best known as Πέτρος toward the latter part
of the first century is shown by the fact that Κηφᾶς appears in
the Gospels only in John 1:42. It is, however, Paul's regular
designation (cf. I Cor. 1:12, 3:22, 9:5, 15:5; Gal. 1:18, 2:9, 11,
14). Bernard[50] thinks its use in John reflects the influence of
אפ כ,and he finds here an indication that Aramaic was the writer's mother-language. Much more probably the Johannine use of
this term represents his literary acquaintance with I Corinthians
and Galatians.

John 1:47   Romans C   II Corinthians C
῍Ιδε ἀληθῶς ᾿Ισραηλείτης.
Rom. 9:4. Οἵτινές εἰσιν ᾿Ισραηλεῖται.   11:1. Γὰρ ἐγὼ
᾿Ισραηλείτης εἰμί (cf. Rom. 2:28, 29,οὐ γὰρ ὁ ἐν τῷ φανερῷ ᾿Ιου-
δαῖος ἐστιν . . . . ἀλλ᾿ ὁ ἐν τῷ κρυπτῷ ᾿Ιουδαῖος).
II Cor. 11:22. ᾿Ισραηλεῖται εἰσιν; κἀγώ.

The term ᾿Ισραηλείτης is used in the New Testament only in
John 1:48, Acts 2:22, 3:12, 5:35, 13:16, 21:28; Rom. 9:4, 11:1;
and II Cor. 11:22. In Romans and II Corinthians, Paul applies it
to himself. If Nathanael serves the Fourth Gospel as a "symboli-
cal counterpart"[51] for Paul, this use of the term may well reflect
the influence of Romans and II Corinthians.

John 1:48   Galatians C
Πρὸ τοῦ σε Φίλιππον φωνῆσαι ὄντα ὑπὸ τὴν συκῆν εἶδόν σε.
Gal. 1:13-16. ᾿Ηκούσατε γὰρ τὴν ἐμὴν ἀναστροφήν ποτε ἐν
τῷ ᾿Ιουδαϊσμῷ, ὅτι καθ᾿ ὑπερβολὴν ἐδίωκον τὴν ἐκκλησίαν τοῦ Θεοῦ
. . . . καὶ προέκοπτον ἐν τῷ ᾿Ιουδαϊσμῷ ὑπὲρ πολλοὺς συνηλικιώτας
ἐν τῷ γένει μου, περισσοτέρως ζηλωτης ὑπάρχων τῶν πατρικῶν μου παρα-

---

[49]Scott, op. cit., pp. 218 and 219.

[50]J. H. Bernard, A Critical and Exegetical Commentary on
the Gospel According to St. John (New York: Charles Scribner's
Sons, 1929), I, 60.

[51]Scott, op. cit., p. 47.

δόσεων. Ὅτε δὲ εὐδόκησεν [ὁ Θεὸς] ὁ ἀφορίσας με ἐκ κοιλίας μητ-
ρός μου καὶ καλέσας διὰ τῆς χάριτος αὐτοῦ ἀποκαλύψαι τὸν υἱὸν αὐτοῦ
ἐν ἐμοὶ ἵνα εὐαγγελίζωμαι αὐτὸν ἐν τοῖς ἔθνεσιν. . . . .

The probable point of the statement regarding Jesus' fore-
knowledge of Nathanael is the assertion of his "predestination to
Christian service while still under the shadow of the Law."[52]
Paul describes himself in exactly this way.

John 1:51   II Corinthians C

Μείζω τούτων ὄψῃ. καὶ λέγει αὐτῷ Ἀμὴν ἀμὴν λέγω ὑμῖν,
ὄψεσθε τὸν οὐρανὸν ἀνεῳγότα καὶ τοὺς ἀγγέλους τοῦ Θεοῦ ἀναβαίνον-
τας καὶ καταβαίνοντας ἐπὶ τὸν υἱὸν τοῦ ἀνθρώπου.
      II Cor. 12:1-4. Ἐλεύσομαι δὲ εἰς ὀπτασίας καὶ ἀποκαλύψεις
Κυρίου. οἶδα ἄνθρωπον ἐν Χριστῷ πρὸ ἐτῶν δεκατεσσάρων,-. . . . .-
ἁρπαγέντα τὸν τοιοῦτον ἕως τρίτου οὐρανοῦ. καὶ οἶδα τὸν τοιοῦτον
ἄνθρωπον,-. . . . ὅτι ἡρπάγη εἰς τὸν παράδεισον καὶ ἤκουσεν ἄρρητα
ῥήματα ἃ οὐκ ἐξὸν ἀνθρώπῳ λαλῆσαι.

The promise to Nathanael is expressed in the imagery of
Gen. 28:12. However, it is entirely likely that the account of
visions in II Corinthians suggested the Johannine promise.

John 2:21   Colossians B   Ephesians B

Ἐκεῖνος δὲ ἔλεγεν περὶ τοῦ ναοῦ τοῦ σώματος αὐτοῦ.
      Col. 1:18. Αὐτός ἐστιν ἡ κεφαλὴ τοῦ σώματος, τῆς ἐκκλη-
σίας. . . . . 24. Ὑπὲρ τοῦ σώματος αὐτοῦ, ὅ ἐστιν ἡ ἐκκλησία.
3:15. Εἰς ἣν καὶ ἐκλήθητε ἐν [ἑνὶ] σώματι.
      Eph. 1:23. Ὑπὲρ πάντα τῇ ἐκκλησίᾳ, ἥτις ἐστὶν τὸ σῶμα
αὐτοῦ. 2:16. Καὶ ἀποκαταλλάξῃ τοὺς ἀμφοτέρους ἐν ἑνὶ σώματι τῷ
Θεῷ. . . . . 21. Ἐν ᾧ πᾶσα οἰκοδομὴ συναρμολογουμένη αὔξει εἰς
ναὸν ἅγιον ἐν κυρίῳ. . . . . 4:4. Ἕν σῶμα. . . . . 13. Εἰς
οἰκοδομὴν τοῦ σώματος τοῦ Χριστοῦ 5:30 καθὼς καὶ ὁ Χριστὸς τὴν
ἐκκλησίαν, ὅτι μέλη ἐσμὲν τοῦ σώματος αὐτοῦ (cf. I Cor. 6:19 and
II Cor. 6:16).

The comment in John 2:21 very probably involves a contrast of the temple and the church. The figure used almost certainly represents a reminiscence of Colossians and Ephesians. In

---

[52]Ibid.

I and II Corinthians the bodies of believers are spoken of as
spiritual temples. But in Colossians and Ephesians, the church
is specifically designated as the body of Christ. The idea is
most elaborately developed in Ephesians, and the interest of
Ephesians and the Fourth Gospel in the church is very similar.

John 2:22   Romans B

῞Οτε οὖν ἠγέρθη ἐκ νεκρῶν . . . . οἱ μαθηταὶ αὐτοῦ . . . .
ἐπίστευσαν τῇ γραφῇ. . . . .

Rom. 10:9-11. Ἐὰν . . . . πιστεύσῃς . . . . ὅτι ὁ Θεὸς
αὐτὸν ἤγειρεν ἐκ νεκρῶν, σωθήσῃ· . . . . λέγει γὰρ ἡ γραφή Πᾶς ὁ
πιστεύων ἐπ᾿ αὐτῷ οὐ καταισχυνθήσεται.

Only in 2:22 is ἐγείρω used of Jesus' Resurrection (cf.
21:14). The use of the Resurrection as a basis of "believing" is
a strong reminder of Rom. 10:8-11. Ἡ γραφή in John has an intelligible significance on the basis of this probable dependence on
Romans and presupposes the quotation which Paul makes from Isa.
28:16.

John 3:2   I Thessalonians C

Οὗτος ἦλθεν πρὸς αὐτὸν νυκτός
I Thess. 5:5, 6, 8. Πάντες γὰρ ὑμεῖς υἱοὶ φωτός ἐστε καὶ
υἱοὶ ἡμέρας. Οὐκ ἐσμὲν νυκτὸς οὐδὲ σκότους . . . . ἡμεῖς δὲ
ἡμέρας ὄντες νήφωμεν.

In I Thessalonians followers of Jesus are called υἱοὶ
φωτός and υἱοὶ ἡμέρας. In the Fourth Gospel τὸ φῶς is a favorite
symbol for Christ.

John 3:3   Ephesians C

Ἐὰν μή τις γεννηθῇ ἄνωθεν, οὐ δύναται ἰδεῖν τὴν βασιλείαν
τοῦ Θεοῦ.
Eph. 4:23, 24. Ἀνανεοῦσθαι δὲ τῷ πνεύματι τοῦ νοὸς ὑμῶν,
καὶ ἐνδύσασθαι τὸν καινὸν ἄνθρωπον τὸν κατὰ Θεὸν κτισθέντα . . . .
(cf. II Cor. 5:17 and Gal. 4:6, 6:15, where the believer is a καινὴ
κτίσις).

John 3:5, 6   Romans B

Ἐὰν μή τις γεννηθῇ ἐξ ὕδατος καὶ πνεύματος, οὐ δύναται
εἰσελθεῖν εἰς τὴν βασιλείαν τοῦ Θεοῦ. τὸ γεγεννημένον ἐκ τῆς

σαρκὸς σάρξ ἐστιν, καὶ τὸ γεγεννημένον ἐκ τοῦ πνεύματος πνεῦμά ἐστιν.

Rom. 8:5-15. Οἱ γὰρ κατὰ σάρκα ὄντες τὰ τῆς σαρκὸς φρονοῦσιν, οἱ δὲ κατὰ πνεῦμα τὰ τοῦ πνεύματος. . . . . οἱ δὲ ἐν σαρκὶ ὄντες Θεῷ ἀρέσαι οὐ δύνανται. Ὑμεῖς δὲ οὐκ ἐστὲ ἐν σαρκὶ ἀλλα ἐν πνεύματι, εἴπερ πνεῦμα Θεοῦ οἰκεῖ ἐν ὑμῖν. εἰ δέ τις πνεῦμα Χριστοῦ οὐκ ἔχει, οὗτος οὐκ ἔστιν αὐτοῦ. . . . . ὅσοι γὰρ πνεύματι Θεοῦ ἄγονται, οὗτοι υἱοὶ Θεοῦ εἰσίν (cf. Eph. 5:26).

Paul makes sonship to God rest on the sanctifying activity of the indwelling Spirit. He lays great stress on the contrariety of σάρξ and πνεῦμα in Rom. 8:5-15. The ἐξ ὕδατος may represent a reminiscence of Eph. 5:26.

John 3:10, 12   I Corinthians B

Σὺ εἶ ὁ διδάσκαλος τοῦ 'Ισραὴλ καὶ ταῦτα οὐ γινώσκεις; . . . . εἰ τὰ ἐπίγεια εἶπον ὑμῖν καὶ οὐ πιστεύετε, πῶς ἐὰν εἴπω ὑμῖν τὰ ἐπουράνια πιστεύσετε;

I Cor. 1:20, 21. Ποῦ σοφός; ποῦ γραμματεύς; ποῦ συνζητητὴς τοῦ αἰῶνος τούτου; οὐχὶ ἐμώρανεν ὁ Θεὸς τὴν σοφίαν τοῦ κόσμου; . . . . . 2:14, 15. Ψυχικὸς δὲ ἄνθρωπος οὐ δέχεται τὰ τοῦ πνεύματος τοῦ Θεοῦ, μωρία γὰρ αὐτῷ ἐστίν, καὶ οὐ δύναται γνῶναι, ὅτι πνευματικῶς ἀνακρίνεται· ὁ δὲ πνευματικὸς ἀνακρίνει μὲν πάντα.

The implications of the question put to Nicodemus have their background exactly in those conceptions that are expressed in I Corinthians. The contrast of τὰ ἐπίγεια and τὰ ἐπουράνια may represent a reminiscence of I Cor. 15:40. 'Επίγειος is found in the New Testament only in John 3:12; I Cor. 15:40; II Cor. 5:1; Phil. 2:10, 3:19; and Jas. 3:15.

John 3:13   Ephesians C

Οὐδεὶς ἀναβέβηκεν εἰς τὸν οὐρανὸν εἰ μὴ ὁ ἐκ τοῦ οὐρανοῦ καταβάς, ὁ υἱὸς τοῦ ἀνθρώπου.

Eph. 4:9, 10. Τὸ δέ 'Ανέβη τί ἐστιν εἰ μὴ ὅτι κατέβη εἰς τὰ κατώτερα μέρη τῆς γῆς; ὁ καταβὰς αὐτός ἐστιν καὶ ὁ ἀναβὰς ὑπεράνω πάντων τῶν οὐρανῶν, ἵνα πληρώσῃ τὰ πάντα (cf. Rom. 10:6; Prov. 30:4; Bar. 3:29).

The allusion in John is to the descent of Christ to earth in the Incarnation instead of the descent into Hades.

John 3:14, 15   Romans C

Καὶ καθὼς Μωυσῆς ὕψωσεν τὸν ὄφιν ἐν τῇ ἐρήμῳ, οὕτως ὑψωθῆ-
ναι δεῖ τὸν υἱὸν τοῦ ἀνθρώπου, ἵνα πᾶς ὁ πιστεύων ἐν αὐτῷ ἔχῃ ζωὴν
αἰώνιον.

Rom. 3:23-25. Πάντες γὰρ ἥμαρτον καὶ ὑστεροῦνται τῆς δόξης
τοῦ Θεοῦ, δικαιούμενοι δωρεὰν τῇ αὐτοῦ χάριτι διὰ τῆς ἀπολυτρώσεως
τῆς ἐν Χριστῷ Ἰησοῦ. ον προέθετο ο Θεος ἱλαστήριον διὰ πίστεως
ἐν τῷ αὐτοῦ αἵματι . . . . (cf. 4:5, 5:1 f., 10:9).

The "lifting-up" of Jesus in John 3:14, 15 clearly refers
to his Crucifixion. Thus, ὑψόω approximates the meaning of προτί-
θεμαι in Rom. 3:25.

John 3:16   Romans B   Ephesians C

Οὕτως γὰρ ἠγάπησεν ὁ Θεὸς τὸν κόσμον ὥστε τὸν υἱὸν τὸν
μονογενῆ ἔδωκεν, ἵνα πᾶς ὁ πιστεύων εἰς αὐτὸν μὴ ἀπόληται ἀλλὰ
ἔχῃ ζωὴν αἰώνιον.

Eph. 2:4, 5. Ὁ δὲ Θεὸς πλούσιος ὢν ἐν ἐλέει, διὰ τὴν
πολλὴν ἀγάπην αὐτοῦ ἥν ἠγάπησεν ἡμᾶς, καὶ ὄντας ἡμᾶς νεκροὺς τοῖς
παραπτώμασιν συνεζωοποίησεν τῷ Χριστῷ.

Rom. 3:24. Δικαιούμενοι δωρεὰν τῇ αὐτοῦ χάριτι διὰ τῆς
ἀπολυτρώσεως τῆς ἐν Χριστῷ Ἰησοῦ· 5:8. Συνίστησιν δὲ τὴν ἑαυτοῦ
ἀγάπην εἰς ἡμᾶς ὁ Θεὸς ὅτι ἔτι ἁμαρτωλῶν ὄντων ἡμῶν Χριστὸς ὑπὲρ
ἡμῶν ἀπέθανεν. 8:32. Ὅς γε τοῦ ἰδίου υἱοῦ οὐκ ἐφείσατο, ἀλλὰ
ὑπὲρ ἡμῶν πάντων παρέδωκεν αὐτόν, πῶς οὐχὶ καὶ σὺν αὐτῷ τὰ πάντα
ἡμῖν χαρίσεται;

Indebtedness to Paul is clear in such a statement as that
of John 3:16. "No other writers of the New Testament save Paul
and those who draw from Paul venture upon the amazing paradox of
his interpretation of the tragedy of Calvary as proof of the love
of God."[53]

John 3:18   Romans B

Ὁ πιστεύων εἰς αὐτὸν οὐ κρίνεται.

Rom. 8:1. Οὐδὲν ἄρα νῦν κατάκριμα τοῖς ἐν Χριστῷ Ἰησοῦ.

---

[53]Bacon, op. cit., p. 209.

The Johannine 'ὁ πιστεύων furnishes a practical equivalent for Paul's ἐν Χριστῷ.

John 3:20, 21   Ephesians B

Πᾶς γὰρ ὁ φαῦλα πράσσων μισεῖ τὸ φῶς καὶ οὐκ ἔρχεται πρὸς τὸ φῶς, ἵνα μὴ ἐλεγχθῇ τὰ ἔργα αὐτοῦ· ὁ δὲ ποιῶν τὴν ἀλήθειαν ἔρχεται πρὸς τὸ φῶς, ἵνα φανερωθῇ αὐτοῦ τὰ ἔργα ὅτι ἐν θεῷ ἐστιν εἰργασμένα.

Eph. 5:8-13. Ἦτε γάρ ποτε σκότος, νῦν δὲ φῶς ἐν κυρίῳ· ὡς τέκνα φωτὸς περιπατεῖτε, ὁ γὰρ καρπὸς τοῦ φωτὸς ἐν πάσῃ ἀγαθω- σύνῃ καὶ δικαιοσύνῃ καὶ ἀληθείᾳ, δοκιμάζοντες τί ἐστιν εὐάρεστον τῷ κυρίῳ   καὶ μὴ συνκοινωνεῖτε τοῖς ἔργοις τοῖς ἀκάρποις τοῦ σκότους, μᾶλλον δὲ καὶ ἐλέγχετε . . . . τὰ δὲ πάντα ἐλεγχόμενα ὑπὸ τοῦ φωτὸς φανεροῦται.

The use of the figure of "light" and the similar use of ἐλέγχω and φανερόω in contexts that so closely resemble one another suggest literary relationship.

John 3:29   Ephesians B

Ὁ ἔχων τὴν νύμφην νύμφιός ἐστιν.

Eph. 5:25. Καθὼς καὶ ὁ Χριστὸς ἠγάπησεν τὴν ἐκκλησίαν. . . . . 27. Ἵνα παραστήσῃ αὐτὸς ἑαυτῷ ἔνδοξον τὴν ἐκκλησίαν. . . . . 28, 31. Ὁ ἀγαπῶν τὴν ἑαυτοῦ γυναῖκα ἑαυτὸν ἀγαπᾷ . . . . τὸ μυστήριον τοῦτο μέγα ἐστίν, ἐγὼ δὲ λέγω εἰς Χριστὸν καὶ [εἰς] τὴν ἐκκλησίαν.

In II Cor. 11:2 there is the germ of the idea of the church as the bride of Christ. The idea is elaborately worked out in Ephesians. This figure as it appears in the Apocalypse (19:7; 21:2) and the Fourth Gospel was probably drawn from Ephesians.

John 3:31   Ephesians C   I Corinthians C

Ὁ ἄνωθεν ἐρχόμενος ἐπάνω πάντων ἐστίν. ὁ ὢν ἐκ τῆς γῆς ἐκ τῆς γῆς ἐστιν καὶ ἐκ τῆς γῆς λαλεῖ· ὁ ἐκ τοῦ οὐρανοῦ ἐρχόμενος ἐπάνω πάντων ἐστίν·

Eph. 4:10. Ὁ καταβὰς αὐτός ἐστιν καὶ ὁ ἀναβὰς ὑπεράνω.

I Cor. 15:47. Ὁ πρῶτος ἄνθρωπος ἐκ γῆς χοϊκός, ὁ δεύτερος ἄνθρωπος ἐξ οὐρανοῦ.

Rom. 9:5. Ὁ ὢν ἐπὶ πάντων.

According to the punctuation of the Greek text, which is probably correct, the phrase quoted from Rom. 9:5 refers to God rather than to Christ.[54] If it could be made to refer to Christ, it would constitute a close parallel for the ἐπάνω πάντων of John. The parallel between John 3:31a and Eph. 4:10 is sufficiently close to make literary dependence probable. In I Cor. 15:47 the contrast of ἄνθρωπος ἐξ οὐρανοῦ with ἄνθρωπος ἐκ γῆς may have suggested the similar contrast in John 3:31b.

John 3:33   II Corinthians B   Ephesians B

῾Ο λαβὼν αὐτοῦ τὴν μαρτυρίαν ἐσφράγισεν ὅτι ὁ Θεὸς ἀληθής ἐστιν.

II Cor. 1:21, 22. ῾Ο δὲ βεβαιῶν ἡμᾶς σὺν ὑμῖν εἰς Χριστὸν καὶ χρίσας ἡμᾶς Θεός, [ὁ] καὶ σφραγισάμενος ἡμᾶς καὶ δοὺς τὸν ἀρραβῶνα τοῦ πνεύματος ἐν ταῖς καρδίαις ἡμῶν.

Eph. 1:13. ᾽Εσφραγίσθητε τῷ πνεύματι τῆς ἐπαγγελίας τῷ ἁγίῳ. . . . . 4:30. ᾽Εν ᾧ ἐσφραγίσθητε εἰς ἡμέραν ἀπολυτρώσεως.

In John it is the believer who "attests" God as true, whereas in II Corinthians and Ephesians it is God who sets his "seal" on the believer. The use of the figure in John, however, is very probably due to his acquaintance with II Corinthians and Ephesians. The verb σφραγίζω is used in the New Testament in a figurative sense in John 3:33, 6:27; II Cor. 1:22; Eph. 1:13, 4:30; and eight times in the Apocalypse.

John 3:34   Ephesians B

῝Ον γὰρ ἀπέστειλεν ὁ Θεὸς τὰ ῥήματα τοῦ Θεοῦ λαλεῖ, οὐ γὰρ ἐκ μέτρου δίδωσιν τὸ πνεῦμα.

Eph. 4:7. Κατὰ τὸ μέτρον τῆς δωρεᾶς τοῦ Χριστοῦ . . . . 13. Εἰς μέτρον ἡλικίας τοῦ πληρώματος τοῦ Χριστοῦ (cf. Gal. 4:4, 5).

The second clause of 3:34 is probably a reflection of the influence of Eph. 4:7, 13. Μέτρον is used in this single instance in John. It is used in each of the Synoptics but not with reference to the Spirit or Christ.

---

[54]The Westcott and Hort text places commas after τὸ κατὰ σάρκα and after πάντων. Souter does not separate πάντων from Θεός with a comma.

John 3:36   Romans B   Colossians C   Ephesians C

'Ο πιστεύων εἰς τὸν υἱὸν ἔχει ζωὴν αἰώνιον· ὁ δὲ ἀπειθῶν τῷ υἱῷ οὐκ ὄψεται ζωήν, ἀλλ' ἡ ὀργὴ τοῦ Θεοῦ μένει ἐπ' αὐτόν.

Rom. 2:8. Τοῖς δὲ ἐξ ἐριθίας καὶ ἀπειθοῦσι τῇ ἀληθείᾳ πειθομένοις δὲ τῇ ἀδικίᾳ ὀργὴ καὶ θυμός.

Eph. 5:6. Διὰ ταῦτα γὰρ ἔρχεται ἡ ὀργὴ τοῦ Θεοῦ ἐπὶ τοὺς υἱοὺς τῆς ἀπειθίας.

Col. 3:6. "Ερχεται ἡ ὀργὴ τοῦ Θεοῦ ἐπὶ τοὺς υἱοὺς τῆς ἀπειθείας.

The thought of John 3:36, although differently expressed, is practically that of 3:18, where dependence is rather clearly on Rom. 8:1. In Rom. 2:8 the use of ἀπειθέω in connection with ὀργή may have influenced John, but the parallels in Colossians and Ephesians are as probably influential.

John 4:10   Romans C   II Corinthians and Ephesians C   I Corinthians B

Εἰ ᾔδεις τὴν δωρεὰν τοῦ Θεοῦ καὶ τίς ἐστιν ὁ λέγων σοι Δός μοι πεῖν, σὺ ἂν ᾔτησας αὐτὸν καὶ ἔδωκεν ἄν σοι ὕδωρ ζῶν.

Rom. 5:15.   Πολλῷ μᾶλλον ἡ χάρις τοῦ Θεοῦ καὶ ἡ δωρεά.

II Cor. 9:15. Χάρις τῷ Θεῷ ἐπὶ τῇ ἀνεκδιηγήτῳ αὐτοῦ δωρεᾷ.

Eph. 3:7. Κατὰ τὴν δωρεὰν τῆς χάριτος τοῦ Θεοῦ. . . . .
4:8. Κατὰ τὸ μέτρον τῆς δωρεᾶς τοῦ Χριστοῦ.

I Cor. 10:4. Πάντες τὸ αὐτὸ πνευματικὸν ἔπιον πόμα.

The noun δωρεά is used this one time in John. Elsewhere in the New Testament it occurs four times in Acts, twice in Romans, once in II Corinthians, twice in Ephesians, and once in Hebrews.

The reference in I Cor. 10:4 to "supernatural drink," whose source is a "supernatural rock," and the identification of this rock as "really Christ" satisfies the imagery of John 4:10 too well to be merely a coincidence.

John 4:21-24   II Corinthians C

Πίστευέ μοι, γύναι, ὅτι ἔρχεται ὥρα ὅτε οὔτε ἐν τῷ ὄρει τούτῳ οὔτε ἐν 'Ιεροσολύμοις προσκυνήσετε τῷ πατρί. . . . . ἀλλὰ ἔρχεται ὥρα καὶ νῦν ἐστίν, ὅτε οἱ ἀληθινοὶ προσκυνηταὶ προσκυνήσουσιν τῷ πατρὶ ἐν πνεύματι καὶ ἀληθείᾳ, καὶ γὰρ ὁ πατὴρ τοιούτους

ζητεῖ τοὺς προσκυνοῦντας αὐτόν· πνεῦμα ὁ Θεός, καὶ τοὺς προσκυνοῦντας αὐτὸν ἐν πνεύματι καὶ ἀληθείᾳ δεῖ προσκυνεῖν.

II Cor. 3:6-9. 'Αλλ' ἡ ἱκανότης ἡμῶν ἐκ τοῦ Θεοῦ, ὃς καὶ
ἱκάνωσεν ἡμᾶς διακόνους καινῆς διαθήκης, οὐ γράμματος ἀλλὰ πνεύματος, τὸ γὰρ γράμμα ἀποκτείνει, τὸ δὲ πνεῦμα ζωοποιεῖ. Εἰ δὲ ἡ
διακονία τοῦ θανάτου ἐν γράμμασιν ἐντετυπωμένη λίθοις ἐγενήθη ἐν
δόξῃ, ... πῶς οὐχὶ μᾶλλον ἡ διακονία τοῦ πνεύματος ἔσται ἐν
δόξῃ; εἰ γὰρ ⌈ἡ διακονία⌉ τῆς κατακρίσεως δόξα πολλῷ μᾶλλον περισ-
σεύει ἡ διακονία τῆς δικαιοσύνης δόξῃ.

In II Corinthians the contrast of "spiritual" with "legal"
is drawn in the way most probably calculated to serve as a suggestion for the Johannine contrast.

John 4:22   Romans C
'Η σωτηρία ἐκ τῶν 'Ιουδαίων ἐστίν.

Rom. 9:4, 5. Οἵτινες εἰσιν 'Ισραηλεῖται, ὧν ἡ υἱοθεσία
καὶ ἡ δόξα καὶ αἱ διαθῆκαι καὶ ἡ νομοθεσία καὶ ἡ λατρεία καὶ αἱ
ἐπαγγελίαι, ὧν οἱ πατέρες, καὶ ἐξ ὧν ὁ Χριστὸς τὸ κατὰ σάρκα.

John 5:21, 25   Ephesians B
"Ωσπερ γὰρ ὁ πατὴρ ἐγείρει τοὺς νεκροὺς καὶ ζωοποιεῖ, οὕτως
καὶ ὁ υἱὸς οὓς θέλει ζωοποιεῖ. . . . . 25. "Ερχεται ὥρα καὶ νῦν
ἐστιν ὅτε οἱ νεκροὶ ἀκούσουσιν τῆς φωνῆς τοῦ υἱοῦ τοῦ Θεοῦ καὶ οἱ
ἀκούσαντες ζήσουσιν.

Eph. 2:5, 6. Καὶ ὄντας ἡμᾶς νεκροὺς τοῖς παραπτώμασιν
συνεζωοποίησεν τῷ Χριστῷ . . . . (cf. Col. 2:13; I Cor. 15:22;
Rom. 6:11, 8:10-11).

The translation of apocalypticism into terms of present
experience together with the similarities of language in these passages make the influence of Ephesians on John probable. Ζωοποιέω
occurs in the New Testament only in Paul's letters, John, and I
Peter. Συνζωοποιέω occurs in Eph. 2:5 and Col. 2:13. In John,
Ephesians, and I Corinthians Christ figures as the significant
figure in the process of "making alive." In I Corinthians the
thought is distinctly eschatological. In John and Ephesians it
is experiential. The use of νεκρός in the two passages is practically the same.

John 5:24   Romans B

Ὁ τὸν λόγον μου ἀκούων καὶ πιστεύων τῷ πέμψαντι με ἔχει ζωὴν αἰώνιον, καὶ εἰς κρίσιν οὐκ ἔρχεται ἀλλὰ μεταβέβηκεν ἐκ τοῦ θανάτου εἰς τὴν ζωήν.

Rom. 8:2. Οὐδὲν ἄρα νῦν κατάκριμα τοῖς ἐν Χριστῷ Ἰησοῦ· . . . . 6:4. Συνετάφημεν οὖν αὐτῷ διὰ τοῦ βαπτίσματος εἰς τὸν θάνατον, ἵνα ὥσπερ ἠγέρθη Χριστὸς ἐκ νεκρῶν διὰ τῆς δόξης τοῦ πατρός, οὕτως καὶ ἡμεῖς ἐν καινότητι ζωῆς περιπατήσωμεν. . . . . 11:15. Τίς ἡ πρόσλημψις εἰ μὴ ζωὴ ἐκ νεκρῶν;

Exemption from future judgment and the present experience of "passage from death to life" as results of a faith relationship to Christ are ideas which the Fourth Gospel probably drew from Romans.

John 5:39, 40   Romans C   II Corinthians C

Ἐραυνᾶτε τὰς γραφάς, ὅτι ὑμεῖς δοκεῖτε ἐν αὐταῖς ζωὴν αἰώνιον ἔχειν· καὶ ἐκεῖναί εἰσιν αἱ μαρτυροῦσαι περὶ ἐμοῦ· καὶ οὐ θέλετε ἐλθεῖν πρός με ἵνα ζωὴν ἔχητε.

Rom. 2:17-20. Εἰ δὲ σὺ Ἰουδαῖος ἐπονομάζῃ καὶ ἐπαναπαύῃ νόμῳ καὶ καυχᾶσθαι ἐν Θεῷ καὶ γινώσκεις τὸ θέλημα καὶ δοκιμάζεις τὰ διαφέροντα κατηχούμενος ἐκ τοῦ νόμου, πέποιθάς τε σεαυτὸν ὁδηγὸν εἶναι τυφλῶν . . . . ἔχοντα τὴν μόρφωσιν τῆς γνώσεως καὶ τῆς ἀληθείας ἐν τῷ νόμῳ.

II Cor. 3:6. Ὃς καὶ ἱκάνωσεν ἡμᾶς διακόνους καινῆς διαθήκης, οὐ γράμματος ἀλλὰ πνεύματος, τὸ γὰρ γράμμα ἀποκτείνει, τὸ δὲ πνεῦμα ζωοποιεῖ (cf. Aboth. 2:8).

The three New Testament passages refute the literalistic doctrine of Scripture which is represented in the New Testament as typically Pharisaic.

John 6:27   Romans C

Ἐργάζεσθε μὴ τὴν βρῶσιν τὴν ἀπολλυμένην ἀλλὰ τὴν βρῶσιν τὴν μένουσαν εἰς ζωὴν αἰώνιον, ἣν ὁ υἱὸς τοῦ ἀνθρώπου ὑμῖν δώσει.

Rom. 2:7. Τοῖς μὲν καθ' ὑπομονὴν ἔργου ἀγαθοῦ δόξαν καὶ τιμὴν καὶ ἀφθαρσίαν ζητοῦσιν ζωὴν αἰώνιον. 6:22, 23. Νυνὶ δέ, ἐλευθερωθέντες ἀπὸ τῆς ἁμαρτίας δουλωθέντες δὲ τῷ Θεῷ, ἔχετε τὸν καρπὸν ὑμῶν εἰς ἁγιασμόν, τὸ δὲ τέλος ζωὴν αἰώνιον. τὰ γὰρ ὀψώνια τῆς ἁμαρτίας θάνατος, τὸ δὲ χάρισμα τοῦ Θεοῦ ζωὴ αἰώνιος ἐν Χριστῷ

'Ιησοῦ τῷ κυρίῳ ἡμῶν.

The figure of "work" in the passages is the same, and the contrasts of transient with eternal rewards correspond. In John and in Romans, chapter 6, "eternal life" is a gift that is mediated through Christ.

John 6:27   II Corinthians B   Ephesians B
Τοῦτον γὰρ ὁ πατὴρ ἐσφράγισεν ὁ Θεός.

The idea of "sealing" by God occurs elsewhere in the New Testament only in II Cor. 1:22 and Eph. 1:13 and 4:30.

John 6:29, 30   Galatians C
Τί ποιῶμεν ἵνα ἐργαζώμεθα τὰ ἔργα τοῦ Θεοῦ; . . . . τοῦτό ἐστιν τὸ ἔργον τοῦ Θεοῦ ἵνα πιστεύητε εἰς ὃν ἀπέστειλεν ἐκεῖνος.
Gal. 2:16. Εἰδότες δὲ ὅτι οὐ δικαιοῦται ἄνθρωπος ἐξ ἔργων νόμου ἐὰν μὴ διὰ πίστεως Χριστοῦ 'Ιησοῦ, καὶ ἡμεῖς εἰς ⌜Χριστὸν 'Ιησοῦν⌝ ἐπιστεύσαμεν, ἵνα δικαιῶμεν ἐκ πίστεως Χριστοῦ καὶ οὐκ ἐξ ἔργων νόμου.

John 6:29, 30 is a sort of epigrammatic summary of Paul's teaching on "faith" and "works." The teaching is common in Paul's letters, and it is difficult to fix dependence on a definite passage. Gal. 2:15, 16 probably furnishes the clearest illustration of Paul's teaching.

John 6:51   I Corinthians B
'Εγώ εἰμι ὁ ἄρτος ὁ ζῶν ὁ ἐκ τοῦ οὐρανοῦ καταβάς· ἐάν τις φάγῃ ἐκ τούτου τοῦ ἄρτου ζήσει εἰς τὸν αἰῶνα, καὶ ὁ ἄρτος δὲ ὃν ἐγὼ δώσω ἡ σάρξ μου ἐστὶν ὑπὲρ τῆς τοῦ κόσμου ζωῆς.
I Cor. 10:3, 4. Καὶ πάντες [τὸ αὐτὸ] πνευματικὸν βρῶμα ἔφαγον καὶ πάντες τὸ αὐτὸ πνευματικὸν ἔπιον πόμα, ἔπινον γὰρ ἐκ πνευματικῆς ἀκολουθούσης πέτρας, ἡ πέτρα δὲ ἦν ὁ Χριστός· 10:16. Τὸ ποτήριον τῆς εὐλογίας ὃ εὐλογοῦμεν, οὐχὶ κοινωνία ἐστιν τοῦ αἵματος τοῦ Χριστοῦ; τὸν ἄρτον ὃν κλῶμεν, οὐχὶ κοινωνία τοῦ σώματος τοῦ Χριστοῦ ἐστίν; 11:23. Καὶ εὐχαριστήσας ἔκλασεν καὶ εἶπεν Τοῦτό μου ἐστιν τὸ σῶμα τὸ ὑπὲρ ὑμῶν·

The typology and contrasts involved in John 6:51 can all be accounted for from I Corinthians.

John 6:56, 57   Romans C   Galatians C
῾Ο τρώγων μου τὴν σάρκα καὶ πίνων μου τὸ αἷμα ἐν ἐμοὶ
μένει κἀγὼ ἐν αὐτῷ.   καθὼς ἀπέστειλεν με ὁ ζῶν πατὴρ κἀγὼ ζῶ διὰ
τὸν πατέρα, καὶ ὁ τρώγων με κἀκεῖνος ζήσει δι᾽ ἐμέ.
     Rom. 5:10. Πολλῷ μᾶλλον . . . . σωθησόμεθα ἐν τῇ ζωῇ
αὐτοῦ (cf. 8:1, 29).
     Gal. 2:20. Ζῶ δὲ οὐκέτι ἐγώ, ζῇ δὲ ἐν ἐμοὶ Χριστός·
3:27. ῞Οσοι γὰρ εἰς Χριστὸν ἐβαπτίσθητε, Χριστὸν ἐνεδύσασθε·

John 6:62   Ephesians C
     ᾽Εὰν οὖν θεωρῆτε τὸν υἱὸν τοῦ ἀνθρώπου ἀναβαίνοντα ὅπου
ἦν τὸ πρότερον;
     Eph. 4:10. ῾Ο καταβὰς αὐτός ἐστιν καὶ ὁ ἀναβὰς ὑπεράνω
πάντων τῶν οὐρανῶν (see the note on 3:13).

John 6:63   II Corinthians B
     Τὸ πνεῦμά ἐστιν τὸ ζωοποιοῦν, ἡ σὰρξ οὐκ ὠφελεῖ οὐδέν·
     II Cor. 3:6. Τὸ γὰρ γράμμα ἀποκτείνει, τὸ δὲ πνεῦμα
ζωοποιεῖ. 17. ῾Ο δὲ κύριος τὸ πνεῦμά ἐστιν (cf. I Cor. 15:45, ὁ
ἔσχατος ᾽Αδὰμ εἰς πνεῦμα ζωποιοῦν).

     There is a close verbal parallel between the second clause
of II Cor. 3:6 and the first clause of John 6:63. The identification of the Lord as the Spirit in II Cor. 3:17 corresponds with
the idea of the Spirit in John.

          John 7:15   I Corinthians B
     ᾽Εθαύμαζον οὖν οἱ ᾽Ιουδαῖοι λέγοντες πῶς οὗτος γράμματα
οἶδεν μὴ μεμαθηκώς;
     I Cor. 1:17-24. Οὐκ ἐν σοφίᾳ λόγου, ... ῾Ο λόγος
γὰρ ὁ τοῦ σταυροῦ τοῖς μὲν ἀπολλυμένοις μωρία ἐστίν, τοῖς δὲ σωζομένοις ἡμῖν δύναμις Θεοῦ ἐστίν. . . . . ποῦ συνζητητὴς τοῦ αἰῶνος
τούτου; οὐχὶ ἐμώρανεν ὁ Θεὸς τὴν σοφίαν τοῦ κόσμου; . . . . ᾽Ιου-
δαῖοι σημεῖα αἰτοῦσιν . . . . ἡμεῖς δὲ κηρύσσομεν Χριστὸν ἐσταυρωμένον, ᾽Ιουδαίοις μὲν σκάνδαλον.

     ᾽Ιουδαῖοι is emphatic in John. They all, like Nicodemus,
have a wisdom that is not spiritually illumined.

John 7:19   Romans B

Οὐ Μωυσῆς ⌜ἔδωκεν⌝ ὑμῖν τὸν νόμον; καὶ οὐδεὶς ἐξ ὑμῶν ποιεῖ τὸν νόμον.

Rom. 2:17-23. See the text in the note on John 5:39, 40.

The Jewish reliance on the Law is evidently the background of the question in John, and the reply is to the effect that their trust is misdirected because they do not keep the Law. These are exactly Paul's ideas in Romans.

John 7:37   I Corinthians B

Ἐάν τις διψᾷ ἐρχέσθω πρός με καὶ πινέτω (cf. Isa. 12:3).
I Cor. 10:4. Ἔπινον γὰρ ἐκ πνευματικῆς ἀκολουθούσης πέτρας, ἡ πέτρα δὲ ἦν ὁ Χριστός (see the note on John 4:10).

John 7:38, 39   II Corinthians C

Ποταμοὶ ἐκ τῆς κοιλίας αὐτοῦ ῥεύσουσιν ὕδατος ζῶντος. Τοῦτο δὲ εἶπεν περὶ τοῦ πνεύματος ⌜οὖ⌝ ἔμελλον λαμβάνειν οἱ πιστεύσαντες εἰς αὐτόν· οὔπω γὰρ ἦν πνεῦμα ὅτι Ἰησοῦς οὔπω ἐδοξάσθη.
II Cor. 3:17. Ὁ δὲ κύριος τὸ πνεῦμα ἐστιν (cf. Gal. 4:6 and I Cor. 12:13).

In Gal. 4:6 the Spirit and the risen Christ are by implication the same, and in II Corinthians their identity is specifically asserted. This is evidently the point in John of γὰρ ἦν πνεῦμα, ὅτι Ἰησοῦς οὔπω ἐδοξάσθη. In I Cor. 12:13 the figure of the Spirit as water is employed, and the same figure differently applied is used in John.

John 8:15   II Corinthians C

Ὑμεῖς κατὰ τὴν σάρκα κρίνετε, ἐγὼ οὐ κρίνω οὐδένα. καὶ ἐὰν κρίνω δὲ ἐγώ, ἡ κρίσις ἡ ἐμὴ ἀληθινή ἐστιν.
II Cor. 5:16. Ὥστε ἡμεῖς ἀπὸ τοῦ νῦν οὐδένα οἴδαμεν κατὰ σάρκα· εἰ καὶ ἐγνώκαμεν κατὰ σάρκα Χριστόν, ἀλλὰ νῦν οὐκέτι γινώσκομεν.

John 8:15 describes the judgments of the Pharisees as false because they judge κατὰ τὴν σάρκα. In II Cor. 5:16, Paul similarly brands as superficial knowledge which is κατὰ σάρκα.

          John 8:23   Colossians C
'Εγὼ ἐκ τῶν ἄνω εἰμί.
Col. 3:1. Τὰ ἄνω ζητεῖτε. . . . . 2. Τὰ ἄνω φρονεῖτε.

     Only in John 8:23 and Col. 3:1, 2 is τὰ ἄνω used in the
New Testament.

          John 8:31, 32   Galatians B
'Εὰν ὑμεῖς μείνητε ἐν τῷ λόγῳ τῷ ἐμῷ, ἀληθῶς μαθηταί μού
ἐστε, καὶ γνώσεσθε τὴν ἀλήθειαν, καὶ ἡ ἀλήθεια ἐλευθερώσει ὑμᾶς.
     Gal. 2:20. Ζῶ δὲ οὐκέτι ἐγώ, ζῇ δὲ ἐν ἐμοὶ Χριστός·
4. Τὴν ἐλευθερίαν ἡμῶν ἣν ἔχομεν ἐν Χριστῷ 'Ιησοῦ. 5:1. ⌐Τῇ
ἐλευθερίᾳ ἡμᾶς Χριστὸς ἠλευθέρωσεν⌐ . . . . 13. ''Υμεῖς γὰρ ἐπ'
ἐλευθερίᾳ ἐκλήθητε, ἀδελφοί·

     The noun ἐλευθερία occurs in the New Testament only in the
Pauline letters (Romans, I and II Corinthians, and Galatians) and
the Catholics (James and I and II Peter). The adjective ἐλεύθερος
occurs in Matt. 17:26, where its meaning is literal, in John 8:33,
36, in the Pauline letters (Romans, I Corinthians, Galatians, and
Colossians), and in Ephesians, I Peter, and the Apocalypse. The
verb ἐλευθερόω occurs in John 8:32, 36 and in Romans and Galatians.

          John 8:33   II Corinthians C
Σπέρμα 'Αβράαμ ἐσμεν.
II Cor. 11:22. Σπέρμα 'Αβραάμ εἰσιν; κἀγώ.

     The phrase σπέρμα 'Αβραάμ occurs in the New Testament only
in the Pauline letters, Hebrews, and John. In John and II Cor.
11:22 it represents a Jewish boast which the Christian writers
refute.

          John 8:34   Romans A
Πᾶς ὁ ποιῶν τὴν ἀμαρτίαν δουλός ἐστιν [τῆς ἀμαρτίας].
     Rom. 6:16-18. Οὐκ οἴδατε ὅτι ᾧ παριστάνετε ἑαυτοὺς δούλους
εἰς ὑπακοήν, δοῦλοί ἐστε ᾧ ὑπακούετε, ἤτοι ἀμαρτίας εἰς θάνατον ἢ
ὑπακοῆς εἰς δικαιοσύνην; χάρις δὲ τῷ θεῷ ὅτι ἦτε δοῦλοι τῆς ἀμαρτίας ὑπηκούσατε δὲ ἐκ καρδίας εἰς ὃν παρεδόθητε τύπον διδαχῆς, ἐλευθερωθέντες δὲ ἀπὸ τῆς ἀμαρτίας ἐδουλώθητε τῇ δικαιοσύνη.

     In John 8:31-47 the argument and language of Gal. 4:21,

5:1 and of Rom. 6:16-23 are clearly employed. The evangelist builds his own distinctive picture on a Pauline foundation. In 8:34 he clearly employs the figure and language of Rom. 6:16-18.

John 8:35   Galatians A

Ὁ δὲ δοῦλος οὐ μένει ἐν τῇ οἰκίᾳ εἰς τὸν αἰῶνα· ὁ υἱὸς μένει εἰς τὸν αἰῶνα.

Gal. 4:30. Ἀλλὰ τί λέγει ἡ γραφή; "Ἔκβαλε τὴν παιδίσκην καὶ τὸν υἱὸν αὐτῆς, οὐ γὰρ μὴ κληρονομήσει ὁ υἱὸς τῆς παιδίσκης μετὰ τοῦ υἱοῦ τῆς ἐλευθέρας.

John is here influenced by the Pauline allegorization of the Genesis story of Hagar and Ishmael (cf. Luke 15:31 and Heb. 3:5). Bernard stresses the fact that the clause ὁ υἱὸς μένει εἰς τὸν αἰῶνα is omitted by ℵ W Γ 33 124 and Clem. Alex., and on this basis advances the possibility that "the whole of v. 35 is an early gloss, brought in from familiarity with such passages as Gal. 4:30, Heb. 3:5."[55] The textual evidence hardly warrants such a conclusion, and the more reasonable position is that both Hebrews and John were directly influenced by Galatians.

John 8:36   Galatians A

Ἐὰν οὖν ὁ υἱὸς ὑμᾶς ἐλευθερώσῃ, ὄντως ἐλεύθεροι ἔσεσθε.

See the text of Gal. 5:1 and the discussion of its influence on John in the note on 8:31, 32.

John 8:37   II Corinthians C

Οἶδα ὅτι σπέρμα Ἀβραάμ ἐστε.

See the text of II Cor. 11:22 and a discussion of its influence on John in the note on 8:33.

John 8:39   Romans B   Galatians B

Εἰ τέκνα τοῦ Ἀβραάμ ἐστε, τὰ ἔργα τοῦ Ἀβραὰμ ⌜ποιεῖτε⌝.
Rom. 4:12. Καὶ πατέρα περιτομῆς τοῖς οὐκ ἐκ περιτομῆς μόνον ἀλλὰ ⌜καὶ τοῖς⌝ στοιχοῦσιν τοῖς ἴχνεσιν τῆς ἐν ἀκροβυστίᾳ πίστεως τοῦ πατρὸς ἡμῶν Ἀβραάμ. 9:7, 8. Οὐδ' ὅτι εἰσὶν σπέρμα Ἀβραάμ, πάντες τέκνα, ἀλλ' Ἐν Ἰσαὰκ κληθήσεταί σοι σπέρμα. τοῦτ' ἔστιν, οὐ τὰ τέκνα τῆς σαρκὸς ταῦτα τέκνα τοῦ θεοῦ.

---

[55]Op. cit., II, 308.

Gal. 3:7. Γινώσκετε ἄρα ὅτι οἱ ἐκ πίστεως, οὗτοι υἱοί εἰσιν 'Αβραάμ. 4:26. Πάντες γὰρ υἱοὶ Θεοῦ ἐστὲ διὰ τῆς πίστεως ἐν Χριστῷ 'Ιησοῦ. . . . . 29. Εἰ δὲ ὑμεῖς Χριστοῦ, ἄρα τοῦ 'Αβραὰμ σπέρμα ἐστέ.

Paul and John make faith the true test of descent from Abraham. Faith is τὸ ἔργον τοῦ Θεοῦ, which Abraham performed. It is Jewish unbelief that John condemns in 8:39.

John 8:41, 42   Romans B   Galatians B

'Υμεῖς ποιεῖτε τὰ ἔργα τοῦ πατρὸς ὑμῶν. εἶπαν αὐτῷ ΄'Ημεῖς ἐκ πορνείας ⌐οὐκ ἐγεννήθημεν⌐· ἕνα πατέρα ἔχομεν τὸν Θεόν. εἶπεν αὐτοῖς [ὁ] 'Ιησοῦς Εἰ ὁ Θεὸς πατὴρ ὑμῶν ἦν ἠγαπᾶτε ἂν ἐμέ, ἐγὼ γὰρ ἐκ τοῦ Θεοῦ ἐξῆλθον καὶ ἥκω·

The discussion of relationship to God in 8:4 f. is in the terms of Galatians and Romans.

John 8:56   Galatians B

'Αβραὰμ ὁ πατὴρ ὑμῶν ἠγαλλιάσατο ἵνα ἴδῃ τὴν ἡμέραν τὴν ἐμήν, καὶ εἶδεν καὶ ἐχάρη.

Gal. 3:8, 9. Προϊδοῦσα δὲ ἡ γραφὴ ὅτι ἐκ πίστεως δικαιοῖ τὰ ἔθνη ὁ Θεὸς προευηγγελίσατο τῷ Αβραὰμ ὅτι 'Ενευλογηθήσονται ἐν σοὶ πάντα τὰ ἔθνη. ὥστε οἱ ἐκ πίστεως εὐλογοῦνται σὺν τῷ πιστῷ 'Αβραάμ.

The evangelist expresses the thoroughly Pauline idea that the promise to Abraham looked forward to the Gospel.

John 8:58   Colossians B

Πρὶν 'Αβραὰμ γενέσθαι ἐγὼ εἰμί.

Col. 1:17. Αὐτὸς ἔστιν πρὸ πάντων.

The absolute use of εἶναι together with the representation of Christ as possessing the timeless being of deity suggest the strong probability of dependence on Colossians.

John 9:5   I and II Corinthians C

'Οταν ἐν τῷ κόσμῳ ὦ, φῶς εἰμὶ τοῦ κόσμου.

For the text of I Cor. 4:5 and II Cor. 4:6 and a discussion of their probable influence on John see the note on 1:9.

John 9:9   Galatians C   II Corinthians C

῎Αλλοι ἔλεγον ὅτι Οὗτός ἐστιν· ἄλλοι ἔλεγον Οὐχί, ἀλλὰ· ὅμοιος αὐτῷ ἐστίν. ἐκεῖνος ἔλεγεν ὅτι ᾿Εγώ εἰμι.

Gal. 2:20. Ζῶ δὲ οὐκέτι ἐγώ, ζῇ δὲ ἐν ἐμοὶ Χριστός· ὁ δὲ· νῦν ζῶ ἐν σαρκί, ἐν πίστει ζῶ τῇ τοῦ υἱοῦ τοῦ Θεοῦ.

II Cor. 5:16, 17. ῞Ωστε ἡμεῖς ἀπὸ τοῦ νῦν οὐδένα οἴδαμεν κατὰ σάρκα· εἰ καὶ ἐγνώκαμεν κατὰ σάρκα Χριστόν, ἀλλὰ· νῦν οὐκέτι γινώσκομεν. ὥστε εἴ τις ἐν Χριστῷ, καινὴ κτίσις· τὰ· ἀρχαῖα παρῆλ-θεν, ἰδοὺ γέγονεν καινά·

The debate about the identity of the healed man suggests Paul's description of himself in Galatians—it is he and yet he is a new and different person. The note of judging κατὰ σάρκα and the description of a man who by virtue of the exercise of faith is ἐν Χριστῷ and therefore καινὴ κτίσις also probably influenced John.

John 9:26, 31   Ephesians C

῍Εν οἶδα ὅτι τυφλὸς ὢν ἄρτι βλέπω . . . . ἤναιξέν μου τοὺς ὀφθαλμούς.

Eph. 1:18. Πεφωτισμένους τοὺς ὀφθαλμοὺς τῆς καρδίας [ὑμῶν] εἰς τὸ εἰδέναι.

In Eph. 1:18 the purpose of the "enlightenment" is εἰς τὸ εἰδέναι. In John the result is ἐν οἶδα.

John 10:10   Romans C

᾿Εγώ· ἦλθον ἵνα ζωὴν ἔχωσιν καὶ περισσὸν ἔχωσιν.

Rom. 5:18-21. ῎Αρα οὖν ὡς δι᾿ ἑνὸς παραπτώματος εἰς πάν-τας ἀνθρώπους εἰς κατάκριμα, οὕτως καὶ δι᾿ ἑνὸς δικαιώματος εἰς πάντας ἀνθρώπους εἰς δικαίωσιν ζωῆς· ὥσπερ γὰρ διὰ τῆς παρακοῆς τοῦ ἑνὸς ἀνθρώπου ἁμαρτωλοὶ κατεστάθησαν οἱ πολλοί, οὕτως καὶ διὰ· τῆς ὑπακοῆς τοῦ ἑνὸς δίκαιοι κατασταθήσονται οἱ πολλοί. . . . . ἵνα ὥσπερ ἐβασίλευσεν ἡ ἁμαρτία ἐν τῷ θανάτῳ, οὕτως καὶ ἡ χάρις βασιλεύσῃ διὰ δικαιοσύνης εἰς ζωὴν αἰώνιον διὰ ᾿Ιησοῦ Χριστοῦ τοῦ κυρίου ἡμῶν.

This conception of Christ as the giver of life was prob-ably derived by John from Paul. Περισσός is used this once in John, and it probably reflects the influence of ὑπερεπερίσσευσεν ἡ χάρις of Romans.

John 10:16   Ephesians A

Καὶ ἄλλα πρόβατα ἔχω ἃ οὐκ ἔστιν ἐκ τῆς αὐλῆς ταύτης·
κἀκεῖνα δεῖ με ἀγαγεῖν, καὶ τῆς φωνῆς μου ἀκούσουσιν, καὶ γενήσον
ται μία ποίμνη, εἷς ποιμήν (cf. 11:52 and 17:20).

Eph. 2:14-17. Αὐτὸς γάρ ἐστιν ἡ εἰρήνη ἡμῶν, ὁ ποιήσας τὰ
ἀμφότερα ἓν καὶ τὸ μεσότοιχον τοῦ φραγμοῦ λύσας, ... ἵνα τοὺς
δύο κτίσῃ ἐν αὐτῷ εἰς ἕνα καινὸν ἄνθρωπον ποιῶν εἰρήνην, καὶ ἀποκαταλλάξῃ τοὺς ἀμφοτέρους ἐν ἑνὶ σώματι τῷ Θεῷ . . . . καὶ ἐλθὼν
εὐηγγελίσατο εἰρήνην ὑμῖν τοῖς μακρὰν καὶ εἰρήνην τοῖς ἐγγύς· 3:6.
Εἶναι τὰ ἔθνη συνκληρονόμα καὶ σύνσωμα καὶ συνμέτοχα τῆς ἐπαγγελίας
ἐν Χριστῷ. . . . .

The Johannine sense of obligation to bring into "one flock"
and under the control of "one shepherd" those " who do not belong
to this fold" is almost certainly a reflection of the influence of
the similar emphasis in Ephesians on the union of the two parties.

John 10:17   Philippians C

Διὰ τοῦτό με ὁ πατὴρ ἀγαπᾷ ὅτι ἐγὼ τίθημι τὴν ψυχήν μου.

Phil. 2:8, 9. Ἐταπείνωσεν ἑαυτὸν γενόμενος ὑπήκοος μέχρι
θανάτου . . . . διὸ καὶ ὁ Θεὸς αὐτὸν ὑπερύψωσεν

John 10:18   Philippians C   II Corinthians C

Οὐδεὶς ⌜ἦρεν⌝ αὐτὴν ἀπ' ἐμοῦ, ἀλλ' ἐγὼ τίθημι αὐτὴν ἀπ'
ἐμαυτοῦ. ἐξουσίαν ἔχω θεῖναι αὐτήν, καὶ ἐξουσίαν ἔχω πάλιν λαβεῖν
αὐτήν·

Phil. 2:5-7. Ὃς ἐν μορφῇ Θεοῦ ὑπάρχων οὐχ ἁρπαγμὸν ἡγήσατο τὸ εἶναι ἴσα Θεῷ, ἀλλὰ ἑαυτὸν ἐκένωσεν μορφὴν δούλου λαβών,
ἐν ὁμοιώματι ἀνθρώπων γενόμενος·

II Cor. 8:9. Γινώσκετε γὰρ τὴν χάριν τοῦ κυρίου ἡμῶν
Ἰησοῦ [Χριστοῦ], ὅτι δι' ὑμᾶς ἐπτώχευσεν πλούσιος ὤν, ἵνα ὑμεῖς
τῇ ἐκείνου πτωχείᾳ πλουτήσητε.

John emphasizes the voluntariness of Jesus' giving of his
life. This is a characteristic element in Paul's Christology.

John 10:28-30   Romans C

Καὶ οὐ μὴ ἀπόλωνται εἰς τὸν αἰῶνα, καὶ οὐχ ἁρπάσει τις
αὐτὰ ἐκ τῆς χειρός μου. ὁ πατήρ μου ⌜ὃ δέδωκέν μοι πάντων μεῖζον
ἐστιν⌝, καὶ οὐδεὶς δύναται ἁρπάζειν ἐκ τῆς χειρὸς τοῦ πατρός.
ἐγὼ καὶ ὁ πατὴρ ἕν ἐσμεν.

Rom. 8:35-39. Τίς ἡμᾶς χωρίσει ἀπὸ τῆς ἀγάπης τοῦ ⌈Χρισ-
τοῦ⌉; θλίψις ἢ στενοχωρία ἢ διωγμὸς ἢ λιμὸς ἢ γυμνότης ἢ κίνδυνος
ἢ μάχαιρα; . . . . πέπεισμαι γὰρ ὅτι οὔτε θάνατος οὔτε ζωὴ οὔτε
. . . . τις κτίσις ἑτέρα δυνήσεται ἡμᾶς χωρίσαι ἀπὸ τῆς ἀγάπης τοῦ
Θεοῦ τῆς ἐν Χριστῷ Ἰησοῦ τῷ κυρίῳ ἡμῶν.

John generalizes where Paul itemizes, but both agree that
nothing in all the universe can endanger the salvation of the person who is true to Christ.

John 11:25, 26   Romans C
Ἐγώ εἰμι ἡ ἀνάστασις καὶ ἡ ζωή· ὁ πιστεύων εἰς ἐμὲ κἂν
ἀποθάνῃ ζήσεται, καὶ πᾶς ὁ ζῶν καὶ πιστεύων εἰς ἐμὲ οὐ μὴ ἀποθάνῃ
εἰς τὸν αἰῶνα·
Rom. 6:9-11. Εἰδότες ὅτι Χριστὸς ἐγερθεὶς ἐκ νεκρῶν οὐκέτι
ἀποθνήσκει, θάνατος αὐτοῦ οὐκέτι κυριεύει· ὁ γὰρ ἀπέθανεν, τῇ ἁμαρτίᾳ ἀπέθανεν ἐφάπαξ· ὁ δὲ ζῇ, ζῇ τῷ Θεῷ. οὕτως καὶ ὑμεῖς λογίζεσθε
ἑαυτοὺς εἶναι νεκροὺς μὲν τῇ ἁμαρτίᾳ ζῶντας δὲ τῷ Θεῷ ἐν Χριστῷ
Ἰησοῦ.

Paul insists that Christ successfully challenged and definitely shattered the lordship of death. John presents the same
ideas in terms of a concrete situation.

John 11:52   Ephesians A
Καὶ οὐχ ὑπὲρ τοῦ ἔθνους μόνον, ἀλλ' ἵνα καὶ τὰ τέκνα τοῦ
Θεοῦ τὰ διεσκορπισμένα συναγάγῃ εἰς ἕν (cf. 10:16 and 17:20).

For dependence of John on Eph. 2:13-18, 3:6, and 4:4-6
see note on John 10:16.

John 12:24   I Corinthians B
Ἀμὴν ἀμὴν λέγω ὑμῖν, ἐὰν μὴ ὁ κόκκος τοῦ σίτου πεσὼν εἰς
τὴν γῆν ἀποθάνῃ, αὐτὸς μόνος μένει· ἐὰν δὲ ἀποθάνῃ, πολὺν καρπὸν
φέρει.
I Cor. 15:36-38. Ἄφρων, σὺ ὃ σπείρεις οὐ ζωοποιεῖται ἐὰν
μὴ ἀποθάνῃ· καὶ ὃ σπείρεις, οὐ τὸ σῶμα τὸ γενησόμενον σπείρεις
ἀλλὰ γυμνὸν κόκκον εἰ τύχοι σίτου ἤ τινος τῶν λοιπῶν· ὁ δὲ Θεὸς
δίδωσιν αὐτῷ σῶμα καθὼς ἠθέλησεν.

The figure employed in the passages is the same, and the

ἐὰν μὴ . . . . ἀποθάνῃ of John is a close verbal parallel for
Paul's ἐὰν μὴ ἀποθάνῃ. The picture may have owed its ultimate
origin to the Eleusinian mysteries and may have been part of the
common background on which Paul and John drew.

John 12:31   Ephesians C

Νῦν κρίσις ἐστὶν τοῦ κόσμου τούτου, νῦν ὁ ἄρχων τοῦ κόσμου τούτου ἐκβληθήσεται ἔξω·

Eph. 2:2. 'Εν αἷς ποτὲ περιπατήσατε κατὰ τὸν αἰῶνα τοῦ
κόσμου τούτου, κατὰ τὸν ἄρχοντα τῆς ἐξουσίας τοῦ ἀέρος, τοῦ πνεύματος τοῦ νῦν ἐνεργοῦντος ἐν τοῖς υἱαῖς τῆς ἀπειθίας (cf. II Cor. 4:4).

The imagery of the three passages may be the reflection of
a common world-view.

John 12:32   Romans C

Κἀγὼ ἂν ὑψωθῶ ἐκ τῆς γῆς, πάντας ἑλκύσω πρὸς ἐμαυτόν.

The idea of 12:32 corresponds with that of 3:14, 15, and
the dependence is probably on Rom. 3:23-25 (see the note on 3:14,
15).

John 12:37-40   Romans C

Οὐκ ἐπίστευον εἰς αὐτόν, ἵνα ὁ λόγος 'Ησαίου τοῦ προφήτου
πληρωθῇ ὃν εἶπεν Κύριε, τίς ἐπίστευσεν τῇ ἀκοῇ ἡμῶν; . . . . διὰ
τοῦτο οὐκ ἠδύναντο πιστεύειν ὅτι πάλιν εἶπεν 'Ησαίας Τετύφλωκεν
αὐτῶν τοὺς ὀφθαλμοὺς καὶ ἐπιώρωσεν αὐτῶν τὴν καρδίαν, ἵνα μὴ ἴδω-
σιν τοῖς ὀφθαλμοῖς καὶ νοήσωσιν τῇ καρδίᾳ καὶ στραφῶσιν, καὶ ἰάσο-
μαι αὐτούς.

Rom. 9:30-31. "Οτι ἔθνη τὰ μὴ διώκοντα δικαιοσύνην κατέ-
λαβεν δικαιοσύνην, δικαιοσύνην δὲ τὴν ἐκ πίστεως· 'Ισραὴλ δὲ διώκων νόμον δικαιοσύνης εἰς νόμον οὐκ ἔφθασεν· διὰ τί; ὅτι οὐκ ἐκ
πίστεως. 10:16. 'Ησαίας γὰρ λέγει Κύριε, τίς ἐπίστευσεν τῇ ἀκοῇ
ἡμῶν; 11:8. αἱ δὲ λοιποὶ ἐπωρώθησαν, καθάπερ γέγραπται "Εδωκεν
αὐτοῖς ὁ Θεὸς πνεῦμα κατανύξεως, ὀφθαλμοὺς τοῦ μὴ βλέπειν καὶ ὦτα
τοῦ μὴ ἀκούειν, ἕως τῆς σήμερον ἡμέρας.

John and Paul both deal with the failure of the Jews. Both
account for it in terms of the divine intention and their repudiation of the faith principle. Both quote Isa. 53:1 (John 12:38 and
Rom. 10:16) to substantiate their positions.

John 13:27   I Corinthians C

Καὶ μετὰ τὸ ψωμίον τότε εἰσῆλθεν εἰς ἐκεῖνον ὁ Σατανᾶς.
I Cor. 11:27-29. Ὥστε ὃς ἂν ἐσθίῃ τὸν ἄρτον ἢ πίνῃ τὸ
ποτήριον τοῦ κυρίου ἀναξίως, ἔνοχος ἔσται τοῦ σώματος καὶ τοῦ
αἵματος τοῦ κυρίου. δοκιμαζέτω δὲ ἄνθρωπος ἑαυτόν, καὶ οὕτως ἐκ
τοῦ ἄρτου ἐσθιέτω καὶ ἐκ τοῦ ποτηρίου πινέτω· ὁ γὰρ ἐσθίων καὶ
πίνων κρίμα ἑαυτῷ ἐσθίει καὶ πίνει μὴ διακρίνων τὸ σῶμα.

The specification that Satan "took possession" of Judas
"after he took the bread" is a probable reminiscence of Paul's
warning that he "eats and drinks a judgment upon himself" who par-
takes of the elements "in a way that is unworthy."

John 13:30   I Thessalonians C

Ἦν δὲ νύξ (cf. 3:2).

For the probability of John's familiarity with I Thess.
5:5, 6, 8 see the note on John 3:2. Nicodemus came to Jesus "at
night," and when Judas parted with Jesus "it was night."

John 14:2   II Corinthians C

Ἐν τῇ οἰκίᾳ τοῦ πατρός μου μοναὶ πολλαί εἰσιν.
II Cor. 5:1. Οἰκοδομὴν ἐκ Θεοῦ ἔχομεν οἰκίαν ἀχειροποίη-
τον αἰώνιον ἐν τοῖς οὐρανοῖς (cf. I En. 39:4, II En. 61:2).

As far as date is concerned, John might be indebted to II
En. 61:2. The probability of dependence on II Corinthians here is
greater, however.

John 14:3   I Thessalonians C

Πάλιν ἔρχομαι καὶ παραλήμψομαι ὑμᾶς πρὸς ἐμαυτόν, ἵνα ὅπου
εἰμὶ ἐγὼ καὶ ὑμεῖς ἦτε.
I Thess. 4:17. Ἔπειτα ἡμεῖς οἱ ζῶντες οἱ περιλειπόμενοι
ἅμα σὺν αὐτοῖς ἁρπαγησόμεθα ἐν νεφέλαις εἰς ἀπάντησιν τοῦ κυρίου
εἰς ἀέρα· καὶ οὕτως πάντοτε σὺν κυρίῳ ἐσόμεθα.

John 14:6   Ephesians B   Colossians C

Ἐγώ εἰμι ἡ ὁδὸς καὶ ἡ ἀλήθεια καὶ ἡ ζωή· οὐδεὶς ἔρχεται
πρὸς τὸν πατέρα εἰ μὴ δι' ἐμοῦ.
For the representation of Christ as (1) ἡ ὁδός see Eph.
2:18, δι' αὐτοῦ ἔχομεν τὴν προσαγωγὴν οἱ ἀμφότεροι . . . . πρὸς

τὸν πατέρα and 3:12, ἐν ᾧ ἔχομεν τὴν παρρησίαν καὶ προσαγωγήν;
(2) ἡ ἀλήθεια, see Eph. 4:21, καθὼς ἔστιν ἀλήθεια ἐν τῷ ’Ιησοῦ;
and (3) ἡ ζωή, see Col. 3:4, ὅταν ὁ Χριστὸς φανερωθῇ, ἡ ζωὴ ἡμῶν.

The phrases πρὸς τὸν πατέρα and δι’ ἐμοῦ seem to be verbal
reminiscences of Eph. 2:18.

John 14:9   II Corinthians C

⌜Τοσοῦτον χρόνον⌝ μεθ’ ὑμῶν εἰμὶ καὶ οὐκ ἔγνωκάς με, Φίλιπ-
πε; ὁ ἑωρακὼς ἐμὲ ἑώρακεν τὸν πατέρα.

II Cor. 4:4. ’Εν οἷς ὁ θεὸς τοῦ αἰῶνος τούτου ἐτύφλωσεν
τὰ νοήματα τῶν ἀπίστων εἰς τὸ μὴ αὐγάσαι τὸν φωτισμὸν τοῦ εὐαγγελίου τῆς δόξης τοῦ Χριστοῦ, ὅς ἐστιν εἰκὼν τοῦ θεοῦ (cf. Col.1:15,17).

The association of ideas of spiritual blindness and of
Christ as the image of God suggests that John was influenced by
II Corinthians.

John 14:16, 26   Romans B

Κἀγὼ ἐρωτήσω τὸν πατέρα καὶ ἄλλον παράκλητον δώσει ὑμῖν
ἵνα ⌜ᾖ μεθ’ ὑμῶν εἰς τὸν αἰῶνα⌝, τὸ πνεῦμα τῆς ἀληθείας. 26. ὁ
δὲ παράκλητος, τὸ πνεῦμα, τὸ ἅγιον ὁ πέμψει ὁ πατὴρ ἐν τῷ ὀνόματί μου.

Rom. 8:26, 27. ‘Ωσαύτως δὲ καὶ τὸ πνεῦμα συναντιλαμβάνεται
τῇ ἀσθενίᾳ ἡμῶν· τὸ γὰρ τί προσευξώμεθα καθὸ δεῖ οὐκ οἴδαμεν,
ἀλλὰ αὐτὸ τὸ πνεῦμα ὑπερεντυγχάνει στεναγμαῖς ἀλαλήτοις, ὁ δὲ
ἐραυνῶν τὰς καρδίας οἶδεν τί τὸ φρόνημα τοῦ πνεύματος, ὅτι κατὰ
θεὸν ἐντυγχάνει ὑπὲρ ἁγίων. . . . . 34. Χριστὸς [’Ιησοῦς] ὁ
ἀποθανών, μᾶλλον δὲ ἐγερθεὶς [ἐκ νεκρῶν], ὅς ἐστιν ἐν δεξιᾷ τοῦ
θεοῦ, ὃς καὶ ἐντυγχάνει ὑπὲρ ἡμῶν·

In John 14:16, 26 there is no logical place for the Spirit.
In Romans, chapter 8, however, Paul has described the Spirit as in
the present "interceding," ὑπὲρ ἁγίων, and also Christ as "interceding" in heaven, ὑπὲρ ἡμῶν. These Pauline conceptions are probably the source of John's idea of Christ and the Spirit as interceding on behalf of men.

John 14:17   I Corinthians C

Τὸ πνεῦμα τῆς ἀληθείας, ὃ ὁ κόσμος οὐ δύναται λαβεῖν, ὅτι
οὐ θεωρεῖ αὐτὸ οὐδὲ γινώσκει· ὑμεῖς γινώσκετε αὐτό.

I Cor. 2:12, 14. ‘Ημεῖς δὲ οὐ τὸ πνεῦμα τοῦ κόσμου ἐλάβομεν ἀλλὰ τὸ πνεῦμα τὸ ἐκ τοῦ θεοῦ, ἵνα εἰδῶμεν τὰ ὑπὸ τοῦ θεοῦ

χαρισθέντα ἡμῖν· . . . . ψυχικὸς δὲ ἄνθρωπος οὐ δέχεται τὰ τοῦ
πνεύματος τοῦ Θεοῦ, μωρία γὰρ αὐτῷ ἐστίν, καὶ οὐ δύναται γνῶναι,
ὅτι πνευματικῶς ἀνακρίνεται·

John 14:18   Romans B

Οὐκ ἀφήσω ὑμᾶς ὀρφανούς, ἔρχομαι πρὸς ὑμᾶς.

Rom. 8:9, 10. Ὑμεῖς δὲ οὐκ ἐστὲ ἐν σαρκὶ ἀλλὰ ἐν πνεύματι, εἴπερ πνεῦμα Θεοῦ οἰκεῖ ἐν ὑμῖν. εἰ δέ τις πνεῦμα Χριστοῦ
οὐκ ἔχει, οὗτος οὐκ ἔστιν αὐτοῦ. εἰ δὲ Χριστὸς ἐν ὑμῖν, τὸ μὲν
σῶμα νεκρὸν διὰ ἁμαρτίαν, τὸ δὲ πνεῦμα ζωὴ διὰ δικαιοσύνην (cf.
II Cor. 3:18).

In John 14:16 a "paraclete" other than the Son is promised.
In 14:18 the coming of the Spirit seems identical with the return
of the Son to abide in the midst of believers. In Rom. 8:9, 10
Paul thinks of the Spirit as at one and the same time the Spirit
of God and of Christ, and, in II Cor. 3:18, he specifically asserts
that "the Lord is the Spirit."

John 14:20, 21   Ephesians C

Γνώσεσθε ὅτι ἐγὼ ἐν τῷ πατρί μου καὶ ὑμεῖς ἐν ἐμοὶ κἀγὼ ἐν
ὑμῖν. ὁ ἔχων τὰς ἐντολάς μου καὶ τηρῶν αὐτὰς ἐκεῖνός ἐστιν ὁ ἀγαπῶν με. ὁ δὲ ἀγαπῶν με ἀγαπηθήσεται ὑπὸ τοῦ πατρός μου, κἀγὼ ἀγα-
πήσω αὐτὸν καὶ ἐμφανίσω αὐτῷ ἐμαυτόν.

Eph. 3:16, 17. Ἵνα δῷ ὑμῖν κατὰ τὸ πλοῦτος τῆς δόξης
αὐτοῦ δυνάμει κραταιωθῆναι διὰ τοῦ πνεύματος αὐτοῦ εἰς τὸν ἔσω ἄνθρωπον, κατοικῆσαι τὸν Χριστὸν διὰ τῆς πίστεως ἐν ταῖς καρδίαις
ὑμῶν ἐν ἀγάπη.

The conception of mystical union in John and Ephesians is
very similar. The emphasis on love in this connection strengthens
the probability of literary relationship.

John 14:23   Ephesians C   Colossians C

Ἐάν τις ἀγαπᾷ με τὸν λόγον μου τηρήσει, καὶ ὁ πατήρ μου
ἀγαπήσει αὐτόν, καὶ πρὸς αὐτὸν ἐλευσόμεθα καὶ μονὴν παρ' αὐτῷ ποιη-
σόμεθα. ὁ μὴ ἀγαπῶν με τοὺς λόγους μου οὐ τηρεῖ·

Col. 3:16. Ὁ λόγος τοῦ ⌜Χριστοῦ⌝ ἐνοικείτω ἐν ὑμῖν
πλουσίως ἐν πάση σοφίᾳ.

See the note on John 14:20, 21 for the text of Eph. 3:16,
17 and a discussion of its influence on John.

The emphasis on ὁ λόγος τοῦ Χριστοῦ is a probable reminiscence of Colossians.

John 14:27   Ephesians B

Εἰρήνην ἀφίημι ὑμῖν, εἰρήνην τὴν ἐμὴν δίδωμι ὑμῖν

Eph. 2:14. Αὐτὸς γάρ ἐστιν ἡ εἰρήνη ἡμῶν. . . . . 17.
Καὶ ἐλθὼν εὐηγγελίσατο εἰρήνην ὑμῖν τοῖς μακρὰν καὶ εἰρήνην τοῖς
ἐγγύς·

John's emphasis on Jesus' bequest of "peace" probably reflects acquaintance with the description of him in Ephesians as
"our Peace."

John 15:1-6   Ephesians C   Romans C

Ἐγώ εἰμι ἡ ἄμπελος ἡ ἀληθινή, καὶ ὁ πατήρ μου ὁ γεωργός
ἐστιν· . . . . μείνατε ἐν ἐμοί, κἀγὼ ἐν ὑμῖν, καθὼς τὸ κλῆμα οὐ
δύναται καρπὸν φέρειν ἀφ' ἑαυτοῦ ἐὰν μὴ μένῃ ἐν τῇ ἀμπέλῳ, οὕτως
οὐδὲ ὑμεῖς ἐὰν μὴ ἐν ἐμοὶ μένητε. ἐγώ εἰμι ἡ ἄμπελος, ὑμεῖς τὰ
κλήματα. ὁ μένων ἐν ἐμοὶ κἀγὼ ἐν αὐτῷ οὗτος φέρει καρπὸν πολύν

Eph. 4:4-7. Ἓν σῶμα καὶ ἓν πνεῦμα, καθὼς [καὶ] ἐκλήθητε
ἐν μιᾷ ἐλπίδι τῆς κλήσεως ὑμῶν· εἷς κύριος, μία πίστις, ἓν βάπτισ-
μα· εἷς Θεὸς καὶ πατὴρ πάντων, ὁ ἐπὶ πάντων καὶ διὰ πάντων καὶ ἐν
πᾶσιν. Ἑνὶ δὲ ἑκάστῳ ἡμῶν ἐδόθη [ἡ] χάρις κατὰ τὸ μέτρον τῆς
δωρεᾶς τοῦ Χριστοῦ.

As far as imagery is concerned, the dependence might be on
Isa. 27:2-6, although it might as well have been suggested by the
καὶ εἰ ἡ ῥίζα ἀγία, καὶ οἱ κλάδοι of Rom. 11:16. The theme is
closer to that of Eph. 4:4-7.

John 15:3   Colossians C   Ephesians C

Ἤδη ὑμεῖς καθαροί ἐστε διὰ τὸν λόγον ὃν λελάληκα ὑμῖν.

See the note on John 14:23 for the probable influence of
Col. 3:16 on John. The καθαροί ἐστε may reflect the influence of
ἵνα αὐτὴν ἁγιάσῃ καθαρίσας κτλ of Eph. 5:26.

John 15:5   Romans C   Galatians C

Ὁ μένων ἐν ἐμοὶ κἀγὼ ἐν αὐτῷ οὗτος φέρει καρπὸν πολύν.

The ideas of union with Christ and of sharing in his life

are probably suggested from Romans and Galatians. See the passages
and the discussion in the note on 6:56, 57.

John 15:13   Romans B

Μείζονα ταύτης ἀγάπην οὐδεὶς ἔχει, ἵνα τις τὴν ψυχὴν
αὐτοῦ θῇ ὑπὲρ τῶν φίλων αὐτοῦ.

Rom. 5:6-8. Μόλις γὰρ ὑπὲρ δικαίου τις ἀποθανεῖται· ὑπὲρ
γὰρ τοῦ ἀγαθοῦ τάχα τις καὶ τολμᾷ ἀποθανεῖν· συνίστησιν δὲ τὴν
ἑαυτοῦ ἀγάπην εἰς ἡμᾶς ὁ Θεὸς ὅτι ἔτι ἁμαρτωλῶν ὄντων ἡμῶν Χριστὸς
ὑπὲρ ἡμῶν ἀπέθανεν.

The death of Christ as the only adequate measure of divine
love is a probable reminiscence of Romans. John's description of
the death of Christ for his friends constitutes a very close parallel to Paul's similar idea in Rom. 5:6-8.

John 15:15   Romans B

Οὐκέτι λέγω ὑμᾶς δούλους, ὅτι ο δοῦλος οὐκ οἶδεν τί ποιεῖ
αὐτοῦ ὁ κύριος·

Rom. 8:15. Οὐ γὰρ ἐλάβετε πνεῦμα δουλείας . . . . ἀλλὰ
ἐλάβετε πνεῦμα υἱοθεσίας.

John 15:15 sounds as though it might be a conscious adaptation of Rom. 8:15.

John 15:26   Romans B   Galatians C

Ὅταν ἔλθῃ ὁ παράκλητος ὃν ἐγὼ πέμψω ὑμῖν παρὰ τοῦ πατρός,
τὸ πνεῦμα τῆς ἀληθείας ὁ παρὰ τοῦ πατρὸς ἐκπορεύεται, ἐκεῖνος μαρτυ-
ρήσει περὶ ἐμοῦ·

Gal. 4:6. Ὅτι δέ ἐστε υἱοί, ἐξαπέστειλεν ὁ Θεὸς τὸ πνεῦμα
τοῦ υἱοῦ αὐτοῦ εἰς τὰς καρδίας ἡμῶν, κρᾶζον Ἀββά ὁ πατήρ.

The indebtedness of John to Romans for his conception of
the Spirit is discussed in the note on 14:16, 26 and 14:18. The
idea of the "sending" of the Spirit to testify of Christ may represent a reminiscence of Gal. 4:6, where Paul says that God sends
τὸ πνεῦμα τοῦ υἱοῦ αὐτοῦ into the hearts of believers.

John 16:8   I Corinthians B

Καὶ ἐλθὼν ἐκεῖνος ἐλέγξει τὸν κόσμον περὶ ἁμαρτίας καὶ περὶ
δικαιοσύνης καὶ περὶ κρίσεως.

I Cor. 14:24, 25. 'Εὰν δὲ πάντες προφητεύωσιν, εἰσέλθη δέ τις ἄπιστος ἢ ἰδιώτης, ἐλέγχεται ὑπὸ πάντων, ἀνακρίνεται ὑπὸ πάντων, τὰ κρυπτὰ τῆς καρδίας αὐτοῦ φανερὰ γίνεται, καὶ οὕτως πεσὼν ἐπὶ πρόσωπον προσκυνήσει τῷ Θεῷ, ἀπαγγέλλων ὅτι "Οντως ὁ Θεὸς ἐν ὑμῖν ἐστίν (cf. Acts 2:36 f.).

John's representation of the Spirit as bringing "conviction to the world about sin and uprightness and judgment" is very probably an adaptation of Paul's description of the functioning of the Spirit in I Corinthians. The use of ἐλέγχω in this connection is a rather clear hint of literary relationship.

John 16:13-16   I Corinthians B

"Οταν δὲ ἔλθη ἐκεῖνος, τὸ πνεῦμα τῆς ἀληθείας, ὁδηγήσει ὑμᾶς ⌐εἰς τὴν ἀλήθειαν πᾶσαν⌐, οὐ γὰρ λαλήσει ἀφ' ἑαυτοῦ, ἀλλ' ὅσα ⌐ἀκούει⌐ λαλήσει, καὶ τὰ ἐρχόμενα ἀναγγελεῖ ὑμῖν.

I Cor. 2:10-16. 'Ημῖν γὰρ ἀπεκάλυψεν ὁ Θεὸς διὰ τοῦ πνεύματος, τὸ γὰρ πνεῦμα πάντα ἐραυνᾷ, καὶ τὰ βάθη τοῦ Θεοῦ. . . . . οὕτως καὶ τὰ τοῦ Θεοῦ οὐδεὶς ἔγνωκεν εἰ μὴ τὸ πνεῦμα τοῦ Θεοῦ. ἡμεῖς δὲ οὐ τὸ πνεῦμα τοῦ κόσμου ἐλάβομεν ἀλλὰ τὸ πνεῦμα τὸ ἐκ τοῦ Θεοῦ, ἵνα εἰδῶμεν τὰ ὑπὸ τοῦ Θεοῦ χαρισθέντα ἡμῖν· . . . . ὁ δὲ πνευματικὸς ἀνακρίνει ⌐μὲν⌐ πάντα, αὐτὸς δὲ ὑπ' οὐδενὸς ἀνακρίνεται. Τίς γὰρ ἔγνω νοῦν Κυρίου, ὃς συνβιβάσει αὐτόν; ἡμεῖς δὲ νοῦν Χριστοῦ ἔχομεν.

John's idea of the Spirit as communicating what is Christ's to men is almost certainly a development of Paul's representation of the functioning of the Spirit in I Cor. 2:10-16 where the spiritually endowed "share the thoughts of Christ."

John 16:25   I Corinthians B

Ταῦτα ἐν παροιμίαις λελάληκα ὑμῖν· ἔρχεται ὥρα ὅτε οὐκέτι ἐν παροιμίαις λαλήσω ὑμῖν ἀλλὰ παρρησίᾳ περὶ τοῦ πατρὸς ἀπαγγελῶ ὑμῖν.

The thought here is the same as in 16:13-16. The spiritual Christ and the Spirit are the same. See the note on 16:13-16 for the text of I Cor. 2:10-16. The idea of I Cor. 3:1, 2 seems also to be present.

        John 16:33   Romans B
    Ἐν τῷ κόσμῳ θλίψιν ἔχετε, ἀλλὰ θαρσεῖτε, ἐγὼ νενίκηκα
τὸν κόσμον.

        Rom. 8:37. Ἀλλ' ἐν τούτοις πᾶσιν ὑπερνικῶμεν διὰ τοῦ
ἀγαπήσαντος ἡμᾶς.   7:24, 25.   τίς με ῥύσεται . . . . ; ⌐χάρις
[δὲ]⌐ τῷ θεῷ διὰ Ἰησοῦ Χριστοῦ τοῦ κυρίου ἡμῶν.   12:21.   Μὴ
νικῶ ὑπὸ τοῦ κακοῦ, ἀλλὰ νίκα ἐν τῷ ἀγαθῷ τὸ κακόν.

    Νικάω is found this once in John. Earlier than John it
occurs in the New Testament in Luke 11:22 and in Romans. The com-
pound form ὑπερνικάω occurs only in Rom. 8:37.

        John 17:5   Colossians B
    Νῦν δόξασον με σύ, πάτερ, παρὰ σεαυτῷ τῇ δόξῃ ᾗ εἶχον
πρὸ τοῦ τὸν κόσμον εἶναι παρὰ σοί.

    For the influence of Phil. 2:6 and Col. 1:15-18 on John
see the note on John 1:1. For the influence of Phil. 2:9 see the
notes on John 12:26 and 17:2.

        John 17:11, 21, 23   Ephesians A
    Ἵνα ὦσιν ἕν καθὼς ἡμεῖς. . . . . 21. Ἵνα πάντες ἕν
ὦσιν, καθὼς σύ, πατήρ, ἐν ἐμοὶ κἀγὼ ἐν σοί, ἵνα αὐτοὶ ἐν ἡμῖν ὦσιν.
. . . . 23. Ἵνα ὦσιν ἕν καθὼς ἡμεῖς ἕν, ἐγὼ ἐν αὐτοῖς καὶ σὺ ἐν
ἐμοί, ἵνα ὦσιν τετελειωμένοι εἰς ἕν.

    For the influence of Eph. 2:14-18, 3:6, and 4:4-6 on John
see the note on John 10:16. The emphasis on unity in Christ which
is common to Ephesians and John almost certainly reflects literary
acquaintance.

        John 17:12   II Thessalonians C
    Καὶ οὐδεὶς ἐξ αὐτῶν ἀπώλετο εἰ μὴ ὁ υἱὸς τῆς ἀπωλείας.
    II Thess. 2:4. Ὁ υἱὸς τῆς ἀπωλείας.

    This particular phrase is found only in John and II Thessa-
lonians. In the one instance the reference is probably to Judas
and in the other to the anti-Christ. It is possible that John
identified Judas with the anti-Christ, for he asserts in 13:27,
τότε εἰσῆλθεν εἰς ἐκεῖνον ὁ Σατανᾶς.

John 17:17   Ephesians C

Ἁγίασον αὐτοὺς ἐν τῇ ἀληθείᾳ· ὁ λόγος ὁ σὸς ἀλήθεια ἐστιν.

Eph. 5:26. Ἵνα αὐτὴν ἁγιάσῃ καθαρίσας τῷ λουτρῷ τοῦ ὕδατος ἐν ῥήματι (cf. I Thess. 5:23 and II Thess. 2:13).

In I Thess. 5:23, Paul prays for the Thessalonians that
God might "consecrate" them "through and through." In II Thess.
2:13 he thinks of God as having chosen them εἰς σωτηρίαν ἐν
ἁγιασμῷ πνεύματος καὶ πίστει ἀληθείας. These conceptions may have
influenced John, but the influence seems clearer in the case of
Ephesians. In John and Ephesians the viewpoint from which redemption is conceived is ἁγιάζειν, the process of its realization in
Ephesians being καθαρίσας . . . . ἐν ῥήματι, and in John 15:3
καθαρὸς διὰ τόν λόγον. The thought of John 17:17 looks back to
that of 15:3.

John 17:20   Romans C

Οὐ περὶ τούτων δὲ ἐρωτῶ μόνον ἀλλὰ καὶ περὶ τῶν πιστευόντων διὰ τοῦ λόγου αὐτῶν εἰς ἐμέ.

Rom. 10:14. Πῶς οὖν ἐπικαλέσωνται εἰς ὃν οὐκ ἐπίστευσαν;
πῶς δὲ πιστεύσωσαν οὗ οὐκ ἤκουσαν; πῶς δὲ ἀκούσωσιν χωρὶς κηρύσσοντος; πῶς δὲ κηρύξωσιν ἐὰν μὴ ἀποσταλῶσιν;

Both writers think of converts won through the preaching
of missionaries.

John 17:22   Ephesians C   Romans C

Κἀγὼ τὴν δόξαν ἥν δέδωκάς μοι δέδωκα.

Eph. 1:18. Εἰς τὸ εἰδέναι ὑμᾶς . . . . τίς ὁ πλοῦτος τῆς
δόξης τῆς κληρονομίας αὐτοῦ ἐν τοῖς ἁγίοις.

Rom. 8:30. Οὓς δὲ ἐδικαίωσεν, τούτους καὶ ἐδόξασεν.
5:10. Πολλῷ μᾶλλον . . . . σωθησόμεθα ἐν τῇ ζωῇ αὐτοῦ·

John makes much of the Pauline idea of sharing in the divine life through Christ. The author of Ephesians also caught
this emphasis from the Pauline letters. John knew Romans and
Ephesians and probably shows the influence of both in this instance.

John 17:24   Ephesians B

Ἠγάπησας με πρὸ καταβολῆς κόσμου.

Eph. 1:4. Ἐξελέξατο ἡμᾶς ἐν αὐτῷ πρὸ καταβολῆς κόσμου.
. . . . 6. Ἐν τῷ ἠγαπημένῳ, ἐν ᾧ εχομεν τὴν ἀπολύτρωσιν.

Καταβολή occurs in the LXX only in II Macc. 2:29. It occurs in the New Testament eleven times, in nine of which it is
followed by κόσμου. Only in John 17:24, Eph. 1:4, and I Pet. 1:20
is it introduced by πρό. The probability of indebtedness to Ephesians is strengthened by the parallel which ἠγάπησας με supplies
for ἐν τῷ ἠγαπημένῳ.

John 17:25   I Corinthians B
Πατὴρ δίκαιε, καὶ ὁ κόσμος σε οὐκ ἔγνω, ἐγὼ δέ σε ἔγνων,
καὶ οὗτοι ἔγνωσαν ὅτι σύ με ἀπέστειλας, καὶ ἐγνώρισα αὐταῖς τὸ
ὄνομα σου καὶ γνωρίσω.
I Cor. 1:21, 22. Ἐπειδὴ γὰρ ἐν τῇ σοφίᾳ τοῦ Θεοῦ οὐκ ἔγνω
ὁ κόσμος διὰ τῆς σοφίας τὸν Θεόν, εὐδόκησεν ὁ Θεὸς διὰ τῆς μωρίας
τοῦ κηρύγματος σῶσαι τοὺς πιστεύοντας.

See the note on John 3:10-12.

John 17:26   Romans C   Ephesians C
Ἵνα ἡ ἀγάπη ἣν ἠγάπησάς με ἐν αὐταῖς ᾖ.
Eph. 2:4, 5. Διὰ τὴν πολλὴν ἀγάπην αὐτοῦ ἣν ἠγάπησεν ἡμᾶς
. . . . συνεζωοποίησεν τῷ Χριστῷ.
Rom. 5:8. Συνίστησιν δὲ τὴν ἑαυτοῦ ἀγάπην εἰς ἡμᾶς ὁ Θεὸς
ὅτι ἔτι ἁμαρτωλῶν ὄντων ἡμῶν Χριστὸς ὑπὲρ ἡμῶν ἀπέθανεν.

See the note on John 3:16.

John 18:37   Ephesians C
Πᾶς ὁ ὢν ἐκ τῆς ἀληθείας ἀκούει μου τῆς φωνῆς.
Eph. 1:13. Ἐν ᾧ καὶ ὑμεῖς ἀκούσαντες τὸν λόγον τῆς ἀληθείας.

John 20:29   II Corinthians B
Ὅτι ἑώρακας με πεπίστευκας; μακάριοι οἱ μὴ ἰδόντες καὶ
πιστεύσαντες.
II Cor. 4:18. Μὴ σκοπούντων ἡμῶν τὰ βλεπόμενα ἀλλὰ τὰ μὴ
βλεπόμενα. . . . . 5:7. Διὰ πίστεως γὰρ περιπατοῦμεν οὐ διὰ εἴδους.
. . . . 16. Εἰ καὶ ἐγνώκαμεν κατὰ σάρκα Χριστόν, ἀλλὰ νῦν οὐκέτι
γινώσκομεν.

Paul and John both stress the primary significance of "faith" and the entirely secondary value of "sight." Those who have known the historical Jesus not only have no advantage over those who lack that experience but may even have found that knowledge an obstacle to a truly spiritual attitude.

John 20:31   Romans C

Ταῦτα δὲ γέγραπται ἵνα πιστεύητε ὅτι ᾽Ιησοῦς ἐστιν ὁ Χριστὸς ὁ υἱὸς τοῦ Θεοῦ, καὶ ἵνα πιστεύοντες ζωὴν ἔχητε ἐν τῷ ὀνόματι αὐτοῦ.

See the notes on John 3:14, 15, 3:16, and 10:10.

Instances of possible literary reminiscence.—John 1:4; cf. Col. 1:17.

John 1:5; cf. I Thess. 5:4, 5. Although differently applied, the analogy employed in these passages is the same. The similar use of καταλαμβάνω may be an additional trace of literary reminiscence.

John 1:18; cf. Col. 1:15.

John 2:17; cf. II Cor. 11:2. Ζῆλος is used this once in John, twice in Acts, twelve times in Paul's letters, once in Hebrews, and once in James. The use of ζηλόω is confined to Acts, I and II Corinthians, Galatians, and James.

John 2:24, 25; cf. I Cor. 2:11.

John 3:17; cf. Gal. 4:4-6.

John 3:19; cf. II Cor. 4:4 and Col. 1:21.

John 3:29; cf. Phil. 2:2.

John 3:35; cf. Col. 1:13 and Eph. 1:7.

John 4:36-38; cf. I Cor. 3:6-8.

John 5:22, 23; cf. Rom. 14:9.

John 5:24; cf. Rom. 8:3. Only in Rom. 8:3 does Paul use πέμπω with reference to the divine mission of Jesus. His favorite word is ἀποστέλλω.

John 5:34; cf. I Cor. 4:3. In both passages human testimony is discounted as of no real value because of its secondary character.

John 5:43; cf. II Cor. 11:19, 20.

John 5:44; cf. I Thess. 2:6. The use of ζητέω tends to relate John to I Thessalonians.

John 5:45; cf. II Cor. 1:10. The verb ἐλπίζω is used this one time in John.

John 5:46, 47; cf. II Cor. 3:6-8. The contrast of γράμματα with ῥήματα reminds of II Cor. 3:6-8.

John 6:45; cf. I Cor. 2:13 and I Thess. 4:9. Διδακτός occurs in the New Testament in I Cor. 2:13 and John 6:45. In the latter instance it is found in a quotation from Isa. 54:13. The only occurrence of Θεοδίδακτος is I Thess. 4:9.

John 7:4; cf. I Cor. 2:7, 8. The ἐν κρυπτῷ of John may have been suggested by ἐν μυστηρίῳ in I Corinthians.

John 7:8; cf. Gal. 4:4 and Eph. 1:10.

John 7:24; cf. Rom. 2:1.

John 8:12; cf. Eph. 5:14. This use of περιπατέω in a figurative sense occurs frequently in Paul's letters and, probably under Pauline influence, in John. The figure of Christ as τὸ φῶς is clearly implied in Ephesians, and this, when taken in connection with περιπατέω, makes Ephesians a possible source of influence.

John 9:39; cf. I Cor. 1:26-29.

John 10:5, 6; cf. Gal. 4:8, 9.

John 10:34; cf. Rom. 3:19. John's method of argument may have been suggested by Romans.

John 11:11; cf. I Thess. 4:13, 14. The use of κοιμάομαι in a context where hope is urged in place of despair and where Jesus appears as the giver of life may indicate dependence.

John 11:55; cf. I Cor. 5:8.

John 12:26; cf. Phil. 2:9, 10.

John 12:35, 36; cf. Eph. 5:8.

John 12:43; cf. Rom. 3:23.

John 13:1; cf. Gal. 4:4 and Eph. 1:10.

John 13:8; cf. Gal. 3:27.

John 13:31, 32; cf. Phil. 2:9.

John 13:34; cf. Rom. 13:8-10. The Johannine emphasis on love as "a new commandment" is the equivalent of Paul's assertion that love is the summing-up of the Law.

John 13:25; cf. Rom. 15:5, 6.

John 14:12; cf. Phil. 4:13.

John 14:14; cf. I Thess. 3:11.

John 15:2; cf. Gal. 5:22.

John 15:5; cf. Eph. 2:12 and Phil. 4:13.

John 15:16; cf. Eph. 1:4. The sense in which 'Εκλέγομαι is used in Ephesians and John suggests literary influence.

John 15:19; cf. Rom. 8:17.

John 16:21; cf. Gal. 4:19 and Rom. 8:22.

John 16:27; cf. I Cor. 16:22. Φιλέω is frequently used in John, but it occurs in the Pauline letters only in I Cor. 16:22.

John 17:1-26; cf. Eph. 1:3-23. In liturgical tone, in confessional character, in portentousness of style, John 17:1-26 reminds of Eph. 1:3-23.

John 17:1; cf. Gal. 4:4 and Eph. 1:10. 'Ελήλυθεν ἡ ὥρα suggests the possible influence of Gal. 4:4 and Eph. 1:10.

John 17:2; cf. Phil. 2:9, 10.

John 17:3; cf. I Thess. 1:9, 10 and Phil. 3:10. God is described in the New Testament as ἀληθινός in I Thess. 1:9, 10, John 17:3, and I John 5:20 (cf. Apoc. 6:10 and 19:11). He is so described, however, in Exod. 34:6, Num. 14:18, Ps. 86:39, and I Esd. 8:39. The basis on which eternal life is possessed in John may be a translation of the distinctly eschatological conception of I Thessalonians. Phil. 3:10 furnishes a more probable source, however, for there Paul relates the knowledge of Christ to the attainment of resurrection-life (cf. Wisd. of Sol. 15:3).

John 17:10; cf. I Cor. 3:22, 23.

John 17:10; cf. I Thess. 2:20 and II Thess. 1:10. In I Thessalonians Paul thinks of himself as "glorified" in his converts. In II Thessalonians he speaks of Christ's eschatological glorification ἐν ταῖς ἀγίοις αὐτοῦ.

John 18:36; cf. I Cor. 4:1. 'Υπηρέτης is used of followers of Jesus only in John 18:36 and I Cor. 4:1 in the New Testament.

John 18:37; cf. Rom. 14:9. The εἰς τοῦτο is emphatic in both passages.

John 19:11; cf. Rom. 13:1. The conception of authority in both passages is the same.

John 19:14; cf. I Cor. 5:7, 8 and 15:20. The Synoptic tradition fixes Nisan 15 as the date of the Crucifixion, whereas John maintains that it took place on Nisan 14. The symbolism of

I Cor. 5:7, 8 and 15:20 accords with the Johannine chronology.
John was written in Ephesus, and it was from Ephesus that Paul
wrote I Corinthians. Paul may have established the quartodeciman
position in Ephesus.

 John 19:30; cf. Eph. 5:2. The representation of παραδί-
δωμι as Jesus' own act may reflect the influence of Ephesians.

 John 19:31; cf. I Cor. 5:7, 8; 15:20.

 Streeter thinks that John used "the ten Epistles of the
Apostle."[56] The probabilities certainly favor acquaintance with
the letters as a collection, and that collection almost certainly
contained our ten letters. However, no traces of acquaintance
with Philemon are found in the present study, and the indications
of familiarity with II Thessalonians are very slight. The evidence
for John's use of Ephesians, Romans, and Galatians is so strong as
to amount to practical certainty.

TABLE OF RESULTS

	A	B	C	Unclassed
Romans..............	2	16	18	14
I Corinthians.......	..	10	8	13
II Corinthians......	..	4	15	7
Galatians..........	2	4	8	10
Ephesians..........	3	12	18	13
Philippians.........	..	..	2	9
Colossians..........	..	6	6	5
I Thessalonians.....	..	..	3	8
II Thessalonians....	..	..	1	2
Philemon...........	..	..	..	....

The Johannine Epistles

 The probabilities are that the Johannine epistles were
written as a corpus rather than as separate letters. The suggestion for the writing of a corpus of letters as a medium of religious

---

[56]Op. cit., p. 371.

instruction would, as was noted with reference to the introductory
letter corpus in the Apocalypse, come naturally through acquaintance with the collected letters of Paul. It is more than a coincidence that the Johannine corpus follows the original sequence
of its Pauline model—an encyclical, a church letter, and a letter to an individual. Concrete evidence and all the probabilities
of the situation indicate that the author of these letters knew
the collected letters of Paul.

There are no quotations from the Old Testament in the
Johannine corpus.

I John 1:3   Philippians C   I Corinthians C
῞Ινα καὶ ὑμεῖς κοινωνίαν ἔχητε μεθ' ἡμῶν· καὶ ἡ κοινωνία
δὲ ἡ ἡμετέρα μετὰ τοῦ πατρὸς καὶ μετὰ τοῦ υἱοῦ αὐτοῦ 'Ιησοῦ Χριστοῦ·
Phil. 1:5. 'Επὶ τῇ κοινωνίᾳ ὑμῶν εἰς τὸ εὐαγγέλιον ἀπὸ τῆς
πρώτης ἡμέρας ἄχρι τοῦ νῦν. . . . . 3:10. Γνῶναι . . . . κοινωνίαν
παθημάτων αὐτοῦ.
I Cor. 1:9. Πιστὸς ὁ Θεὸς δι' οὗ ἐκλήθητε εἰς κοινωνίαν
τοῦ υἱοῦ αὐτοῦ 'Ιησοῦ Χριστοῦ τοῦ κυρίου ἡμῶν (cf. John 17:21).

The term κοινωνία occurs in the New Testament once in
Acts, thirteen times in Paul's letters, once in Hebrews, and four
times in I John. Its use in I John 1:3 corresponds with that of
Phil. 1:5 in the one instance and in the other with its use in
I Cor. 1:9. The second half of the Johannine statement sounds
like a free quotation of I Cor. 1:9. The verb κοινωνέω is limited
in the New Testament to the Pauline corpus, I Timothy, Hebrews,
I Peter, and II John.

I John 1:6   II Corinthians C
'Εὰν εἴπωμεν ὅτι κοινωνίαν ἔχομεν μετ' αὐτοῦ καὶ ἐν τῷ
σκότει περιπατῶμεν, ψευδόμεθα καὶ οὐ ποιοῦμεν τὴν ἀλήθειαν·
II Cor. 6:14. ῝Η τίς κοινωνία φωτὶ πρὸς σκότος;

The figurative use of "light" and "darkness" was widespread
in Jewish and early Christian writings (Philo, De somn. 1.75, De
abr. 205; Test. Levi 19:1; Test. Napth. 2:7; II En. 30:15; Ps. 92:
16; John 1:5-9; Jas. 1:13, 17). It is the combination of the figure with κοινωνία that suggests dependence on II Corinthians. For
the use of κοινωνία and κοινωνέω in the New Testament see the note
on I John 1:3.

I John 1:7   Colossians C

'Εὰν δὲ ἐν τῷ φωτὶ περιπατῶμεν ὡς αὐτὸς ἔστιν ἐν τῷ φωτὶ, κοινωνίαν ἔχομεν μετ' ἀλλήλων καὶ τὸ αἷμα 'Ιησοῦ τοῦ υἱοῦ αὐτοῦ καθαρίζει ἡμᾶς ἀπὸ πάσης ἁμαρτίας.

Col. 1:13, 14. ˚Ος ἐρύσατο ἡμᾶς ἐκ τῆς ἐξουσίας τοῦ σκότους καὶ μετέστησεν εἰς τὴν βασιλείαν τοῦ υἱοῦ τῆς ἀγάπης αὐτοῦ, ἐν ᾧ ⌜ἔχομεν⌝ τὴν ἀπολύτρωσιν, τὴν ἄφεσιν τῶν ἁμαρτιῶν· . . . . 20. Καὶ δι' αὐτοῦ ἀποκαταλλάξαι τὰ πάντα εἰς αὐτόν, εἰρηνοποιήσας διὰ τοῦ αἵματος τοῦ σταυροῦ αὐτοῦ, [δι' αὐτοῦ] εἴτε τὰ ἐπὶ τῆς γῆς εἴτε τὰ ἐν τοῖς οὐρανοῖς·

Like Colossians, I John combines the figurative use of light and darkness with the idea of purification from sin through the blood of Jesus Christ.

I John 2:1   Romans B

Καὶ ἐάν τις ἁμάρτῃ, παράκλητον ἔχομεν πρὸς τὸν πατέρα 'Ιησοῦν Χριστόν.

Rom. 8:34. Χριστὸς ['Ιησοῦς] . . . . ὅς ἐστιν ἐν δεξιᾷ τοῦ Θεοῦ, ὃς καὶ ἐντυγχάνει ὑπὲρ ἡμῶν (cf. Gal. 6:1).

The term παράκλητος occurs in the New Testament only in John 14:16, 26, 15:26, 16:7, and I John 2:1. The idea in the epistle differs, however, in that Christ's advocacy on the sinner's behalf is in heaven, whereas in John the place of his activity is on earth. Furthermore, in John the ministry of the Paraclete is to remind men of the meaning of Christ's message. The thought of I John finds a closer parallel in Rom. 8:34.

I John 2:2   Romans B

Αὐτὸς ἱλασμός ἐστιν περὶ τῶν ἁμαρτιῶν ἡμῶν, οὐ περὶ τῶν ἡμετέρων δὲ ⌜μόνον⌝ ἀλλὰ καὶ περὶ ὅλου τοῦ κόσμου.

Rom. 3:23-25. Πάντες γὰρ ἥμαρτον καὶ ὑστεροῦνται τῆς δόξης τοῦ Θεοῦ, δικαιούμενοι δωρεὰν τῇ αὐτοῦ χάριτι διὰ τῆς ἀπολυτρώσεως τῆς ἐν Χριστῷ 'Ιησοῦ· ὃν προέθετο ὁ Θεὸς ἱλαστήριον διὰ πίστεως ἐν τῷ αὐτοῦ αἵματι.

Paul's teaching in Romans on propitiation almost certainly has influenced I John. The description of Christ as ἱλασμὸς περὶ τῶν ἁμαρτιῶν ἡμῶν, together with the accompanying stress on the

universality of Christ's saving mission, corresponds closely with
the thought of Romans. Ἱλασμός is used in the New Testament only
in I John 2:3 and 4:10, and ἱλαστήριον only in Rom. 3:25 and Heb.
9:5. In I Cor. 1:30 Christ is called ἁγιασμός (cf. Gal. 3:13).

I John 2:3, 4   I Corinthians C

Καὶ ἐν τούτῳ γινώσκομεν ὅτι ἐγνώκαμεν αὐτόν, ἐὰν τὰς
ἐντολὰς αὐτοῦ τηρῶμεν.   ὁ λέγων ὅτι ᾿Έγνωκα αὐτόν καὶ τὰς ἐντολὰς
αὐτοῦ μὴ τηρῶν ψεύστης ἐστίν, καὶ ἐν τούτῳ ἡ ἀλήθεια οὐκ ἔστιν·
I Cor. 8:3, 4. Ἡ γνῶσις φυσιαῖ, ἡ δὲ ἀγάπη οἰκοδομεῖ.
εἴ τις δοκεῖ ἐγνωκέναι τι, οὔπω ἔγνω καθὼς δεῖ γνῶναι· εἰ δέ τις
ἀγαπᾷ τὸν Θεόν, οὗτος ἔγνωσται ὑπ᾽ αὐτοῦ (cf. John 14:21, 23 and 15:10).

The distinction between true and counterfeit "gnosis" and
the suggestion that ethical standards are the proper basis for
discriminating between the two probably indicates acquaintance
with I Corinthians. ᾿Έγνωκα αὐτόν may have been a sort of Gnostic
watchword to which Paul and the author of I John allude.

I John 2:8   Romans C   I Corinthians C
Ἡ σκοτία παράγεται καὶ τὸ φῶς τὸ ἀληθινὸν ἤδη φαίνει.
Rom. 13:12. Ἡ νὺξ προέκοψεν, ἡ δὲ ἡμέρα ἤγγικεν. ἀποθώ-
μεθα οὖν τὰ ἔργα τοῦ σκότους, ἐνδυσώμεθα [δὲ] τὰ ὅπλα τοῦ φωτός.
ὡς ἐν ἡμέρᾳ εὐσχημόνως περιπατήσωμεν.
I Cor. 7:31. Παράγει γὰρ τὸ σχῆμα τοῦ κόσμου τούτου

The teaching of I John regarding the Parousia is clearer
than that of the Pauline letters. Παράγω occurs in the Pauline
letters only in I Cor. 7:31. It is used in the New Testament, in
an eschatological sense only, in I Cor. 7:31 and I John 2:8, 17.
The context, however, agrees more closely with that of Rom. 13:12,
where the same eschatological ideas appear and where the figures
of light and darkness are an added point of resemblance.

I John 2:17   Romans C   I Corinthians C
Καὶ ὁ κόσμος παράγεται καὶ ἡ ἐπιθυμία [αὐτοῦ], ὁ δὲ ποιῶν
τὸ θέλημα τοῦ Θεοῦ μένει εἰς τὸν αἰῶνα.

For the text of Rom. 13:12 and I Cor. 7:31 and a discussion of their probable influence on I John see the note on 2:8.

I John 2:20, 21, 27   I Corinthians

Καὶ ὑμεῖς χρίσμα ἔχετε ἀπὸ τοῦ ἁγίου· ⌜οἴδατε πάντες _⌝ οὐκ ἔγραψα ὑμῖν ὅτι οὐκ οἴδατε τὴν ἀλήθειαν, ἀλλ' ὅτι οἴδατε αὐτήν, ... καὶ ὑμεῖς τὸ χρίσμα ὃ ἐλάβετε ἀπ' αὐτοῦ μένει ἐν ὑμῖν, καὶ οὐ χρείαν ἔχετε ἵνα τις διδάσκῃ ὑμᾶς ἀλλ' ὡς τὸ αὐτοῦ χρίσμα διδάσκει ὑμᾶς περὶ πάντων.

I Cor. 2:14, 15. Ψυχικὸς δὲ ἄνθρωπος οὐ δέχεται τὰ τοῦ πνεύματος τοῦ θεοῦ, μωρία γὰρ αὐτῷ ἐστίν, καὶ οὐ δύναται γνῶναι, ὅτι πνευματικῶς ἀνακρίνεται· ὁ δὲ πνευματικὸς ἀνακρίνει ⌜μὲν⌝ πάντα, αὐτὸς δὲ ὑπ' οὐδενὸς ἀνακρίνεται. 12:4. Διαιρέσεις δὲ χαρισμάτων εἰσίν . . . . 10. Ἄλλῳ [δὲ] διακρίσεις πνευμάτων.

Supernatural endowment as a prerequisite for the apprehension of spiritual truth is an emphasis that the author of I John may have received from Paul. With both writers the "gift discernment" is held in high regard.

I John 3:2, 3   Colossians C   Romans C

Ἀγαπητοί, νῦν τέκνα θεοῦ ἐσμέν, καὶ οὔπω ἐφανερώθη τί ἐσόμεθα. οἴδαμεν ὅτι ἐὰν φανερωθῇ ὅμοιοι αὐτῷ ἐσόμεθα, ὅτι ὀψόμεθα αὐτὸν καθώς ἐστιν. Καὶ πᾶς ὁ ἔχων τὴν ἐλπίδα ταύτην ἐπ' αὐτῷ ἁγνίζει ἑαυτὸν καθὼς ἐκεῖνος ἁγνός ἐστιν.

Col. 3:4. Ὅταν ὁ Χριστὸς φανερωθῇ, ἡ ζωὴ ⌜ἡμῶν⌝ τότε καὶ ὑμεῖς σὺν αὐτῷ φανερωθήσεσθε ἐν δόξῃ.

Rom. 8:17-20. Ἐσμὲν τέκνα θεοῦ. εἰ δὲ τέκνα, καὶ κληρονόμοι· κληρονόμοι μὲν θεοῦ, συνκληρονόμοι δὲ Χριστοῦ, ... Λογίζομαι γὰρ ὅτι οὐκ ἄξια τὰ παθήματα τοῦ νῦν καιροῦ πρὸς τὴν μέλλουσαν δόξαν ἀποκαλυφθῆναι εἰς ἡμᾶς. ἡ γὰρ ἀποκαραδοκία τῆς κτίσεως τὴν ἀποκάλυψιν τῶν υἱῶν τοῦ θεοῦ ἀπεκδέχεται·

The use of φανερόω in connection with the Parousia and the way in which the future of the believer is linked with that of the glorified Christ tends to relate I John 3:2 f. rather clearly to Col. 3:4.

The thought of the passage also resembles that of Rom. 8:17-20, and the emphasis on ἐλπίς points to a probable literary dependence. The "hope" described in both passages is the same in content. In the clause ὅτι ὀψόμεθα αὐτὸν καθώς ἐστιν there is a possible reminiscence of the thought of I Cor. 13:12.

I John 3:5   II Corinthians C
Καὶ οἴδατε ὅτι ἐκεῖνος ἐφανερώθη ἵνα τὰς ἁμαρτίας ἄρῃ,
καὶ ἁμαρτία ἐν αὐτῷ οὐκ ἔστιν.
II Cor. 5:21. Τὸν μὴ γνόντα ἁμαρτίαν ὑπὲρ ἡμῶν ἁμαρτίαν
ἐποίησεν, ἵνα ἡμεῖς γενώμεθα δικαιοσύνη Θεοῦ ἐν αὐτῷ.

The assertion of the sinlessness of Christ, who yet bore
the sin of men and took it away, is a probable reminiscence of II
Cor. 5:21.

I John 3:7, 8   Romans C
⌐Τεκνία⌐, μηδεὶς πλανάτω ὑμᾶς· ὁ ποιῶν τὴν δικαιοσύνην
δίκαιός ἐστιν, καθὼς ἐκεῖνος δίκαιός ἐστιν· ὁ ποιῶν τὴν ἁμαρτίαν
ἐκ τοῦ διαβόλου ἐστίν.
Rom. 6:1, 2. Τί οὖν ἐροῦμεν; ἐπιμένωμεν τῇ ἁμαρτίᾳ, ἵνα
ἡ χάρις πλεονάσῃ; μὴ γένοιτο· αἵτινες ἀπεθάνομεν τῇ ἁμαρτίᾳ,
πῶς ἔτι ζήσομεν ἐν αὐτῇ;

Both writers undertake to combat antinomianism. The "de-
ception" against which each warns is essentially the same, and the
opinion given is to the same effect.

I John 3:11   I Thessalonians C
Αὕτη ἐστὶν ἡ ἀγγελία ἣν ἠκούσατε ἀπ᾽ ἀρχῆς, ἵνα ἀγαπῶμεν
ἀλλήλους·
I Thess. 4:9. Περὶ δὲ τῆς φιλαδελφίας οὐ χρείαν ἔχετε
γράφειν ὑμῖν, αὐτοὶ γὰρ ὑμεῖς θεοδίδακτοί ἐστε εἰς ἀγαπᾶν ἀλλή-
λους· καὶ γὰρ ποιεῖτε αὐτὸ εἰς πάντας τοὺς ἀδελφοὺς [τοὺς] ἐν
ὅλῃ τῇ Μακεδονίᾳ.

The "teaching" to which reference is made is probably
early Christian teaching, although the use of Cain as an illustration in the succeeding context may mean that ἀπ᾽ ἀρχῆς looks
back to Genesis. It more probably has the sense of I Clem. 47:2,
Ἐν ἀρχῇ τοῦ εὐαγγελίου (cf. Polyc. 7:2, Ἐπὶ τὸν ἐξ ἀρχῆς ἡμῖν
παραδοθέντα λόγον ἐπιστρέψωμεν).

I John 4:1-3   I Corinthians B   I Thessalonians C
Ἀγαπητοί, μὴ παντὶ πνεύματι πιστεύετε, ἀλλὰ δοκιμάζετε
τὰ πνεύματα εἰ ἐκ τοῦ Θεοῦ ἐστίν, ὅτι πολλοὶ ψευδοπροφῆται ἐξελη-
λύθασιν εἰς τὸν κόσμον. Ἐν τούτῳ γινώσκετε τὸ πνεῦμα τοῦ Θεοῦ·

πᾶν πνεῦμα ὃ ὁμολογεῖ 'Ιησοῦν Χριστὸν ἐν σαρκὶ ⌜ἐληλυθότα⌝ ἐκ
τοῦ Θεοῦ ἐστίν, καὶ πᾶν πνεῦμα ὃ ⌜μὴ ὁμολογεῖ⌝ τὸν 'Ιησοῦν ἐκ
τοῦ Θεοῦ οὐκ ἔστιν·

I Cor. 12:3. Διὸ γνωρίζω ὑμῖν ὅτι οὐδεὶς ἐν πνεύματι Θεοῦ
λαλῶν λέγει 'Ανάθεμα 'Ιησοῦς, καὶ οὐδεὶς δύναται εἰπεῖν Κύριος
'Ιησοῦς εἰ μὴ ἐν πνεύματι ἁγίῳ. 10. "Αλλῳ [δὲ] διακρίσεις πνευμάτων.

I Thess. 5:20, 21. Τὸ πνεῦμα μὴ σβέννυτε . . . . πάντα [δὲ]
δοκιμάζετε, τὸ καλὸν κατέχετε. . . . (cf. Did.11:8-12, Hermas Mand. x1. 7-16).

In I Cor. 12:10 Paul indicates the need for discrimination
between "spirits," and in 12:3 he insists that a correct Christology is the proper basis on which a spirit is judged. The christo-
logical test indicated in I John is probably an adaptation of the
original Pauline test. The use of δοκιμάζω in connection with
πνεῦμα suggests acquaintance with I Thessalonians, the verb being
used in this sense in the New Testament only in I John and I Thessalonians.

I John 4:9-11   Romans B
'Εν τούτῳ ἐφανερώθη ἡ ἀγάπη τοῦ Θεοῦ ἐν ἡμῖν, ὅτι τὸν
υἱὸν αὐτοῦ τὸν μονογενῆ ἀπέσταλκεν ὁ Θεὸς εἰς τὸν κόσμον ἵνα
ζήσωμεν δι' αὐτοῦ. ἐν τούτῳ ἐστὶν ἡ ἀγάπη, οὐχ ὅτι ἡμεῖς ⌜ἠγαπή-
καμεν⌝ τὸν Θεόν, ἀλλ' ὅτι αὐτὸς ἠγάπησεν ἡμᾶς καὶ ἀπέστειλεν τὸν
υἱὸν αὐτοῦ ἱλασμὸν περὶ τῶν ἁμαρτιῶν ἡμῶν.

The author of I John seems to combine the ideas of Paul
as expressed in Rom. 5:8 (see the text and discussion in the note
on 3:1) and Rom. 3:23-25 (see the text and discussion in the note
on 2:2). The description of Christ as ἱλασμὸς περὶ τῶν ἁμαρτιῶν
ἡμῶν is a particularly strong reminder of Romans.

I John 4:16-18   Romans C
'Ο Θεὸς ἀγάπη ἐστίν, καὶ ὁ μένων ἐν τῇ ἀγάπῃ ἐν τῷ Θεῷ
μένει καὶ ὁ Θεὸς ἐν αὐτῷ [μένει]. 'Εν τούτῳ τετελείωται ἡ ἀγάπη
μεθ' ἡμῶν, ἵνα παρρησίαν ἔχωμεν ἐν τῇ ἡμέρᾳ τῆς κρίσεως, ὅτι καθὼς
ἐκεῖνός ἐστιν καὶ ἡμεῖς ἐσμεν ἐν τῷ κόσμῳ τούτῳ. φόβος οὐκ ἔστιν
ἐν τῇ ἀγάπῃ, ἀλλ' ἡ τελεία ἀγάπη ἔξω βάλλει τὸν φόβον.

Rom. 8:38, 39. Πέπεισμαι γὰρ ὅτι οὔτε θάνατος οὔτε ζωὴ
οὔτε ἄγγελοι . . . . οὔτε τις κτίσις ἑτέρα δυνήσεται ἡμᾶς χωρίσαι
ἀπὸ τῆς ἀγάπης τοῦ Θεοῦ τῆς ἐν Χριστῷ 'Ιησοῦ τῷ κυρίῳ ἡμῶν.

It is probable, as Carpenter suggests, that I John 4:16-18
is "a translation into Johannine speech of the impassioned experience of Paul, who defies the world and all its powers to separate
him from the love of God in Christ."[57]

II John 1   Ephesians C
'Ο Πρεσβύτερος ἐκλεκτῇ κυρίᾳ.

An examination of the data supplied by the letter and by
current literary practice makes it practically certain that II
John was addressed to a church and not to an individual.[58] This
description of a church as κυρία may be a reminiscence of the
representation of the church as the "bride of Christ" in Eph.
5:25-32. Windisch notes this as a possibility but regards it as
very questionable.[59] Moffatt does not urge the point but is more
impressed by it than Windisch seems to be.[60] The probable relation between the Johannine letters and the Pauline corpus being
what it is, the Ephesian origin of the figure is at least probable.

II John 3, 6   I Thessalonians C
'Εν ἀληθείᾳ καὶ ἀγάπῃ· . . . . καὶ αὕτη ἐστὶν ἡ ἀγάπη,
ἵνα περιπατῶμεν κατὰ τὰς ἐντολὰς αὐτοῦ· αὕτη ἡ ἐντολή ἐστιν,
καθὼς ἠκούσατε ἀπ' ἀρχῆς, ἵνα ἐν αὐτῇ περιπατῆτε (cf. Eph. 4:15
and 5:2).
For the text of I Thess. 4:9 see the note on 3:11.

II John 7   I Corinthians C
"Οτι πὀλλοὶ πλάνοι ἐξῆλθαν εἰς τὸν κόσμον, οἱ μὴ ὁμολο-
γοῦντες 'Ιησοῦν Χριστὸν ἐρχόμενον ἐν σαρκί· οὗτός ἐστιν ὁ πλάνος
καὶ ὁ ἀντίχριστος.

---

[57] J. Estlin Carpenter, The Johannine Writings (London:
Constable & Co., Ltd., 1927), p. 345.

[58] A. E. Brooke, A Critical and Exegetical Commentary on
the Johannine Epistles (New York: Charles Scribner's Sons, 1912),
pp. 166-69.

[59] Hans Windisch, Die katholischen Briefe (Tübingen:
J. C. B. Mohr, 1911), p. 133.

[60] Introduction, p. 476.

See the note on I John 4:1-3 for the text of I Cor. 12:3 and a discussion of the influence of that passage on the Johannine letters. The author probably conceives of the "anti-Christ" as being the embodiment of a false spirit and so adduces the christo-logical test whereby false spirits are distinguished.

Instances of possible literary reminiscence.—I John 1:1; cf. Phil. 2:16. The phrase ὁ λόγος τῆς ζωῆς occurs in the New Testament only in the two passages cited; cf. John 3:34 and 6:68.

I John 1:4; cf. II Cor. 1:24.

I John 1:8, 9; cf. Rom. 3:23.

I John 1:9; cf. Eph. 5:26. The use of καθαρίζω in I John 1:9 may reflect the influence of Eph. 5:26. The verb is used in the letters of the Pauline corpus in II Cor. 5:7 and Eph. 5:26. Its use in the Gospels is mainly in a literal or liturgical sense.

I John 2:1; cf. Gal. 4:19. The exact phrase τεκνία μου is found in the New Testament only in I John 2:1 and Gal. 4:19. In John 13:33 τεκνία without μου is used, and the use of τεκνίον occurs in John 13:33, Gal. 4:19, and seven times in I John.

I John 2:5, 6; cf. Phil. 3:8. The ἐν αὐτῷ of I John 2:6 has a distinctly Pauline connotation. It certainly indicates acquaintance with the Pauline type of Christianity and probably with the Pauline letters. The vocabulary of I John 2:5, 6, as well as its emphases, tends to relate it to Phil. 3:8-17. Note the use of τελειόω and περιπατέω, together with the emphasis on following the example of Christ as though this were involved in being ἐν αὐτῷ.

I John 2:9, 10; cf. Gal. 5:14 and Rom. 14:13.

I John 2:11; cf. II Cor. 4:4. The verb τυφλόω occurs in the New Testament only in John 12:40, II Cor. 4:4, and I John 2:11. In John 12:40 it is in a quotation of Isa. 6:10.

I John 2:12; cf. I Cor. 6:11.

I John 2:16; cf. Gal. 5:16. The sense in which ἐπιθυμία is used in I John 2:16 is Pauline. The contrast involved is fre-quently employed in Paul's letters, but most strikingly in Gal. 5:16-24.

I John 2:18; cf. II Thess. 2:3-12. The actual word ἀντίχριστος appears in the New Testament only in I John 2:18, 22, 4:3, and II John 7. Its sense is the equivalent of παρείσκαται ψευδάδελφοι of Gal. 2:4. The eschatological emphasis of the passage reminds one strongly of II Thess. 2:3-12, where the appearance of ὁ ἄνθρωπος τῆς ἀνομίας, ὁ υἱὸς ἀπωλείας heralds the end of the age.

I John 2:28; cf. Col. 3:4.

I John 3:1; cf. Rom. 5:8 and 8:17.

I John 3:16; cf. II Cor. 5:14, 15.

I John 3:22; cf. Eph. 3:12. The use of παρρησία in description of the attitude of Christians toward God suggests indebtedness to Ephesians or, possibly, to Hebrews.

I John 3:24; cf. Rom. 8:9.

I John 4:7; cf. I Cor. 8:3.

I John 5:1; cf. I Cor. 12:3.

I John 5:10; cf. Rom. 8:16.

II John 8; cf. Gal. 4:11.

II John 12; cf. II Cor. 3:3. Μέλας is used in the sense of ink only in II Cor. 3:3, II John, chapter 12, and III John, chapter 13 in the New Testament. There is the bare possibility that in II and III John there is a play on the word and an indirect allusion to II Cor. 3:3.

III John 1; cf. Rom. 16:23 and I Cor. 1:14. The practice in pseudepigraphic writings of using the names of known characters to give the atmosphere of reality to their compositions suggests the possibility that the author of II John has used Gaius of Paul's letters in this way. He seems to have been a man who might appropriately be addressed as ὁ ἀγαπητός.

III John 4; cf. I Cor. 4:15.

III John 6; cf. I Thess. 2:12. Ἀξίως is used in the New Testament only in the Pauline letters and II John. The phrase ἀξίως τοῦ Θεοῦ occurs only in I Thess. 2:12 and III John 6.

III John 7, 8; cf. I Cor. 4:12, 9:6, and 16-18. Repeatedly in I Corinthians Paul affirms his right to support and yet insists by example and assertion that his real rewards are spiritual. This position may be reflected in III John.

TABLE OF RESULTS

	A	B	C	Unclassed
Romans..............	.	3	5	6
I Corinthians.......	.	1	6	7
II Corinthians......	.	.	2	4
Galatians...........	.	.	.	5
Ephesians...........	.	.	1	3
Philippians.........	.	.	1	2
Colossians..........	.	.	2	1
I Thessalonians.....	.	.	3	1
II Thessalonians....	.	.	.	1
Philemon............	.	.	.	....

The Epistles of St. Ignatius

The conditions under which Ignatius wrote his letters must be kept in mind in an examination of his allusions to literature. He was a prisoner under guard. His own description of his circumstances implies an environment adverse to careful literary reference. He says (Rom. 5:1): Ἀπὸ Συρίας μέχρι ᾽Ρώμης θηριομαχῶ, διὰ γῆς καὶ θαλάσσης, νυκτὸς καὶ ἡμέρας, δεδεμένος δέκα λεοπάρδοις, ὅ ἐστιν στρατιωτικὸν τάγμα. οἳ καὶ εὐεργετούμενοι χείρους γίνονται. This statement and the other data of the letters indicate that Ignatius was without any manuscripts and that all his allusions to the writings of our Old and New Testaments were from memory. His allusions are, accordingly, free and inexact. Nevertheless, it is entirely clear in given instances that his recollection looks back to literary sources.

His references to the Old Testament writings are comparatively rare. In some instances they are introduced with such formulas as: Eph. 5:3, γέγραπται γάρ; ᾽Υπερηφάνοις ὁ Θεὸς ἀντιτάσσεται; and Magn. 12:1, ὡς γέγραπται, ὅτι ὁ δίκαιος ἑαυτοῦ κατήγορος. Philad. 8:2 refers to the Old Testament as Scripture with the formula ὅτι γέγραπται, but without a specific passage in mind. Most frequently his allusions to Old Testament writings are without introductory formulas—as Eph. 15:1, cf. Ps. 33:9; Magn. 10:3, cf. Isa. 66:18; Magn. 13:1, cf. Ps. 1:3; Trall. 8:2, cf. Isa. 52:5; Smyrn. 1:2, cf. Isa. 5:26.

In the concluding statement of Eph. 12:2, Ignatius reveals
his knowledge of a collection of Pauline letters: Παύλου . . . .
ὃς ἐν πάσῃ ἐπιστολῇ μνημονεύει ὑμῶν ἐν Χριστῷ 'Ιησοῦ.[61] There
are, however, no direct quotations of the letters by Ignatius, although there are many unmistakable allusions in which their use is
clear.

Ignatius to the Ephesians

| Inscription | Ephesians B |

'Ιγνάτιος, ὁ καὶ Θεοφόρος, τῇ εὐλογημένῃ ἐν μεγέθει Θεοῦ
πατρὸς πληρώματι, τῇ προωρισμένῃ πρὸ αἰώνων εἶναι διὰ παντὸς εἰς
δόξαν παράμονον ἄτρεπτον, ἡνωμένη καὶ ἐκλελεγμένη ἐν πάθει ἀληθινῷ,
ἐν θελήματι τοῦ πατρὸς καὶ 'Ιησοῦ Χριστοῦ τοῦ Θεοῦ ἡμῶν, τῇ ἐκκλησίᾳ τῇ ἀξιομακαρίστῳ, τῇ οὔσῃ ἐν 'Εφέσῳ τῆς 'Ασίας, πλεῖστα ἐν 'Ιησοῦ Χριστῷ καὶ ἐν ἀμώμῳ χαρᾷ χαίρειν.

Eph. 1:3-12. Εὐλογητὸς ὁ Θεὸς καὶ πατὴρ . . . . ὁ εὐλογήσας ἡμᾶς ἐν πάσῃ εὐλογίᾳ . . . . καθὼς ἐξελέξατο ἡμᾶς . . . . πρὸ
καταβολῆς κόσμου, εἶναι ἡμᾶς . . . . ἀμώμους . . . . προορίσας ἡμᾶς
. . . . κατὰ τὴν εὐδοκίαν τοῦ θελήματος αὐτοῦ . . . . διὰ τοῦ αἵματος αὐτοῦ . . . . τοῦ πληρώματος τῶν καιρῶν . . . . προορισθέντες
κατὰ πρόθεσιν τοῦ τὰ πάντα ἐνεργοῦντος κατὰ τὴν βουλὴν τοῦ θελήματος αὐτοῦ, εἰς τὸ εἶναι ἡμᾶς εἰς ἔπαινον δόξης αὐτοῦ.

The phrases noted in Eph. 1:3-12 have parallels in the inscription to Ignatius' letter to the Ephesians. They constitute
evidence for literary acquaintance that is cumulative in character. The propriety with which Ignatius might have adopted the
language of his predecessor strengthens the probability that he
did so. Many of the expressions are almost certainly reminiscences
of Ephesians. They are used in special adaptation to Ignatius'
purpose; but that is to be expected in free quotation, and it does
not reduce the likelihood that Ignatius was indebted to Ephesians.

| Eph. 1:1 | Ephesians C |

Μιμηταὶ ὄντες Θεοῦ.
Eph. 5:1. Γίνεσθε οὖν μιμηταὶ τοῦ Θεοῦ.

---

[61]Goodspeed, New Solutions, p. 37; and Harnack, op. cit.,
p. 72.

It is probable that the expression was borrowed from Ephesians 5:1, which is its only occurrence in the New Testament. The
context with its exhortation to kindliness and forgiveness strengthens this probability.

Eph. 2:1   Colossians B
Περὶ δὲ τοῦ συνδούλου μου Βούρρου, τοῦ κατὰ Θεὸν διακόνου
ὑμῶν.

Col. 1:7. Καθὼς ἐμάθετε ἀπὸ 'Επαφρᾶ τοῦ ἀγαπητοῦ συνδούλου ἡμῶν, ὅς ἐστιν πιστὸς ὑπὲρ ⌐ἡμῶν⌐ διάκονος τοῦ Χριστοῦ.   4:7.
Τὰ κατ' ἐμὲ πάντα γνωρίσει ὑμῖν Τύχικος ὁ ἀγαπητὸς ἀδελφὸς καὶ·
πιστὸς διάκονος καὶ σύνδουλος ἐν κυρίῳ.

The term σύνδουλος occurs in the Pauline letters only in
Col. 1:7 and 4:7. In the one instance it is applied to Epaphras
and in the other to Tychicus. In each case πιστὸς διάκονος is a
further element in the characterization. In the letters of
Ignatius the term occurs in Eph. 2:1, Philad. 4:1, and Smyrn. 12:2,
each time in connection with διάκονος. The usage in these instances
strongly suggests acquaintance with Colossians. Lightfoot[62] and
Bauer[63] are both of the opinion that Ignatius is influenced by the
passages in Colossians.

Eph. 8:2   Romans C
Οἱ σαρκικοὶ τὰ πνευματικὰ πράσσειν οὐ δύνανται, οὐδε οἱ
πνευματικοὶ· τὰ σαρκινά.

Rom. 8:5, 8. Οἱ γὰρ κατὰ σάρκα ὄντες τὰ τῆς σαρκὸς φρονοῦσιν, οἱ δὲ κατὰ πνεῦμα τὰ τοῦ πνεύματος . . . . οἱ δὲ ἐν σαρκὶ
ὄντες Θεῷ ἀρέσαι οὐ δύνανται.

Ignatius' employment of σάρξ in the strong ethical sense
so characteristic of Paul suggests dependence on Rom. 8:5, 8. The
contrasts into which his thought is cast strengthen this suggestion.

-----

[62] J. B. Lightfoot, St. Paul's Epistles to Colossians and
Philemon9 (1890), p. 234.

[63] Walter Bauer, Die Briefe des Ignatius von Antiochia und
des Polykarpbrief (Tübingen: J. C. B. Mohr, 1920), p. 199.

Eph. 12:2   Ephesians B

Παύλου συμμύσται τοῦ ἡγιασμένου. τοῦ μεμαρτυρημένου, ἀξιο-
μακαρίστου, οὗ γένοιτό μοι ὑπὸ τὰ ἴχνη εὑρεθῆναι, ὅταν Θεοῦ ἐπιτύχω, ὃς ἐν πάσῃ ἐπιστολῇ μνημονεύει ὑμῶν ἐν Χριστῷ 'Ιησοῦ.

Eph. 1:9. Τὸ μυστήριον τοῦ θελήματος αὐτοῦ.   3:3, 4, 9.
Κατὰ ἀποκάλυψιν ἐγνωρίσθη μοι τὸ μυστήριον . . . . ἐν τῷ μυστηρίῳ
τοῦ Χριστοῦ . . . . καὶ φωτίσαι τίς ἡ οἰκονομία τοῦ μυστηρίου τοῦ
ἀποκεκρυμμένου ἀπὸ τῶν αἰώνων ἐν τῷ Θεῷ.   5:32. Τὸ μυστήριον τοῦ-
τα μέγα ἐστίν.   6:19. 'Εν παρρησίᾳ γνωρίσαι τὸ μυστήριον [τοῦ εὐαγ-
γελίου].

The phrase συμμύσται Παύλου may be a reminiscence of the
presentation of Christianity as a μυστήριον in Ephesians. Whether
that be true or not, Ignatius almost certainly had Ephesians in
mind. 'In the phrase ἐν πάσῃ ἐπιστολῇ he reflects acquaintance
with a number of letters, perhaps a corpus, which circulate under
Paul's name.   Interpreted literally, as Bauer feels is required,[64]
the statement is simply hyperbole, for, excluding the Pastorals
(I Tim. 1:3; II Tim. 1:18 and 4:12), Ephesus is mentioned only in
I Cor. 15:32 and 16:8, although it is probably in mind in Rom.
16:5, I Cor. 16:19, and II Cor. 1:8.   There is no necessity for
stressing the hyperbole or for maintaining that Ignatius had just
the passages enumerated in mind or for holding that he knew only
those letters in which there are allusions to Ephesus and to Asian
Christianity.   The probabilities are that there is here the reflection of a corpus of Pauline letters assembled at Ephesus and introduced by our Ephesians, which would make every letter in the corpus
a reminder of the city and group where the publication took place.[65]
In this case Ephesians would clearly be in Ignatius' thought.

Eph. 15:3   I Corinthians C
Πάντα οὖν ποιῶμεν ὡς αὐτοῦ ἐν ἡμῖν κατοικοῦντος, ἵνα ὦμεν
αὐτοῦ ναοὶ καὶ αὐτὸς ἐν ἡμῖν Θεὸς ἡμῶν.

I Cor. 3:16, 17. Οὐκ οἴδατε ὅτι ναὸς Θεοῦ ἐστὲ καὶ τὸ
πνεῦμα τοῦ Θεοῦ ⌜ἐν ὑμῖν οἰκεῖ⌝. . . . ὁ γὰρ ναὸς τοῦ Θεοῦ ἅγιος
ἐστιν οἵτινές ἐστε ὑμεῖς (cf. II Cor. 6:16).

_____
[64]Ibid., p. 212.

[65]E. J. Goodspeed, Formation of the New Testament (Chicago:
University of Chicago Press, 1926), p. 28; and New Solutions, p. 8.

The analogy and its essential application are the same in
Ignatius and Paul. A proper self-respect and development are the
common objectives of their exhortations. Both insist on their positions in view of the relationship to God in which the Christian
stands and the service to God which he should perform. The more
extended development of the figure in I Corinthians affords more
points of similarity, but it is entirely possible that II Corinthians also contributed to Ignatius' thought.

Eph. 16:1   I Corinthians B

Μὴ πλανᾶσθε, ἀδελφαί μου. αἱ οἰκοφθόραι βασιλείαν Θεοῦ
οὐ κληρονομήσουσιν.

I Cor. 6:9, 10. ᾿Η οὐκ οἴδατε ὅτι ἄδικοι Θεοῦ βασιλείαν
οὐ κληρονομήσουσιν; μὴ πλανᾶσθε. οὔτε πόρναι οὔτε εἰδωλολάτραι
οὔτε μοιχοὶ οὔτε μαλακοὶ . . . . βασιλείαν Θεοῦ κληρονομήσουσιν.

The οἰκοφθόραι of Ignatius has a close parallel in μοιχοί
of I Corinthians. Ignatius uses the warning against seduction to
illustrate the seriousness of disrupting the unity of the church
by false teaching. He frequently adapts his unmistakable allusions in this fashion, but the adaptations do not reduce the probability of literary dependence.

Eph. 18:1   I Corinthians A

Περίψημα τὸ ἐμὸν πνεῦμα τοῦ σταυροῦ, ὅ ἐστιν σκάνδαλον
τοῖς ἀπιστοῦσιν, ἡμῖν δὲ σωτηρία καὶ ζωὴ αἰώνιος. ποῦ σοφός;
ποῦ συζητητής; ποῦ καύχησις τῶν λεγομένων συνετῶν;

I Cor. 1:18-23. ῾Ο λόγος γὰρ ὁ τοῦ σταυροῦ τοῖς μὲν ἀπολλυμένοις μωρία ἐστίν, τοῖς δὲ σωζομένοις ἡμῖν δύναμις Θεοῦ ἐστίν.
γέγραπται γάρ, ᾿Απολῶ τὴν σοφίαν τῶν σοφῶν, καὶ τὴν σύνεσιν τῶν
συνετῶν ἀθετήσω. ποῦ σοφός; ποῦ γραμματεύς; ποῦ συνζητητὴς τοῦ
αἰῶνος τούτου . . . . ἡμεῖς δὲ κηρύσσομεν Χριστὸν ἐσταυρωμένον,
᾿Ιουδαίοις μεν σκάνδαλον (cf. Gal. 5:11 and Isa. 29:14 and 33:18).

The phrase τὸ σκάνδαλον τοῦ σταυροῦ of Gal. 5:11 is a
striking one and may have been in Ignatius' mind along with I Cor.
1:18-23. The terms all occur in the latter passage, however; and,
since that passage almost certainly influenced Ignatius, the terms
of this phrase could as well have come from it.

Paul's ποῦ σοφός κτλ. represents a free quotation of Isa.

33:18. Ignatius very evidently follows Paul rather than the **LXX**
in his series of rhetorical questions. The clause ποῦ καύχησις
τῶν λεγομένων συνετῶν is Ignatius' own, but, as Lightfoot suggests,
it was probably "suggested by the quotation from Isa. 29:14 . . . .
which S. Paul introduced into his context (1:19), combined with
other expressions of the Apostle in this neighborhood (1:31)."[66]

Eph. 18:2   Romans B

'Εκ σπέρματος μὲν Δαυείδ, πνεύματος δὲ ἁγίου (cf. Smyrn.
1:1).

Rom. 1:3, 4. Τοῦ γενομένου ἐκ σπέρματος Δαυεὶδ κατὰ σάρκα,
τοῦ ὁρισθέντος υἱοῦ Θεοῦ ἐν δυνάμει κατὰ πνεῦμα ἁγιωσύνης.

Emphasis on the Davidic descent of Jesus was common in
early Christian thought. Ignatius' phraseology is distinctly
Pauline, however, and this is more pronounced if the present passage be taken together with Smyrn. 1:1.

Eph. 19:3   Romans C

"Αγνοια καθηρεῖτα, παλαιὰ βασιλεία διεφθείρετο Θεοῦ ἀνθρω-
πίνως φανερουμένου εἰς καινότητα αἰδίου ζωῆς.

Rom. 6:4. Οὕτως καὶ ἡμεῖς ἐν καινότητι ζωῆς περιπατήσωμεν.
7:6. "Ωστε δουλεύειν [ἡμᾶς] ἐν καινότητι πνεύματος.

The only occurrences of καινότης in the New Testament are
Rom. 6:4 and 7:6. In the writings of the Apostolic Fathers the
term occurs twice, both times in Ignatius' letters (Magn. 9:1, εἰς
καινότητα ἐλπίδος). In the present instances each writer is describing the purpose of God's self-disclosure in Christ.

Eph. 20:1   Ephesians C

Προσδηλώσω ὑμῖν ἧς ἡρξάμην οἰκονομίας εἰς τὸν καινὸν ἄνθρωπον 'Ιησοῦν Χριστόν.

Eph. 2:15. "Ινα τοὺς δύο κτίσῃ ἐν αὐτῷ εἰς ἕνα καινὸν ἄνθρωπον ποιῶν εἰρηνην. 4:24. Καὶ ἐνδύσασθαι τὸν καινὸν ἄνθρωπον
τὸν κατὰ Θεὸν (cf. I Cor. 15:45, 47).

The thought of Ignatius finds an equivalent in I Cor. 15:45,
47, but his phraseology is more nearly akin to that of Ephesians.

---

[66]Apostolic Fathers, II, Part II, 1, 74.

Eph. 20:2   Romans B

'Εν 'Ιησοῦ Χριστῷ, τῷ κατὰ σάρκα ἐκ γένους Δαυείδ, τῷ υἱῷ ἀνθρώπου καὶ υἱῷ Θεοῦ.

Rom. 1:3, 4. For the text and a discussion of the probable influence of this passage on Ignatius see the comment on Eph. 18:2.

Ignatius to the Magnesians

Magn. 2:1   Colossians B

Καὶ τοῦ συνδούλου μου διακόνου Ζωτίωνος.

Col. 1:7 and 4:7. For the text and discussion see the note on Ign. Eph. 2:1.

Magn. 10:2   I Corinthians B

'Υπέρθεσθε οὖν τὴν κακὴν ζύμην, τὴν παλαιωθεῖσαν καὶ ἐνοξίσασαν, καὶ μεταβάλεσθε εἰς νέαν ζύμην ὅ ἐστιν 'Ιησοῦς Χριστός.

I Cor. 5:7. Οὐκ οἴδατε ὅτι μικρὰ ζύμη ὅλον τὸ φύραμα ζυμαῖ; ἐκκαθάρατε τὴν παλαιὰν ζύμην, ἵνα ἦτε νέον φύραμα, καθώς ἐστε ἄζυμοι. καὶ γὰρ τὸ πάσχα ἡμῶν ἐτύθη Χριστός.

Ignatius seems to be making a free quotation of I Cor. 5:7. He carries the metaphor through more logically in that he makes Christ the "new yeast," whereas Paul makes him the new Passover.

Ignatius to the Trallians

Trall. 2:3   I Corinthians B

Δεῖ δὲ καὶ τοὺς διακόνους ὄντας μυστηρίων 'Ιησοῦ Χριστοῦ κατὰ πάντα τρόπον πᾶσιν ἀρέσκειν.

I Cor. 4:1. Οὕτως ἡμᾶς λογιζέσθω ἄνθρωπος ὡς ὑπηρέτας Χριστοῦ καὶ οἰκονόμους μυστηρίον Θεοῦ. 10:32, 33. 'Απρόσκοποι καὶ 'Ιουδαίοις γίνεσθε καὶ "Ελλησιν καὶ τῇ ἐκκλησίᾳ τοῦ Θεοῦ, καθὼς κἀγὼ πάντα πᾶσιν ἀρέσκω, μὴ ζητῶν τὸ ἐμαυτοῦ σύμφορον ἀλλὰ τὸ τῶν πολλῶν, ἵνα σωθῶσιν.

There are rather clear traces of I Cor. 4:1 and of 10:32, 33 in Trall. 2:3. Τοὺς διακόνους ὄντας μυστηρίων 'Ιησοῦ Χριστοῦ appears to be an echo of ὑπηρέτας Χριστοῦ καὶ οἰκονόμους μυστηρίων Θεοῦ. Κατὰ πάντα τρόπον πᾶσιν ἀρέσκειν is with equal probability a reminiscence of κἀγὼ πάντα πᾶσιν ἀρέσκω.

Trall. 5:1   I Corinthians B

Μὴ οὐ δύναμαι ὑμῖν τὰ ἐπουράνια γράψαι; ἀλλὰ φοβοῦμαι,
μὴ νηπίοις οὖσιν ὑμῖν βλάβην παραθῶ. καὶ συγγνωμονεῖτέ μοι, μή-
ποτε οὐ δυνηθέντες χωρῆσαι στραγγαλωθῆτε.

I Cor. 3:1-3. Κἀγώ, ἀδελφοί, οὐκ ἠδυνήθην λαλῆσαι ὑμῖν
ὡς πνευματικοῖς ἀλλ' ὡς σαρκίνοις, ὡς νηπίοις ἐν Χριστῷ. γαλα
ὑμᾶς ἐπότισα, οὐ βρῶμα, οὔπω γὰρ ἐδύνασθε. ἀλλ' οὐδὲ [ἔτι] νῦν
δύνασθε.

In his characterization of the Trallians, Ignatius seems
to make a free paraphrase of I Cor. 3:1-3. The order of the items
enumerated and the description of each remind one unmistakably of
the Corinthians passage. The Pauline picture of the children who
could take no stronger nourishment than milk was almost certainly
in Ignatius' memory.

Trall. 5:2   Colossians C

Καὶ τὰς συστάσεις τὰς ἀρχοντικάς, ὁρατά τε καὶ ἀόρατα.

Col. 1:16. Ἐν αὐτῷ ἐκτίσθη τὰ πάντα ἐν τοῖς οὐρανοῖς
καὶ ἐπὶ τῆς γῆς, τὰ ὁρατά, καὶ τὰ ἀόρατα, εἴτε θρόνοι εἴτε κυριό-
τητες εἴτε ἀρχαὶ εἴτε ἐξουσίαι.

Ignatius has reproved the Trallians for their spiritual
immaturity. In comparison with that immaturity he describes his
own ability as a mature disciple to understand τὰ ἐπουράνια καὶ
τὰς τοποθεσίας τὰς ἀγγελικὰς καὶ τὰς συστάσεις τὰς ἀρχοντικάς,
ὁρατά τε καὶ ἀόρατα. These are the things which Paul says in
Colossians were created by the pre-existent Christ.

Trall. 10:1   I Corinthians B

Ἐγὼ τί δέδεμαι, τί δὲ καὶ εὔχομαι θηριομαχῆσαι; δωρεὰν
οὖν ἀποθνήσκω. ἄρα οὖν καταψεύδομαι τοῦ κυρίου.

I Cor. 15:14, 15, 32. Εἰ δὲ Χριστὸς οὐκ ἐγήγερται, κενὸν
ἄρα τὸ κήρυγμα ἡμῶν, κενὴ καὶ ἡ πίστις ⌜ἡμῶν⌝, εὑρισκόμεθα δὲ καὶ
ψευδομάρτυρες τοῦ Θεοῦ . . . . εἰ κατὰ ἄνθρωπον ἐθηριομάχησα ἐν
Ἐφέσῳ, τί μοι τὸ ὄφελος;

The argument of I Cor. 15:15 is clearly reflected in ἄρα
οὖν καταψεύδομαι τοῦ κυρίου of Trall. 10:1, as is also the allusion
to fighting with wild beasts in verse 32.

Trall. 12:3   I Corinthians C

Ἵνα μὴ ἀδόκιμος εὑρεθῶ.

I Cor. 9:27. Μή πως ἄλλοις κηρύξας αὐτὸς ἀδόκιμος γένωμαι.

The imagery of both statements is that of the race.
Ignatius' concern lest he as a leader should miss the Christian
goal sounds very much like Paul.

Ignatius to the Romans

Rom. 2:1   I Thessalonians C

Οὐ γὰρ θέλω ὑμᾶς ἀνθρωπαρεσκῆσαι, ἀλλὰ Θεῷ ἀρέσαι, ὥσπερ
καὶ ἀρέσκετε.

I Thess. 2:4. Οὐχ ὡς ἀνθρώποις ἀρέσκοντες ἀλλὰ Θεῷ τῷ
δοκιμάζοντι τὰς καρδίας ἡμῶν (cf. Gal. 1:10, ἢ ζητῶ ἀνθρώποις ἀρέσκειν; Eph. 6:6 and Col. 3:22, ὡς ἀνθρωπάρεσκοι).

The verb ἀνθρωπαρεσκεῖν is used neither in the Old nor in
the New Testament nor in contemporary Greek. The noun occurs in
Col. 3:22, Eph. 6:6, and Ps. 52:6. The contrast involved in
Ignatius' statement is found in I Thess. 2:4 and Gal. 1:10, but
more fully in the former than in the latter.

Rom. 4:3   I Corinthians B

'Ἀλλ' ἐὰν πάθω, ἀπελεύθερος γενήσομαι 'Ιησοῦ Χριστοῦ ἀνα-
στήσομαι ἐν αὐτῷ ἐλεύθερος.

I Cor. 7:22. Ὁ γὰρ ἐν κυρίῳ κληθεὶς δοῦλος ἀπελεύθερος
κυρίου ἐστίν. ὁμοίως ὁ ἐλεύθερος κληθεὶς δοῦλος ἐστιν Χριστοῦ.

The expression ἀπελεύθερος κυρίου of I Cor. 7:22 is probably reflected in ἀπελεύθερος γενήσομαι 'Ιησοῦ Χριστοῦ of Ignatius.
The term ἀπελεύθερος occurs in the New Testament only in I Cor.
7:22.

Rom. 5:1   I Corinthians A

'Ἐν δὲ τοῖς ἀδικήμασιν αὐτῶν μᾶλλον μαθητεύομαι, ἀλλ' οὐ
παρὰ τοῦτο δεδικαίωμαι.

I Cor. 4:4. Οὐδὲν γὰρ ἐμαυτῷ σύνοιδα, ἀλλ' οὐκ ἐν τούτῳ
δεδικαίωμαι, ὁ δὲ ἀνακρίνων με κύριός ἐστιν.

The second clause of Ignatius' statement is apparently a

free quotation of the second clause of I Cor. 4:4. Παρὰ τοῦτο is
substituted for ἐν τούτῳ, but this does not alter the sense, and
it is the kind of variation that is natural in free quotation.

    Rom. 6:1   I Corinthians C

Καλόν μοι ἀποθανεῖν εἰς Χριστὸν 'Ιησοῦν, ἢ βασιλεύειν τῶν
περάτων τῆς γῆς.

    I Cor. 9:15. Οὐκ ἔγραψα δὲ ταῦτα ἵνα οὕτως γένηται ἐν
ἐμοί, καλὸν γάρ μοι μᾶλλον ἀποθανεῖν ἢ τὸ καύχημά μου οὐδεὶς κενώσει.

    The context of these passages is entirely different. The
probability of literary relationship is suggested by the phrase
καλὸν μοι ἀποθανεῖν, which seems to be an echo of καλὸν γάρ μοι
μᾶλλον ἀποθανεῖν ἤ.

    Rom. 7:3   Romans B

Τοῦ ἐκ σπέρματος Δαυείδ.

    Rom. 1:3. For the text and the probability of its influ-
ence on Ignatius see the discussion of Ign. Eph. 18:2.

    Rom. 9:2   I Corinthians A

'Εγὼ δὲ αἰσχύνομαι ἐξ αὐτῶν λέγεσθαι. οὐδὲ γὰρ ἄξιος
εἰμι, ὧν ἔσχατος αὐτῶν καὶ ἔκτρωμα. ἀλλ' ἠλέημαι τις εἶναι, ἐὰν
Θεοῦ ἐπιτύχω.

    I Cor. 15:8, 9. "Εσχατον δὲ πάντων ὡσπερεὶ τῷ ἐκτρώματι
ὤφθη κἀμοί. 'Εγὼ γὰρ εἰμι ὁ ἐλάχιστος τῶν ἀποστόλων, ὃς οὐκ εἰμὶ
ἱκανὸς καλεῖσθαι ἀπόστολος . . . . χάριτι δὲ Θεοῦ εἰμὶ ὃ εἰμι.

    The word ἔκτρωμα occurs in the New Testament only in I
Corinthians. It is used in the sense in which Paul employed it in
the LXX (Num. 12:12, Job 3:16, Eccles. 6:3), and Paul's usage may
have been suggested by that source. Ignatius' application of the
term, however, and the passage as a whole show the clear influence
of I Cor. 15:8, 9.

Ignatius to the Philadelphians

    Philad. 1:1   Galatians C

῝Ον ἐπίσκοπον ἔγνων οὐκ ἀφ' ἑαυτοῦ οὐδὲ δι ἀνθρώπων κεκτῆσ-
θαι τὴν διακονίαν τὴν εἰς τὸ κοινὸν ἀνήκουσαν οὐδὲ κατὰ κενοδοξίαν.

    Gal. 1:1. Παυλος ἀπόστολος, οὐκ ἀπ' ἀνθρώπων οὐδὲ δι' ἀν-
θρώπου ἀλλὰ διὰ 'Ιησοῦ Χριστοῦ καὶ Θεοῦ πατρός (cf. Phil. 2:16).

Ignatius was concerned to exalt the episcopal office. As a means to that end he insists on the divine commission under which bishops work. Paul's description of the origin of his own call in Gal. 1:1 as οὐκ ἀπ' ἀνθρώπων οὐδὲ δι' ἀνθρώπου would suit Ignatius' purpose most acceptably, and it is probably echoed in οὐδὲ δι' ἀνθρώπων of Philad. 1:1. His further descriptive phrase οὐδὲ κατὰ κενοδοξίαν is a possible trace of the influence of Phil. 2:16.

Philad. 3:3   I Corinthians C
Μὴ πλανᾶσθε, ἀδελφοί μου. εἴ τις σχίζοντι ἀκολουθεῖ βασιλείαν Θεοῦ οὐ κληρονομεῖ.

The μὴ πλανᾶσθε and βασιλείαν Θεοῦ οὐ κληρονομεῖ of Philadelphians are reminders of I Cor. 6:9, 10 (cf. Gal. 5:21 and Eph. 5:5). The evidence for dependence is not so strong as in the case of Ign. Eph. 16:1, however, because there is no item in the list of vices in I Corinthians to correspond with the "schismatics" condemned by Ignatius, unless, indeed, they were generally understood to be immoral. In I Cor. 1:10-17 Paul deals with the problem of schism in the church, and it is possible that Ignatius had the thought of the two passages from Corinthians in mind.

Philad. 4:1   I Corinthians B
Μία γὰρ σὰρξ τοῦ κυρίου ἡμῶν 'Ιησοῦ Χριστοῦ καὶ ἓν ποτήριον εἰς ἕνωσιν τοῦ αἵματος αὐτοῦ.
I Cor. 10:16, 17. Τὸ ποτήριον . . . . οὐχὶ κοινωνία ἐστὶν τοῦ αἵματος τοῦ Χριστοῦ; . . . . ὅτι εἷς ἄρτος, ἓν σῶμα οἱ πολλοί ἐσμεν, οἱ γὰρ πάντες ἐκ τοῦ ἑνὸς ἄρτου μετέχομεν.

The traces of acquaintance with I Corinthians are rather clear.

Philad. 6:3   II Corinthians C
Εὐχαριστῶ δὲ τῷ Θεῷ μου, ὅτι εὐσυνείδητός εἰμι ἐν ὑμῖν καὶ οὐκ ἔχει τις καυχήσασθαι οὔτε λάθρα οὔτε φανερῶς, ὅτι ἐβάρησά τινα ἐν μικρῷ ἢ ἐν μεγάλῳ.
II Cor. 1:12. Ἡ γὰρ καύχησις ἡμῶν αὕτη ἐστίν, τὸ μαρτύριον τῆς συνειδήσεως ἡμῶν. . . . . 11:9, 10. Καὶ παρὼν πρὸς ὑμᾶς καὶ ὑστερηθεὶς οὐ κατενάρκησα οὐθενός . . . . καὶ ἐν παντὶ ἀβαρῆ ἐμαυτὸν ὑμῖν ἐτήρησα καὶ τηρήσω. . . . . ἡ καύχησις αὕτη οὐ φραγήσεται εἰς ἐμέ. . . . . 12:16. 'Εγὼ οὐ κατεβάρησα ὑμᾶς.

Ignatius' gladness for his clear conscience and his thank-
fulness that he has not been a burden to anyone sound very much
like Paul's statements in II Corinthians. There are probable
echoes of his language in εὐσυνείδητος, καυχήσασθαι, and ἐβάρησα.

Philad. 7:1   I Corinthians C
'Αλλὰ τὸ πνεῦμα . . . . τὰ κρυπτὰ ἐλέγχει.
I Cor. 2:10. Τὸ γὰρ πνεῦμα πάντα ἐραυνᾷ, καὶ τὰ βάθη τοῦ
Θεοῦ.

Philad. 7:2   I Corinthians C
Τὴν σάρκα ὑμῶν ὡς ναὸν Θεοῦ τηρεῖτε.

For the text and a discussion of the probability of the
influence of I Cor. 3:16 on Ignatius see the note on Ign. Eph. 15:3.

Ignatius to the Smyrnaeans

Smyrn. Inscr.   I Corinthians C
'Εκκλησίᾳ Θεοῦ πατρὸς καὶ τοῦ ἠγαπημένου 'Ιησοῦ Χριστοῦ
. . . . ἀνυστερήτῳ οὔσῃ παντὸς χαρίσματος.
I Cor. 1:1, 7. Τῇ ἐκκλησίᾳ τοῦ Θεοῦ . . . . ἠγιασμένοις
ἐν Χριστῷ 'Ιησοῦ . . . . ὥστε ὑμᾶς μὴ ὑστερεῖσθαι ἐν μηδενὶ χαρίσ-
ματι.

The general resemblance of Ignatius' salutation to that of
Paul, together with the rather striking parallel in ἀνυστερήτῳ
οὔσῃ παντὸς χαρίσματος, makes dependence on I Corinthians probable.

Smyrn. 1:1   Romans B
'Αληθῶς ὄντα ἐκ γένους Δαυεὶδ κατὰ σάρκα, υἱὸν Θεοῦ κατὰ
θέλημα καὶ δύναμιν Θεοῦ.
Rom. 1:3, 4. Τοῦ γενομένου ἐκ σπέρματος Δαυεὶδ κατὰ σάρκα,
τοῦ ὁρισθέντος υἱοῦ Θεοῦ ἐν δυνάμει κατὰ πνεῦμα ἁγιωσύνης ἐξ ἀναστάσεως νεκρῶν.

In Smyrn. 1:1, A and Theodoret omit Θεοῦ after δύναμιν,
but G L C contain it. Lightfoot regards the addition of Θεοῦ as
a "transcriber's expedient, owing to ignorance of this absolute
use of θέλημα,"[67] and he accordingly omits it from his text. Lake

---

[67]Ibid., p. 290.

refers to Lightfoot's note[68] but does not share his opinion. The
insertion or omission of Θεοῦ is not very material for the present
comparison.

Smyrn. 1:2   Ephesians C

"Ινα ἄρη σύσσημον εἰς τοὺς αἰῶνας διὰ τῆς ἀναστάσεως εἰς
τοὺς ἁγίους καὶ πιστοὺς αὐτοῦ, εἴτε ἐν 'Ιουδαίοις εἴτε ἐν ἔθνεσιν,
ἐν ἑνὶ σώματι τῆς ἐκκλησίας αὐτοῦ.

Eph. 2:15, 16. ''Ο ποιήσας τὰ ἀμφότερα ἓν . . . . ἵνα
τοὺς δύο κτίση ἐν αὐτῷ εἰς ἕνα καινὸν ἄνθρωπον ποιῶν εἰρήνην, καὶ
ἀποκαταλλάξη τοὺς ἀμφοτέρους ἐν ἑνὶ σώματι τῷ Θεῷ (cf. Col. 1:18,
καὶ αὐτός ἐστιν ἡ κεφαλὴ τοῦ σώματος, τῆς ἐκκλησίας).

The parallel use of the phrase ἐν ἑνὶ σώματι to describe
the church creates the strong probability of literary acquaintance.
The context of the passages strengthens this probability.

Smyrn. 4:2   Philippians C

Μόνον ἐν τῷ ὀνόματι 'Ιησοῦ Χριστοῦ εἰς τὸ συμπαθεῖν αὐτῷ
πάντα ὑπομένω, αὐτοῦ με ἐνδυναμοῦντος τοῦ τελείου ἀνθρώπου.

Phil. 4:13. Πάντα ἰσχύω ἐν τῷ ἐνδυναμουντί με (cf. Rom.
8:17).

There is a rather clear echo of Phil. 4:13 in Ignatius'
assertion: πάντα ὑπομένω, αὐτοῦ με ἐνδυναμοῦντος. The probability
that it indicates literary acquaintance is heightened by the fact
that the statement forms the climax of an enumeration of the sufferings Ignatius had endured. Both men testify to their spiritual
empowerment for all trials through their fellowship with Christ.

It is barely possible that in εἰς τὸ συμπαθεῖν αὐτῷ there
is a trace of the influence of Rom. 8:17.

Smyrn. 11:3   Philippians C

Τέλειοι ὄντες τέλεια καὶ φρονεῖτε.

Phil. 3:15. "Οσοι οὖν τέλειοι, τοῦτο φρονῶμεν.

Smyrn. 11:3 may easily be a free quotation of Phil. 3:15a.
The immediately succeeding context is sufficiently similar to Phil.

---

[68]K. Lake, The Apostolic Fathers (London: William Heine-
mann, 1925), I, 257.

3:15b, 16 to strengthen the likelihood that the one passage is a reminiscence of the other.

Ignatius to Polycarp

Polyc. 1:2   Ephesians C

Τῆς ἑνώσεως φρόντιζε, ἧς οὐδὲν ἄμεινον . . . . πάντων ἀνέχου ἐν ἀγάπῃ.

Eph. 4:2-4. ᾿Ανεχόμενοι ἀλλήλων ἐν ἀγάπῃ, σπουδάζοντες τηρεῖν τὴν ἑνότητα τοῦ πνεύματος ἐν τῷ συνδέσμῳ τῆς εἰρήνης.

The points of resemblance are:

Τῆς ἑνώσεως φρόντιζε ἧς οὐδὲν ἄμεινον	Σπουδάζοντες τηρεῖν τὴν ἑνότητα τοῦ πνεύματος
Πάντων ἀνέχου ἐν ἀγάπῃ	᾿Ανεχόμενοι ἀλλήλων ἐν ἀγάπῃ

Polyc. 5:1, 2   Ephesians B

Παράγγελλε ἐν ὀνόματι ᾿Ιησοῦ Χριστοῦ, ἀγαπᾶν τὰς συμβίους ὡς ὁ κύριος τὴν ἐκκλησίαν. εἴ τις δύναται ἐν ἁγνείᾳ μένειν εἰς τιμὴν τῆς σαρκὸς τοῦ κυρίου, ἐν ἀκαυχησίᾳ μενέτω.

Eph. 5:25, 29. Οἱ ἄνδρες, ἀγαπᾶτε τὰς γυναῖκας, καθὼς καὶ ὁ Χριστὸς ἠγάπησεν τὴν ἐκκλησίαν . . . . ὅτι μέλη ἐσμὲν τοῦ σώματος αὐτοῦ.

Eph. 5:21—6:9 is a "Haustafel," which seems to be an elaboration of Col. 3:18 ff. Ignatius' injunction to husbands to love their wives as Christ loved the church sounds like a free quotation of Eph. 5:25. The phrase εἰς τιμὴν τῆς σαρκὸς τοῦ κυρίου may have been suggested by ὅτι μέλη ἐσμὲν τοῦ σώματος αὐτοῦ of Eph. 5:29.

Polyc. 6:2   Ephesians C

Τὸ βάπτισμα ὑμῶν μενέτω ὡς ὅπλα, ἡ πίστις ὡς περικεφαλαία, ἡ ἀγάπη ὡς δόρυ, ἡ ὑπομονὴ ὡς πανοπλία.

Ignatius' extended development of the figure of spiritual armor was probably suggested by his familiarity with Eph. 6:13-17 (cf. I Thess. 5:8).

Instances of possible literary reminiscence.— Inscription; cf. Rom. 15:29. The τῇ εὐλογημένῃ . . . . πληρώματι of Ignatius'

Inscription is a possible reminiscence of Rom. 15:29. The context does not suggest acquaintance, however, and the dependence is more probably on Ephesians 1:3.

Eph. 1:3; cf. Rom. 15:5. Ignatius is pleading for proper regard for one another. Beyond this very general element of agreement there is a trace of resemblance in the phrase κατὰ Ἰησοῦν Χριστόν. The secondary reading of Westcott and Hort is ʼΙησοῦν Χριστόν.

Eph. 2:1; cf. I Cor. 16:18. There is a possible trace of acquaintance with I Cor. 16:18 in the similar use of ἀναπαύω. The verb is similarly used in Philem. 7 and 20.

Eph. 2:2; cf. Philem. 20. The verb ὀνίνημι occurs in the New Testament only in Philem. 20 (cf. Sir. 30:2). It is apparently used there as a play on the name ʼΟνήσιμος. That name occurs in the immediate context of the passage in Ignatius, and yet, though supported (Eph. 2:1) by ἀναπαύω (cf. Philem. 7, 20), it does not constitute more than a possible trace of influence. The verb is a favorite one with Ignatius, occurring in Eph. 2:2; Magn. 2:1, 12:1; Rom. 5:2; Polyc. 1:1, 6:2.

Eph. 2:2; cf. I Cor. 1:10. There is a trace of possible kinship between the passages in their parallel use of κατηρτισμένοι.

Eph. 4:2; cf. I Cor. 6:15. The representation of Christians as μέλη ὄντας τοῦ υἱοῦ αὐτοῦ may reflect the influence of I Cor. 6:15.

Eph. 9:1; cf. I Cor. 3:10-17. The λίθοι ναοῦ πατρός may represent a point of contact with the imagery of I Cor. 3:10-17.

Eph. 9:1; cf. Eph. 2:20-22. There is the same general agreement between Ign. Eph. 9:1 and Eph. 2:20 as was noted above with I Cor. 3:10-17. In addition to this, there is an agreement in the emphasis placed on the Christian group into which the individual is to build himself.

Eph. 10:1; cf. I Thess. 5:17. The phrase ἀδιαλείπτως προσεύχεσθε suggests the possibility of literary dependence on I Thessalonians. The suggestion is weakened by the doubtfulness of the text of Ignatius' letter, however, G L g read ἀδιαλείπτως but Σ A omit it. Lake's text includes it without a note. Lightfoot's text also includes it but with the following note: "The Syriac

and Armenian have simply 'pray,' and simply 'be constant' in Polyc.
1. In the passage before us therefore the ἀδιαλείπτως is highly
suspicious and may easily have been inserted from S. Paul."[69]

Eph. 10:2; cf. Col. 1:23. Forms of ἑδραῖος occur in the
New Testament in I Cor. 7:37, 15:58, and Col. 1:23. Only in
Colossians is it used in connection with πίστις, however. The
same quality of "steadfastness" is stressed in Rom. 4:20 and I
Cor. 16:13, but these instances show no verbal parallel to the
Ignatian passage.

Eph. 10:3; cf. I Thess. 1:6. The phrase μιμηταὶ δὲ τοῦ
κυρίου finds its closest New Testament parallel in I Thess. 1:6,
of which it is clearly a possible reminiscence.

Eph. 17:2; cf. I Cor. 1:24, 30 and Col. 2:2. The trace of
possible influence of either or both of the Pauline passages lies
in Ignatius' conception of Christ as θεοῦ γνῶσιν. The equivalent
of this phrase is present in I Cor. 1:24, 30 and in Col. 2:2.

Eph. 9:2; cf. Eph. 3:9 and Col. 1:26. The wording of
Ignatius' statement may have been influenced by the language of
Ephesians and Colossians.

Magn. 1:2; cf. Eph. 3:1 and Philem. 9, 13. Ignatius'
conception of his imprisonment as expressed in Magn. 1:2 may reflect the influence of the similar passages in Ephesians and
Philemon.

Magn. 5:2; cf. Gal. 5:6. Ignatius' phrase πιστοὶ ἐν ἀγάπῃ
may reflect his recollection of the phrase πίστις δι' ἀγάπης
ἐνεργουμένη in Galatians. The emphasis in both passages is upon
the possession of the same qualities of character.

Magn. 5:2; cf. Phil. 3:10. Ignatius' idea of sharing the
suffering of Christ, even to the point of death, as a condition of
sharing his divine life resembles phases of Paul's thought (as in
Rom. 6:5, 8:17, 29; I Cor. 4:10; Phil. 3:10). The phraseology
used tends to relate the present passage to Philippians. The εἰς
τὸ αὐτοῦ πάθος may be a reminiscence of κοινωνίαν παθημάτων.

Magn. 6:2; cf. Rom. 6:17. Ignatius' phrase εἰς τύπον καὶ
διδαχήν may represent a dim recollection of τύπον διδαχῆς in Rom.
6:17.

----

[69]_Apostolic Fathers_, II, Part II, i, 58.

Magn. 9:1; cf. Col. 2:16. The abrogation of the Sabbath
for Christians and the basis on which it is placed may reflect the
influence of Col. 2:16.

Magn. 13:1; cf. II Cor. 13:13. The threefold enumeration
ἐν υἱῷ καὶ πατρὶ καὶ ἐν πνεύματι may be a reminiscence of II Cor.
13:13.

Trall. 4:1; cf. II Cor. 10:12, 13. The ideas of self-
measurement and the desirability of humility relate the passages
in thought. It is possible that ἑαυτοὺς μετροῦντες . . . . ἡμεῖς
δὲ οὐκ εἰς τὰ ἄμετρα καυχησόμεθα finds an echo in Trall. 4:1.

Trall. 6:1; cf. I Cor. 7:10. Ignatius and Paul are discussing different themes—the one heresy and the other marriage.
Yet each feels that his utterance has the sanction of Christ, and
this common conviction finds expression in the very similar clauses
οὐκ ἐγώ, ἀλλ' ἡ ἀγάπη 'Ιησοῦ Χριστοῦ and οὐκ ἐγὼ ἀλλὰ ὁ κύριος.

Trall. 9:2; cf. II Cor. 4:14. The Resurrection of Christ
and of believers through the act of the Father is the common theme
of the two passages. The one may represent a faint trace of the
influence of the other.

Trall. 11:12; cf. I Cor. 12:12. The concluding statement
of Trallians links the passage more closely to I Cor. 12:12 than
to the other instances in which Paul uses the figure.

Trall. 12:2; cf. Eph. 3:1 and Philem. 9, 13. See the note
on Ign. Magn. 1:2.

Rom. 2:2; cf. Phil. 2:17. Martyrdom seems to be the pros-
pect in each of these passages, and the writers regard themselves
as in a sense a sacrificial libation. The verb σπένδομαι occurs
in the New Testament writings only in Phil. 2:17 and II Tim. 4:16.
In II Timothy it may be borrowed from Philippians. If there is
literary dependence on the part of Ignatius it is to Philippians.

Rom. 3:8; cf. I Cor. 2:4. Ignatius emphasizes the efficacy
of Christianity. This emphasis and the contrast in which it is expressed correspond closely with Paul's description of his own
preaching at Corinth.

Rom. 4:2; cf. Phil. 2:17. The θυσία of Romans may be a
reminiscence of the ἐπὶ τῇ θυσίᾳ of Philippians (cf. Ign. Rom. 2:2).

Rom. 5:1; cf. I Cor. 15:32. The figure involved in θηριομαχῶ may reflect the influence of Paul's language in I Cor. 15:32.

Rom. 6:1; cf. Gal. 4:19. Ignatius' metaphor, differently applied as it is, may have been suggested by Paul's imagery in Gal. 4:19. His martyrdom represented the "pangs of motherhood" out of which he expected to emerge a heavenly being, spiritually refined. Paul's spiritual agony was on behalf of his converts, that Christ might more fully possess their lives in the present.

Rom. 7:2; cf. Gal. 6:14. It is possible that ὁ ἐμὸς ἔρως ἐσταύρωται is an echo of δι' οὗ ἐμοὶ κόσμος, εσταύρωται κἀγὼ κόσμῳ.

Rom. 10:2; cf. II Thess. 3:5. The phrase ἐν ὑπομονῇ Ἰησοῦ Χριστοῦ may reflect the influence of the similar phrase of II Thess. 3:5.

Philad. 2:1; cf. Eph. 5:8, 9. The expression τέκνα οὖν φωτὸς ἀληθείας seems to be Ignatius' distinctive coinage. It may, however, have been suggested by the τέκνα φωτός of Eph. 5:9.

Philad. 2:2; cf. I Cor. 9:24-26 and Gal. 5:7. Θεοδρόμος (cf. Ign. Polyc. 7:2) is not used in the Pauline figure, but Ignatius' coinage may have been suggested by the passages indicated.

Philad. 7:2; cf. I Thess. 1:6.

Philad. 8:2; cf. Phil. 2:3, 5. The μηδὲν κατ' ἐριθείαν of Philadelphians suggests a possible trace of the influence of Phil. 2:3. It is possible that κατὰ χριστομαθίαν is another trace of the influence of Philippians, in that it refers to the example of Jesus. It might be taken as the equivalent of τοῦτο φρονεῖτε ἐν ὑμῖν ὁ καὶ ἐν Χριστῷ Ἰησοῦ. This is exceedingly dubious, however. The term χριστομαθίαν seems to be Ignatius' coinage.

Philad. 10:1; cf. II Cor. 5:20 and Eph. 6:20. The conception of a Christian leader as an envoy of God suggests familiarity with II Cor. 5:20 and Eph. 6:20, the two instances in the New Testament where πρεσβεύω is used in this sense.

Smyrn. 1:1; cf. Col. 2:14. The resemblance between these passages consists in the phrases καθηλωμένους ἐν τῷ σταυρῷ and προσηλώσας αὐτὸ τῷ σταυρῷ. Ignatius uses the figure to describe the completeness of the consecration of the Smyrnaeans, and Paul to picture Christ's removal of sin through his death.

Smyrn. 13:2; cf. Col. 1:23.

Polyc. 1:3; cf. I Thess. 5:17. See the note on Ign. Eph. 10:1.

Polyc. 1:3 and 2:3; cf. I Cor. 9:25. The discipline required of a successful athlete is the analogy common to these passages.

Polyc. 4:3; cf. I Cor. 7:21, 22. It is faintly possible that κρείττονος ἐλευθερίας ἀπὸ Θεοῦ reflects the influence of I Cor. 7:21, 22.

It is clear that Ignatius knew I Corinthians, Romans, and Ephesians and that he very probably knew Galatians, Philippians, and Colossians. He may also have known II Corinthians, I and II Thessalonians, and Philemon.

TABLE OF RESULTS

	A	B	C	Unclassed
Romans..............	.	4	2	4
I Corinthians.......	2	7	7	13
II Corinthians......	.	.	1	5
Galatians...........	.	.	1	5
Ephesians...........	.	3	5	6
Philippians.........	.	.	2	6
Colossians..........	.	2	1	6
I Thessalonians.....	.	.	1	4
II Thessalonians....	.	.	.	1
Philemon............	.	.	.	3

The Epistle to the Philippians of St. Polycarp

Polycarp made an exceedingly limited use of the Old Testament. The few instances of such use are allusive and informal in character, with a tendency to freedom of rendering as though he were quoting from memory. Instead of making his references direct and formal, he usually works the ideas and expressions into statements of his own.

In 12:1 he clearly follows Eph. 4:26, but he seems to be aware that the original source of the quotation is Ps. 4:5. This instance furnishes about the nearest approach to a formula of citation that is found in the letter: "Modo, ut his scripturis dictum

est, irascimini et nolite peccare." Other illustrations of his
practice are: (a) 6:3, ἀλλὰ προνοοῦντες ἀεὶ τοῦ καλοῦ ἐνώπιον
Θεοῦ καὶ ἀνθρώπων, which seems to be an allusion to Prov. 3:4,
καὶ προνοοῦ καλὰ ἐνώπιον κυρίου καὶ ἀνθρώπων; (b) 10:2, "quia
eleemosyna de morte liberat" (cf. Tob. 12:9, ἐλεημοσύνη ἐκ θανάτου
ῥύεται); and (c) 11:2, "qui ignorant iudicum domini" (cf. Jer.
5:4, οὐκ ἔγνωσαν ὁδὸν κυρίου καὶ κρίσιν Θεοῦ).

Interesting instances in which Polycarp is apparently following an oral tradition of the teaching of Jesus are: (a) 2:3,
μνημονεύοντες δὲ ὧν εἶπεν ὁ κύριος διδάσκων. μὴ κρίνετε, ἵνα μὴ
κριθῆτε (cf. Matt. 7:1); and (b) καθὼς εἶπεν ὁ κύριος. τὸ μὲν
πνεῦμα πρόθυμον, ἡ δὲ σὰρξ ἀσθενής (cf. Matt. 26:41, Mark 14:38).

In some instances (4:1, 5:1, and 6:1) where the references
are seemingly to Christian writings, he uses the formula εἰδότες
ὅτι. In 11:2, where the allusion is clearly to I Cor. 6:2, he refers to Paul by name: "Aut nescimus quia sancti mundum iudicabunt?
sicut Paulus docet."

In several passages Polycarp shows that he writes under
the conscious influence of Paul and his letters. In 11:2 he mentions Paul in a specific reference to his teaching. Paul stands
as the climax in his list of heroes in 9:1. In 3:2 and 11:3 he
refers to Paul as a writer of letters, and it is entirely possible
that he has in mind a corpus of these letters. It is to be expected, therefore, that his allusions will bear numerous traces
of the influence of Paul's letters.[70]

The characteristics of his use of the Old Testament are in
general true of his use of Paul's letters. There is some tendency
to exactness in the shorter citations, but the general tendency is
toward freedom. He compresses, conflates, omits, and alters the
order to suit his own purposes.

    Polyc. 1:1   Philippians B
Συνεχάρην ὑμῖν μεγάλως ἐν τῷ κυρίῳ ἡμῶν Ἰησοῦ Χριστῷ.
 Phil. 2:17. Χαίρω καὶ συνχαίρω πᾶσιν ὑμῖν. 4:10. Ἐχά-
ρην δὲ ἐν κυρίῳ μεγάλως ὅτι ἤδη ποτὲ ἀνεθάλετε τὸ ὑπὲρ ἐμοῦ φρονεῖν.

---

[70]Leipoldt, op. cit., p. 189.

The verbal correspondence between the passages is considerable when Phil. 2:17 and 4:10 are taken together. Moffatt lists Polyc. 1:1 among what he terms "indubitable echoes"[71] of Philippians.

Polyc. 1:2   I Thessalonians C

Καὶ ὅτι ἡ βεβαία τῆς πίστεως ὑμῶν ῥίζα, ἐξ ἀρχαίων καταγγελλομένη χρόνων, μέχρι νῦν διαμένει καὶ καρποφορεῖ εἰς τὸν κύριον ἡμῶν Ἰησοῦν Χριστόν.

I Thess. 1:7, 8. Ὥστε γενέσθαι ὑμᾶς ⌜τύπον⌝ πᾶσιν ταῖς πιστεύουσιν ἐν τῇ Μακεδονίᾳ καὶ ἐν τῇ Ἀχαίᾳ. ἀφ' ὑμῶν γὰρ ἐξήχηται ὁ λόγος τοῦ κυρίου οὐ μόνον ἐν τῇ Μακεδονίᾳ καὶ Ἀχαίᾳ, ἀλλ' ἐν παντὶ τόπῳ η πίστις ὑμῶν ἡ πρὸς Θεὸν ἐξελήλυθεν (cf. Phil. 4: 15 and Col. 1:5, 6).

In Phil. 4:15 Paul praises the Philippians for their early and enduring fidelity to him. The ἐν ἀρχῇ τοῦ εὐαγγελίου of this passage may be reflected in the ἐξ ἀρχαίων of Polycarp. Harnack argues that I Thessalonians, addressed as it is to a Macedonian church, was regarded by Polycarp as also intended for the Philippian church and that he applied the commendatory introduction of I Thessalonians to the Philippians in the present instance.[72] There is a considerable degree of probability that this conjecture is correct and that Polycarp had I Thess. 1:8 in mind.

It is possible that καρποφορεῖ is a reminiscence of καρποφορούμενον in Col. 1:6, although no great stress can be placed on the coincidence of terms.

Polyc. 1:3   Ephesians A

Εἰδότες, ὅτι χάριτί ἐστε σεσωμένοι, οὐκ ἐξ ἔργων, ἀλλὰ θελήματι Θεοῦ διὰ Ἰησοῦ Χριστοῦ.

Eph. 2:5, 8, 9. Χάριτί ἐστε σεσωμένοι . . . . τῇ γὰρ χάριτί ἐστε σεσωμένοι διὰ πίστεως. καὶ τοῦτο οὐκ ἐξ ὑμῶν, Θεοῦ τὸ δῶρον. οὐκ ἐξ ἔργων, ἵνα μὴ τις καυχήσηται.

---

[71]Introduction, p. 176.

[72]A. Harnack, "Patristische Miscellen," Texte und Untersuchungen zur Geschichte der altchristlichen Literatur (Leipzig: J. C. Hinrichs, 1900), XX, ii, 91.

The introductory εἰδότες ὅτι may indicate that Polycarp was consciously quoting a written source. His thought and the wording employed bear an unmistakable resemblance to Eph. 2:5, 8, 9. He has compressed his source somewhat but has omitted no essential idea or term. All that he says can be accounted for from the Ephesian passage.

Polyc. 2:1   Philippians C   I Corinthians C

ᵀῼι ὑπετάγη τὰ πάντα ἐπουράνια καὶ ἐπίγεια . . . . οὗ τὸ αἷμα ἐκζητήσει ὁ Θεὸς ἀπὸ τῶν ἀπειθούντων αὐτῷ.

Phil. 2:10. Ἵνα ἐν τῷ ὀνόματι Ἰησοῦ πᾶν γόνυ κάμψῃ ἐπουρανίων καὶ ἐπιγείων καὶ καταχθονίων. 3:21. Ὑποτάξαι αὐτῷ τὰ πάντα. I Cor. 15:28. Ὅταν δὲ ὑποταγῇ αὐτῷ τὰ πάντα.

The subjection of everything to Christ is the central idea in Phil. 3:21 and I Cor. 15:28. In this same connection ἐπουράνια and ἐπίγεια occur in Phil. 2:10. Polycarp probably combined ὅταν δὲ ὑποταγῇ αὐτῷ τὰ πάντα of I Cor. 15:28 or the ὑποτάξαι αὐτῷ τὰ πάντα of Phil. 3:21 with the πᾶν γόνυ κάμψῃ ἐπουρανίων καὶ ἐπιγείων of Phil. 2:10. The suggested conflation of the passages accords with his way of using his sources.

Polyc. 2:2   II Corinthians C

Ὁ δὲ ἐγείρας αὐτὸν ἐκ νεκρῶν καὶ ἡμᾶς ἐγερεῖ.

II Cor. 4:14. Εἰδότες ὅτι ὁ ἐγείρας τὸν [κύριον] Ἰησοῦν καὶ ἡμᾶς σὺν Ἰησοῦ ἐγερεῖ.

The thought of Polycarp is similar to that of Rom. 8:11 and I Cor. 6:14, but the combination of thought and verbal resemblance is with II Cor. 4:14. The clauses ὁ ἐγείρας and καὶ ἡμᾶς ἐγερεῖ very probably reflect a recollection of that passage. Except for the substitution of αὐτόν for τὸν [κύριον] Ἰησοῦν and the omission of σὺν Ἰησοῦ, there is complete verbal agreement between the passages.

Polyc. 3:2   Philippians A

Οὔτε γὰρ ἐγὼ οὔτε ἄλλος ὅμοιος ἐμοὶ δύναται κατακολουθῆσαι τῇ σοφίᾳ τοῦ μακαρίου καὶ ἐνδόξου Παύλου, ὃς γενόμενος ἐν ὑμῖν κατὰ πρόσωπον τῶν τότε ἀνθρώπων ἐδίδαξεν ἀκριβῶς καὶ βεβαίως τὸν περὶ ἀληθείας λόγον, ὃς καὶ ἀπὼν ὑμῖν ἔγραψεν ἐπιστολάς.

Phil. 3:1. Τὰ αὐτὰ γράφειν ὑμῖν ἐμοι μὲν οὐκ ὀκηρόν, ὑμῖν δὲ ἀσφαλές.

The point of major interest for the present study in Polyc. 3:2 is the meaning of the clause καὶ ἀπὼν ἔγραψεν ἐπιστολάς. Lightfoot argues that ἐπιστολάς meant a single letter and that the allusion is specifically to our canonical Philippians.[73] Bauer grants the grammatical possibility of Lightfoot's position but maintains that, in view of current usage (I Clem. 47:1; Ign. Eph. 12:2, Smyr. 11:3, Polyc. 8:1) and Polycarp's own discrimination (13:2) between the singular and plural, the proper position is to take the plural as a real plural.[74] Taken as plural, he thinks ἐπιστωλάς may include the Thessalonian letters as directed to all Macedonian churches but that the most probable meaning is that from Phil. 3:1 Polycarp concluded that Paul had written to the Philippians many times.[75] Harnack argues that ἐπιστωλάς should be taken as plural on the ground that Polycarp had reference to the whole collection of Paul's letters as embodying a message for particular churches.[76] Perhaps no absolute decision is possible in the case as between Bauer and Harnack, but the probabilities lie in their direction rather than in Lightfoot's. The use of Philippians by Polycarp is certain, apart from the present passage. The statement under consideration either refers to Philippians specifically or else has it in view as one of a group of Pauline letters.

Polyc. 3:3   Galatians C

Εἰς τὴν δοθεῖσαν ὑμῖν πίστιν. ἥτις ἐστὶν μήτηρ πάντων ἡμῶν.

Gal. 4:27. Ἡ δὲ ἄνω Ἱερουσαλὴμ ἐλευθέρα ἐστίν, ἥτις ἐστὶν μήτηρ ἡμῶν.[77]

---

[73]Epistle to the Philippians[4] (London: Macmillan & Co., Ltd., 1878), p. 138.

[74]Op. cit., p. 287.   [75]Ibid.

[76]"Patristische Miscellen," p. 89.

[77]Textual note on Gal. 4:27: ἡμῶν 𝔫[*] B C[*] D G 33 424[**] al. Latin (vt. and vg.) Syr. (vg. hl. mg.) Eg. (sah. and boh.) Gothic Eth. Mcion Orig. saepius Eus. saepius Chr. Cyr. Tert. Hil. Ambst. Greg. Aug. al. plur.; πάντων ἡμῶν 𝔫[C] A C3 ω Syr. (hl. pal) Arm. Iren. lat. Orig. lat. bis. Cyr. Hier. Cosm. Victorin. Theod. Mops. lat. Cassiod. al. plur.

Very probably πάντων was inserted in the later texts of
Galatians under the influence of Polyc. 3:3. The τὴν δοθεῖσαν
ὑμῖν πίστιν may be a way of describing the faith dispensation
which is pictured in ἡ δὲ ἄνω 'Ιερουσαλήμ. The πάντων which Polycarp adds has the effect of making explicit what he probably took
to be implicit in Paul's position in Galatians. Except for the
addition of πάντων, the second clauses agree completely.

   Polyc. 3:2, 3   I Corinthians C
  Εἰς τὴν δοθεῖσαν ὑμῖν πίστιν . . . . ἐπακολουθούσης τῆς
ἐλπίδος, προαγούσης τῆς ἀγάπης τῆς εἰς Θεὸν καὶ Χριστὸν καὶ εἰς
τὸν πλησίον.
  I Cor. 13:13. Νυνὶ δὲ μένει πίστις, ἐλπίς, ἀγάπη. τὰ
τρία ταῦτα, μείζων δὲ τούτων ἡ ἀγάπη.

  The sequence πίστιν . . . . ἐλπίδος . . . . ἀγάπης suggests acquaintance with I Cor. 13:13. The terms appear in I Thess.
1:3 and Col. 1:4, 5 but in shifted order. In the passages under
comparison Polycarp and Paul emphasize the graces that are supreme
in Christianity. In the succeeding context Polycarp exalts love
as inclusive and supreme, ὁ γὰρ ἔχων ἀγάπην μακράν ἐστιν πάσης ἁμαρτίας.
   Polyc. 3:3   Romans C
  Προαγούσης τῆς ἀγάπης τῆς εἰς Θεὸν καὶ Χριστὸν καὶ· εἰς
τὸν πλησίον. ἐὰν γὰρ τις τούτων ἐντὸς ᾖ, πεπλήρωκεν ἐντολὴν δικαιοσύνης.
  Rom. 13:8-10. Μηδενὶ μηδὲν ὀφείλετε, εἰ μὴ τὸ ἀλλήλους
ἀγαπᾶν. ὁ γὰρ ἀγαπῶν τὸν ἔτερον νόμον πεπλήρωκεν. τὸ γὰρ . . . .
καὶ εἴ τις ἐτέρα ἐντολή, ⌜ἐν τῷ λόγῳ τούτῳ⌝ ἀνοκεφαλαιοῦται, [ἐν
τῷ] ἀγαπήσεις τὸν πλησίον σου ὡς σεαυτόν. ἡ ἀγάπη τῷ πλησίον κακὸν
οὐκ ἐργάζεται. πλήρωμα οὖν νόμου ἡ ἀγάπη (cf. Gal. 5:14).

  Polycarp's emphasis on love to neighbor reflects the spirit
of Rom. 13:8-10 and Gal. 5:14. The thought of Romans is more fully
developed, and its influence on Polycarp is more evident, than that
of Galatians, although the influence of the latter may be allowed
as a possibility. The clause ἐὰν γὰρ τις τούτων ἐντὸς ᾖ πεπλήρωκεν ἐντολὴν δικαιοσύνης very probably reflects acquaintance with
ὁ γὰρ ἀγαπῶν τὸν ἔτερον νόμον πεπλήρωκεν of Rom. 13:8.

Polyc. 5:1   Galatians B

Εἰδότες, οὖν, ὅτι Θεὸς οὐ μυκτηρίζεται, ὀφείλομεν ἀξίως
τῆς ἐντολῆς αὐτοῦ καὶ δόξης περιπατεῖν.

Gal. 6:7, 10. Μὴ πλανᾶσθε, Θεὸς οὐ μυκτηρίζεται . . . .
ἄρα οὖν ὡς καιρὸν ἔχωμεν, ἐργαζώμεθα τὸ ἀγαθὸν πρὸς πάντος.

The clause Θεὸς οὐ μυκτηρίζεται occurs in each instance as
a preface to moral exhortation. The formula εἰδότες, οὖν, ὅτι may
indicate that Polycarp was consciously quoting, and μὴ πλανᾶσθε
may indicate as much for Paul. Both may have had some familiar
saying in mind, and yet, in view of other evidence that Polycarp
knew Galatians, it is probable that there is a reminiscence of
that writing here.

Polyc. 5:3   I Corinthians A

Καὶ οὔτε πόρνοι οὔτε μαλακοὶ οὔτε ἀρσενοκαῖται βασιλείαν
Θεοῦ κληρονομήσουσιν, οὔτε οἱ ποιοῦντες τὰ ἄτοπα.

I Cor. 6:9, 10. ῍Η οὐκ οἴδατε ὅτι ἄδικοι Θεοῦ βασιλείαν
οὐ κληρονομήσουσιν; . . . . οὔτε πόρνοι οὔτε εἰδωλολάτραι οὔτε
μοιχοὶ οὔτε μαλακοὶ οὔτε ἀρσενοκαῖται οὔτε κλέπται οὔτε πλεονέκται,
οὐ μέθυσοι, οὐ λοίδοροι, οὐχ ἅρπαγες βασιλείαν Θεοῦ κληρονομήσουσιν.

The indications are that Polyc. 5:3 is a compressed quotation of I Cor. 6:9, 10. Bauer characterizes the influence of I
Cor. 6:9, 10 on Polycarp as "unverkennbar,"[78] and his term is ac-
curate. Except for his omissions, Polycarp's list of vices which
exclude from the Kingdom is verbally identical with Paul's. It is
probable that the quotation was from memory and that he included
under the blanket classification τὰ ἄτοπα the whole manner of life
which Paul condemned.

Polyc. 6:2   Romans B   II Corinthians B

Καὶ πάντας δεῖ παραστῆναι τῷ βήματι τοῦ Χριστοῦ καὶ ἕκαστον ὑπὲρ αὐτοῦ λόγον δοῦναι.

Rom. 14:10, 12. Πάντες γὰρ παραστησόμεθα τῷ βήματι τοῦ
Θεοῦ . . . . ἄρα [οὖν] ἕκαστος ἡμῶν περὶ ἑαυτοῦ λόγον δώσει [τῷ Θεῷ].

II Cor. 5:10. Τοὺς γὰρ πάντας ἡμᾶς φανερωθῆναι δεῖ ἔμπροστεν

---

[78]Op. cit., p. 289.

τοῦ βήματος τοῦ Χριστοῦ, ἵνα κομίσηται ἕκαστος τὰ διὰ τοῦ σώματος
πρὸς ἃ ἔπραξεν, εἴτε ἀγαθὸν εἴτε φαῦλον·

In Polyc. 6:2 there seems to be a conflation of Rom. 14:
10, 12 and II Cor. 5:10. The passage is verbally closer to the
former than to the latter, but the influence of II Cor. 5:10 appears in δεῖ and τοῦ Χριστοῦ (cf. Romans, τοῦ Θεοῦ).

Polyc. 9:1, 2   Philippians B
Καὶ ἐν αὐτῷ Παύλῳ καὶ ταῖς λοιπαῖς ἀποστόλοις . . . . ὅτι
οὗτοι πάντες οὐκ. . . . . εἰς κενὸν ἔδραμον.
Phil. 2:16. Ὅτι οὐκ εἰς κενὸν ἔδραμον (cf. Gal. 2:2).

The specific mention of Paul, the eschatological note in
the contexts, and the verbal parallel in the phrase εἰς κενὸν
ἔδραμον make dependence on Phil. 2:16 highly probable. The same
figure is employed in Gal. 2:2, but the difference in contexts and
application make Polycarp's dependence on Philippians much more
evident.

Polyc. 10:1   Romans C
Fraternitatis amatores, diligentes invicem, in veritate
sociati, mansuetudine domini alterutri praestolantes nullum des-
picientes. Lightfoot's translation: Τῇ φιλαδελφίᾳ εἰς ἀλλήλους
φιλόστοργοι, τῇ ἀληθείᾳ κοινωνοῦντες, τῇ ἐπιεικείᾳ τοῦ κυρίου
ἀλλήλους προηγούμενοι, μηδενὸς καταφρονοῦντες.
Rom. 12:10. Τῇ φιλαδελφίᾳ εἰς ἀλλήλους φιλόστοργοι, τῇ
τιμῇ ἀλλήλους προηγούμενοι.

There seems to be here what Bauer characterizes as "ein
Rückgriff auf Paul. Rom. 12:10."[79] Lightfoot's Greek for the passage presents a verbal correspondence that is complete for the
first clause, and this is accentuated by ἀλλήλους προηγούμενοι
in the second clause. These coincidences cannot be too strongly
urged because they represent a translation.

Polyc. 11:2   I Corinthians A
Aut nescimus, quia sancti mundum judicabunt? sicut
Paulus docet. Lightfoot's translation: Ἢ οὐκ οἴδαμεν ὅτι οἱ

[79]Ibid., p. 293.

ἅγιοι τὸν κόσμον κρινοῦσιν; ὡς Παῦλος διδάσκει.

I Cor. 6:2. ˹Ἢ οὐκ οἴδατε ὅτι οἱ ἅγιαι τὸν κόσμον ˹κρι-
νοῦσιν˺;

Lightfoot's translation presents a verbatim agreement with
I Cor. 6:2. There would be little room to doubt the influence of
Corinthians on Polycarp even if the clause "sicut Paulus docet"
were absent; but the direct reference to Paul makes such influence
indubitable.

        Polyc. 11:3   II Thessalonians B
     Ego autem nihil tale sensi in vobis vel audivi, in quibus
laboravit beatus Paulus, qui estis in principio epistulae eius.
De vobis etenim gloriatur in omnibus ecclesiis, quae dominum solae
tunc cognoverant; nos autem nondum cognoveramus. Lightfoot's translation: Ἐγὼ δὲ οὐδὲν τοιοῦτο ἔγνων ἐν ὑμῖν οὐδὲ ἤκουσα, ἐν οἷς
ἐκοπίασεν ὁ μακάριος Παῦλος, ταῖς οὖσιν ἐν ἀρχῇ ἐπιστολαῖς αὐτοῦ.
περὶ ὑμῶν γὰρ καυχᾶται ἐν πάσαις ταῖς ἐκκλησίαις, αἵτινες μόναι
τότε τὸν κύριον ἔγνωσαν, ἡμεῖς δὲ οὔπω ἐγνώκειμεν.
     II Thess. 1:3, 4. Εὐχαριστεῖν ὀφείλομεν τῷ Θεῷ πάντοτε
περὶ ὑμῶν ἀδελφοί, καθὼς ἄξιον ἐστιν, ὅτι ὑπεραυξάνει ἡ πίστις
ὑμῶν καὶ πλεονάζει ἡ ἀγάπη ἑνὸς ἑκάστου πάντων ὑμῶν εἰς ἀλλήλους,
ὥστε αὐτοὺς ἡμᾶς ἐν ὑμῖν ἐνκαυχᾶσθαι ἐν ταῖς ἐκκλησίαις τοῦ Θεοῦ.

     The specific mention of Paul and his "letter" or "letters,"
as the case may be, shows conclusively that Polycarp was writing
under Pauline influence. The problem of determining the exact nature of the dependence is one of interpretation and issues in
widely differing solutions.
     Lightfoot treats "epistulae" as a nominative and translates
"qui estis in principio epistulae eius" as ταῖς οὖσιν ἐν ἀρχῇ
ἐπιστολαῖς αὐτοῦ: "Ye who in the beginning [of the Gospel] were
his letters [of commendation]."[80] Lake believes that the Greek
was probably ταῖς οὖσιν ἐν ἀρχῇ ἐπιστολαῖς αὐτοῦ, and he feels with
Lightfoot that it represented a reminiscence of II Cor. 3:2.[81] He

_____

[80] Apostolic Fathers, II, Part II, ii, 926.

[81] Op. cit., p. 297.

does not, however, incorporate this conjecture in his translation
of the Latin text.

Harnack protests this interpretation of Polycarp's thought
and insists that the clause together with what follows be regarded
as a reference to II Thess. 1:3, 4.[82] He concludes:

Nun versteht man es auch, warum etenim (καὶ γάρ) und nicht
einfach γάρ steht. Der zweite Satz ist nämlich keine Begründung
im strengen Sinne, sondern eine begründende Epexegese: schon im
ersten Satz schwebte dem Polykarp 2 Thess 1:4 vor; er giebt in ihm
gleichsam eine Regeste jener Worte, um dann im zweiten Satz die
Worte selbst anzuführen.[83]

As Harnack points out, the second half of Polycarp's statement strongly resembles II Thess. 1:4. Polycarp knew the letters
of Paul as a collection, and he probably regarded the message of
each letter as for every congregation. He might, therefore, very
logically take II Thess. 1:3, 4 as applicable to the Philippians.
Harnack's résumé gives excellent statement to the position which
is here accepted:

Haben wir die Stelle richtig verstanden, so folgt (1) dass
Polykarp die ganze Paulinische Briefsammlung im Kopfe hatte . . . .
(2) dass er reine richtige Vorstellung von der Zeit der Gründung
der Gemeinde zu Thessalonich und der Abfassung der Thessalonicherbriefe besass, (3) dass er die Thessalonicherbriefe auch als für
Philippi bestimmte Briefe beurteilt hat; denn sonst hätte er nicht
behaupten können, das 2 Thess 1:3 f gespendete Lob gelte dieser
Gemeinde.[84]

Though not thoroughly conclusive, Harnack's view carries a high
degree of probability. In Polyc. 11:4 there is a probable reminiscence of II Thess. 3:15, which serves to strengthen the case for
dependence on II Thessalonians in Polyc. 11:3.

Bauer feels that all the elements in Polycarp's statement
can be accounted for in terms of Phil. 1:3-11,[85] and his position
is recognized as representing a possible interpretation of the
passage.

---

[82]"Patristische Miscellen," p. 91.

[83]Ibid.   [84]Ibid., p. 89.

[85]Op. cit., p. 295.

Polyc. 11:4 II Thessalonians C

Et non sicut inimicos tales existimetis, sed sicut passibilia membra et errantia eos revocate, ut omnium vestrum corpus salvetis. Lightfoot's translation: Καὶ μὴ ὡς ἐχθροὺς ἡγεῖσθε τοὺς τοιούτους, ἀλλ' ὡς μέλη παθητὰ καὶ πλανώμενα ἐπιστρέψατε, ἵνα πάντων ὑμῶν τὸ σωματεῖον σώζηται.

II Thess. 3:15. Καὶ μὴ ὡς ἐχθρὸν ἡγεῖσθε, ἀλλὰ νουθετεῖτε ὡς ἀδελφόν (cf. I Cor. 12:26).

The passages in Polycarp and II Thessalonians both deal with the reclamation of Christians who have sinned. The wording of the first clause in Polycarp so strongly resembles that of II Thess. 3:15 as to make literary acquaintance probable. The exhortation of this clause is enforced in the following sentence by what seems to be an allusion to I Cor. 12:26. Polycarp may have been unconsciously conflating II Thess. 3:15 and I Cor. 12:26.

Polyc. 12:1 Ephesians B

Modo, et his scripturis dictum est, irascimini et nolite peccare, et sol non occidat super iracundiam vestram. Lightfoot's translation: Μόνον, ὡς ταῖς γραφαῖς εἴρηται, ὀργίζεσθε καὶ μὴ ἁμαρτάνετε, καὶ ὁ ἥλιος μὴ ἐπιδυέτω ἐπὶ παροργισμῷ ὑμῶν.

Eph. 4:26. Ὀργίζεσθε καὶ μὴ ἁμαρτάνετε. ὁ ἥλιος μὴ ἐπιδυέτω ἐπὶ παροργισμῷ ὑμῶν (cf. Ps. 4:5, Jer. 15:9, Deut. 14:13).

The first clause of Eph. 4:26 is a direct quotation of the LXX of Ps. 4:5. The second may show reminiscences of Jer. 15:9 and Deut. 24:13, although they are not clear. The admonition in Polycarp is in verbatim agreement with Ephesians except for the insertion of the conjunction "et" between the clauses.

The introductory formula "ut his scripturis dictum est" probably indicates that Polycarp recognized that Ephesians quoted Ps. 4:5, and the "et" may reflect his awareness of the Old Testament allusions in the second clause.

Lightfoot[86] and Bauer[87] call attention to the rule of the Pythagoreans (Plut. Mor. 488B): Εἴποτε προαχθεῖεν εἰς λοιδορίας ὑπ' ὀργῆς, πρὶν ἢ τὸν ἥλιον δῦναι τὰς δεξιὰς ἐμβάλλοντες καὶ

---

[86] Apostolic Fathers, p. 929.   [87] Op. cit., p. 297.

ἀσπασάμεναι διελύοντο. The rule supplies an interesting thought parallel but is hardly evidence for any literary indebtedness in that direction on the part of Polycarp.

Unless Polycarp was directly indebted to Ephesians, it is necessary to suppose that he and the author of Ephesians both quoted some popular proverb; that, however, would leave "ut scripturis dictum est" unaccounted for.

Polyc. 12:3   Philippians B

Orate . . . . pro inimicis crucis. Lightfoot's translation: Προσεύχεσθε . . . . ὑπὲρ τῶν ἐχθρῶν τοῦ σταυροῦ.

Phil. 3:18. Τοὺς ἐχθροὺς τοῦ σταυροῦ τοῦ Χριστοῦ.

The phrase "pro inimicis crucis" is a striking one. The only parallel for it in the New Testament is the phrase in Philippians. It does not occur elsewhere in the Apostolic Fathers.

Instances of possible literary reminiscence.—Polyc. 4:1; cf. Rom. 13:12 and II Cor. 6:7. The imagery and wording of 4:1 may reflect influence of the Pauline passages.

Polyc. 4:3; cf. I Cor. 14:25. The phrases τῶν κρυπτῶν καρδίας and τὰ κρυπτὰ τῆς καρδίας suggest the possibility of literary relationship between the passages.

Polyc. 5:2; cf. Phil. 1:27.

Polyc. 6:1; cf. Rom. 12:17 and II Cor. 8:21 (cf. Prov. 3:4). Paul clearly depends on Proverbs in both passages, and although Polycarp makes very infrequent use of the Old Testament it must be granted that he may have used it here. In 6:2, however, he rather clearly depends on Rom. 14:10, 12 and II Cor. 5:10, so that it is possible that he has these letters in mind in the present instance.

Polyc. 6:1; cf. Rom. 3:9.

Polyc. 9:2; cf. Rom. 8:17.

Polyc. 10:1; cf. I Cor. 15:58 and Col. 1:23. A common note is sounded in the three passages. Both Pauline statements have ἑδραῖοι in common with Polycarp. I Corinthians has the adjective ἀμετακίνητοι with Polycarp, whereas Colossians uses the participle μετακινούμενοι. On the other hand, Colossians has τῇ πίστει with Polycarp, and I Corinthians lacks it.

Polyc. 10:2; cf. Eph. 5:21.

Polyc. 11:2; cf. Col. 3:5 and Eph. 5:5. The identification

of "avarice" or "covetousness" with "idolatry" is common to the three passages.

Polyc. 12:2; cf. Col. 1:12, 23. The first and last clauses of Polycarp's statement resemble phrases from Colossians.

Polyc. 12:2; cf. Gal. 1:1. "Et deum" is included in the Latin MSS r p m f and omitted from osvsbscsts. There is nothing in the contexts of these passages to relate them. The close parallel between "Iesum Cristum et ipsius patrem, qui resuscitavit eum a mortuis" and Gal. 1:1 is the basis of the suggestion of possible literary acquaintance. It would seem from Col. 2:12 and I Pet. 1:21 that such phrases might have become stereotyped in Christian usage.

Polyc. 12:3; cf. Col. 2:10 (cf. Jas. 1:4). The verbal agreement is closer with James than with Colossians, but James lacks an equivalent for "in illo" such as is supplied by the ἐν αὐτῷ of Colossians.

The position is frequently taken that Polycarp knew and used the Pastorals.[88] That view is open to serious question.

The data and procedure in Harnack's discussion[89] are fairly representative of those who share his views. He admits that such instances of resemblance as 4:1 and I Tim. 6:7, 10, 4:3; and I Tim. 5:5, 5:2; and I Tim. 3:8-11 may be accounted for by supposing a joint use of widely current truisms, although he does not so regard them. He insists, however, that 5:2 and II Tim. 2:12, 9:2 and II Tim. 4:10, 12:3 and I Tim. 2:1 can be properly interpreted only as indications of literary acquaintance with the Pastorals on the part of Polycarp. He does not consider the possibility of acquaintance with Polycarp on the part of the author of the Pastorals. While admitting that I Tim. 6:20, 21 was apparently directed against Marcion's _Antitheses_ and belongs to the fifth decade of the second century, that the discussions of offices in I Tim. 3:1-13 and Titus 1:7-9 breathe the atmosphere of the middle of the second century, and that I Tim. 5:17-22 cannot be dated earlier

---

[88]A. Harnack, _Die Briefsammlung_, p. 72; _Die Chronologie der altchristlichen Litteratur bis Eusebius_ (Leipzig: J. C. Hinrichs, 1897), I, 481; Leipoldt, _op. cit._, p. 189; and E. Jacquier, _Le Nouveau Testament dans l'église chrétienne_, p. 57.

[89]_Die Chronologie_, I, 481-83.

than A.D. 130 and probably belongs several decades later, he insists that these are interpolations and that the original date for
the group of letters is A.D. 90-110. He insists that this early
date made it possible and even certain that Polycarp knew the Pastorals, and then he guarantees the early date of the Pastorals by
saying that Polycarp knew them.

     An alternative, and, it is here maintained, a more logical
interpretation of the data is that the passages which Harnack regards as interpolations are the true watermarks of the age out of
which the Pastorals came and are the determining considerations in
dating them. The parallels that Harnack insists show that Polycarp used the Pastorals may as easily be allowed to show the latter's use of Polycarp but are more properly, perhaps, to be understood in terms of their common use of paranesis. The Pastorals
seem to belong to the atmosphere of the sectarian conflicts of the
middle of the century and after, which, of course, precludes any
use of them in Polycarp's letter to the Philippians.

     The canon of Christian Scripture reflected in the Pastorals
approximates that of II Peter, which points to a date later than
Polycarp's epistle. When in A.D. 180 the Scilitan martyrs were
asked before their execution what their church chests contained,
they replied: "The books and the letters of Paul." That reply
sounds interestingly like "the books, especially the parchments"
that seem to be so highly treasured in II Tim. 4:13.

     The martyrological interest of the Pastorals furnishes
data that tend to place them near the middle of the second century.
The probably technical meaning of such terms as "confess" and "witness" (I Tim. 6:12, cf. Acts. Just. 4:6 and 6:1), the use of the
figure of "fighting" in illustration of the Christian life (cf.
Acts Scil. Mart. 17), the martyrological use of the trial of Jesus
(I Tim. 6:13, cf. Mart. Polyc. 1:1), the careful identification of
Jesus (I Tim. 6:15) in all probability as over against the emperor
(cf. Mart. Polyc. 9:3, Acts Scil. Mart. 2, 3, 6, 9), the exemplary
use of Paul as a martyr (II Tim. 2:3, 3:10-12, 4:7, 8) tend to
bring the Pastorals into the atmosphere that permeates the martyrological literature. On the basis of a convincing review of the
relevant data, Riddle suggests that the approximate date of the
Pastorals is "not far in time from those untoward actions which

occurred during the periods of Marcus Aurelius and Antonius Pius
(reflected in the letter of the Christians of Lyons and Vienne, the
Martyrdom of Polycarp, the Acts of the Scilitan Martyrs, and the
Acts of Justin)."[90]

Harnack takes the position that the Pauline letter collection circulated in two forms during the first half of the second
century, one containing ten letters (the form in which Marcion
knew the collection) and the other containing thirteen letters.
It is his conviction that Polycarp knew the corpus with a content
of thirteen letters,[91] although in enumerating the letters of which
he finds traces in Polycarp he mentions only I Corinthians, Galatians, Romans, II Thessalonians, Ephesians, Philippians, and I and
II Timothy.[92]

Leipoldt is certain that Polycarp knew and used Romans,
I Corinthians, Galatians, Ephesians, Philippians, II Thessalonians,
I and II Timothy, and perhaps II Corinthians.[93] Jacquier's list
agrees with Liepoldt's, except that he expresses no doubt regarding II Corinthians.[94] Goodspeed is in general agreement with the
three positions described except for his omission of the Pastorals.
He finds traces in Polycarp of Romans, I and II Corinthians, Galatians, Ephesians, and II Thessalonians.[95]

The results of the present study are decisively against
the inclusion of the Pastorals in Polycarp's corpus of Pauline letters. There is reasonable certainty that the letter of Polycarp
shows traces of the influence of Romans, I Corinthians, Ephesians,
and Philippians. There is a high degree of probability that the
letter shows acquaintance with II Corinthians, Galatians, and II
Thessalonians and the reasonable possibility that it evidences
traces of the influence of Colossians and I Thessalonians. No
trace of Philemon is found.

---

[90]D. W. Riddle, The Martyrs: A Study in Social Control
(Chicago: University of Chicago Press, 1931), p. 156.

[91]Die Briefsammlung, p. 6.   [92]Ibid., p. 72.

[93]Op. cit.   [94]Op. cit.

[95]New Solutions, p. 38.

TABLE OF RESULTS

	A	B	C	Unclassed
Romans................	.	1	2	4
I Corinthians........	2	.	2	3
II Corinthians.......	.	1	1	3
Galatians............	.	1	1	3
Ephesians............	1	1	.	2
Philippians..........	1	3	1	3
Colossians...........	.	.	.	5
I Thessalonians......	.	.	1	....
II Thessalonians.....	.	1	1	....
Philemon.............	.	.	.	....

III

THE SUBSIDENCE OF THE POPULARITY OF THE LETTERS

During the first half of the second century, and very definitely during the second quarter of that century, Paul's letters
waned in their popularity. This was apparently due to the espousal
of Paul by heretical groups as the truest exponent of Christianity.
The literature of the period that has been preserved almost entirely lacks reminiscences of the letters.

The Epistle of James

Mayor argues for the authenticity of James[1] and insists
that such literary dependence as may exist between it and the letters of Paul is on the part of the latter.[2] The critical position
of Mayor is generally abandoned, and James is recognized as belong-
ing among the latest writings that found a place in the New Testament. The location of the letter in the opening quarter of the
second century[3] makes the acquaintance of its author with the collected letters of Paul easily possible. Such data of resemblance,
therefore, as may require explanation in terms of literary dependence will certainly point to such dependence on the part of James.

The use of literature by James is difficult to trace because it is allusive and indirect. There are no direct quotations
of Christian writings and very few of the Old Testament.

In five instances allusion to the LXX is by the use of
formulas of citation: 2:8, κατὰ τὴν γραφήν; 2:11, ὁ γὰρ εἰπών
. . . . εἶπεν; 2:23, ἡ γραφὴ ἡ λέγουσα; 4:5, ἡ γραφὴ.

---

[1] J. B. Mayor, The Epistle of St. James[3] (London: Macmillan
& Co., Ltd., 1910), p. lxvi.

[2] Ibid., pp. xci-ci.

[3] Otto Stählin, Die altchristliche griechische Literatur
(München: C. H. Becksche, 1924), p. 1156.

Jas. 1:2-4   Romans B

Πᾶσαν χαρὰν ἡγήσασθε, ἀδελφοί μου, ὅταν πειρασμαῖς περιπέ-
σητε ποικίλοις, γινώσκοντες ὅτι τὸ δοκίμιον ὑμῶν τῆς πίστεως κατεργάζεται ὑπομονήν· ἡ δὲ ὑπομονὴ ἔργον τέλειον ἐχέτω, ἵνα ἦτε τέλειοι
καὶ ὁλόκληροι, ἐν μηδενὶ λειπόμενοι.

Rom. 5:3, 4. ᾽Αλλὰ καὶ ⌜καυχώμεθα⌝ ἐν ταῖς θλίψεσιν, εἰδότες ὅτι ἡ θλίψις ὑπομονὴν κατεργάζεται, ἡ δὲ ὑπομονὴ δοκιμήν, ἡ δὲ
δοκιμὴ ἐλπίδα (cf. I Thess. 5:23).

The view of trial expressed in James first makes its appearance in Christian literature in Rom. 5:3.[4] The agreement in
the form and wording of James's statement with that of Romans suggests literary dependence. The similar use of ὁλόκληρος in James
and I Thessalonians may represent literary acquaintance. The word
occurs in the New Testament only in these two instances.

Jas. 1:4, 6   Ephesians C

῞Ινα ἦτε τέλειοι καὶ ὁλόκληροι, ἐν μηδενὶ λειπόμενοι. . . .
ὁ γὰρ διακρινόμενος ἔοικεν κλύδωνι θαλάσσης ἀνεμιζομένῳ καὶ ῥιπι-
ζομένῳ.

Eph. 4:13, 14. Μέχρι καταντήσωμεν οἱ πάντες. . . . εἰς
ἄνδρα τέλειον, εἰς μέτρον ἡλικίας τοῦ πληρώματος τοῦ Χριστοῦ, ἵνα
μηκέτι ὦμεν νήπιοι, κλυδωνιζόμενοι καὶ περιφερόμενοι παντὶ ἀνέμῳ
τῆς διδασκαλίας.

The use of τέλειος in the New Testament is limited to
Matt. 5:48, 19:21; the Pauline letters, where it occurs eight
times; Heb. 5:14, 9:11; Jas. 1:4, 17, 25, 3:2; and I John 4:18.
Its use in James and Ephesians is practically identical.

Jas. 1:10   I Corinthians C

Καυχάσθω δὲ [ὁ] ἀδελφὸς ὁ ταπεινὸς ἐν τῷ ὕψει αὐτοῦ, ὁ
δὲ πλούσιος ἐν τῇ ταπεινώσει αὐτοῦ.

I Cor. 1:26-29. Βλέπετε γὰρ τὴν κλῆσιν ὑμῶν, ἀδελφοί,
. . . . ἀλλὰ τὰ μωρὰ τοῦ κόσμου ἐξελέξατο ὁ Θεός, ἵνα καταισχύνῃ
τοὺς σοφούς . . . . ὅπως μὴ καυχήσηται πᾶσα σὰρξ ἐνώπιον τοῦ Θεοῦ.

---

[4]Hans Windisch cites similar statements from non-Christian
writings in Die katholischen Briefe (Tübingen: J. C. B. Mohr,
1911), p. 4.

The contrasts involved in the two passages are substantially the same. The use of καυχάομαι in the New Testament is restricted to the Pauline letters and James. Its use in connection
with the contrast that is common to the passages creates the probability of literary dependence.

Jas. 1:18   Ephesians C
Βουληθεὶς ἀπεκύησεν ἡμᾶς λόγῳ ἀληθείας.
Eph. 1:5. Προορίσας ἡμᾶς εἰς υἱοθεσίαν . . . . κατὰ τὴν
εὐδοκίαν τοῦ θελήματος αὐτοῦ . . . . 13.   Τὸν λόγον τῆς ἀληθείας,
τὸ εὐαγγέλιον τῆς σωτηρίας ὑμῶν. . . . .

God's will as the source of salvation and the gospel as
the means employed for the communication of life are ideas common
to James and Ephesians. The description of the gospel as ὁ λόγος
τῆς ἀληθείας (cf. Col. 1:5) probably influenced James.

Jas. 1:22   Romans C
Γίνεσθε δὲ ποιηταὶ λόγου καὶ μὴ ἀκροαταὶ μόνον . . . .
(25, ὁ δὲ παρακύψας εἰς νόμον κτλ).
Rom. 2:13. Οὐ γὰρ οἱ ἀκροαταὶ νόμου δίκαιοι παρὰ [τῷ]
Θεῷ, ἀλλ' οἱ ποιηταὶ νόμου δικαιωθήσονται.
I Macc. 2:67. Τοὺς ποιητὰς τοῦ νόμου.

'Ακροατής is used in the New Testament only in these passages. Ποιητής is used in this sense only in Rom. 2:13 and James.
In Acts 17:28—its only other occurrence in the New Testament—it
is used in an entirely different sense. The reference to the .
"faultless law" in Jas. 1:25 strengthens the probability of dependence on Rom. 2:13.

The antithesis between hearing and doing is entirely familiar (cf. Ezek. 33:32, Pirke Aboth 1:16, Matt. 7:24, Apoc. 1:3, etc.),
but the terms employed in James and Romans create the probability
of literary dependence.

Jas. 1:25   Galatians C
'Ο δὲ παρακύψας εἰς νόμον τέλειον τὸν τῆς ἐλευθερίας καὶ
παραμείνας, οὐκ ἀκροατὴς ἐπιλησμονῆς γενόμενος ἀλλὰ ποιητὴς ἔργου,
οὗτος μακάριος ἐν τῇ ποιήσει αὐτοῦ ἔσται.
Gal. 4:31. Διό, ἀδελφοί, οὐκ ἐσμὲν παιδίσκης τέκνα ἀλλὰ

τῆς ἐλευθέρας.   5:1. ⌜Τῇ ἐλευθερίᾳ ἡμᾶς Χριστὸς ἠλευθέρωσεν⌝·
στήκετε οὖν καὶ μὴ πάλιν ζυγῷ δουλείας ἐνέχεσθε. 13. Ὑμεῖς γὰρ
ἐπ’ ἐλευθερίᾳ ἐκλήθητε, ἀδελφαί.   6:2. Καὶ οὕτως ἀναπληρώσατε
τὸν νόμον τοῦ Χριστοῦ.

In Gal. 6:2 Paul thinks in terms of ὁ νόμος τοῦ Χριστοῦ
(cf. Rom. 3:27, διὰ νόμου πίστεως; and I Cor. 9:21, ἔννομος Χριστοῦ). James thinks of Christianity as ὁ νόμος τέλειος, and his
further characterization of it as τῆς ἐλευθερίας strongly suggests
Galatians. The noun ἐλευθερία occurs in the New Testament in
Paul's letters and three of the Catholics (James, I and II Peter).
The verb ἐλευθερόω occurs in Romans, Galatians, and the Fourth
Gospel. The adjective ἐλεύθερος occurs in Matt. 17:26, the Pauline
letters, the Fourth Gospel, I Peter, and the Apocalypse.

Jas. 2:5   I Corinthians C
Ἀκούσατε, ἀδελφαί μου ἀγαπητοί. οὐχ ὁ Θεὸς ἐξελέξατο
τοὺς πτωχοὺς τῷ κόσμῳ πλουσίους ἐν πίστει καὶ κληρονόμους τῆς
βασιλείας ἧς ἐπηγγείλατο τοῖς ἀγαπῶσιν αὐτόν;
I Cor. 1:26, 27. Βλέπετε γὰρ τὴν κλῆσιν ὑμῶν, ἀδελφαί,
. . . . τὰ μωρὰ τοῦ κόσμου ἐξελέξατο ὁ Θεός, ἵνα καταισχύνῃ τοὺς
σοφούς κτλ (cf. II Cor. 6:10, ὡς πτωχοὶ πολλοὺς δὲ πλουτίζοντες).

The form and character of the contrast employed in James
reminds one of I Cor. 1:26, 27. The final clause may show the influence of I Cor. 2:9, ὅσα ἡτοίμασεν ὁ Θεὸς τοῖς ἀγαπῶσιν αὐτόν.

Jas. 2:10, 11   Romans C
Ἐλεγχόμενοι ὑπὸ τοῦ νόμου ὡς παραβάται. . . . . Ὁ γὰρ
εἰπών Μὴ μοιχεύσῃς εἶπεν καί Μὴ φονεύσῃς· εἰ δὲ οὐ μοιχεύεις
φονεύεις δέ, γέγονας παραβάτης νόμου.
Rom. 2:21-25. Ὁ κηρύσσων μὴ κλέπτειν κλέπτεις; ὁ λέγων
μὴ μοιχεύειν μοιχεύεις; . . . . ὃς ἐν νόμῳ καυχᾶσαι, διὰ τῆς παρα-
βάσεως τοῦ νόμου τὸν Θεὸν ἀτιμάζεις; . . . . περιτομὴ μὲν γὰρ
ὠφελεῖ ἐὰν νόμον πράσσῃς· ἐὰν δὲ παραβάτης νόμου ᾖς, ἡ περιτομή
σου ἀκροβυστία γέγονεν.

Paul and James both insist that practice conform with
teaching. Both use the term παραβάτης to designate the type of
person whom they denounce. The term occurs in the New Testament

only in Rom. 2:25, 27, Gal. 2:18; and James 2:9, 11. It is used
only three times in the LXX.

          Jas. 2:12   Romans C   Galatians C
'Ὡς διὰ νόμου ἐλευθερίας μέλλοντες κρίνεσθαι.
          Rom. 2:12. ῞Οσοι γὰρ ἀνόμως ἥμαρτον, ἀνόμως καὶ ἀπολοῦν-
ται· καὶ ὅσοι ἐν νόμῳ ἥμαρτον, διὰ νόμου κριθήσονται.

        Paul draws a contrast between ὅσοι . . . . ἀνόμως and ὅσοι
ἐν νόμῳ, and he thinks of the difference involved as determining
the basis on which God will judge them. James seems to have a
similar contrast and a similar basis of judgment in mind.
        The emphasis on ἐλευθερία in this connection may indicate
the influence of Galatians. See the note on Jas. 1:25.

          Jas. 2:18   Romans C
Τὴν πίστιν σου χωρὶς τῶν ἔργων.
Rom. 3:28. Πίστει . . . . χωρὶς ἔργων νόμου.

        The use of χωρίς with ἔργον is found in the New Testament
only in Rom. 3:28, 4:6, and Jas. 2:18, 20, 26. The contrast implied and the similarity of phrasing make literary reminiscence
probable.

          Jas. 2:19-24   Romans B
Σὺ πιστεύεις ὅτι εἷς ⌜Θεὸς ἔστιν⌝; . . . . ὅτι ἡ πίστις
χωρὶς τῶν ἔργων ἀργή ἐστιν; 'Αβραὰμ ὁ πατὴρ ἡμῶν οὐκ ἐξ ἔργων ἐδικαιώθη, ἀνενέγκας 'Ισαὰκ τὸν υἱὸν αὐτοῦ ἐπὶ τὸ θυσιαστήριον; βλέ-
πεις ὅτι ἡ πίστις συνήργει τοῖς ἔργοις αὐτοῦ καὶ ἐκ τῶν ἔργων ἡ
πίστις ἐτελειώθη, καὶ ἐπληρώθη ἡ γραφὴ ἡ λέγουσα 'Επίστευσεν δὲ
'Αβραὰμ τῷ θεῷ, καὶ ἐλογίσθη αὐτῷ εἰς δικαιοσύνην, καὶ φίλος Θεοῦ
ἐκλήθη. ὁρᾶτε ὅτι ἐξ ἔργων δικαιοῦται ἄνθρωπος καὶ οὐκ ἐκ πίστεως μόνον.
        Rom. 3:28, 29. Λογιζόμεθα ⌜γὰρ⌝ δικαιοῦσθαι πίστει ἄνθρω-
πον χωρὶς ἔργων νόμου. ἢ 'Ιουδαίων ὁ Θεὸς ⌜μόνον⌝; οὐχὶ καὶ ἐθνῶν;
ναὶ καὶ ἐθνῶν, εἴπερ εἷς ὁ Θεός. . . . . 4:1-5. 'Αβραὰμ τὸν
προπάτορα ἡμῶν κατὰ σάρκα; εἰ γὰρ 'Αβραὰμ ἐξ ἔργων ἐδικαιώθη, ἔχει
καύχημα· ἀλλ' οὐ πρὸς Θεόν, τί γὰρ ἡ γραφὴ λέγει; 'Επίστευσεν δὲ
'Αβραὰμ τῷ Θεῷ, καὶ ἐλογίσθη αὐτῷ εἰς δικαιοσύνην. τῷ δὲ ἐργαζομένῳ ὁ μισθὸς οὐ λογίζεται κατὰ χάριν ἀλλὰ κατὰ ὀφείλημα· τῷ δὲ

μὴ ἐργαζομένῳ, πιστεύοντι δὲ ἐπὶ τὸν δικαιοῦντα τὸν ἀσεβῆ, λογίζεται ἡ πίστις αὐτοῦ εἰς δικαιοσύνην.

In the note on 2:18 attention is called to the restriction
of the use of χωρὶς τῶν ἔργων in the New Testament to James and
Romans. In 2:19-24 there is in common with Romans the argument
from the unity of God, the reference to Abraham as ὁ πατὴρ ἡμῶν
(cf. Rom. 4:1, τὸν προπάτορα ἡμῶν), the quotation of Gen. 15:6 in
which James agrees with Romans against the LXX in the insertion
of δέ before 'Αβραάμ and the argument concerning the basis of
Abraham's justification.

Jas. 3:15   I Corinthians C

Οὐκ ἔστιν αὕτη ἡ σοφία ἄνωθεν κατερχομένη, ἀλλὰ ἐπίγειος,
ψυχική, δαιμονιώδης·
        I Cor. 2:13, 14. Ἃ καὶ λαλοῦμεν οὐκ ἐν διδακταῖς ἀνθρω-
πίνης σοφίας λόγοις . . . . ψυχικὸς δὲ ἄνθρωπος οὐ δέχεται τὰ τοῦ
πνεύματος τοῦ Θεοῦ. . . . .

The use of ψυχικός in the New Testament is restricted to
I Cor. 2:14, 15:44; Jas. 3:15; and Jude 19. Its use in I Cor.
2:14 and Jas. 3:15 in connection with σοφία probably shows the
influence of one on the other. 'Επίγειος occurs in the New Testament in Paul's letters, John 3:12, and Jas. 3:15. In I Cor.
15:40 it occurs in a context with ψυχικός which somewhat strengthens the probability of dependence on the part of James.

Jas. 3:18   Philippians C

Καρπὸς δὲ δικαιοσύνης ἐν εἰρήνῃ σπείρεται τοῖς ποιοῦσιν
εἰρήνην.
        Phil. 1:11. Πεπληρωμένοι καρπὸν δικαιοσύνης (cf. Heb. 12:
11).

The phrase καρπὸς δικαιοσύνης occurs in the New Testament
only in James and Philippians.

Jas. 4:1   Romans C

Οὐκ ἐντεῦθεν, ἐκ τῶν ἡδονῶν ὑμῶν τῶν στρατευομένων ἐν τοῖς
μέλεσιν ὑμῶν;
        Rom. 7:23. Βλέπω δὲ ἕτερον νόμον ἐν τοῖς μέλεσίν μου ἀν-

τιστρατευόμενον τῷ νόμῳ τοῦ νοός μου καὶ αἰχμαλωτίζοντά με [ἐν]
τῷ νόμῳ τῆς ἀμαρτίας τῷ ὄντι ἐν ταῖς μέλεσίν μου.

The picture of inner struggle and the similarity of phrasing that appears in the use of στρατεύομαι and ἐν ταῖς μέλεσιν
point toward literary reminiscence.

Jas. 4:4, 5, 7   Romans C   Galatians C
Οὐκ οἴδατε ὅτι ἡ φιλία τοῦ κόσμου ἔχθρα τοῦ Θεοῦ ἐστίν;
. . . . Ὑοτάγητε οὖν τῷ Θεῷ.
Rom. 8:7.   Διότι τὸ φρόνημα τῆς σαρκὸς ἔχθρα εἰς Θεόν, τῷ
γὰρ νόμῳ τοῦ Θεοῦ οὐχ ὑποτάσσεται.
Gal. 5:17. Ἡ γὰρ σὰρξ ἐπιθυμεῖ κατὰ τοῦ πνεύματος, τὸ
δὲ πνεῦμα κατὰ τῆς σαρκός, ταῦτα γὰρ ἀλλήλοις ἀντίκειται.

The question in James sounds like a quotation, and there
are some indications that the allusion may be to Rom. 8:7. Ἔχθρα
occurs in the New Testament only in Luke 23:12; Rom. 8:7; Gal. 5:
20; Eph. 2:15, 16; and Jas. 4:4. The ἔχθρα τοῦ Θεοῦ may echo the
ἔχθρα εἰς Θεόν of Romans. In the New Testament ὑποτάσσω occurs in
Luke 2:51, 10:17, 20; the Pauline letters; and the later letters
that were influenced by the Pauline collection. The same fundamental antithesis of the carnal and the spiritual is found in Gal.
5:17. The reference to τὸ πνεῦμα in this context tends to strength-
en the likelihood of acquaintance with Galatians. It is to be
noted, however, that τὸ πνεῦμα in James corresponds more closely
with its connotation in Hermas than in Paul's letters.

Jas. 5:3, 5   Romans C
Ὡς πῦρ ἐθησαυρίσατε ἐν ἐσχάταις ἡμέραις . . . . ἐθρέψατε
τὰς καρδίας ὑμῶν ἐν ἡμέρᾳ σφαγῆς.
Rom. 2:5. Θησαυρίζεις σεαυτῷ ὀργὴν ἐν ἡμέρᾳ ὀργῆς.

The play on θησαυρίζω is not unusual, but only in Jas. 5:3
and Rom. 2:5 is it used in the New Testament of storing up that
which is "evil." It is so used, however, in the LXX (cf. Prov. 1:
18 and 16:27). The ἐν ἡμέρᾳ σφαγῆς may be a reminiscence of ἐν
ἡμέρᾳ ὀργῆς.

Instances of possible literary reminiscence.—Jas. 1:1;
cf. Rom. 1:1. The author of James may have imitated Romans in his
self-designation.

Jas. 1:1; cf. Eph. 1:1. The encyclical character of the address of James may reflect the influence of Ephesians.

Jas. 1:6; cf. Rom. 4:19, 20. The use of διακρίνω in the sense of these passages does not appear in writings earlier than those of the New Testament.

Jas. 1:12; cf. I Cor. 2:9 and Rom. 5:3 ff. For the possibility of acquaintance with Rom. 5:3 ff. see the note on 1:2-4. The close parallel between the final clause of Jas. 1:12 and that of I Cor. 2:9 may reflect literary dependence. The imagery of the first half of Jas. 1:12 is substantially that of I Cor. 9:25. Στέφανος is employed in its figurative sense in the New Testament only in Paul's letters and the later writings that were influenced by them. The occurrence of the exact phrase in the Apocalypse reduces the probability which might otherwise be predicated of the dependence of James on I Corinthians for the figure, however.

Jas. 1:13; cf. I Cor. 10:13. Paul's exhortation in I Corinthians is different in form from that of James, but it is very similar in import.

Jas. 1:14; cf. Rom. 7:5. The explanation of the origin of temptation here is very similar to that given in Romans.

Jas. 1:16; cf. I Cor. 6:9, 15:33, and Gal. 6:7. This negative exhortation Μὴ πλανᾶσθε occurs in James and in I Cor. 6:9, 15:33, and Gal. 6:7.

Jas. 1:17; cf. II Cor. 4:6. The representation of God as the source of light and blessing is a utilization of imagery that was quite familiar in Jewish and early Christian literature.

Jas. 1:18; cf. Rom. 8:23. The use of ἀπαρχή in the New Testament is limited to the Pauline letters, James, and the Apocalypse. It appears once each in the last two writings. Its use in connection with the idea of redemption may reflect the influence of Romans. Κτίσις and κτίζω are used figuratively in the New Testament in the Pauline letters and the later writings.

Jas. 1:21, 15, 26, 18; cf. Eph. 4:22-25. The conjunction of ideas in contexts that are markedly similar suggests the possibility of literary dependence, however, and may represent common paranetic emphases. Note the similar use of ἀποτίθεμαι.

Jas. 1:21; cf. Rom. 1:16. The conception of the gospel in terms of δύναμις and the use of this term in connection with σώζω may reflect the influence of Rom. 1:16.

Jas. 1:22; cf. Col. 2:4. Παραλογίζομαι is used only in these two instances in the New Testament.

Jas. 1:23; cf. I Cor. 13:12 and II Cor. 3:18. The figure of the "mirror" occurs in the New Testament only in the three passages cited. In James and I Corinthians the noun ἔσοπτρον is used. The figure is familiar from Jewish literature (Sir. 12:11, Wisd. of Sol. 7:26) and in Greek writings.

Jas. 1:26; cf. I Cor. 3:18 and Gal. 6:3. The similar use of δοκέω and the use of ἀπατάω in connection with it may reflect literary acquaintance with Paul's statements in I Corinthians and Galatians. The latter verb and the compounds in question occur in the New Testament only in the Pauline writings and the books that they influenced.

Jas. 2:1; cf. Eph. 6:9 and Col. 3:25. The noun προσωπο-λημψία occurs in the New Testament in Rom. 2:11, Eph. 6:9, and Col. 3:25 in addition to its use in Jas. 2:1. In Romans it describes the disposition of God, and in Ephesians the disposition of Christ. James is closer to Ephesians and Colossians than to Romans.

Jas. 2:8; cf. Gal. 5:14 and Rom. 13:9. James is in agreement with both Pauline passages in that he represents love as "the supreme law."

Jas. 2:9; cf. Eph. 6:9 and Col. 3:25.

Jas. 2:10; cf. Gal. 5:3. Paul insists that the acceptance of the legal principle carries with it the obligation to keep all precepts. It is possible that Jas. 2:10 reflects the influence of this position.

Jas. 2:14, 17, 24; cf. Rom. 3:28 and Gal. 2:16. The opposition of "faith" and "works" in James may reflect the influence of the similar contrast in Romans and Galatians. It is possible that James intended to refute the Pauline position, or at least to counteract wrong conclusions that had been drawn on the basis of it.

Jas. 2:18; cf. I Cor. 15:35. The exact verbal correspondence of these phrases suggests the possibility of literary dependence. Both writers, however, may merely be using a device of the diatribe, and the likelihood of this is sufficiently strong to make any emphasis on the resemblance unwarranted.[5]

Jas. 3:10; cf. Rom. 12:14.

Jas. 3:14, 16; cf. II Cor. 12:20 and Eph. 4:31. The terms
employed by James may indicate acquaintance with letters of the
Pauline collection. The sequence of terms reminds one particularly
of II Cor. 12:20. Ζῆλος occurs in the New Testament in Heb. 10:2;
John 2:17; Jas. 3:14, 16; and Acts. 5:17 and 13:45 outside the
Pauline corpus. It is used eleven times in Paul's letters. Πικρός
occurs only in Jas. 3:11, 14, but πικρία occurs in Acts 8:23, Rom.
3:14, Eph. 4:31, and Heb. 12:15. 'Εριθία is found only in Paul's
letters and in James. 'Ακαταστασία occurs in Luke 21:9, I Cor.
14:33, II Cor. 6:5 and 12:20, and Jas. 3:16.

Jas. 4:7; cf. Eph. 4:27. Διάβολος does not appear in any
Pauline letter but is found in the New Testament in Matthew, Luke-
Acts, John, Ephesians, the Pastorals, Hebrews, the Catholics, and
the Apocalypse. 'Ανθίστημι is used in Matthew, Luke-Acts, Romans,
Galatians, Ephesians, II Timothy, James, and I Peter.

Jas. 4:11, 12; cf. Rom. 2:1.

Jas. 5:8; cf. Phil. 4:5. The nearness of the Parousia is
frequently made a basis of appeal in the New Testament. The content of the exhortation and the language in which the appeal is
expressed suggest acquaintance with Philippians.

Jas. 5:12; cf. II Cor. 1:17 (cf. Matt. 5:37). The mode of
speech in the three passages is the same, but the form of James is
closer to that of II Corinthians than to that of Matthew.

Jas. 5:13; cf. Eph. 5:19 and 6:18. The exhortation to
prayer and song reminds one of Ephesians. Ψάλλω occurs in the New
Testament in Rom. 15:9, I Cor. 14:15, Eph. 5:19, and Jas. 5:13.

Ropes is inclined to explain resemblances between James
and the Pauline letters in terms of indebtedness to Hellenistic
Christianity rather than direct literary indebtedness. If any
literary influence at all exists, he would restrict it to Romans

---

[5]Ibid., p. 16; cf. also R. Bultmann, *Der Stil der Paulinischen Predigt und die kynisch-stoische Diatribe* (Göttingen: Vandenhoeck & Ruprecht, 1910).

and Galatians.[6] Goodspeed[7] and Moffatt[8] both affirm the fact of
James's literary indebtedness to the Pauline letters, and both regard acquaintance with Romans, I Corinthians, and Galatians as
clear. Goodspeed thinks acquaintance with Ephesians probable,[9]
but Moffatt is somewhat less certain.[10]

The present study finds the evidence for Romans, I Corinthians, and Galatians strongest. Furthermore, Ephesians was so
certainly in the first Pauline corpus that acquaintance with it
is hardly less probable. The data are extremely meager, however,
and may reflect a misunderstanding of Pauline teaching that made
it an embarrassment to the author of James.

TABLE OF RESULTS

	A	B	C	Unclassed
Romans	.	2	7	10
I Corinthians	.	.	3	6
II Corinthians	.	.	.	3
Galatians	.	.	3	5
Ephesians	.	.	2	7
Philippians	.	.	1	1
Colossians	.	.	.	3
I Thessalonians	.	.	.	1
II Thessalonians	.	.	.	....
Philemon	.	.	.	....

---

[6] J. H. Ropes, A Critical and Exegetical Commentary on the
Epistle of St. James (New York: Charles Scribner's Sons, 1916),
p. 21.

[7] New Solutions of New Testament Problems (Chicago: University of Chicago Press, 1927), p. 40.

[8] James Moffatt, An Introduction to the Literature of the
New Testament (New York: Charles Scribner's Sons, 1927), p. 466.

[9] Loc. cit.   [10] Loc. cit.

The Epistle of Jude

Jude resembles Ephesians in that it is an encyclical. Its author may have conceived the idea of addressing a letter to all Christians as a result of his acquaintance with Ephesians.

Specific evidence that indicates acquaintance with Ephesians and the other letters of the Pauline corpus is almost entirely lacking. In no instance does it go beyond the line of possibility.

The use of the Old Testament is allusive in character, and there is no employment of formulas of citation.

Jude 1; cf. Rom. 1:1-7 and I Thess. 1:4. The use of ἀγαπάω in the phrase in which it occurs in Jude, Romans, and I Thessalonians is confined in the New Testament to those writings. The use of the singular δοῦλος Ἰησοῦ Χριστοῦ in a salutation is found in Paul's letters only in Romans (cf. Phil. 1:1, where the plural is used). The use of this phrase in Jude, together with the way in which ἀγαπάω and κλητός are employed, may indicate acquaintance with Romans. Windisch is probably right, however, when, although noting that "die Anschauung 'berufen. geliebt. in Christus bewahrt' ist auch Paulinisch-Johanneisch," he adds, "warscheinlich allgemein urchristlich."[11]

Jude 4; cf. Gal. 2:4. Compounds with παρεις occur in the New Testament only in the Pauline corpus, Jude, and II Peter. The whole statement in Jude 4 is very similar to that of Gal. 2:4. The emphasis on the coming judgment of these "godless persons" may reflect the influence of Gal. 5:10, although the reference may be to Jewish prophecy (cf. Isa. 37:26 and Heb. 1:1).

Jude 6; cf. I Cor. 10:5. The allusion in each writing is probably to the Old Testament story of Num. 14:35. The possibility that Jude depended on I Corinthians, however, is allowed.

Jude 10, 19; cf. I Cor. 2:14, 15. The same contrast between the "spiritual" and the "fleshly" is involved in both passages. Ψυχικός is used in the New Testament only in I Cor. 2:14, 15:44, 46; James 3:15; and Jude 19.

Jude 20; cf. Rom. 8:26, 27. The assistance of the Spirit in prayer may be an idea for which Jude is indebted to Romans.

---

[11] Op. cit., p. 36.

Jude 24; cf. Eph. 1:4.

Jude 24, 25; cf. Rom. 16:25-27. The resemblance in tone
and expression between these doxologies may be due to literary dependence. It may, however, be due to the use of stereotyped forms
of benediction.[12] The verses in Romans are un-Pauline. They are
distinctly liturgical and probably represent an editorial addition
of a later day when the liturgical emphasis in the church was on
the increase.

TABLE OF RESULTS

	A	B	C	Unclassed
Romans...............	.	.	.	3
I Corinthians........	.	.	.	2
II Corinthians.......	.	.	.	....
Galatians............	.	.	.	1
Ephesians............	.	.	.	1
Philippians..........	.	.	.	....
Colossians...........	.	.	∘	....
I Thessalonians......	.	.	.	....
II Thessalonians.....	.	.	.	....
Philemon.............	.	.	.	....

The Shepherd of Hermas

The Shepherd of Hermas is difficult to date with any
great degree of confidence. The specific statement of the Muratorian Canon would seem to require its assignment to about the
middle of the second century,[13] except that this datum is discounted
as a "by-product of anti-Montanist polemic"[14] and that the allusions

---

[12]Moffatt, Introduction, pp. 135 and 348.

[13]"Pastorem vero nuperrime temporibus mostris in urbe Roma
Hermas conscripsit sedente cathedra urbis Romae ecclesiae Pio
episcopo fratre eius: et ideo legi eum quidem oportet, se publicare
vero in ecclesia populo neque inter prophetas completo numero neque
inter apostolos in fine temporum potest."

[14]B. H. Streeter, The Four Gospels (London: Macmillan &
Co., Ltd., 1936), p. 528.

to Clement (Vis. II. iv. 3) and to persecution suggest that it be
dated as early as A.D. 95.[15] However, the reference to Clement
does not require that he be alive at the time, and the persecutions, which seem to lie in the past, can as well have been those
under Trajan as under Domitian, with the result that the third or
fourth decade of the second century more nearly satisfies all the
data than any other time.[16]

The Shepherd affords no instance of the direct quotation
of the writings that constitute the Old and New Testaments. The
single exception to the author's allusive and indefinite use of
his sources is found in Vis. II. iii. 4, where there is a direct
quotation from the book of Eldad and Modat: Ἐγγὺς κύριος ταῖς
ἐπιστρεφομένοις, ὡς γέγραπται ἐν τῷ Ἐλδὰδ καὶ Μωδάτ, ταῖς προφ-
ητεύσασιν ἐν τῇ ἐρήμῳ τῷ λαῷ.

There are instances where the language points to an Old or
a New Testament source, but there is generally an element of un-
certainty because of the content with which the terms are filled.
Again, ideas that are familiar in biblical sources are so presented
as to make the confident affirmation of definite literary indebtedness impossible.

Mand. IV. iv. 1, 2   I Corinthians C
Ἐὰν γυνή, ... ἢ πάλιν ἀνήρ τις κοιμηθῇ καὶ γαμήσῃ
τις ἐξ αὐτῶν μήτι ἁμαρτάνει ὁ γαμῶν; Οὐχ ἁμαρτάνει, φησίν. ἐὰν
δὲ ἐφ' ἑαυτῷ μείνῃ τις, περισσοτέραν ἑαυτῷ τιμὴν καὶ μεγάλην δόξαν
περιποιεῖται πρὸς τὸν κύριον. ἐὰν δὲ καὶ γαμήσῃ, οὐχ ἁμαρτάνει.
I Cor. 7:28, 39, 40. Ἐὰν δὲ καὶ γαμήσῃς, οὐχ ἥμαρτες
. . . . ἐὰν δὲ κοιμηθῇ ὁ ἀνήρ, ἐλευθέρα ἐστὶν ᾧ θέλει γαμηθῆναι
. . . . μακαριωτέρα δέ ἐστιν ἐὰν οὕτως μείνῃ.

Both passages deal with the problem of the remarriage of
widows. The position taken by Hermas is the same as that taken
by Paul in I Corinthians, chapter 7. A second marriage for widows
is allowed, but the single state is preferred. As in I Corinthians,

---

[15] W. J. Wilson, "The Career of the Prophet Hermas," Harvard
Theological Review, January, 1927, pp. 21-62.

[16] M. Dibelius, Der Hirt des Hermas (Tübingen: J. C. B.
Mohr, 1923), p. 422.

a rigoristic ideal is paralleled with a less desirable, yet, at
the same time, allowable, alternative. The agreement in thought
between Hermas and Paul and the considerable coincidence of language create the probability of literary relationship.

Sim. IX. xiii. 5, 7   Ephesians C

Οἱ πιστεύσαντες τῷ κυρίῳ διὰ τοῦ υἱοῦ αὐτοῦ καὶ ἐνδιδυσκό-
μενοι τὰ πνεύματα ταῦτα ἔσονται εἰς ἓν πνεῦμα, ἓν σῶμα . . . . καὶ
ἦν αὐτῶν ἓν πνεῦμα καὶ ἓν σῶμα καὶ ἓν ἔνδυμα.

Eph. 4:4. ῝Εν σῶμα καὶ ἓν πνεῦμα . . . . ἓν μιᾷ ἐλπίδι
. . . . εἷς κύριος, μιὰ πίστις, ἓν βάπτισμα· εἷς Θεός κτλ.

See the note on I Clem. 46:6 for a discussion of the background and ultimate derivation of this "unity formula" in Ephesians. It represents a Christianization of a Hellenistic conception,[17] and in the form in which it appears in Ephesians it has
a distinctly liturgical ring to it. It is probable that its impressive statement in Ephesians is echoed in the several repeti-
tions of the formula in later Christian writings. There is close
verbal agreement and a common emphasis in the two passages under
consideration.

Sim. IX. xvii. 4, 5   Ephesians C

Λαβόντες οὖν τὴν σφραγῖδα μίαν φρόνησιν ἔσχον καὶ ἕνα νοῦν,
καὶ μία πίστις αὐτῶν ἐγένετο καὶ μία ἀγάπη . . . . καὶ γενέσθαι
ἓν σῶμα.

Eph. 4:4. See the note on Sim. IX. xiii. 5, 7 for the
text and discussion.

Sim. IX. xviii. 4   Ephesians C

῎Εσται ἡ ἐκκλησία τοῦ Θεοῦ ἓν σῶμα, μία φρόνησις, εἷς
νοῦς, μία πίστις, μία ἀγάπη.

Eph. 4:4. See the note on Sim. IX. xiii. 5, 7 for the
text and discussion.

Instances of possible literary reminiscence.—Vis. II. ii.
7, 8; cf. Col. 3:4. The reference to Christ (if the text is ac-
curate) as τῆς ζωῆς αὐτῶν may be a reminiscence of ἡ ζωὴ ⌜ἡμῶν⌝

---

[17]M. Dibelius, "Die Christianisierung einer hellenistischen
Formel," in Neue Jahrbücher für das klassische Altertum, Geschichte,
und deutsche Literatur, XXXV (1915), 224-36.

of Col. 3:4.

Vis. II. iv. 1; cf. Eph. 1:4. The idea of the church as πάντων πρώτη ἐκτίσθη may reflect the influence of Eph. 1:4.

Vis. III. v. 1; cf. I Cor. 15:6. Paul is speaking of the "more than five hundred brothers" to whom Christ appeared after the resurrection, "most of whom" were "still alive," but some of whom had "fallen asleep." Hermas is speaking of the bishops, teachers, and deacons who "walked according to the majesty of God, and served the elect of God," of whom, he says, some "are fallen asleep and some are still alive."

Vis. III. vi. 3; cf. I Thess. 5:14. The close correspondence between καὶ μὴ εἰρηνεύοντες ἐν ἑαυταῖς and the similar clause in I Thessalonians creates the possibility of literary reminiscence.

Vis. III. viii. 3-5; cf. I Cor. 13:13. Hermas begins his catalogue of virtues with πίστις and closes it with ἀγάπη, which may reflect the influence of the Pauline sequence. A significant feature of Hermas' list is that his virtues number seven. This feature is paralleled by the similar list from the Corpus Hermeticum xiii. 8bc, 9. In Sim. IX. xv. 1-3 a list of twelve virtues (the first being πίστις and the last ἀγάπη is contrasted with a corresponding list of twelve vices. The influence of the Hermetic literature is as probable in such instances as any other.[18]

Vis. III. ix. 2; cf. I Thess. 5:14.

Vis. III. ix. 2; cf. Rom. 15:7.

Mand. I. 1; cf. Rom. 4:17. It is possible that the passage in Hermas was influenced by Rom. 4:17, but it as probably represents the employment of a devotional conception that had passed into liturgical form.

Mand. II. 1; cf. I Cor. 14:20. Ἀλλὰ τῇ κακίᾳ νηπιάζετε (I Cor. 14:20) may find an echo in Hermas.

Mand. II. 4; cf. Eph. 4:28 and Rom. 12:8. Hermas may have picked the phrase ἐργάζου τὸ ἀγαθόν from Ephesians and δίδου ἁπλῶς from Romans.

Mand. III. 1; cf. Eph. 4:30 (Clem. Hom. IX. 9-23, Recog. IV. 15-19). Although Eph. 4:30 seems to relate truthfulness or

---

[18]R. Reitzenstein, Poimandres: Studien zur griechisch-ägyptischen und frühchristlichen Literatur (1904), p. 231.

its opposite to pleasing or "grieving" the Holy Spirit, it must
be noted that the conception of τὸ πνεῦμα τὸ ἅγιον in Ephesians is
radically different from the conception as found in the Shepherd.
The only New Testament equivalent for the latter is found in Jas.
4:5.

Mand. X. i. 2; ii. 2, 4, 5; cf. II Cor. 7:10 and Eph. 4:
30. The καὶ πάλιν σώζει of Mand. X. i. 2 seems at first glance
to draw the distinction that is drawn in II Cor. 7:10 between ἡ
λύπη κατὰ Θεόν and ἡ λύπη τοῦ κόσμου. Similarly, the several
exhortations against "grieving the Holy Spirit" bring to mind the
exhortation of Eph. 4:30. The resemblance in each instance is
purely verbal, and the clauses in Hermas have to be isolated from
their context for the maintenance of any relationship with the
passages in II Corinthians and Ephesians. The association of λύπη
with διψυχία and ὀξυχολία indicates that it is regarded with the
cardinal vices. In Sim. IX. xv. 3 λύπη is one of a series of
twelve vices, just as it is in Corpus Hermeticum xiii. 7b.[19]

Mand. XII. ii. 4; cf. Eph. 6:13. The metaphor of spiritual
armor is used in the two passages.

Sim. V. iii. 8; cf. Phil. 4:18. Ἔσται ἡ θυσία σου δεκτὴ
παρὰ τῷ Θεῷ may be a reminiscence of Phil. 4:18.

Sim. V. v. 2; cf. Eph. 3:10.

Sim. V. v. 5; cf. Phil. 2:7.

Sim. VII. 4; cf. Eph. 3:9. Ὁ τὰ πάντα κτίσας may reflect
acquaintance with Eph. 3:9.

Sim. VIII. v. 6; cf. I Cor. 15:23. Ἕκαστος εἰς τὸ ἴδιον
τάγμα may be a verbal reminiscence of I Cor. 15:23.

Sim. VIII. vii. 2; cf. I Thess. 5:14. Καὶ μηδέποτε εἰρηνεύοντες εἰς ἑαυτούς may look back to I Thess. 5:14.

Sim. IX. iv. 3; cf. Eph. 2:20. The figure of the tower
may have been suggested by Eph. 2:20-22. The reference to prophets,
apostles, and teachers in xv. 4 may strengthen the case for dependence.

Sim. IX. xi. 7; cf. I Thess. 5:17.

Sim. IX. xii. 1; cf. I Cor. 10:4.

Sim. IX. xvi. 2, 3; cf. Eph. 2:1, 5.

_____

[19]Ibid., p. 233.

Leipoldt finds it likely that Hermas used Ephesians and I Corinthians,[20] and Jacquier that he used Ephesians, Romans, and I Thessalonians.[21]

The present study finds possible traces of acquaintance with Ephesians, I Corinthians, Romans, I Thessalonians, Philippians, and Colossians, listing them in the order of the evidence of literary influence on Hermas. The strongest case can be made for Ephesians and I Corinthians. In no instance, however, is there warrant for certainty that Hermas used a letter of the Pauline collection.

TABLE OF RESULTS

	A	B	C	Unclassed
Romans...............	•	•	•	3
I Corinthians.......	•	•	1	5
II Corinthians......	•	•	•	....
Galatians...........	•	•	•	....
Ephesians...........	•	•	3	9
Philippians.........	•	•	•	2
Colossians..........	•	•	•	1
I Thessalonians.....	•	•	•	4
II Thessalonians....	•	•	•	....
Philemon............	•	•	•	....

The Epistle of Barnabas

The Epistle of Barnabas is made up largely of allegorical interpretation of Old Testament passages. By this method of interpretation the author retains the Old Testament for Christian use and turns it into a sourcebook of proof texts for Christian apologetic, although he despises its literal sense.

He uses the Old Testament in an indiscriminate and arbi-

---

[20] J. Leipoldt, Geschichte des neutestamentlichen Kanons (Leipzig: J. C. Hinrichs, 1907), p. 189.

[21] E. Jacquier, Nouveau Testament dans l'église chrêtienne (Paris: J. Gabalde & Co., 1911), p. 78.

trary manner. He will arrange a series of irrelevant passages
side by side and by a prefatory or concluding exposition make them
prove his point (cf. 2:4-10, 3:1-6, 6:1-5, 9:1-3, etc.). Or,
again, he will intersperse his comments throughout a collection
of proof texts (6:8-19, 7:3-11, 11:6-11, 15:1-7). Still a third
resort is to cite or take extracts from narratives and interpret
them to serve the end he has in view (4:6-8, 9:6-9, 12:5-7, 13:1-
7). He conflates widely separated passages as though they were
continuous, and he makes little apparent effort to present the
text with accuracy. He omits from and otherwise alters his sources
at will.

His formulas of citation are varied and instructive. Most
frequently God or the Lord or the Spirit are represented as speaking: 5:5, εἶπεν ὁ θεός; 5:12, λέγει . . . . ὁ θεός; 6:12, εἶπεν
κύριος; 9:2, τὸ πνεῦμα κυρίου προφητεύει. In other instances the
formulas are without a subject, as λέγει (6:1, 9:8); φησίν (7:7);
λέγει ἡ γραφή (4:7, 5:4, 6:12); and γεγραμμένης ἐντολῆς (7:3).
References to the sources of quotations and allusions are generally indefinite, as ἐν ἑτέρῳ λέγει (15:2) and λέγει κύριος ἐν τῷ
προφήτῃ (9:1). In 15:1 the reference is unusually precise: ἔτι
οὖν καὶ περὶ τοῦ σαββάτου γέγραπται ἐν ταῖς δέκα λόγοις. In addition to these more usual formulas, there are ascriptions of statements to inspired persons, sometimes by name (Daniel, 4:5; Moses,
6:8; David, 10:10; Jacob, 13:4), sometimes merely as prophets, as
λέγει ὁ προφήτης (4:4).

In 4:14 there is the quotation of a saying that appears in
Matt. 22:14, and Barnabas introduces it with the formula ὡς
γέγραπται. This may mean that he regarded the statement as authoritative as coming from Jesus or that he confusedly thought of it as
from the Old Testament or, least probably, that he regarded Matthew
as a scriptural book.

There are no direct citations of the Pauline letters, nor
are there any references to Paul. The writer probably knew Paul's
letters, but their literary influence on him was negligible beyond
the general consideration that he adopted the epistle as a literary
medium for religious instruction.[22]

----

[22]Stählin, op. cit., pp. 1223, 1229.

Barn. 2:1; cf. Eph. 5:16, 17. The view that the "days are evil" because Satan rules is the general conception of early Christianity. The practical exhortation, ὀφείλομεν κτλ, is paralleled in Eph. 5:17. This combination of coincidence of apocalyptic imagery and moral exhortation is interesting and may indicate literary dependence.

Barn. 3:6; cf. Eph. 1:5, 6. The conception in Barn. 3:6 and the language in which it is expressed may show the influence of Jewish apocalyptic (cf. Isa. 44:2, IV Ezra 6:58, II Bar. 14:18) or of Christian writings other than Ephesians (cf. Herm. Sim. IX. xii. 5). The resemblance to Ephesians is sufficiently strong, however, to make it a possible source of influence for Barnabas.

Barn. 4:1; cf. I Thess. 5:22. The eschatological ideas which form the background of the exhortation in Barnabas are similar to those found in I Cor. 7:26, 29, 31; I Thess. 5:1-11; and II Thess 2:3, 7-12. The immediate context of the exhortation in I Thess. 5:22 does not relate to the eschatological section in 5:1-11 but rather to testing utterances inspired by the Spirit.

Barn. 4:9; cf. II Thess. 2:4, 8. In Barn. 4:3 the clause τὸ τέλειον σκάνδαλον ἤγγικεν would suggest II Thess. 2:3 ff. (cf. Matt. 24:15) but for the fact that the author indicates that he has a passage from Enoch in mind (cf. 89:61-64, 90:17). In 4:9 he may still have the Enoch passage in mind, but the influence of II Thessalonians is reasonably possible.

Barn. 4:11; cf. I Cor. 3:1, 16, 18. Paul's designation for true Christians is πνευματικοί (I Cor. 2:13, 15; 3:1; 14:37; Gal. 6:1). In I Corinthians he combines this conception of Christians with the kindred conception of them as ναὸς Θεοῦ. The idea of a "spiritual temple" is not confined to Paul or, for that matter, to Christian writings, but the conjunction of ideas in Barn. 4:11 and I Corinthians, chapter 3, makes it possible that the former reflects the influence of the latter. It is to be noted, however, that for Barnabas πνευματικοί are those who "in the fear of God" strive to "keep his commandments," which misses Paul's fundamental idea.

Barn. 4:12; cf. II Cor. 5:10. The resemblances between the passages may be explained in terms of their common dependence on Ecclus. 32:15, 16, 24. There remains the possibility, however, of the influence of II Corinthians.

Barn. 6:11, 13-15; cf. Eph. 2:10 and II Cor. 5:17. The
idea of spiritual re-creation in Barnabas resembles the thought
of Ephesians and II Corinthians. The indiscriminate combination
of Old Testament materials in Barnabas would make it easy to be-
lieve that he had Ephesians and II Corinthians in mind, if dependence of any kind be judged probable. The conjunction of the ideas
of spiritual re-creation and of the re-created hearts of men as a
temple of God argues for the influence of Ephesians.

Barn. 9:6; cf. Rom. 4:11. Barn. 9:6 probably had as its
background some such Jewish teaching as is found in Jubil. 15:26.
It is possible, however, that there is a conscious effort to
controvert the position of Rom. 4:11.

Barn. 12:7, 8; cf. Col. 1:16, 17.

Barn. 13:2, 3; cf. Rom. 9:7-13. The allusion in Barnabas
and Romans is to the same Old Testament story. Each illustration
is made to turn on the phrase that is common to them—ὁ μείζων
δουλεύσει τῷ ἐλάσσονι. Barnabas, however, makes the statement a
specific prophecy of Christianity, whereas Paul uses it to illustrate and establish the general principle of election.

    Barn. 13:7   Romans C

Τί οὖν λέγει τῷ 'Αβραάμ, ὅτε μόνος πιστεύσας ἐτέθη εἰς
δικαιοσύνην; 'Ιδού, τέθεικά σε, 'Αβραάμ, πατέρα ἐθνῶν τῶν πιστευόντων δι' ἀκροβυστίας τῷ θεῷ.

Rom. 4:3, 10. Τί γὰρ ἡ γραφὴ λέγει; 'Επίστευσεν δὲ 'Αβραὰμ
τῷ θεῷ, καὶ ἐλογίσθη αὐτῷ εἰς δικαιοσύνην . . . . πῶς οὖν ἐλογίσθη;
ἐν περιτομῇ ὄντι ἢ ἐν ἀκροβυστίᾳ; οὐκ ἐν περιτομῇ ἀλλ' ἐν ἀκροβυστίᾳ . . . . εἰς τὸ εἶναι αὐτὸν πατέρα πάντων τῶν πιστευόντων δι'
ἀκροβυστίας.

The phrase τῶν πιστευόντων δι' ἀκροβυστίας in Barnabas
represents an addition to the Old Testament source employed. It
may mean that the writer was conflating his Old Testament illustration with Rom. 4:10.

Barn. 15:5; cf. II Thess. 2:8, 12.

Barn. 21:6; cf. I Thess. 4:9. The contexts of the passages are different. The term θεοδίδακτοι occurs in the Apostolic
Fathers and the New Testament only in the instances cited.

Leipoldt is certain that the author of Barnabas was acquainted with Paul's letters, but he finds clear traces of Romans and probable traces of Ephesians only.[23]   These are the two letters of which Goodspeed finds traces in Barnabas.[24]   Windisch finds clear acquaintance with Romans but thinks that knowledge of Ephesians is not established.[25]   Harnack finds the clearest use of Romans and II Corinthians.[26]

The present study finds no instances that require explanation in terms of literary indebtedness to Paul's letters on the part of Barnabas. The traces of Romans are clearer than of any other letters of the Pauline collection. Ephesians is a close second to Romans, and II Corinthians and the two Thessalonian letters were also possibly used.

TABLE OF RESULTS

	A	B	C	Unclassed
Romans	·	·	1	2
I Corinthians	·	·	·	1
II Corinthians	·	·	·	2
Galatians	·	·	·	··········
Ephesians	·	·	·	3
Philippians	·	·	·	··········
Colossians	·	·	·	1
I Thessalonians	·	·	·	2
II Thessalonians	·	·	·	2
Philemon	·	·	·	··········

The Didache

The Didache makes no direct use of the Old Testament. In those instances where allusions point to an Old Testament source,

---

[23] Op. cit., p. 189.   [24] Op. cit., p. 41.

[25] H. Windisch, Der Barnabasbrief (Tübingen: J. C. B. Mohr, 1920), p. 314.

[26] A. Harnack, Die Chronologie der altchristlichen Literatur bis Eusebius (Leipzig: J. C. Hinrichs, 1897), I, 415.

the usual formulas of citation are wanting. In 16:7, where the
influence of Zech. 14:5 (cf. I Thess. 3:13) may be present, the
introductory formula is ἀλλ' ὡς ἐρρέθη.

In the author's addition to his "Two Ways" source (1:3—
2:1) there is a saying from an unidentified source introduced by
ἀλλὰ καὶ περὶ τούτου δὲ εἴρηται. This is the only instance in
the first six chapters where any introductory formula is used.
There is evidence of dependence on sources in other instances in
this section; but the cases are allusive rather than formal, and
the statements and ideas are interwoven with the author's own
without specific acknowledgment.

Other illustrations of the author's practice are: 8:2 (cf.
Matt. 6:9-13), ἀλλ' ὡς ἐκέλευσεν ὁ κύριος ἐν τῷ εὐαγγελίῳ αὐτοῦ;
and 9:5 (cf. Matt. 7:6), εἴρηκεν ὁ κύριος.

In the "Two Ways" section (1—6, except 1:3—2:1), the author of the Didache evidently draws on a source which was either
the Epistle of Barnabas or a document used in common with that
epistle. This makes it impossible to maintain acquaintance with
the Pauline letters on the part of the Didache in its present
form, even if the parallels were more impressive than they actually
are. The passages that are at all similar and that on any view of
the date and character of the writing have been regarded as bearing traces of the influence of Paul's letters are listed for the
sake of completeness.

In other sections of the Didache traces of the possible influence of Paul's letters are found, but they are in all instances
extremely vague.

Did. 1:2; cf. Rom. 13:9a-10b. The clause τὸν πλησίον σου
ὡς σεαυτόν is common to the two passages. The negative form of
the "Golden Rule" in the Didache has some resemblance to the negative teaching about love to neighbor in Rom. 13:10a (Barnabas has
no parallel for this part of the passage). A closer parallel is
found, however, in Tob. 4:15.

Did. 1:5; cf. I Cor. 7:7. The phrase that seems to indicate the influence of I Corinthians is ἐκ τῶν ἰδίων χαρισμάτων.
In a list of "gifts" in Rom. 12:8, one specification is ὁ μεταδι-
δοὺς ἐν ἁπλότητι, which is in line with the meaning in Did. 1:5.
The real parallel and the probable source for Did. 1:5, however,

is Herm. Mand. II. 4: Πᾶσιν γάρ ὁ Θεὸς δίδοσθαι θέλει ἐκ τῶν ἰδίων δωρημάτων.

Did. 1:5; cf. II Thess. 3:10-12. The whole situation reflected in the passages and the contexts in which they occur is different. The better parallel and the probable source for the Didache passage are Herm. Mand. II. 5: Οἱ οὖν λαμβάνοντες ἀποδώσουσιν λόγον τῷ Θεῷ, διατί ἔλαβον καὶ εἰς τί. οἱ μὲν γὰρ λαμβάνοντες θλιβόμενοι οὐ δικασθήσονται, οἱ δὲ ἐν ὑποκρίσει λαμβάνοντες τίσουσιν δίκην.

Did. 2:1-7; cf. Rom. 13:9, 13. The Didache list of the commandments does contain the items listed by Paul, but it is so greatly expanded and developed as to leave little basis for the predication of dependence on Romans.

Did. 2:6; cf. I Cor. 5:10. Ἡ πλεονέκτης and ἢ ἅρπαξ are used in close connection in each of the passages. Paul's list of vices is more or less conventional and in accordance with the practice of the times. The Didache is not necessarily dependent because its list contains two items in Paul's list.

Did. 3:1; cf. I Thess. 5:22. A more probable source than I Thess. 5:22 is Barn. 4:1 or Job 1:1 and 2:3.

Did. 3:3; cf. Col. 3:8. The adjective αἰσχρολόγος occurs neither in the New Testament nor in the LXX. In the writings of the Apostolic Fathers it is used only in Did. 3:3 and 5:1. The noun is used in the New Testament in Col. 3:9, where it occurs in a list of vices.

Did. 4:3; cf. I Cor. 1:10; 6:5.

Did. 4:5; cf. Rom. 12:8.

Did. 4:8; cf. Rom. 15:27.

Did. 4:10; cf. Rom. 8:29, 30.

Did. 4:11; cf. Eph. 6:5, 6.

Did. 5:1; cf. Rom. 1:29-31. Such lists of vices are thoroughly conventional.

Did. 5:2; cf. Rom. 12:9.

Did. 6:2; cf. I Cor. 7:36. In I Cor. 7:25-40 Paul gives a series of instances where two permissible courses of action are offered. The parallel in Barn. 19:8 for Did. 6:2 is not so close as in most of the instances noted.

Did. 6:3; cf. I Cor. 8:4. There is no parallel for this

passage in Barnabas. The interesting coincidences in theme and
language may indicate acquaintance with I Corinthians.

Did. 6:3; cf. I Cor. 7:1, 25, 8:1, 12:1, 16:1, 12. In I
Corinthians Paul introduces the several sections of his letter
with the formula περὶ δέ. After the close of the "Two Ways" section, the author of the Didache uses the same formula in 6:3, 7:1,
9:1-3, and 11:2. This does not necessarily mean acquaintance with
I Corinthians. In the epistle of "Claudius to the Alexandrians"[27]
this same parallel in structure may be observed, and it is entirely
out of the question to suppose that Claudius was influenced by I
Corinthians. He was simply following the usual form for making the
various divisions of his thought distinct.

Did. 9:2, 3; cf. I Cor. 10:16, 21. The Didache order of
the "cup" and the "bread" is illustrated in I Corinthians. The
only other parallel for this order in early Christian literature
is Luke 22:14 f. In Did. 9:5 there is a recurrence to the usual
order, just as is the case in I Cor. 11:28. It is possible that
this order in I Corinthians suggested the order and the separate
blessing of the "cup" and the "bread" in the Didache. The data in
both instances may, however, be accounted for on the basis of Jewish
custom.

Did. 9:4; cf. I Cor. 10:17. The figure of grains scattered
on the mountain and then gathered together in one loaf may be a
development of Paul's illustration (cf. John 11:52). It is to be
noted, however, that the prayer in the Didache is distinctly eschatological.

Did. 10:6; cf. I Cor. 16:22. The ἀμήν with which the Didache closes its prayer may be an echo of I Cor. 14:16. Μαρὰν
ἀθά may be from I Cor. 16:22, but it is probably a liturgical formula for which the author of the Didache would not have to refer
to I Corinthians.

Did. 11:2, 3; cf. I Cor. 12:28. Nothing is said about
"apostles" after Did. 11:6, and they are assigned no duties in
the instances where they are mentioned. It is possible that in
the church of the time of the Didache they were no longer real

---

[27]H. I. Bell, _Jews and Christians in Egypt_ (London: Oxford
University Press, 1924).

functionaries and that περὶ δὲ τῶν ἀποστόλων καὶ προφητῶν is a
reminiscence of I Cor. 12:28.

Did. 11:7; cf. I Cor. 12:10. It is barely possible that
the author of the Didache was consciously taking issue with and
deliberately correcting Paul when he warns: καὶ πάντα προφήτην
λαλοῦντα ἐν πνεύματι οὐ πειράσετε οὐδὲ διακρινεῖτε.

Did. 11:11; cf. Eph. 5:32. The meaning of the Didache
clause ποιῶν εἰς μυστήριον κοσμικὸν ἐκκλησίας is not clear. The
writer may have the idea and language of Ephesians in mind.

Did. 12:3; cf. II Thess. 3:10. The practical purpose and
advice of these passages are the same. The author of the Didache
may have been influenced by Paul's directions in II Thessalonians
when he says regarding visiting brethren: εἰ δὲ θέλει πρὸς ὑμᾶς
καθῆσθαι, τεχνίτης ὤν, ἐργαζέσθω καὶ φαγέτω.

Did. 13:1, 2; cf. I Cor. 9:14.

Did. 16:4; cf. II Thess. 2:3, 4, 8. The points of similarity between the passages are as follows:

Κοσμοπλανής (cf. Apoc. 12:9)	Ὁ ἄνθρωπος τῆς ἀνομίας (cf. Matt. 24:15)
Ὡς υἱὸς Θεοῦ	Ὥστε αὐτὸν εἰς τὸν ναὸν τοῦ Θεοῦ καθίσαι, ἀποδεικνύντα ἑαυτὸν ὅτι ἔστιν Θεός. (cf. Apoc. 13:11)
Σημεῖα καὶ τέρατα	Σημείοις καὶ τέρασιν (cf. Matt. 24:24, Mark 13:22)

The specific and personal doctrine of the anti-Christ may
be a reminiscence of II Thessalonians (but see Barnabas, chap. 4).

Did. 16:6; cf. II Thess. 4:16, 17, and I Cor. 15:52. The
general scheme of Did. 16:6 agrees with that of I Thess. 4:16 f.—
the revelation of the Messiah from heaven, the trumpet, the resurrection of the dead. The φωνῆς σάλπιγγος may be a reminiscence
of I Cor. 15:52.

Did. 16:7; cf. I Thess. 3:13. Ἥξει ὁ κύριος καὶ πάντες
οἱ ἅγιοι μετ' αὐτοῦ may reflect the influence of I Thess. 3:13,
but it may, with equal probability, reflect the influence of Zech.
14:5.

Harnack finds no instance where the use of any Pauline letter is really evident.[28] Leipoldt describes the result of his examination of the Didache for traces of Paul's letters as "unbe-
stimmtere."[29]

The present study finds that the strongest case can be
made for acquaintance with I Corinthians, but the evidence, even
here, is inconclusive. Next in line of possibility come I and II
Thessalonians, with a still weaker likelihood for acquaintance
with Ephesians and Colossians.

TABLE OF RESULTS

	A	B	C	Unclassed
Romans............	•	•	•	7
I Corinthians.......	•	•	•	13
II Corinthians......	•	•	•	....
Galatians..........	•	•	•	....
Ephesians..........	•	•	•	2
Philippians.........	•	•	•	....
Colossians..........	•	•	•	1
I Thessalonians.....	•	•	•	2
II Thessalonians....	•	•	•	4
Philemon...........	•	•	•	....

The Second Epistle of Clement
to the Corinthians

The use of the Old Testament in II Clement is characterized
by freedom rather than by exactness. The method of reference is
illustrated in 6:8, where a loose quotation of Ezek. 14:18, 20 is
introduced with the formula λέγει δὲ καὶ ἡ γραφὴ ἐν τῷ Ἰεζεκιήλ.
In 11:2 f. there is a quotation of an unknown apocryphal writing

---

[28]A. Harnack, "Die Lehre der zwölf Apostl," Texte und
Untersuchungen zur Geschichte der altchristlichen Literatur (1884),
II, 87, 88; "Apostellehre," Hauck's Realencyklopäedie (1896), I,
716.

[29]Op. cit., p. 190.

with the introductory formula λέγει γὰρ καὶ ὁ προφητικὸς λόγος.

Illustrations of formulas of citation for material from
the canonical gospels are: 6:1, λέγει δὲ ὁ κύριος; 8:5, λέγει
γὰρ ὁ κύριος ἐν τῷ εὐαγγελίῳ; 9:11, καὶ γὰρ εἶπεν ὁ κύριος.

In two instances gospel material is quoted as though it
were Scripture: 2:4, καὶ ἑτέρα δὲ γραφὴ λέγει, ὅτι οὐκ ἦλθον
καλέσαι δικαίους, ἀλλὰ ἁμαρτωλούς; and 13:4, ὅταν γὰρ ἀκούσωσιν
παρ' ἡμῶν, ὅτι λέγει ὁ Θεός, Οὐ χάρις ὑμῖν, εἰ ἀγαπᾶτε τοὺς ἀγα-
πῶντας ὑμᾶς.

In 14:2 a Christian writing (or writings) is apparently
co-ordinated with the writings of the Old Testament: λέγει γὰρ ἡ
γραφή . . . . καὶ ἔτι τὰ βιβλία καὶ οἱ ἀπόστολοι τὴν ἐκκλησίαν
οὐ νῦν εἶναι λέγουσιν. It is to be noted, however, that οἱ
ἀπόστολοι are not included in τὰ βιβλία, which probably constituted
the writer's Scripture. Nor is it possible to determine the content of οἱ ἀπόστολοι.

There are no formal quotations of the Pauline letters.
The allusions to these letters are so general and free that in no
instance is there certainty of literary dependence.

    II Clem. 7:1   I Corinthians C

῞Ωστε οὖν, ἀδελφαί μου, ἀγωνισώμεθα εἰδότες, ὅτι ἐν χερσὶν
ὁ ἀγὼν καὶ ὅτι εἰς τοὺς φθαρτοὺς ἀγῶνας καταπλέουσιν πολλοί, ἀλλ'
οὐ πάντες στεφανοῦνται, εἰ μὴ οἱ πολλὰ κοπιάσαντες καὶ καλῶς ἀγω-
νισάμενοι.

I Cor. 9:24, 25. Οὐκ οἴδατε ὅτι οἱ ἐν σταδίῳ τρέχοντες
πάντες μὲν τρέχουσιν, εἷς δὲ λαμβάνει τὸ βραβεῖον; οὕτως τρέχετε
ἵνα καταλάβητε. πᾶς δὲ ὁ ἀγωνιζόμενος πάντα ἐγκρατεύεται, ἐκεῖνοι
μὲν οὖν ἵνα φθαρτὸν στέφανον λάβωσιν, ἡμεῖς δὲ ἄφθαρτον.

The athletic metaphor was a popular one.[30] Its employment
by II Clement does not of itself show literary acquaintance with
I Corinthians. The similarity of the context, the contrast of
corruptible with incorruptible prizes, the insistence that only he
who runs well deserves a crown, the similarity of the terms used
in developing the figure do, however, when taken together, tend to

---

[30]P. Wendland, Die hellenistisch-römische Kultur: Die
urchristlichen Literaturformen (Tübingen: J. C. B. Mohr, 1912),
p. 357.

create a reasonable probability that in II Clem. 7:1 there is an echo of I Cor. 9:24, 25.

II Clem. 9:3, 4   I Corinthians C

Δεῖ οὖν ἡμᾶς ὡς ναὸν Θεοῦ φυλάσσειν τὴν σάρκα. ὃν τρόπον γὰρ ἐν τῇ σαρκὶ ἐκλήθητε, καὶ ἐν τῇ σαρκὶ ἐλεύσεσθε.

I Cor. 6:19. Ἢ οὐκ οἴδατε ὅτι τὸ σῶμα ὑμῶν ναὸς τοῦ ἐν ὑμῖν ⌐ἁγίου πνευματός ἐστιν⌐, οὗ ἔχετε ἀπὸ Θεοῦ; καὶ οὐκ ἐστὲ ἑαυτῶν, ἠγοράσθητε γὰρ τιμῆς. δοξάσατε δὴ τὸν Θεὸν ἐν τῷ σώματι ὑμῶν.

Paul and II Clement both undertake to inculcate purity of living by insisting that Christ has redeemed the whole life. They assert that the body is, accordingly, the temple of God and that as such it must be kept free from defilement. There is the alternative possibility that this imagery had become popularized and that II Clement reflects common usage (cf. Ign. Philad. 7:2 and Eph. 15:3).

II Clem. 11:7   I Corinthians B

'Εὰν οὖν ποιήσωμεν τὴν δικαιοσύνην ἐναντίον τοῦ Θεοῦ, εἰ- σήξομεν εἰς τὴν βασιλείαν αὐτοῦ καὶ ληψόμεθα τὰς ἐπαγγελίας ἃς οὓς οὐκ ἤκουσεν οὐδὲ ὀφθαλμὸς εἶδεν, οὐδὲ επὶ καρδίαν ἀνθρώπου ἀνέβη.

I Cor. 2:9. See the text and discussion in connection with I Clem. 34:8.

II Clem. 14:1   Ephesians C

Ὥστε, ἀδελφοί, ποιοῦντες τὸ θέλημα τοῦ πατρὸς ἡμῶν Θεοῦ ἐσόμεθα ἐκ τῆς ἐκκλησίας τῆς πρώτης, τῆς πνευματικῆς, τῆς πρὸ ἡλίου καὶ σελήνης ἐκτισμένης.

Eph. 1:4, 5. Καθὼς ἐξελέξατο ἡμᾶς ἐν αὐτῷ πρὸ καταβολῆς κόσμου, εἶναι ἡμᾶς ἁγίους καὶ ἀμώμους κατενώπιον αὐτοῦ ἐν ἀγάπη. 2:22. 'Εν ᾧ καὶ ὑμεῖς συνοικοδομεῖσθε εἰς κατοικητήριον τοῦ Θεοῦ ἐν πνεύματι.

The τῆς πνευματικῆς and τῆς πρὸ ἡλίου καὶ σελήνης ἐκτι- σμένης of II Clement are interesting parallels for the ὑμεῖς συνοικοδομεῖσθε εἰς κατοικητήριον τοῦ Θεοῦ ἐν πνεύματι and πρὸ καταβολῆς κόσμου of Ephesians.

II Clem. 14:2   Ephesians C

Οὐκ οἴομαι δὲ ὑμᾶς ἀγνοεῖν, ὅτι ἐκκλησία ζῶσα σῶμα ἐστιν
Χριστοῦ. λέγει γὰρ ἡ γραφή. ἐποίησεν ὁ θεὸς τὸν ἄνθρωπον ἄρσεν
καὶ θῆλυ. τὸ ἄρσεν ἐστιν ὁ Χριστός, τὸ Θῆλυ ἡ ἐκκλησία.

Eph. 1:22. Καὶ αὐτὸν ἔδωκεν κεφαλὴν ὑπὲρ πάντα τῇ ἐκκλησίᾳ, ἥτις ἐστὶν τὸ σῶμα αὐτοῦ, τὸ πλήρωμα τοῦ τὰ πάντα ἐν πᾶσιν
πληρουμένου. 5:23, 31. ῞Οτι ⌜ἀνήρ ἐστιν κεφαλῆ⌝ τῆς γυναικὸς ὡς
ὁ Χριστὸς κεφαλὴ τῆς ἐκκλησίας, αὐτὸς σωτὴρ τοῦ σώματος . . . .
τὸ μυστήριον τοῦτο μέγα ἐστίν, ἐγὼ δὲ λέγω εἰς Χριστὸν καὶ [εἰς]
τὴν ἐκκλησίαν.

The points of similarity between these passages are the
description of the church as the body of Christ (cf. Rom. 12:6;
I Cor. 10:16 f., 12:27; Col. 1:18, 24, 2:19, and 3:15) and the
portrayal of the relation between Christ and the church as analogous to that of husband and wife. The first phase of the figure
receives its most extended development in Ephesians (1:23, 2:16,
4:4, 12-16). The second phase with its extended allegorical exposition probably discloses a recollection of Eph. 5:31, 32, where,
after quoting Gen. 2:24, the author comments τὸ μυστήριον τοῦτο
μέγα ἐστίν, ἐγὼ δὲ λέγω εἰς Χριστὸν καὶ [εἰς] τὴν ἐκκλησίαν. The
entire metaphor and particularly this application of it bear the
marks of having been suggested by Ephesians.

II Clem. 14:5   I Corinthians C

Οὔτε ἐξειπεῖν τις δύναται οὔτε λαλῆσαι ἃ ἡτοίμασεν ὁ κύριος
τοῖς ἐκλεκτοῖς αὐτοῦ.

For the text and discussion of I Cor. 2:9 see the note on
I Clem. 34:8.

Instances of possible literary reminiscence.—II Clem. 1:8;
cf. Rom. 4:17. ᾿Εκάλεσεν γὰρ ἡμᾶς οὐκ ὄντας καὶ ἠθέλησεν ἐκ μὴ
ὄντος εἶναι ἡμᾶς may represent a reminiscence of Romans in II
Clement. The likelihood of this is reduced by the equally striking parallel in Philo, De spec. leg. iv. 7. 187: Τὰ γὰρ μὴ ὄντα
ἐκάλεσεν εἰς τὸ εἶναι.

II Clem. 2:1; Cf. Gal. 4:27. Paul and II Clement both re-
produce the LXX of Isa. 54:1. Clement omits the introductory formula γέγραπται γάρ, very probably because the passage has just been

read to the congregation before the sermon (cf. 15:1, 17:3, 19:1).
Paul and II Clement both allegorize the passage to the same general effect, the one using it to contrast two dispensations and
the other to illustrate the divinely intended progress of gentile
Christianity as over against Judaism. This allegorizing of the
passage for the purpose of contrasting two religious groups may
have been suggested by Galatians.

   II Clem. 6:3-5; cf. Eph. 2:1-3. The dualism of II Clement is similar to that of Eph. 2:1-3 and of the Pauline letters
(cf. Rom. 12:2, I Cor. 2:6, II Cor. 4:4, Gal. 1:4). The comparison is made with the Ephesian passage because in its detailed
character it more closely resembles II Clement. Both view the
present age as transitory, as under the control of evil, as doomed
to destruction, and therefore to be renounced. Paul inherited
this general conception from Jewish apocalypticism, modifying it
in the light of his Christian experience and faith. In a similarly
modified form it was shared by Christians quite generally (Jas.
4:4, I John 5:19, Hermas Sim. I., etc.; cf. IV Ezra 7:50 and Apoc.
Bar. 44:9, 12).

   II Clem. 8:1; cf. Rom. 9:21. Paul's use of Jeremiah's
figure of the potter and the clay may have suggested the employment
of it in II Clement. The development of the imagery in the latter, however, suggests direct dependence on Jer. 18:4 ff.

   II Clem. 13:1; cf. Col. 3:22 and Eph. 6:6. The word
ἀνθρωπάρεσκοι occurs in the New Testament only in Col. 3:22 and
Eph. 6:6, and in the writings of the Apostolic Fathers only in
II Clem. 13:1. It does occur in Ps. 52:6, however (ὁ θεὸς διε-
σκόρπισεν ὀστᾶ ἀνθρωπαρέσκων), and in Ps. Sol. 4:8, 10, 21. The
interest of II Clement in the effect of the conduct of Christians
on ταῖς ἔξω ἀνθρώποις parallels a similar interest of Col. 4:5,
and the two coincidences create the possibility that Colossians
influenced II Clement.

   II Clem. 17:3; cf. Rom. 12:16. Ἵνα πάντες τὸ αὐτὸ
φρονοῦντες represents a type of moral exhortation that had perhaps
become a commonplace in Christian preaching.

   II Clem. 19:2; cf. Eph. 4:18 and Rom. 1:2. Καὶ ἐσκοτίσμεθα
τὴν διάνοιαν may indicate acquaintance with Ephesians and Romans.
See the text of Eph. 4:18 and Rom. 1:21 and the note on I Clem. 36:2.

The only letters of the Pauline collection of which fairly clear traces are found are I Corinthians and Ephesians. The data for any influence of Romans, Galatians, and Colossians are scanty and indecisive.

TABLE OF RESULTS

	A	B	C	Unclassed
Romans..............	•	•	•	4
I Corinthians.......	•	1	3	....
II Corinthians......	•	•	•	....
Galatians...........	•	•	•	1
Ephesians...........	•	•	2	3
Philippians.........	•	•	•	....
Colossians..........	•	•	•	1
I Thessalonians.....	•	•	•	....
II Thessalonians....	•	•	•	....
Philemon............	•	•	•	....

The Martyrdom of St. Polycarp,
Bishop of Smyrna

There are no direct quotations of Old or New Testament writings in the Martyrdom of Polycarp. There are allusions and narratives of fact that indicate acquaintance with certain of these writings, but the data for the determination of literary relationships are meager.

There are no allusions to Paul and no specific mention of his letters. The author presumably knew the Pauline letter collection and his adoption of the letter form for the presentation of his message may testify to the influence of that collection upon him. There is, however, no single instance that warrants the certainty of definite literary indebtedness to a letter of the Pauline corpus.

Mart. Polyc. Inscr.   I Corinthians C

ʽΗ ἐκκλησία τοῦ Θεοῦ ἡ παροικοῦσα Σμύρναν τῇ ἐκκλησίᾳ τοῦ Θεοῦ τῇ παροικούσῃ ἐν Φιλομηλίῳ καὶ πάσαις ταῖς κατὰ πάντα τόπον τῆς ἁγίας καὶ καθολικῆς ἐκκλησίας παροικίαις.

I Cor. 1:2. Παυλος κλητὸς ἀπόστολος . . . . τῇ ἐκκλησίᾳ
τοῦ Θεοῦ τῇ οὔσῃ ἐν Κορίνθῳ . . . . σὺν πᾶσιν ταῖς ἐπικαλουμέναις
τὸ ὄνομα τοῦ κυρίου ἡμῶν Ἰησοῦ Χριστοῦ ἐν παντὶ τόπῳ αὐτῶν καὶ
ἡμῶν·

The parallelism in the form and language of the two in-
scriptions is considerable:

Τῇ ἐκκλησίᾳ τοῦ Θεοῦ τῇ   Τῇ ἐκκλησίᾳ τοῦ Θεοῦ τῇ
παροικοῦσῃ ἐν Φιλομηλίῳ καὶ   οὔσῃ ἐν Κορίνθῳ . . . . σὺν
πάσαις ταῖς κατὰ πάντα τόπον   πᾶσιν ταῖς . . . . ἐν παντὶ
                                 τόπῳ

Mart. Polyc. 1:2   Philippians C

"Ινα μιμηταὶ καὶ ἡμεῖς αὐτοῦ γενώμεθα, μὴ μόνον σκοποῦντες
τὸ καθ᾽ ἑαυτούς, ἀλλὰ καὶ τὸ κατὰ τοὺς πέλας.

Phil. 2:4. Μὴ τὰ ἑαυτῶν ⌜ἕκαστοι⌝ σκοποῦντες, ἀλλὰ καὶ τὰ
⌐ἑτέρων ἕκαστοι. . . . ⌐

Mart. Polyc. 2:3   I Corinthians B

Καὶ τοῖς τῆς καρδίας ὀφθαλμαῖς ἀνέβλεπον τὰ τηρούμενα ταῖς
ὑπομείνασιν ἀγαθά, ἃ οὔτε οὖς ἤκουσεν οὔτε ὀφθαλμὸς εἶδεν οὔτε ἐπὶ
καρδίαν ἀνθρώπου ἀνέβη.

I Cor. 2:9. For the text and discussion see the note on
I Clem. 34:8. There is the same futuristic emphasis in Mart.
Polyc. as in I Clement, but dependence on I Corinthians is prob-
able in both cases.

Instances of possible literary reminiscence.—Mart. Polyc.
1:2; cf. I Cor. 11:1 and I Thess. 1:6. The "imitation" of a heroic
follower of Jesus who himself conceived of discipleship in terms of
imitation of his Lord is the point of the statement in Mart. Polyc.
There is a definitely martyrological interest in the statement that
does not exist in the Pauline letters, but the later writer may
have used the earlier conception and language in an adapted sense.

Mart. Polyc. 2:2; cf. II Cor. 5:6. The τῆς σαρκὸς ἀπεδή-
μουν may indicate the influence of II Cor. 5:6.

Mart. Polyc. 10:2; cf. Rom. 13:1. The attitude toward governmental authorities and the possible implications of δεδιδάγμεθα
may point to the influence of Rom. 13:1.

Mart. Polyc. 17:3; cf. I Cor. 1:1 and I Thess. 1:6. Μιμητὰς τοῦ κυρίου may be an echo of Paul's figure.

Mart. Polyc. 20:2; cf. Rom. 16:25-27. The peroration of 20:2 may be in imitation of Rom. 16:25-27. The passage has a strongly liturgical tone, however.

The present study finds that acquaintance with I Corinthians and Philippians is probable and that acquaintance with Romans, I Thessalonians, and II Corinthians is possible.

TABLE OF RESULTS

	A	B	C	Unclassed
Romans...............	•	•	•	2
I Corinthians.......	•	1	1	2
II Corinthians......	•	•	•	1
Galatians...........	•	•	•	....
Ephesians...........	•	•	•	....
Philippians.........	•	•	1	....
Colossians..........	•	•	•	....
I Thessalonians.....	•	•	•	2
II Thessalonians....	•	•	•	....
Philemon............	•	•	•	....

The Apology of Aristides

The Apology of Aristides was written toward the middle of the second century and addressed to Antoninus Pius, the emperor.[31] Its concern is with the questions that occupied popular philosophic thought in the second century.

The writer makes very meager use of the writings of the Old and New Testaments. There are no direct quotations, nor are any of the books of our New Testament mentioned by name. There are instances, however, where the influence of their language and ideas seems to be reflected. In chapter 15 (οὗ τὸ κλέος τῆς παρουσίας ἐκ τῆς παρ' αὐταῖς καλουμένης εὐαγγελικῆς ἁγίας γραφῆς

---

[31] J. Geffcken, Zwei griechische Apologeten (Leipzig: B. G. Teubner, 1907), and Stählin, op. cit., p. 1280.

ἔξεστί σοι γνῶναι, βασιβεῦ, ἐὰν ἐντύχης) one or more of the Gospels seem to be in mind, and the Christology of the section (σάρκα
ἀνέλαβε) may indicate acquaintance with John 1:14. In 16:5 ("Capi-
te igitur scripturas eorum et legite in eis") the availability of
the Christian writings for persons interested in consulting them
is clearly indicated. In 15:4 (καὶ τοὺς πλησίον φιλοῦσι) there is
a possible allusion to material from the Synoptics (cf. Matt. 19:
19, 22:39; Mark 12:31, 33; Luke 10:27), and similarly in 16:2 ("et
dona sua celant sicut qui thesaurum invenit et abscondit"; cf. Matt.
13:44).

        Arist. 1:5; cf. Col. 1:17. Aristides speaks of God, and
Paul of Christ, but there may be a reminiscence of Paul's language
in δι' αὐτοῦ δὲ τὰ πάντα συνέστηκεν.

        Arist. 3:1; cf. Rom. 1:25 and Col. 2:8. Robinson thinks
that the μὴ εἰδότες Θεὸν ἐπλανήθησαν ὀπίσω τῶν στοιχείων καὶ
ἤρξαντο σέβεσθαι τὴν κτίσιν παρὰ τὸν κτίσαντα αὐτούς of Arist. 3:1
is "clearly based on Rom. 1:25."[32] His statement is, perhaps, too
strong, and yet the resemblance in idea and language is sufficiently striking to make literary reminiscence possible. The verbal
similarity to Colossians is less convincing and is as probably due
to a common Hellenistic background as to literary influence.

        Arist. 4:1; cf. Rom. 1:23. The sense in which φθαρτός and
ἄφθαρτος are used may indicate literary relationship. The usage
is as probably due to a common religious inheritance.

        Arist. 7:4; cf. Rom. 1:24. Both writers are condemning
idolatry, and the resemblances in their language may indicate literary dependence.

        Arist. 8:2; cf. Rom. 1:22.

        Arist. 11:7; cf. Rom. 7:8. The sense here is different,
but ὅθεν λαμβάνοντες οἱ ἄνθρωποι ἀφορμὴν ἀπὸ τῶν Θεῶν αὐτῶν ἔπρατ-
τον πᾶσαν ἀνομίαν καὶ ἀσέλγειαν καὶ ἀσέβειαν may involve a sort of
echo of Romans.

        Arist. 13:7; cf. Rom. 7:12. Νυνὶ δὲ οἱ νομοί καλοί εἰσι
καὶ δίκαιοι has some resemblance to the similar description in
Romans.

_____

        [32]J. A. Robinson, "The Apology of Aristides," Texts and
Studies[2] (Cambridge: Cambridge University Press, 1893), I, 83.

Arist. 15:7; cf. Col. 3:12. Aristides' description of the manner in which Christians lived ("et in omni humilitate et benignitate ambulant et mendacium apud eos non invenitur") may reflect the influence of Colossians.

TABLE OF RESULTS

	A	B	C	Unclassed
Romans..............	•	•	•	6
I Corinthians.......	•	•	•	....
II Corinthians......	•	•	•	....
Galatians...........	•	•	•	....
Ephesians...........	•	•	•	....
Philippians.........	•	•	•	....
Colossians..........	•	•	•	3
I Thessalonians.....	•	•	•	....
II Thessalonians....	•	•	•	....
Philemon............	•	•	•	....

IV

THE RETURN TO POPULARITY

The second half of the second century was marked by the gradual return to popularity of Paul's letters, culminating in their inclusion in the Muratorian Canon. The author of II Peter refers with some embarrassment to the letters and his actual use of them is characterized by extreme reserve, and yet his specific mention of them (3:16) testifies to the favorable trend that was developing.

Justin avoided the mention of Paul's name but made liberal use of the content of the letters. The Pastorals are written in Paul's name and employ his language in the delivery of their message on church polity. In the Pastorals, Paul is completely redeemed from the heretics and is presented to the Church as the patron saint of orthodoxy. In more or less the same effective way in which Ephesians had originally presented the Pauline letter collection as embodying a message to the entire church, the Pastorals restored the corpus to general usage as the primary source for guidance in church discipline and doctrine.

The Preaching of Peter and the Apology of Quadratus are fragmentarily preserved in other writings. The several small fragments of the one are found in the writings of Clement of Alexandria. The single extant fragment of the other is found in Eusebius HE iv. 3, 2. There are no references to the books of the New Testament in these fragments that can be identified.

The Second Epistle of Peter

The author of II Peter makes very meager use of the Old Testament. Three allusions to Isaiah, one to a Psalm, and one to Proverbs exhaust his employment of Old Testament material. In 2:22, where the reference is to Prov. 26:11, there occurs the nearest approach to a formula of citation: Συμβέβηκεν αὐτοῖς τὸ τῆς

ἀληθοῦς παροιμίας. In the other instances he gives no evidence
of conscious literary indebtedness.

The writer's acquaintance with Christian writings is
clearer and more extensive. He seems to have known the Fourfold
Gospel, Acts, some of the Catholics, and a corpus of Pauline letters. In the central section of his letter he incorporates the
body of the epistle of Jude but without the slightest indication
that he has done so.

The allusion to Paul's letters in 3:15, 16 is most significant. He knows them as a collection (ἐν πάσαις ἐπιστολαῖς
λαλῶν), and he seems to accord them a status that approximates
that of Scripture (ὡς καὶ τὰς λοιπὰς γραφάς). Yet they are a
source of difficulty, and even embarrassment, to him (ἐν αἷς
ἐστὶν δυσνόητά τινα, ἃ οἱ ἀμαθεῖς καὶ ἀστήρικτοι στρεβλοῦσιν
. . . . πρὸς τὴν ἰδίαν αὐτῶν ἀπώλειαν). It is possible that the
use of Paul's letters by heretics caused the author of II Peter
his difficulty and led him to use the letters sparingly.

II Pet. 1:1, 2   Ephesians B

⌜Σίμων⌝ Πέτρος δοῦλος καὶ ἀπόστολος Ἰησοῦ Χριστοῦ τοῖς
ἰσότιμον ἡμῖν λαχοῦσιν πίστιν ἐν δικαιοσύνη τοῦ Θεοῦ ἡμῶν καὶ
σωτῆρος Ἰησοῦ Χριστοῦ· Χάρις ὑμῖν καὶ εἰρήνη πληθυνθείη ἐν ἐπιγνώσει τοῦ Θεοῦ.

Eph. 1:1, 2. Παῦλος ἀπόστολος Χριστοῦ Ἰησοῦ διὰ θελήματος Θεοῦ τοῖς ἁγίοις τοῖς οὖσιν . . . . καὶ πιστοῖς ἐν Χριστῷ
Ἰησοῦ· Χάρις ὑμῖν καὶ εἰρήνη ἀπὸ Θεοῦ (cf. Rom. 1:1, 3:29, 30).

Resemblances to the salutation of I Peter are clear in II
Pet. 1:1, 2. In its catholic character it also resembles Ephesians, and that writing was probably its model. The fundamental
basis of personal religion for II Peter is indicated in the phrase
ἐν ἐπιγνώσει τοῦ Θεοῦ, and this probably reflects the influence
of Eph. 1:17, ἐν ἐπιγνώσει αὐτοῦ. Ἐπίγνωσις is used in the New
Testament only in the Pauline letters and in the later letters that
were influenced by them (Ephesians, the Pastorals, Hebrews, and
II Peter).

The writer's description of himself as δοῦλος καὶ ἀπόστολος
Ἰησοῦ Χριστοῦ suggests acquaintance with Paul's self-introduction
in Romans as δοῦλος Ἰησοῦ Χριστοῦ, κλητὸς ἀπόστολος. The concep-

tion of the essential democracy of Christian faith is not unlike that of Rom. 3:29, 30, ἢ 'Ιουδαίων ὁ Θεὸς μόνον; οὐχὶ καὶ ἐθνῶν; ναὶ καὶ ἐθνῶν, εἴπερ εἷς ὁ Θεός κτλ.

II Pet. 1:10   Romans C

Σπουδάσατε βεβαίαν ὑμῶν τὴν κλῆσιν καὶ ἐκλογὴν ποιεῖσθαι. ταῦτα γὰρ ποιοῦντες οὐ μὴ πταίσητέ ποτε·

The vocabulary and thought of II Peter are strongly reminiscent of Romans. The fundamental thought is that of Rom. 8:28-30, ταῖς κατὰ πρόθεσιν κλητοῖς οὖσιν . . . . οὓς δὲ προώρισεν, τούτους καὶ ἐκάλεσεν· καὶ οὓς ἐκάλεσεν, τούτους καὶ ἐδικαίωσεν. The noun ἐκλογή occurs in the New Testament only in Acts 9:15; Rom. 9:11, 11:5, 7, 28; I Thess. 1:4; and II Pet. 1:10. The verb πταίω is found in the New Testament only in Rom. 11:11; Jas. 2:10, 3:2; and II Pet. 1:10. In II Peter and Romans it is used in the discussion of ἐκλογή.

II Pet. 1:13, 14   II Corinthians C

'Εφ' ὅσον εἰμὶ ἐν τούτῳ τῷ σκηνώματι, διεγείρειν ὑμᾶς ἐν ὑπομνήσει, εἰδὼς ὅτι ταχινή ἐστιν ἡ ἀπόθεσις τοῦ σκηνώματος μου, καθὼς καὶ ὁ κύριος ἡμῶν 'Ιησοῦς Χριστὸς ἐδήλωσεν μοι· σπουδάσω δὲ καὶ ἑκάστοτε.

II Cor. 5:1. Οἴδαμεν γὰρ ὅτι ἐὰν ἡ ἐπίγειος ἡμῶν οἰκία τοῦ σκήνους καταλυθῇ, οἰκοδομὴν ἐκ Θεοῦ ἔχομεν. . . . . 4. Καὶ ἐνδυσάμενοι οὐ γυμνοὶ εὑρεθησόμεθα. καὶ γὰρ οἱ ὄντες ἐν τῷ σκήνει στενάζομεν βαρούμενοι ἐφ' ᾧ οὐ θέλομεν ἐκδύσασθαι ἀλλ' ἐπενδύσασθαι, ἵνα καταποθῇ τὸ θνητὸν ὑπὸ τῆς ζωῆς.

Σκήνωμα occurs in the New Testament only in Acts 7:46 and II Pet. 1:13, 14. The thought of II Peter corresponds so closely with that of II Corinthians, however, as to create the likelihood of literary dependence.

II Pet. 2:18, 19   Galatians C

Δελεάζουσιν ἐν ἐπιθυμίαις σαρκὸς ἀσελγείαις τοὺς ὀλίγως ἀποφεύγοντας τοὺς ἐν πλάνη ἀναστρεφομένους, ἐλευθερίαν αὐταῖς ἐπαγγελλόμενοι, αὐτοὶ δοῦλοι ὑπάρχοντες τῆς φθορᾶς·

Gal. 5:13. 'Υμεῖς γὰρ ἐπ' ἐλευθερίᾳ ἐκλήθητε, ἀδελφοί· μόνον μὴ τὴν ἐλευθερίαν εἰς ἀφορμὴν τῇ σαρκί, ἀλλὰ διὰ τῆς ἀγάπης δουλεύετε ἀλλήλοις·

The use of ἐλευθερία in the New Testament is confined to
the Pauline corpus and the Catholic epistles. The contrast in II
Peter with δοῦλοι and the exhortation against obedience to fleshly
desires relate the passage rather closely to Gal. 5:13.

II Pet. 2:19   Romans B

Ὧι γάρ τις ἥττηται, τούτῳ δεδούλωται.

Rom. 6:16. Οὐκ οἴδατε ὅτι ᾧ παριστάνετε ἑαυτοὺς δούλους
εἰς ὑπακοήν, δοῦλοί ἐστε ᾧ ὑπακούετε, ἤτοι ἁμαρτίας εἰς θάνατον ἢ
ὑπακοῆς εἰς δικαιοσύνην; (cf. II Cor. 12:13).

Ἡττάομαι occurs in the New Testament only in II Cor. 12:
13 and II Pet. 2:19, 20. This verb is the only point of contact
between the passages. The thought is identical with that of Rom.
6:16, and the general point of the two contexts is so nearly the
same as to create the strong presumption in favor of literary dependence.

II Pet. 3:9   Romans C

Οὐ βραδύνει Κύριος τῆς ἐπαγγελίας, ὥς τινες βραδυτῆτα
ἡγοῦνται, ἀλλὰ μακροθυμεῖ εἰς ὑμᾶς, μὴ βουλόμενος τινας ἀπολέσθαι
ἀλλὰ πάντας εἰς μετάνοιαν χωρῆσαι.

Rom. 2:4. Ἢ τοῦ πλούτου τῆς χρηστότητος αὐτοῦ καὶ τῆς
ἀνοχῆς καὶ τῆς μακροθυμίας καταφρονεῖς, ἀγνοῶν ὅτι τὸ χρηστὸν τοῦ
Θεοῦ εἰς μετάνοιάν σε ἄγει;

The idea in II Peter seems to represent a development from
Rom. 2:4. The delay of the Parousia is explained in terms of God's
patience and the divine desire that men repent. This is Paul's
explanation of the delay of impending judgment. This idea is expressed in the New Testament only in Rom. 2:4, 9:22, and II Pet.
3:15 (cf. I Pet. 3:20).

II Pet. 3:10   I Thessalonians C

Ἥξει δὲ ἡμέρα Κυρίου ὡς κλέπτης.

I Thess. 5:2. Ἡμέρα Κυρίου ὡς κλέπτης ἐν νυκτὶ οὕτως
ἔρχεται.

This saying is found in the New Testament only in II Peter
and I Thessalonians. The saying may have become proverbial, and
the author of II Peter may have used it as such without any

conscious indebtedness to a written source.

| II Pet. 3:15 | Romans C |

Καὶ τὴν τοῦ κυρίου ἡμῶν μακροθυμίαν σωτηρίαν ἡγεῖσθε, καθὼς καὶ ὁ αγαπητὸς ἡμῶν ἀδελφὸς Παῦλος . . . . ἔγραψεν ὑμῖν, ὡς καὶ ἐν πάσαις ἐπιστολαῖς λαλῶν. . . . .

The allusion here is to a collection of Paul's letters. The author probably thinks of the letters as a unit and in this sense can feel that what he finds in any one of them is the teaching of the whole collection. The passages that best satisfy the teaching on "patience" are Rom. 2:4 and 9:22 (see the text in the note on II Pet. 3:9).

| II Pet. 3:15 | Ephesians C |

Κατὰ τὴν δοθεῖσαν αὐτῷ σοφίαν.

Eph. 3:2-10. Εἴ γε ἠκούσατε τὴν οἰκονομίαν τῆς χάριτος τοῦ θεοῦ τῆς δοθείσης μοι εἰς ὑμᾶς, [ὅτι] κατὰ ἀποκάλυψιν ἐγνωρίσθη μοι τὸ μυχτήριον, καθὼς προέγραψα ἐν ὀλίγῳ πρὸς ὃ δύνασθε ἀναγινώσκοντες νοῆσαι τὴν σύνεσίν μου ἐν τῷ μυστηρίῳ τοῦ Χριστοῦ . . . . ἵνα γνωρισθῇ . . . . ἡ πολυπαίκιλος σοφία τοῦ Θεοῦ.

The most impressive assertion of Paul's insight into the "many-sided wisdom of God" which the New Testament contains is that found in Ephesians. The author of Ephesians thinks of Paul as a writer of letters (καθὼς προέγραψα ἐν ὀλίγῳ). This Ephesian representation of Paul must have impressed the author of II Peter.

Possible instances of literary reminiscence.— II Pet. 1: 3, 4; cf. I Cor. 4:4, 6. The clause διὰ τῆς ἐπιγνώσεως τοῦ καλέσαντος ἡμᾶς διὰ δόξης may reflect the influence of the ideas and language of II Cor. 4:4, 6. The use of ἐπάγγελμα (used in the New Testament only in II Peter) may reflect an acquaintance with II Cor. 7:1.

II Pet. 1:4; cf. I Cor. 10:18, 20. The use of κοινωνός in II Peter more nearly resembles its use in I Cor. 10:18, 20 (cf. II Cor. 1:7) than any other instance in the New Testament. The language of Hellenistic piety is as probable a source of influence, however.

II Pet. 1:4; cf. Eph. 4:22. The sense in which ἐπιθυμία is used in II Peter is the sense in which it is generally used in

the Pauline letters. The context in which it occurs here tends
to relate it to Eph. 4:22 more closely than to any other New Testament passage.

        II Pet. 1:5-7; cf. Gal. 5:22, 23 and Rom. 5:4, 5. The lit-
erary form and vocabulary of II Peter 1:5-7 may have been influenced by the Pauline letters. 'Επιχορηγέω occurs in the New Testament in II Cor. 9:10, Gal. 3:5, Col. 2:19, and II Pet. 1:5, 11.
'Αρετή is found in Phil. 4:8, I Pet. 2:9, and II Pet. 1:3, 5. It
is also found in the LXX in Wisd. of Sol. 4:1, 5:13, 8:1; II Macc.
10:28, 15:17. Γνῶσις occurs in Luke, the Pauline letters, and the
later writings that were influenced by those letters. Its most
frequent occurrence is in the letters of the Pauline corpus.
'Εγκράτεια occurs in Acts 24:25, Gal. 5:23, and II Pet. 1:6. In
the LXX it is found in Ecclus. 18:15, 30 and IV Macc. 5:34. In
Galatians and II Peter it is an item in an enumeration of Christian
virtues (cf. ἐγκρατεύομαι, I Cor. 7:9 and 9:25). 'Υπομονή occurs
in Luke, the Pauline corpus, and the later New Testament writings.
In Rom. 5:3 and II Pet. 1:6 it is an item in lists of virtues.
Εὐσέβεια is not a Pauline word but is found in the New Testament
in Acts, the Pastorals, and II Peter. Φιλαδελφία is found in Rom.
12:10, I Thess. 4:9, Heb. 13:1, I Pet. 1:22, and II Pet. 1:7. In
the LXX it is found in IV Macc. 13:23, 26 and 14:1. The series
in II Peter begins with πίστις and ends with ἀγάπη (cf. I Cor. 13:
13, Ign. Eph. 14:1, Herm. Vis. III. viii. 3-5). The vocabulary
and literary form of II Pet. 1:5-7 may reflect the influence of
Paul's letters, but, on the other hand, Paul's letters and II Peter
may both reflect the influence of a common Hellenistic background.

        II Pet. 1:12; cf. Rom. 1:11, 16:25, and Eph. 3:17. Στηρίζω
occurs in the New Testament in Luke-Acts, Romans, I and II Thessalonians, James, I and II Peter, and the Apocalypse. Its use in
II Peter corresponds closely with that in Rom. 1:11, 16:25; I
Thess. 3:2, 13; II Thess. 2:17, 3:3. The thought and form of the
statement remind one of Eph. 3:17, ἐν ἀγάπη ἐρριζωμένοι καὶ τεθεμελιωμένοι.

        II Pet. 2:1; cf. I Cor. 6:20. There is clearly the rela-
tionship of dependence between II Pet. 2:1 and Jude 4. Yet ἀγορά-
σαντα is an emphasis which II Peter adds to what is found in Jude.
In the sense in which it is used in II Peter, ἀγοράζω is found

elsewhere in the New Testament in I Cor. 6:20 and 7:23 and in Apoc. 5:9, 14:3, 4.

II Pet. 2:3; cf. I Thess. 2:5. Only in II Pet. 2:3 and I Thess 2:5 is πλεονεξία mentioned in the New Testament in connection with the preaching of the Christian message.

II Pet. 2:9; cf. I Cor. 10:13.

II Pet. 3:1; cf. Phil. 1:10. Ειλικρινής occurs in the New Testament in these two instances only. In the LXX its only occurrence is Wisd. of Sol. 7:25.

II Pet. 3:2; cf. Eph. 2:20. The reverence for the apostles and prophets expressed in Ephesians may have influenced II Peter.

II Pet. 3:13, 14; cf. II Cor. 7:1. Peter's exhortation, made in view of promises that refer to the future, may look back to a Pauline model such as is supplied in II Cor. 7:1.

II Pet. 3:18; cf. Rom. 16:25, 27. II Peter, like Romans, closes with a laudation instead of with greetings.

TABLE OF RESULTS

	A	B	C	Unclassed
Romans..............	.	1	3	4
I Corinthians.......	.	.	.	3
II Corinthians......	.	.	1	3
Galatians...........	.	.	1	1
Ephesians...........	.	1	1	3
Philippians.........	.	.	.	1
Colossians..........	.	.	.	....
I Thessalonians.....	.	.	1	1
II Thessalonians....	.	.	.	....
Philemon............	.	.	.	....

Tatian's Address to the Greeks

There is some difference of opinion regarding the date of Tatian's Address to the Greeks. Stählin is inclined to accept Eusebius' interpretation of chapter 19 to the effect that Tatian refers to the martyrdom of Justin (HE iv. 16. 8 f.). He accordingly makes A.D. 163-67 the terminus post quem for the

writing.[1] Goodspeed[2] and Harnack[3] hold, with better warrant, that
the date of the Address is about A.D. 155. Harnack is convinced
that Eusebius misunderstood Tatian's reference to Justin and that
the Address was written prior to Justin's death.

The character of the writing is distinctly that of an
apology. Greek philosophy and morality are ridiculed, and their
deficiencies are used as arguments for the superiority of Christianity.

As a pupil of Justin, Tatian presumably knew the writings
with which his master shows acquaintance. However, he does not in
the Address refer to any Christian writing specifically. There
are allusions that indicate acquaintance with the Fourth Gospel
and probably with Matthew, with several letters of the Pauline
corpus, and with Hebrews.

There is practically no use made of the Old Testament in
the Address. In 5:1 and 15:1 there may be faint allusions to
Genesis, and in 15:4 there is a direct quotation (with slight
verbal variations) of Ps. 8:6 with the introductory formula κατὰ
τὸν εἰπόντα λόγον.

In several instances there are rather clear reflections of
acquaintance with the Fourth Gospel, and in 13:1 Tatian quotes
John 1:5 (with slight verbal variations) with the introductory
formula τὸ εἰρημένον.

Address 4:2   Romans C

Τοῦτον διὰ τῆς ποιήσεως αὐτοῦ ἴσμεν καὶ τῆς δυνάμεως αὐτοῦ
τὸ ἀόρατον τοῖς ποιήμασι καταλαμβανόμεθα.

Rom. 1:20. Τὰ γὰρ ἀόρατα αὐτοῦ ἀπὸ κτίσεως κόσμου τοῖς
ποιήμασιν νοούμενα καθορᾶται, ἥ τε ἀίδιος αὐτοῦ δύναμις καὶ Θειότης.

Tatian and Paul agree in their ideas that God is knowable
through his creation. The language employed by Tatian adds weight

---

[1]Otto Stählin, Die altchristliche griechische Literatur
(München: C. H. Becksche Verlagsbuchhandlung, 1924), p. 1288.

[2]E. J. Goodspeed, Die ältesten Apologeten (Göttingen: Van-
den Hoeck & Ruprecht, 1914), p. 266.

[3]A. Harnack, Die Chronologie der altchristlichen Literatur
bis Eusebius (Leipzig: J. C. Hinrichs, 1900), I, 284 f.

to the probability that he was influenced here by Romans.

Address 5:1   Colossians C

῎Εργον πρωτότοκον τοῦ πατρός.

See the discussion and the text of Col. 1:15 in the note on Justin Apol. 23:2.

Address 11:2   Romans C   Colossians C

'Απόθνησκε τῷ κόσμῳ . . . . ζῆθι τῷ Θεῷ διὰ τῆς αὐτοῦ καταλήψεως τὴν παλαιὰν γένεσιν παραιτούμενος.

Rom. 6:10. ῞Ο γὰρ ἀπέθανεν, τῇ ἁμαρτίᾳ ἀπέθανεν ἐφάπαξ· ὁ δὲ ζῇ, ζῇ τῷ Θεῷ.

Col. 2:20. Εἰ ἀπεθάνετε σὺν Χριστῷ ἀπὸ τῶν στοιχείων τοῦ κόσμου, τί ὡς ζῶντες ἐν κόσμῳ δογματίζεσθε. . . . . 3:1. Εἰ οὖν συνηγέρθητε τῷ Χριστῷ, τὰ ἄνω ζητεῖτε, οὗ ὁ Χριστός ἐστιν.

This conception of ceasing to live in relationship to the physical order and of becoming alive to the spiritual order need not necessarily have been borrowed from the Pauline letters, but the probabilities favor that source.

Address 11:2   Romans C

Δοῦλοι γεγόναμεν οἱ ἐλεύθεροι, διὰ τὴν ἁμαρτίαν ἐπράθημεν. Rom. 7:14. Πεπραμένος ὑπὸ τὴν ἁμαρτίαν.

Instances of possible literary reminiscence.—Address 11:1; cf. I Cor. 7:21. Tatian's statement has certain verbal resemblances to that of Paul: δοῦλος ἐὰν ᾦ, τὴν δουλείαν ὑπομένω· κᾶν ἐλεύθερος ὑπάρχω, τὴν εὐγένειαν οὐ σεμνύνομαι. The context of the statement in the Address fails to make any very definite connection with the thought of I Cor. 7. The ideas of the passages under comparison are sufficiently similar to suggest literary indebtedness.

Address 15:2; cf. I Cor. 3:16 and Eph. 2:21, 22. Tatian uses the figure of the "spiritual temple": εἰ μὲν ὡς ναὸς εἴη, κατοικεῖν ἐν αὐτῷ Θεὸς βούλεται διὰ τοῦ πρεσβεύοντος πνεύματος· The Spirit is the intermediary in the Address and in I Corinthians and Ephesians. Tatian's thought is closer to that of I Corinthians than to that of Ephesians (cf. II Cor. 6:16).

Address 16:2; cf. Eph. 6:14. Θώρακι γὰρ πνεύματος ἐπουρανίου καθωπλισμένος may reflect acquaintance with Ephesians (cf. I Thess. 5:8).

Address 30:1; cf. Eph. 4:22 and Col. 3:9. Τούτων οὖν τὴν κατάληψιν πεποιημένος βούλομαι καθάπερ τὰ νήπια τῶν βρεφῶν . . . . ἀποδύσασθαι may show the influence of Eph. 4:22 and Col. 3:9.

Leipoldt finds traces of acquaintance with Romans, I Corinthians, Ephesians, and Colossians in Tatian's Address,[4] and Westcott traces of acquaintance with I Corinthians, Galatians, and Colossians.[5]

The present study finds reasonable probability of acquaintance with Romans and Colossians. In all instances of apparent literary indebtedness, however, the parallels are of the type that might have resulted from a common inheritance rather than from direct literary dependence.

TABLE OF RESULTS

	A	B	C	Unclassed
Romans...........	•	•	3	....
I Corinthians.....	•	•	•	2
II Corinthians....	•	•	•	....
Galatians.........	•	•	•	....
Ephesians.........	•	•	•	3
Philippians.......	•	•	•	....
Colossians........	•	•	2	1
I Thessalonians...	•	•	•	....
II Thessalonians..	•	•	•	....
Philemon..........	•	•	•	....

The Writings of Justin

The writings of Justin belong to the decade A.D. 150-60. His authentic extant works are the Apology, the Appendix, and the Dialogue with Trypho. Justin's objective in these writings was

[4] J. Leipoldt, Geschichte des neutestamentlichen Kanons (Leipzig: J. C. Hinrichs, 1907), I, 193.

[5] B. F. Westcott, A General Survey of the History of the Canon of the New Testament5 (London: Macmillan & Co., Ltd., 1881), p. 171.

the defense of Christianity against the various attacks to which
it was subject and to set forth the true character of the Christian
message. In the pursuit of this purpose he made frequent use of
material from the Old and New Testaments.

The Apology and the Dialogue are of chief significance for
this study. The Appendix makes no reference to any New Testament
book, either direct or indirect.

Justin's use of the Old and New Testaments frequently takes
the form of definite quotation, usually introduced by formulas of
citation. At times he quotes accurately but in other instances
freely from memory. He not infrequently conflates several passages.

Except in the case of the Gospels and the Apocalypse, he
does not refer to any New Testament book by name, nor does he any-
where mention the name of Paul. He was unquestionably acquainted
with Paul's letters, but he never cites them formally, and his indebtedness to them is smaller than to the Gospels.

The following illustrations are typical of his usage with
reference to the Old Testament, and they shed light on his understanding of its inspiration:

1. Inspired men speak:

Apol. 32:1. Μωυσῆς μὲν οὖν, πρῶτος τῶν προφητῶν γενόμενος,
εἶπεν αὐτολεξεὶ οὕτως·

Apol. 32:12. Καὶ 'Ησαΐας δέ, ἄλλος προφήτης ....οὕτως
εἶπεν·

Apol. 34:1. 'Ως προεῖπεν ἕτερος προφήτης ὁ Μιχαΐας

Dial. 14:3. Εἴρηνται δὲ ὑπὸ τοῦ 'Ησαΐου οὕτως

Dial. 15:2. Κέκραγε δὲ 'Ησαΐας οὕτως·

2. The "prophetic Spirit" speaks through the writer:

Apol. 35:3. 'Ο αὐτὸς προφήτης 'Ησαΐας θεοφορούμενος τῷ
πνεύματι τῷ προφητικῷ ἔφη

Apol. 41:1. Καὶ πάλιν δι' ἄλλης προφητείας μηνύον τὸ προφητικὸν πνεῦμα δι' αὐτοῦ τοῦ Δαυεὶδ

Apol. 44:1. 'Εδίδαξε δὲ ἡμᾶς ταῦτα τὸ ἅγιον προφητικὸν
πνεῦμα, διὰ Μωσέως

3. This Spirit is conceived as from Christ:

Apol. 38:1. "Οταν δὲ ἀπὸ προσώπου τοῦ Χριστοῦ λέγῃ τὸ προφητικὸν πνεῦμα, οὕτως φθέγγεται·

4. God is conceived as speaking directly through the writer:

Dial. 16:1.   Καὶ διὰ Μωσέως κέκραγεν ὁ Θεὸς αὐτός, οὕτως λέγων

5.   The more usual formulas are also employed:

Dial. 34:6.   Καὶ ἐπὶ τέλει τοῦ ψαλμοῦ τούτου, οὗ ἔφην, γέγραπ-
ται·

Dial. 55:1.   ῝Α γέγραπται·

Dial. 56:8.   ῾Ως γέγραπται

In Apol. 66:3, where several passages are conflated (Luke 22:
19, 20, Matt. 26:26, 27, Mark 14:22-23), our Gospels are spoken of
as "memoirs" of the Apostles: αἱ γὰρ ἀπόστολοι ἐν τοῖς γενομένοις
ὑπ' αὐτῶν ἀπομνημονεύμασιν, ἃ καλεῖται εὐαγγέλια, οὕτως καρέδωκαν
ἐντετάλθαι αὐταῖς·   These "memoirs" are frequently mentioned in
the Dialogue: (1) as "memoirs of his [Jesus'] apostles" (100:4,
101:3, 102:5, and 104:1); (2) as "memoirs of the apostles" (103:6
and 106:1); and (3) as simply "the memoirs" (105:1, 5, 6).   In
Apol. 66:3 the Gospels are spoken of as εὐαγγελίαι, and in Dial.
100:1 (cf. Matt. 11:27, Luke 10:22) they are spoken of collective-
ly as containing the message of Jesus in the clause, καὶ ἐν τῷ
εὐαγγελίῳ δὲ γέγραπται εἰπών·   In Dial. 67:3 the public reading of
the "memoirs" is described in a way that may indicate their achieve-
ment of the status of Scripture: καὶ τῇ τοῦ ἡλίου λεγομένῃ ἡμέρᾳ
πάντων κατὰ πόλεις ἢ ἀγροὺς μενόντων ἐπὶ τὸ αὐτὸ συνέλευσις γίνεται,
καὶ τὰ ἀπομνημονεύματα τῶν ἀποστόλων ἢ τὰ συγγράμματα τῶν προφητῶν
ἀναγινώσκεται, μέχρις ἐγχωρεῖ.

Formulas of citation indicate that the "memoirs" were valued
because they recorded Jesus' words: Apol. 15:9, ταῦτα ἐδίδαξεν;
16:5, οὕτως παρεκελεύσατα; 16:9, εἶπε γὰρ οὕτως; 17:4, ὡς ὁ Χριστὸς
ἐμηνύσεν εἰπών; 61:4, ὁ Χριστὸς εἶπεν; Dial. 17:4, καὶ ἐβόα; 49:5,
διὸ καὶ ὁ ἡμέτερος Χριστὸς εἰρήκει.

In Dial. 81:4 Justin refers to the Apocalypse of John as
inspired, and he attributes it to John the disciple of Jesus: καὶ
ἔπειτα καὶ παρ' ἡμῖν ἀνήρ τις, ᾧ ὄνομα ᾿Ιωάννης, εἷς τῶν ἀποστόλων
τοῦ Χριστοῦ, ἐν ἀποκαλύψει γενομένῃ αὐτῷ κτλ.

Apol. 19:4   I Corinthians C

Αφθαρσίαν ἐνδύσασθαι.

I Cor. 15:33.   Δεῖ γὰρ τὸ φθαρτὸν τοῦτο ἐνδύσασθαι ἀφθαρσίαν.

The discussion in Apol. 19 and I Cor. 15 centers about the

possibility of resurrection. Paul and Justin undertake to make
belief in resurrection rational. The context combines with the
resemblance in phrasing to make literary reminiscence probable.

Apol. 23:2   Colossians B

'Ιησοῦς Χριστὸς . . . . λόγος αὐτοῦ ὑπάρχων καὶ πρωτότοκος καὶ δύναμις.

Col. 1:15. Ὅς ἐστιν . . . . πρωτότοκος πάσης κτίσεως.

Πρωτότοκος occurs in the New Testament in Luke, Romans,
Colossians, Hebrews, and the Apocalypse. Its use in Hebrews and
the Apocalypse probably was influenced by Colossians. The sense
in which Justin uses the term corresponds most nearly with its use
in Colossians and very probably reflects acquaintance with that
writing. On the basis of this and other similar passages (Apol.
33:6, 46:2, 63:15; Dial. 84:2, 85:2, 100:2, 125:3, and 138:2),
Zahn concludes: "So ist doch nicht zu bezweifeln, dass Justin den
Kolosserbrief als die Quelle dieser Lehre gekannt und anerkannt
hat."[6]

Apol. 28:3   Romans B

Ὥστ' ἀναπολόγητον εἶναι ταῖς πᾶσιν ἀνθρώποις παρὰ τῷ Θεῷ·

Rom. 1:20. Εἰς τὸ εἶναι αὐτοὺς ἀναπολογήτους.

Justin and Paul both argue that in view of the way God has
made men and the world, rational creatures are without excuse in
their failure to know and do the divine will. The quality of
thought and the verbal coincidence represented in the use of
ἀναπολόγητος argue strongly for Justin's acquaintance with Romans.

Apol. 60:11   I Corinthians B

Οὐ σοφίᾳ ἀνθρωπείᾳ ταῦτα γεγονέναι, ἀλλὰ δυνάμει Θεοῦ λέγεσθαι.

I Cor. 2:4, 5. Καὶ ὁ λόγος μου . . . . οὐκ ἐν πιθαῖς σοφίας
λόγοις ἀλλ' ἐν ἀποδείξει πνεύματος καὶ δυνάμεως, ἵνα ἡ πίστις ὑμῶν
μὴ ᾖ ἐν σοφίᾳ ἀνθρώπων ἀλλ' ἐν δυνάμει Θεοῦ.

Both writers draw the same essential contrast between
σοφία ἀνθρώπων and δύναμις Θεοῦ.

---

[6]Theodor Zahn, "Paulus und Justin," Geschichte des Neues-
testamentlichen Kanons (Erlangen: Deichert, 1881), I, ii, 567.

Dial. 11:5   Romans A

Ἰσραηλιτικὸν γὰρ τὸ ἀληθινόν, πνευματικόν, καὶ Ἰούδα
γένος καὶ Ἰακὼβ καὶ Ἰσαὰκ καὶ Ἀβραάμ, τοῦ ἐν ἀκροβυστίᾳ ἐπὶ
τῇ πίστει μαρτυρηθέντος ὑπὸ τοῦ Θεοῦ καὶ εὐλογηθέντος καὶ πατρὸς
πολλῶν ἐθνῶν κληθέντος, ἡμεῖς ἐσμεν.

Rom. 2:26-28. Ἐὰν οὖν ἡ ἀκροβυστία τὰ δικαιώματα τοῦ
νόμου φυλάσσῃ, οὐχ ἡ ἀκροβυστία αὐτοῦ εἰς περιτομὴν λογισθήσεται;
. . . . οὐ γὰρ ὁ ἐν τῷ φανερῷ Ἰουδαῖός ἐστιν, ... ἀλλ' ὁ ἐν
τῷ κρυπτῷ Ἰουδαῖος. 4:9-11. Ἐλογίσθη τῷ Ἀβραὰμ ἡ πίστις
εἰς δικαιοσύνην. πῶς οὖν ἐλογίσθη; ἐν περιτομῇ ὄντι ἢ ἐν ἀκροβυστίᾳ; οὐκ ἐν περιτομῇ ἀλλ' ἐν ἀκροβυστίᾳ· καὶ σημεῖον ἔλαβεν περιτομῆς, ... εἰς τὸ εἶναι αὐτὸν πατέρα πάντων τῶν πιστευόντων
δι' ἀκροβυστίας.

The distinction between the "true Israel" and the racial
Israel is exactly the distinction that Paul draws, and the description of Abraham as "approved" on account of his faith while yet
ἐν ἀκροβυστίᾳ is in effect the point made in Rom. 4:9 ff.

Dial. 14:2   I Corinthians C

Τοῦτο γάρ ἐστι τὸ σύμβολον τῶν ἀζύμων, ἵνα μὴ τὰ παλαιὰ
τῆς κακῆς ζύμης ἔργα πράττητε . . . . νέαν ζύμην φυρᾶσαι ἑαυταῖς
ὁ Θεὸς παρήγγειλε, τοῦτ' ἔστιν ἄλλων ἔργων πρᾶξιν καὶ μὴ τῶν
παλαιῶν καὶ φαύλων τὴν μίμησιν.

I Cor. 5:7-9. Ἐκκαθάρατε τὴν παλαιὰν ζύμην, ἵνα ἦτε νέον
φύραμα, καθώς ἐστε ἄζυμοι. . . . . ὥστε ἑορτάζωμεν μὴ ἐν ζύμῃ
παλαιᾷ μηδὲ ἐν ζύμῃ κακίας καὶ πονηρίας, ἀλλ' ἐν ἀζύμοις εἰλικρι-
νίας καὶ ἀληθείας.

Justin and Paul use the same figures to represent the for-
saking of wrong ways of living and the assumption of new attitudes.
They may have done this independently, but the probabilities favor
Justin's dependence on Paul.

Dial. 23:4   Romans A

Ὁ Ἀβραὰμ ἐν ἀκροβυστίᾳ ὢν διὰ τὴν πίστιν, ἣν ἐπίστευσε
τῷ Θεῷ, ἐδικαιώθη καὶ εὐλογήθη, ὡς ἡ γραφὴ σημαίνει· τὴν δὲ περιτομὴν εἰς σημεῖον, ἀλλ' οὐκ εἰς δικαιοσύνην ἔλαβεν.

See the text of Rom. 4:9-11 and a discussion of its influence on Justin in the note on Dial. 11:5.

            Dial. 27:3   Romans A
    Πάντες γὰρ ἐξέκλιναν . . . . πάντες ἄρα ἠχρειώθησαν· οὐκ
ἔστιν ὁ συνίων, οὐκ ἔστιν ἕως ἑνός. ταῖς γλώσσαις αὐτῶν ἐδολιοῦσαν, τάφος ἀνεῳγμένος ὁ λάρυγξ αὐτῶν, ἰὸς ἀσπίδων ὑπὸ τὰ χείλη
αὐτῶν, σύντριμμα καὶ ταλαιπωρία ἐν ταῖς ὁδαῖς αὐτῶν, καὶ ὁδὸν εἰρήνης οὐκ ἔγνωσαν.
    Rom. 3:12. Πάντες ἐξέκλιναν, ἅμα ἠχρεώθησαν· 11. Οὐκ
ἔστιν δίκαιος οὐδὲ εἷς, οὐκ ἔστιν συνίων. . . . . 13. Τάφος ἀνεῳγμένος ὁ λάρυγξ αὐτῶν, ταῖς γλώσσαις αὐτῶν ἐδολιοῦσαν, ἰὸς ἀσπίδων
ὑπὸ τὰ χείλη αὐτῶν. . . . . 16. Σύντριμμα καὶ ταλαιπωρία ἐν ταῖς
ὁδαῖς αὐτῶν, καὶ ὁδὸν εἰρήνης οὐκ ἔγνωσαν.

    Justin and Paul both conflate passages from the Old Testa-
ment. The order of the passages in Justin is Ps. 14:3, 5:10,
140:4, and Isa. 59:7b, 8a. The order in Romans is the same, although within the passages there are minor differences in sequence
of phrases. In Romans the conflation is more extensive, so that
Justin gives the impression of having abbreviated his source or
else quoted it from memory.
    The most plausible explanation of this coincidence of con-
flation is that Justin was familiar with Romans. The only alternative would be that offered by Rendel Harris,[7] who is convinced that
Christian leaders very early assembled collections of proof texts
which were widely used in meeting Jewish opposition and which were
of value in establishing the antiquity of the new religion by root-
ing it in the Old Testament.

            Dial. 28:4   Colossians A   Romans B
    Κἂν Σκύθης ᾖ τις ἢ Πέρσης, ἔχει δὲ τὴν τοῦ Θεοῦ γνῶσιν
καὶ τοῦ Χριστοῦ αὐτοῦ . . . . περιτέτμηται τὴν καλὴν καὶ ὠφέλιμον
περιτομήν, καὶ φίλος ἐστὶ τῷ Θεῷ.
    Col. 3:11. Ὅπου οὐκ ἔνι Ἕλλην καὶ Ἰουδαῖος, περιτομὴ
καὶ ἀκροβυστία, βάρβαρος, Σκύθης . . . . ἀλλὰ πάντα καὶ ἐν πᾶσιν
Χριστός.
    See the text of Rom. 2:25-28 in the note on Dial. 11:5.
With the certainty of acquaintance with Romans in Dial. 11:5, there

_____
    [7]Testimonies (Cambridge: University Press, 1916).

is a high degree of probability of acquaintance here. The clause
περιτέτμηται τὴν καλὴν καὶ ὠφέλιμον περιτομήν looks rather definitely in the direction of Rom. 2:25 ff.

The passage looks as definitely in the direction of Colossians. Σκύθης occurs in the New Testament only in Col. 3:11, and
its use in both instances in an enumeration of exactly the same
type and for the illustration of the same point makes literary dependence a matter of practical certainty.

Dial. 32:4   II Thessalonians B

Τὸν τῆς ἀνομίας ἄνθρωπον.

II Thess. 2:4. Ὁ ἄνθρωπος τῆς ⌜ἀνομίας⌝, ὁ υἱὸς τῆς ἀπωλείας, ὁ ἀντικείμενος καὶ ὑπεραιρόμενος ἐπὶ πάντα λεγόμενον Θεὸν
ἢ σέβασμα.

It is conceivable that Justin might have gotten from Dan.
7:25 the conception of a blasphemous "anti-Christ." He refers
specifically to Daniel in the immediately preceding context, ὃν
καιρὸν καὶ καιροὺς καὶ ἥμισυ καιροῦ διακαθέξειν Δανιὴλ μηνύει.
It is, however, difficult to conceive of his having hit upon the
phrase τὸν τῆς ἀνομίας ἄνθρωπον in independence of II Thessalonians.
As far as known sources go, II Thessalonians is the most probable.

Dial. 39:1, 2   Romans A

Καὶ γὰρ Ἠλίας περὶ ὑμῶν πρὸς τὸν Θεὸν ἐντυγχάνων οὕτως
λέγει· Κύριε, τοὺς προφήτας σου ἀπέκτειναν καὶ τὰ θυσιαστήριά
σου κατέσκαψαν   κἀγὼ ὑπελείφθην μόνος, καὶ ζητοῦσι τὴν ψυχήν μου.
καὶ ἀποκρίνεται αὐτῷ· Ἔτι εἰσί μοι ἑπτακισχίλιοι ἄνδρες, οἳ οὐκ
ἔκαμψαν γόνυ τῇ Βάαλ. ὃν οὖν τρόπον διὰ τοὺς ἑπτακισχιλίους ἐκείνους τὴν ὀργὴν οὐκ ἐπέφερε τότε ὁ Θεός.

Rom. 11:2-5. Ἢ οὐκ οἴδατε ἐν Ἠλείᾳ τί λέγει ἡ γραφή, ὡς
ἐντυγχάνει τῷ Θεῷ κατὰ τοῦ Ἰσραήλ; Κύριε, τοὺς προφήτας σου ἀπέκτειναν, τὰ θυσιαστήριά σου κατέσκαψαν, κἀγὼ ὑπελείφθην μόνος, καὶ
ζητοῦσιν τὴν ψυχήν μου. ἀλλὰ τί λέγει αὐτῷ ὁ χρηματισμός; Κατέλιπον ἐμαυτῷ ἑπτακισχιλίους ἄνδρας, οἵτινες οὐκ ἔκαμψαν γόνυ τῇ
Βάαλ. οὕτως οὖν καὶ ἐν τῷ νῦν καιρῷ λίμμα κατ' ἐκλογὴν χάριτος
γέγονεν.

Again Justin conflates Old Testament passages in agreement
with Romans. Variations from the LXX in which Justin agrees with

Romans are the following: (1) He omits the first line of verse 10 and adds Κύριε. The whole quotation is introduced with a preliminary statement that is absent from the LXX and that must have been taken from Romans. (2) He omits ἐν ῥομφαίᾳ and reverses the order of the phrases about the slaughter of the prophets and the destruction of the altars. (3) He has κἀγὼ ὑπελείφθην μόνος instead of καὶ ὑπολέλειμμαι ἐγὼ μονώτατος. (4) He omits λαβεῖν αὐτήν after τὴν ψυχήν μου. (5) Verse 18 immediately follows verse 10 in answer to its assertion. (6) Instead of καὶ καταλείψεις ἐν 'Ισραὴλ, Rom. 11:4 reads κατέλιπον ἐμαυτῷ and Justin "Ετι εἰσί μοι. (7) Justin has οἱ (Romans, οἵτινες) οὐκ ἔκαμψαν γόνυ τῇ Βάαλ, whereas the LXX reads πάντα γόνατα ἃ οὐκ ὤκλασαν γόνυ τῷ Βάαλ.

Furthermore, the application of the story in Dial. 39:2 is very similar to that of Rom. 11:5, and this strengthens the case of literary dependence.

It is difficult to account for this conflation of passages and the points of difference from the LXX in which Justin and Paul agree except in terms of literary dependence.

Dial. 39:2   I Corinthians B
Οἱ καὶ λαμβάνουσι δόματα ἕκαστος ὡς ἄξιοι εἰσι . . . . ὁ μὲν γὰρ λαμβάνει συνέσεως πνεῦμα, ὁ δὲ βουλῆς, ὁ δὲ ἰσχύος, ὁ δὲ ἰάσεως, ὁ δὲ προγνώσεως, ὁ δὲ διδασκαλίας, ὁ δὲ φόβου Θεοῦ.

I Cor. 12:7-10. Ἑκάστῳ δὲ δίδοται ἡ φανέρωσις τοῦ πνεύματος πρὸς τὸ συμφέρον. ᾧ μὲν γὰρ διὰ τοῦ πνεύματος δίδοται λόγος σοφίας, ἄλλῳ δὲ λόγος γνώσεως . . . . ἄλλῳ δὲ χαρίσματα ἰαμάτων . . . . ἄλλῳ [δὲ] προφητείᾳ.

The language of Isa. 11:2 and the thought of I Corinthians both seem to have influenced Justin. The description of the distribution of "gifts of the Spirit" almost certainly evidences the influence of I Corinthians.

Dial. 39:4   Ephesians A
'Ανέβη εἰς ὕψος, ἠχμαλώτευσεν αἰχμαλωσίαν, ἔδωκε δόματα τοῖς ἀνθρώποις.

Eph. 4:7, 8. Ἑνὶ δὲ ἑκάστῳ ἡμῶν ἐδόθη [ἡ] χάρις . . . . διὸ λέγει 'Αναβὰς εἰς ὕψος ἠχμαλώτευσεν αἰχμαλωσίαν, [καὶ] ἔδωκεν δόματα τοῖς ἀνθρώποις.

Justin and the author of Ephesians are both discussing the distribution of "gifts" through Christ. Both quote Ps. 67:19, but so changed as to make a point very different from the original meaning of the Psalm. Justin, except for his substitution of ἀνέβη for ἀναβάς, agrees with Ephesians in the latter's differences from the LXX. Both have ἔδωκε instead of ἔλαβες with the LXX, and both have τοῖς ἀνθρώποις instead of ἐν ἀνθρώπῳ with the LXX.

Dial. 42:3   I Corinthians B

᾽Οπαῖον καὶ ἐπὶ τοῦ σώματος ἔστιν ἰδεῖν· πολλῶν ἀριθμου-μένων μελῶν τὰ σύμπαντα ἓν καλεῖται καὶ ἔστι σῶμα· . . . . καὶ γὰρ δῆμος καὶ ἐκκλησία, πολλοὶ τὸν ἀριθμὸν ὄντες ἄνθρωποι, ὡς ἓν ὄντες πρᾶγμα.

I Cor. 12:12. Καθάπερ γὰρ τὸ σῶμα ἕν ἐστιν καὶ μέλη πολλὰ ἔχει, πάντα δὲ τὰ μέλη τοῦ σώματος πολλὰ ὄντα ἕν ἐστιν σῶμα.

With the practical certainty that Justin knew I Corinthians there can be little doubt that he is here influenced by its thought. The multiplicity of members in the unity of a body is the figure employed by both writers as an analogy for the Christian group.

Dial. 43:2   Colossians A

Καὶ ἡμεῖς, οἱ διὰ τούτου προσχωρήσαντες τῷ Θεῷ, οὐ ταύτην τὴν κατὰ σάρκα παρελάβομεν περιτομήν, ἀλλὰ πνευματικήν . . . . ἡμεῖς δὲ διὰ τοῦ βαπτίσματος αὐτήν, ἐπειδὴ ἁμαρτωλοὶ ἐγεγόνειμεν, διὰ τὸ ἔλεος τὸ παρὰ τοῦ Θεοῦ ἐλάβομεν.

Col. 2:11-13. ᾽Εν ᾧ καὶ περιετμήθητε περιτομῇ ἀχειροποιήτῳ ἐν τῇ ἀπεκδύσει τοῦ σώματος τῆς σαρκός, ἐν τῇ περιτομῇ τοῦ Χριστοῦ, συνταφέντες αὐτῷ ἐν τῷ βαπτίσματι, ... καὶ ὑμᾶς νεκροὺς ὄντας τοῖς παραπτώμασιν καὶ τῇ ἀκροβυστίᾳ τῆς σαρκὸς ὑμῶν, συνεζωοποίησεν ⌜ὑμᾶς⌝ σὺν ⌜αὐτῷ·⌝ χαρισάμενος ἡμῖν πάντα τὰ παραπτώματα. . . . .⌝

The association of "spiritual circumcision" with baptism and the accompanying forgiveness of sin almost certainly reflects Justin's acquaintance with Colossians.

Dial. 46:6   Romans A

᾽Αλλ᾽ ἐπὶ ᾽Ηλίου ονομάζων τὸν ἀριθμὸν τῶν μὴ καμψάντων γόνυ τῇ Βάαλ, ἑπτακισχιλίους τὸν ἀριθμὸν ὄντας εἶπε.

See the text of Rom. 11:4 in the note on Dial. 39:1, 2.
Similar agreements between the Dialogue and Romans in variations
from the LXX are to be noted here as were noted there: κάμπτω is
used instead of ὀκλάζω, and ἑπτακισχιλίους instead of ἑπτὰ χιλιά-
δας. The argument for dependence on Romans here is to the same
effect as in the case of Dial. 39:1, 2.

Dial. 47:5   Romans C

ʽΗ γὰρ χρηστότης καὶ ἡ φιλανθρωπία τοῦ Θεοῦ καὶ τὸ ἄμετρον
τοῦ πλούτου αὐτοῦ τὸν μετανοοῦντα ἀπὸ τῶν ἁμαρτημάτων, ὡς δι' ᾽Ιεζε-
κιὴλ μηνύει, ὡς δίκαιον καὶ ἀναμάρτητον ἔχει

Rom. 2:4. ʽΗ τοῦ πλούτου τῆς χρηστότητος αὐτοῦ καὶ τῆς
ἀνοχῆς καὶ τῆς μακροθυμίας καταφρονεῖς, ἀγνοῶν ὅτι τὸ χρηστὸν τοῦ
Θεοῦ εἰς μετάνοιαν σε ἄγει;

Ezek. 33:19. Καὶ ἐν τῷ ἀποστρέψαι τὸν ἁμαρτωλὸν ἀπὸ τῆς
ἀνομίας αὐτοῦ καὶ ποιήσῃ κρίμα καὶ δικαιοσύνην, ἐν αὐταῖς αὐτὸς
ζήσεται.

Justin refers to Ezekiel, but his language is that of the
New Testament.

Dial. 87:6   Ephesians A

᾽Ανέβη εἰς ὕψος, ἠχμαλώτευσεν αἰχμαλωσίαν, ἔδωκε δόματα
ταῖς υἱοῖς τῶν ἀνθρώπων.

See the note on Dial. 39:4 for the discussion and for the
text of Eph. 4:7, 8.

Dial. 89:2   Galatians B

Εἰ δὲ καὶ ἀτίμως οὕτως σταυρωθῆναι τὸν Χριστόν, ἀποροῦμεν·
ἐπικατάρατος γὰρ ὁ σταυρούμενος ἐν τῷ νόμῳ λέγεται εἶναι·

Gal. 3:13. Χριστὸς ἡμᾶς ἐξηγόρασεν ἐκ τῆς κατάρας τοῦ
νόμου γενόμενος ὑπὲρ ἡμῶν κατάρα, ὅτι γέγραπται ᾽Επικατάρατος πᾶς
ὁ κρεμάμενος ἐπὶ ξύλου.

The whole dilemma about the cross is probably suggested to
Justin by Paul, and he seems to undertake to explain it in terms
of Gal. 3:13.

Dial. 92:3   Romans A

Οὐδὲ γὰρ ᾽Αβραὰμ διὰ τὴν περιτομὴν δίκαιος εἶναι ὑπὸ τοῦ
Θεοῦ ἐμαρτυρήθη, ἀλλὰ διὰ τὴν πίστιν· πρὸ τοῦ γὰρ περιτμηθῆναι

αὐτὸν εἴρηται περὶ αὐτοῦ οὕτως· Ἐπίστευσε δὲ Ἀβραὰμ τῷ Θεῷ,
καὶ ἐλογίσθη αὐτῷ εἰς δικαιοσύνην.

    Rom. 4:3. Τί γὰρ ἡ γραφὴ λέγει; Ἐπίστευσεν δὲ Ἀβραὰμ
τῷ Θεῷ, καὶ ἐλογίσθη αὐτῷ εἰς δικαιοσύνην.   9-11. Λέγομεν γὰρ
Ἐλογίσθη τῷ Ἀβραὰμ ἡ πίστις εἰς δικαιοσύνην. πῶς οὖν ἐλογίσθη;
ἐν περιτομῇ ὄντι ἢ ἐν ἀκροβυστίᾳ, οὐκ ἐν περιτομῇ ἀλλ' ἐν ἀκροβυστίᾳ·

Justin and Paul both quote Gen. 15:6. The limits of the
quotation in the two instances are the same. The point that makes
dependence on Romans clear is that Justin emphasizes the fact that
Abraham was "justified" before he was circumcised and that his ap-
proval was on the basis of faith and depended in no sense on his
circumcision.

    Dial 92:4   Romans A
    Καὶ ἡμεῖς οὖν, ἐν ἀκροβυστίᾳ τῆς σαρκὸς ἡμῶν πιστεύοντες
τῷ Θεῷ διὰ τοῦ Χριστοῦ καὶ περιτομὴν ἔχοντες τὴν ὠφελοῦσαν ἡμᾶς
τοὺς κεκτημένους, τοῦτ' ἔστι τῆς καρδίας.
    Rom. 2:29. Καὶ περιτομὴ καρδίας ἐν πνεύματι οὐ γράμματι,
οὗ ὁ ἔπαινος οὐκ ἐξ ἀνθρώπων ἀλλ' ἐκ τοῦ Θεοῦ.

    Dial 95:1   Galatians A
    Καὶ γὰρ πᾶν γένος ἀνθρώπων εὑρεθήσεται ὑπὸ κατάραν ὃν κατὰ
τὸν νόμον Μωσέως· Ἐπικατάρατος γὰρ εἴρηται πᾶ ς ὃς οὐκ ἐμμένει
ἐν τοῖς γεγραμμένοις ἐν τῷ βιβλίῳ τοῦ νόμου τοῦ ποιῆσαι αὐτά.
    Gal. 3:10. Ὅσοι γὰρ ἐξ ἔργων νόμου εἰσὶν ὑπὸ κατάραν
εἰσίν, γέγραπται γὰρ ὅτι Ἐπικατάρατος πᾶς ὃς οὐκ ἐμμένει πᾶσιν
τοῖς γεγραμμένοις ἐν τῷ βιβλίῳ τοῦ νόμου τοῦ ποιῆσαι αὐτά.

The statements with which the quotation from Deut. 27:26
are introduced in the Dialogue and Galatians are very similar. In
addition there are convincing agreements of the Dialogue with
Galatians against the LXX: ἄνθρωπος after πᾶς is lacking, and
there is ἐν τοῖς γεγραμμένοις ἐν τῷ βιβλίῳ τοῦ νόμου τοῦ ποιῆσαι
αὐτά instead of ἐν πᾶσιν τοῖς λόγοις τοῦ νόμου τούτου ποιῆσαι
αὐτούς.

    Dial. 96:1   Galatians A
    Καὶ γὰρ τὸ εἰρημένον ἐν τῷ νόμῳ, ὅτι Ἐπικατάρατος πᾶς
ὁ κρεμάμενος ἐπὶ ξύλου.

Gal. 3:13. Ὅτι γέγραπται 'Επικατάρατος πᾶς ὁ κρεμάμενος ἐπὶ ξύλου.

Points in which Justin agrees with Galatians against the LXX in the quotations from Deut. 21:23 are: (1) ἐπικατάρατος instead of κεχαταραμένος; (2) the omission of ὑπὸ Θεοῦ; and (3) the insertion of ὁ before κρεμάμενος.

Dial. 110:2   II Thessalonians B
'Η δὲ δευτέρα, ἐν ᾗ μετὰ δόξης ἀπὸ τῶν οὐρανῶν παρέσται, ὅταν καὶ ὁ τῆς ἀποστασίας ἄνθρωπος, ὁ καὶ εἰς τὸν ὕψιστον ἔξαλλα λαλῶν, ἐπὶ τῆς γῆς ἄνομα τολμήσῃ εἰς ἡμᾶς τοὺς Χριστιανούς.

See the note on Dial. 32:4 for the discussion and for the text of II Thess. 2:4.

Dial. 111:3   I Corinthians A
'Ην γὰρ τὸ πάσχα ὁ Χριστός, ὁ τυθεὶς ὕστερον.
I Cor. 5:8. Καὶ γὰρ τὸ πάσχα ἡμῶν; ἐτύθη Χριστός.

Dial. 113:7   Romans A
Καρδίας περιτομήν (cf. 114:4, τὴν δευτέραν περιτομήν).
See the text of Rom. 2:29 in the note on Dial. 92:4.

Dial. 114:4   Ephesians B
Διὰ τῶν λόγων τῶν διὰ τῶν ἀποστόλων τοῦ ἀκρογωνιαίου λίθου καὶ τοῦ ἄνευ χειρῶν τμηθέντος.
Eph. 2:20. 'Εποικοδομηθέντες ἐπὶ τῷ θεμελίῳ τῶν ἀποστόλων καὶ προφητῶν, ὄντος ἀκρογωνιαίου αὐτοῦ Χριστοῦ 'Ιησοῦ.

Dial. 116:1, 3   Galatians C
Τὰ ῥυπαρὰ πάντα, ἃ ἠμφιέσμεθα, κακὰ ἀπεδυσάμεθα . . . . ἐνδῦσαι ἡμᾶς τὰ ἡτοιμασμένα ἐνδύματα . . . . οὕτως ἡμεῖς, οἱ διὰ τοῦ 'Ιησοῦ ὀνόματος ὡς εἰς ἄνθρωπος πιστεύσαντες εἰς τὸν ποιητὴν τῶν ὅλων Θεόν, διὰ τοῦ ὀνόματος τοῦ πρωτοτόκου αὐτοῦ υἱοῦ τὰ ῥυπαρὰ ἱμάτια τοῦτ' ἔστι τὰς ἁμαρτίας, ἀπημφιεσμένοι, πυρωθέντες διὰ τοῦ λόγου τῆς κλήσεως αὐτοῦ, ἀρχιερατικὸν τὸ ἀληθινὸν γένος ἐσμὲν τοῦ Θεοῦ.
Gal. 3:27, 28. Πάντες γὰρ υἱοὶ Θεοῦ ἐστὲ διὰ τῆς πίστεως ἐν Χριστῷ 'Ιησοῦ. ὅσοι γὰρ εἰς Χριστὸν ἐβαπτίσθητε Χριστὸν ἐνεδύσασθε. . . . . πάντες γὰρ ὑμεῖς εἷς ἐστὲ ἐν Χριστῷ 'Ιησοῦ.

The figure of soiled and fresh clothing as an analogy for
the transformation effected through relation to Christ and the
idea of the unity of those who exercise faith are ideas that probably came to Justin through his acquaintance with Galatians.

Dial. 119:5, 6   Galatians B

Καὶ σὺν τῷ ᾿Αβραὰμ τὴν ἁγίαν κληρονομήσομεν γῆν, εἰς τὸν
ἀπέραντον αἰῶνα τὴν κληρονομίαν ληψόμενοι, τέκνα τοῦ ᾿Αβραὰμ διὰ
τὴν ὁμοίαν πίστιν ὄντες . . . . ἐπίστευσε καὶ ἐλογίσθη αὐτῷ εἰς
δικαιοσύνην.

Gal. 3:9. ῞Ωστε οἱ ἐκ πίστεως εὐλογοῦνται σὺν τῷ πιστῷ
᾿Αβραάμ. 7. Γινώσκετε ἄρα ὅτι οἱ ἐκ πίστεως, οὗτοι υἱοί εἰσιν
᾿Αβραάμ. 6. Καθὼς ᾿Αβραὰμ ἐπίστευσεν τῷ θεῷ, καὶ ἐλογίσθη αὐτῷ
εἰς δικαιοσύνην.

The inclusion of Christians among the beneficiaries of the
promises made to Abraham, the identification of Abraham's children
as those who have his faith, and the quotation of Gen. 15:6, apparently under the influence of Gal. 3:6, are indications that
Justin was here influenced by Galatians.

Dial. 120:6   Ephesians C

. . . . μάγῳ Σίμωνι, ὃν θεὸν ὑπεράνω πάσης ἀρχῆς καὶ ἐξουσίας καὶ δυνάμεως εἶναι λέγουσι.

Eph. 1:21. ῾Υπεράνω πάσης ἀρχῆς καὶ ἐξουσίας καὶ δυνάμεως.

There is verbal identity in the phrases that are common to
these passages. Their application is entirely different, but as
familiar as Justin was with Ephesians it is entirely probable that
he used the phrase for the different application.

Dial. 135:6   Galatians C

Δύο σπέρματα ᾿Ιούδα καὶ δύο γένη, ὡς δύο οἴκους ᾿Ιακώβ,
τὸν μὲν ἐξ αἵματος καὶ σαρκός, τὸν δὲ ἐκ πίστεως καὶ πνεύματος
γεγεννημένον.

Gal. 3:16. Τῷ δὲ ᾿Αβραὰμ ἐρρέθησαν αἱ ἐπαγγελίαι καὶ τῷ
σπέρματι αὐτοῦ· οὐ λέγει Καὶ τοῖς σπέρμασιν, ὡς ἐπὶ πολλῶν, ἀλλ᾿
ὡς ἐφ᾿ ἑνός Καὶ τῷ σπέρματί σου, ὅς ἐστιν Χριστός. 4:22-23.
᾿Αβραὰμ δύο υἱοὺς ἔσχεν, ἕνα ἐκ τῆς παιδίσκης καὶ ἕνα ἐκ τῆς ἐλευ-
θέρας· ἀλλ᾿ ὁ [μὲν] ἐκ τῆς παιδίσκης κατὰ σάρκα γεγέννηται. . . . .
24. Αὗται γὰρ εἰσιν δύο διαθῆκαι . . . . . 29. Κατὰ ᾿Ισαὰκ

ἐπαγγελίας τέκνα ἐσμέν· ἀλλ' ὥσπερ τότε ὁ κατὰ σάρκα γεννηθεὶς ἐδίωκε τὸν κατὰ πνεῦμα, οὕτως καὶ νῦν.

The phraseology of Dial. 135:6 may be influenced by that of John 1:13, but the ideas are rather clearly those of Galatians. The emphasis on δύο σπέρματα, and the nature of the contrast drawn between the "two houses" point rather clearly to dependence on Galatians.

Instances of possible literary reminiscence.—Apol. 5:4; cf. Phil. 2:7. Τοῦ λόγου μορφωθέντος καὶ ἀνθρώπου γενομένου καὶ Ἰησοῦ Χριστοῦ κληθέντος suggests the language and Christology of Philippians.

Apol. 9:1; cf. Phil. 2:6. Καὶ Θεοῦ μορφὴν μὴ ἔχοντα represents a purely verbal parallel to Philippians. It is possible that Paul's phraseology had stuck in Justin's mind.

Apol. 14:5; cf. Rom. 1:16. Both writers characterize the Christian message as δύναμις Θεοῦ.

Apol. 40:1-4; cf. Rom. 10:18. Paul and Justin both quote Ps. 19:4. The quotation in Romans is briefer, and the only suggestion of dependence on the part of the Apology consists in the use of the quotation as a prophecy of Jesus. The probability of such dependence is reduced by the fact that in the immediately succeeding context other Psalms are quoted by Justin without Pauline parallels.

Apol. 49:2-4; cf. Rom. 10:20. Justin and Paul use Isa. 65:1-3 to similar effect.

Apol. 52:5, 6; cf. Rom. 14:11. Justin conflates two passages here and introduces his statement with ἐρρήθη δὲ διὰ Ἰεζεκιὴλ τοῦ προφήτου οὕτως· His rendering of Ezek. 37:7 is evidently from memory. The variations in his quotation of Isa. 45:23 might be explained similarly but for the agreement with Romans against Isaiah in the use of ἐξομολογέω, which suggests literary acquaintance. It is to be remembered, however, that the LXX text of Isa. 45:23 is somewhat uncertain (ἐξομολογήσεται א[c.] [b mg] A Q), and this variation in the text may explain the usage of Paul and of Justin.

Apol. 53:5; cf. Gal. 4:27. Justin in Apol. 53:5 and Paul in Gal. 4:27 quote the words of Isa. 54:1 verbatim. The limits of the quotation in the two writings are identical. Justin intro-

duces the quotation in a way that shows that his application of
it was strikingly similar to its application by Paul—the two
women represent the two racial groups of early Christianity.

Apol. 67:5; cf. I Cor. 14:16. The association of the
terms εὐχαριστία and 'Αμήν may represent literary reminiscence.

Dial. 12:3; cf. Phil. 3:3. Justin tells the Jews that
they need a "second circumcision" and that they glory greatly "in
the flesh." In Philippians Paul speaks of the "true circumcision"
and means thereby that it is different from the literal, and in
the same connection he asserts that Christians do not rely on
"physical advantages."

Dial. 13:1; cf. Rom. 3:20. Justin and Paul both insist on
the inefficacy of legal provisions for dealing with sin and on the
complete efficaciousness of the sacrifice of Christ when taken advantage of by faith.

Dial. 16:4; cf. I Thess. 2:15. The sequence in the two
enumerations of Jewish persecutions is the same.

Dial. 32:2; cf. Rom. 9:27-29. Paul quotes from Isa. 10:
22 and 1:9, and Justin may be alluding to the same Old Testament
passages in complete independence of Paul. The allusive character
of his reference and the certainty of his acquaintance with Romans
in other instances suggest the likelihood that in the present instance he writes under the influence of Romans.

Dial. 32:5; cf. I Cor. 1:19. Justin and Paul both quote
Isa. 29:14, and the quotation in the former is not limited by the
confines of the quotation in the latter. This indicates that
Justin's dependence was directly on Isaiah, and yet, in view of
Justin's highly probable acquaintance with I Corinthians, this
common use of the same Old Testament passage is worth noting.

Dial. 33:2; cf. Phil. 2:8, 9. The contrast between ταπει-
νός and ὑψωθείς suggests acquaintance with Philippians. Justin,
however, seems to feel that the contrast has been suggested by Ps.
109:7. It is possible that the Psalm took on this connotation for
him because he knew Philippians also.

Dial. 35:3; cf. I Cor. 11:18, 19 and Gal. 3:19, 20.
῎Εσονται σχίσματα καὶ αἱρέσεις may reflect acquaintance with I
Corinthians and Galatians. Αἵρεσις occurs in the New Testament
in Acts 5:17, 15:5, 24:5, 14, 26:5, and 28:22 and in I Cor. 11:19,

Gal. 5:20, and II Pet. 2:1. Σχίσμα occurs in Matt. 9:16; Mark 2:21; John 7:43, 9:16, 10:19; I Cor. 1:10, 11:18, 12:25.

Dial. 35:3; cf. II Cor. 11:13. Ψευδαπόστολος occurs in the New Testament only in II Cor. 11:13.

Dial. 40:1; cf. I Cor. 3:16. The influence of the LXX of Gen. 2:7 is clear in Dial. 40:1, ὅτι γὰρ τὸ πλάσμα, ὃ ἔπλασεν ὁ Θεὸς τὸν 'Αδάμ, οἶκος ἐγένετο τοῦ ἐμφυσήματος τοῦ παρὰ τοῦ Θεοῦ, καὶ πάντες νοεῖν δύνασθε. There seems to be in addition to this a reminiscence of I Corinthians in the idea of man as the dwelling place of the Spirit of God.

Dial. 42:1, 2; cf. Rom. 10:16. Justin and Paul insist that the Old Testament writers they quote looked forward to Christianity. Both quote Ps. 18:5 and Isa. 53:1, 2 to authenticate their arguments, although Justin reverses the order of the quotations and uses the common sources at greater length.

Dial. 44:1; cf. Rom. 9:6-9.

Dial. 49:8; cf. Eph. 1:21 and Col. 2:10. There is a clear reference to Exod. 17:16 in Dial. 49:8. It is in the christological application of the reference that the possibility of influence from Ephesians appears. The influence of Ephesians is given precedence over that of Colossians because of the more elaborate development and greater impressiveness of the picture that is found there.

Dial. 55:3; cf. II Cor. 3:14.

Dial. 55:3; cf. Rom. 9:27-29. See the note on Dial. 32:2.

Dial. 64:2; cf. Rom. 9:27-29. See the note on Dial. 32.

Dial. 82:1; cf. I Cor. 1:7.

Dial. 91:1; cf. Rom. 8:29. Justin may have been following Romans in his substitution of ἐν ἀδελφαῖς for ἐπ' ἀδελφαῖς in his use of Deut. 33:16.

Dial. 119:2; cf. Rom. 10:19. Justin and Paul both quote from Deuteronomy to show that the passage of the gospel from the Jews to the Gentiles was foretold. Justin, however, quotes more extensively than Paul does (Deut. 32:16-23 as against 32:21). It is possible that Paul's reference suggested Justin's fuller use of the common source.

Dial. 134:5; cf. Phil. 2:7, 8.

Dial. 135:3; cf. Phil. 3:3.

Leipoldt finds in Justin's writings evidence of acquaintance with Romans, I and II Corinthians, Galatians, Ephesians, Philippians, Colossians, and I and II Thessalonians.[8] Westcott finds traces of the influence of "all St. Paul's Epistles with the exception of the Pastoral Epistles and those to Philippians and Philemon."[9]

The findings of the present study are in general accord with those mentioned. No traces of acquaintance with the Pastorals are found. Of the Pauline letters, no traces of acquaintance with Philemon are found, and indications of acquaintance with II Corinthians and I Thessalonians are exceedingly weak.

TABLE OF RESULTS

	A	B	C	Unclassed
Romans	8	2	1	12
I Corinthians	1	3	2	5
II Corinthians	.	.	.	2
Galatians	2	2	2	2
Ephesians	2	1	1	1
Philippians	.	.	.	6
Colossians	2	1	.	1
I Thessalonians	.	.	.	1
II Thessalonians	.	2	.	....
Philemon	.	.	.	....

The Greek Fragments of the Writings of Melito

Fragments of the writings of Melito of Sardis are preserved in other works. The Greek fragments are found in conveniently edited form in Goodspeed's Die ältesten Apologeten. The works which these fragments represent probably come from the decade A.D. 170-80.

In Fragment III (Eusebius HE iv. 26. 14) Melito writes: καὶ ἀκριβῶς μαθὼν τὰ τῆς παλαιᾶς διαθήκης βιβλία, ὑποτάξας ἔπεμψά- σοι· He then proceeds to list the "acknowledged Scriptures of the

---

[8]Op. cit., I, 192.   [9]Op. cit., p. 171.

Old Covenant." The implications are that he also knew τὰ βιβλία τῆς καινῆς διαθήκης, and a catalogue of the latter may originally have followed the catalogue that is here preserved in Fragment III.[10]

In Fragments IX and XII allusions to the Old Testament are introduced by the simple formula φησί. In Fragment XII occurs the only other reference to the Old Testament, and it is introduced with οὕτω καὶ ᾽Ιεζεκιήλ.

There are no direct allusions to, or citations of, the writings that constitute the New Testament. There are, however, indirect allusions that indicate acquaintance with the Christian writings.

Fragment II; cf. Eph. 4:6. Οὐκ ἐσμὲν λίθων οὐδεμίαν αἴσθησιν ἐχόντων θεραπευταί, ἀλλὰ μόνου Θεοῦ τοῦ πρὸ πάντων καὶ ἐπὶ πάντων καὶ τοῦ Χριστοῦ αὐτοῦ ὄντος Θεοῦ λόγου πρὸ αἰώνων ἐσμὲν θρησκευταί.

Eph. 4:6. Εἷς κύριος . . . . εἷς Θεὸς καὶ πατὴρ πάντων, ὁ ἐπὶ πάντων.

The resemblances in phrasing to Rom. 9:5 and I Cor. 2:7 are probably due to general usage in religious speech. The conceptions of the passage are sufficiently akin to those of Eph. 4:5, 6 to suggest literary reminiscence, and the similarities of phrasing strengthen that as a possibility.

Fragment VIII. 4; cf. Eph. 4:9. ῾Ο Χριστὸς . . . . ἥλιος ἀνατολῆς, ὃς καὶ τοῖς ἐν ᾅδου νεκραῖς ἐφάνη καὶ τοῖς ἐν κόσμῳ βροτοῖς, καὶ μόνος ἥλιος οὗτος ἀνέτειλεν ἀπ᾽ οὐρανοῦ.

Eph. 4:9. Τὸ δέ ᾽Ανέβη τί ἐστιν εἰ μὴ ὅτι καὶ κατέβη εἰς τὰ κατώτερα μέρη τῆς γῆς; . . . . 5:14. Καὶ ἐπιφαύσει σοι ὁ Χριστός.

The probabilities all favor an acquaintance with Paul's letters on the part of Melito. It is interesting to note that the two possible traces of acquaintance which the Fragments show indicate a knowledge of Ephesians.

Athenagoras' Supplication for the Christians

Athenagoras was a contemporary of Melito and Tatian. Very little is known of the circumstances of his life except as these

---

[10]Vernon Bartlett, "Melito the Author of the Muratorian Canon," Expositor, June, 1906, pp. 481-95.

appear from what he wrote. In about A.D. 177 he addressed an
apology to Marcus Aurelius and Commodus. His effort in this plea
was to refute the principal charges that had been urged against
Christians and the Christian movement.

In about A.D. 177 No book that is found in our New Testament is mentioned in
the Supplication, nor are there any direct quotations of the books.
There are allusions, however, that indicate acquaintance with the
Gospels, several of the letters of the Pauline collection, and
probably Hebrews and the Apocalypse.

In 9:1 it is taken for granted that everyone knows the
writings of the Old Testament: Νομίζω δὲ καὶ ὑμᾶς φιλομαθεστάτους
καὶ ἐπιστημονεστάτους ὄντας οὐκ ἀνοήτους γεγονέναι οὔτε τῶν
Μωυσέως οὔτε των Ἡσαΐου καὶ Ἱερεμίου καὶ τῶν λοιπῶν προφητῶν.
Athenagoras' conception of inspiration is indicated in the statement of the immediately succeeding context: οἱ κατ' ἔκστασιν τῶν
ἐν αὐτοῖς λογισμῶν, κινήσαντος αὐτοὺς τοῦ θείου πνεύματος, συγχρη-
σαμένου τοῦ πνεύματος ὡς εἰ καὶ αὐλητὴς αὐλὸν ἐμπνεῦσαι. In 10:1,
where the reference is to Prov. 8:22, the introductory formula is
συνᾴδει δὲ τῷ λόγῳ καὶ τὸ προφητικὸν πνεῦμα· Κύριος γάρ, φησίν.
. . . .

Supplic. 13:2   Romans B
Δέον ἀναίμακτον θυσίαν τὴν λογικὴν προσάγειν λατρείαν;
Rom. 12:1. Παρακαλῶ οὖν ὑμᾶς, ἀδελφοί, διὰ τῶν οἰκτιρμῶν
τοῦ θεοῦ παραστῆσαι τὰ σώματα ὑμῶν θυσίαν ζῶσαν ἁγίαν ⌜τῷ θεῷ
εὐάρεστον⌝, τὴν λογικὴν λατρείαν ὑμῶν.

The representation of the sacrifice that pleases God is in
both instances the same.

Supplic. 16:2   Galatians B
Οὐ παραλιπόντες προσκυνεῖν τὸν αἴτιον τῆς κινήσεως τοῦ
σώματος θεὸν ἐπὶ τὰ πτωχὰ καὶ ἀσθενῆ στοιχεῖα καταπίπτομεν.
Gal. 4:8, 9. Ἀλλὰ τότε μὲν οὐκ εἰδότες θεὸν ἐδουλεύσατε
τοῖς φύσει μὴ οὖσι θεοῖς· νῦν δὲ γνόντες θεόν, μᾶλλον δὲ γνω-
σθέντες ὑπὸ θεοῦ, πῶς ἐπιστρέφετε πάλιν ἐπὶ τὰ ἀσθενῆ καὶ πτωχὰ
στοιχεῖα, οἷς πάλιν ἄνωθεν ⌜δουλεῦσαι⌝ θέλετε;

Geffcken suggests that Athenagoras has conflated his quotation from Plato (Polit. 269 D) with Galatians,[11] and the suggestion seems to be a sound one. Both writers contrast the worship of the true God with the pagan worship of the physical order. This similarity of theme is accompanied by an equally impressive resemblance in phraseology.

Supplic. 34:1   Romans C

Καὶ μηδὲ τῶν ἀρσένων φειδόμενοι, ἄρσενες ἐν ἄρσεσι τὰ δεινὰ κατεργαζόμενοι.

Rom. 1:27. Ὁμοίως τε καὶ οἱ ἄρσενες ἀφέντες τὴν φυσικὴν χρῆσιν τῆς θηλείας ἐξεκαύθησαν ἐν τῇ ὀρέξει αὐτῶν εἰς ἀλλήλους ἄρσενες ἐν ἄρσεσιν, τὴν ἀσχημοσύνην κατεργαζόμενοι.

Both writers severely arraign pagan morality. The specification of moral degradation that is common to the two passages is probably due to literary relationship.

Instances of possible literary reminiscence.—Supplic. 5:2; cf. Rom. 1:20. Athenagoras describes God as visible in creation: Τὸν δὲ ἀπὸ τῶν ἔργων, ὄψιν τῶν ἀδήλων νοῶν τὰ φαινόμενα ἐφώρα αἰθέρος γῆς. This view was probably the common possession of ancient thought. It may represent in this instance familiarity with Romans, however.

Supplic. 12:1; cf. Rom. 8:18. Athenagoras' representation of the Christian life and hope has possible points of contact with Romans: Οὐδὲν τηλικοῦτον πείσεσθαι κακὸν ἐνταῦθα νομίζοντες κἂν τῆς ψυχῆς ἡμᾶς ἀφαιρῶνται τινες, ὧν ἐκεῖ κομιούμεθα.

Supplic. 12:2; cf. I Cor. 15:32. It is possible that Athenagoras was influenced by I Corinthians rather than by Isaiah in the statement: Εἶθ' οἱ μὲν τὸν βίον τοῦτον νομίζοντες Φάγωμεν καὶ πίωμεν, αὔριον γὰρ ἀποθνήσκομεν. There can be no certainty of this, however, because the two versions of the quotations from Isa. 22:13 are verbally the same. The context in the Supplication might argue somewhat more strongly for dependence on I Corinthians, since in both cases the transiency of death is urged.

Supplic. 16:1; cf. I Cor. 15:28 and Col. 3:11. Ὑμᾶς δὲ πάντα ἐν πᾶσιν ἄγουσι τῇ δόξῃ may reflect the influence of I Corinthians and Colossians.

[11] J. Geffcken, Zwei griechische Apologeten (Leipzig: B. G. Teubner, 1907), p. 192.

TABLE OF RESULTS

	A	B	C	Unclassed
Romans..............	.	1	1	2
I Corinthians.......	.	.	.	2
II Corinthians......	.	.	.	....
Galatians...........	.	1	.	....
Ephesians...........	.	.	.	....
Philippians.........	.	.	.	....
Colossians..........	.	.	.	1
I Thessalonians.....	.	.	.	....
II Thessalonians....	.	.	.	....
Philemon............	.	.	.	....

The Pastoral Epistles

The Pastorals seem to have had no circulation as separate
letters. The indications are that they were written as a letter
corpus and that from the beginning they circulated in the form of
a collection. The suggestion for the writing of a letter collection in the name of Paul would naturally come through acquaintance
with an existing Pauline letter collection. Among the probable
motives of the author of the Pastorals was the rescue of the Pauline letters from the disfavor into which they seem to have fallen
toward the middle of the second century as a result of their popularity among the Marcionites.

The use of the Old Testament in the Pastorals is very limited. The list of allusions given in Westcott and Hort, The New
Testament in Greek, number only six, as follows: I Tim. 5:18 (cf.
Deut. 25:4); I Tim. 5:19 (cf. Deut. 19:15); II Tim. 2:19 (cf. Num.
16:5 and Isa. 26:13); II Tim. 4:14 (cf. Ps. 62:12 and Prov. 24:12);
II Tim. 4:17 (cf. Ps. 22:21); Titus 2:14 (cf. Ps. 130:8, Ezek. 37:
23, and Deut. 14:2). In only one of these instances is the allusion in the form of a direct quotation; in I Tim. 5:18 there is the
introductory formula λέγει γὰρ ἡ γραφή. The remainder of the instances are informally introduced as though they were the writer's
own ideas.

I Tim. 1:1   Colossians C
Καὶ Χριστοῦ Ἰησοῦ τῆς ἐλπίδος ἡμῶν.
Col. 1:28. ⌜Ὅ⌝ ἐστιν Χριστὸς ἐν ὑμῖν, ἡ ἐλπὶς τῆς δόξης.

Ἐλπίς is predominantly a Pauline word in the New Testament. It occurs in Acts, the Pauline letters, the Pastorals, Hebrews, and the Catholics. It is applied figuratively to Christ
only in Colossians and I Timothy (cf. Ign. Eph. 21:2, ἐν Ἰησοῦ
Χριστῷ, τῇ κοινῇ ἐλπίδι ἡμῶν; also Philad. 11:2 and Magn. 11).
This phrase in I Timothy and Ignatius has a formal sound that is
absent in Colossians, and yet both were probably influenced by
Colossians.

I Tim. 1:1   Philippians B
Τιμοθέῳ γνησίῳ τέκνῳ ἐν πίστει (cf. I Tim. 1:18).
Phil. 2:9. Ἐλπίζω . . . . Τιμόθεον ταχέως πέμψαι ὑμῖν.
. . . . 20.   Ἔχω ἰσόψυχον ὅστις γνησίως τὰ περὶ ὑμῶν μεριμνήσει.
. . . . 22.   Ὡς πατρὶ τέκνον σὺν ἐμοὶ ἐδούλευσεν εἰς τὸ εὐαγγέλιον.
4:3. Γνήσιε σύνζυγε . . . . (cf. I Cor. 4:17; cf. Corpus Hermeticum xiii. 3 [I, 240 (Scott)]: Μὴ φθόνει μοι, πάτηρ· γνήσιος υἱός
εἰμι. διάφρασον μοι τῆς παλιγγενεσίας τὸν τρόπον).

The reference to Timothy was very probably a reflection of
the influence of Philippians, and possibly of I Corinthians. In
I Cor. 4:17 and Phil. 2:22, Paul calls Timothy his "child." The
use of γνήσιος makes dependence on Philippians clearer, the term
being used in the New Testament only in II Cor. 8:8, Phil. 4:3,
I Tim. 1:1, and Titus 1:4. The sense in which it is used here
corresponds with its use in Phil. 4:3 and was probably suggested
by the use of the adverbial form in Phil. 2:20.

I Tim. 1:3   I Corinthians C
Καθὼς παρεκάλεσά σε προσμεῖναι ἐν Ἐφέσῳ πορευόμενος εἰς
Μακεδονίαν, ... ἵνα παραγγείλῃς τισὶν μὴ ἑτεροδιδασκαλεῖν.
I Cor. 16:5-11. Ἐλεύσομαι δὲ πρὸς ὑμᾶς ὅταν Μακεδονίαν
διέλθω, Μακεδονίαν γὰρ διέρχομαι, ... ἐπιμένω δὲ ἐν Ἐφέσῳ ἕως
τῆς πεντηκοστῆς· . . . . . Ἐὰν δὲ ἔλθῃ Τιμόθεος, βλέπετε ἵνα ἀφόβως γένηται πρὸς ὑμᾶς, ... προπέμψατε δὲ αὐτὸν ἐν εἰρήνῃ, ἵνα
ἔλθῃ πρός με.

The situation implied in I Tim. 1:3 is best explained as
literary fiction. The effort to create a real situation is dis-
appointing. The material for the situation was probably derived
from Paul's description of his own and Timothy's movements in I
Cor. 16:5-11. He is in Ephesus and has sent Timothy to Corinth
but expects him to return. In Ephesus there are ἀντικείμενοι
πολλοί.

I Tim. 1:4 Colossians C

Αἵτινες ἐκζητήσεις παρέχουσι μᾶλλον ἢ οἰκονομίαν Θεοῦ τὴν
ἐν πίστει.

Col. 1:25. ᵗΗς ἐγενόμην ἐγὼ διάκονος κατὰ τὴν οἰκονομίαν
τοῦ Θεοῦ τὴν δοθεῖσάν μοι εἰς ὑμᾶς πληρῶσαι τὸν λόγον τοῦ Θεοῦ.

The only occurrences of οἰκονομία in the New Testament are
Luke 16:2-4; I Cor. 9:17; Eph. 1:10, 3:2, 9; Col. 1:25; and I Tim.
1:4. Its use in Colossians in connection with τὸν λόγον τοῦ Θεοῦ
is a probable source of influence for I Timothy, where false teaching is described as creating controversy instead of οἰκονομίαν
Θεοῦ.

I Tim. 1:7 Galatians C

Θέλοντες εἶναι νομοδιδάσκαλοι, μὴ νοοῦντες μήτε ἃ λέγουσιν
μήτε περὶ τίνων διαβεβαιοῦνται.

Gal. 4:21-27. Λέγετέ μοι, οἱ ὑπὸ νόμον θέλοντες εἶναι,
τὸν νόμον οὐκ ἀκούετε; γέγραπται γὰρ ὅτι Ἀβραὰμ δύο υἱοὺς ἔσχεν,
ἕνα ἐκ τῆς παιδίσκης καὶ ἕνα ἐκ τῆς ἐλευθέρας· . . . . ἅτινά ἐστιν
ἀλληγορούμενα· αὗται γάρ εἰσιν δύο διαθῆκαι . . . . ἡ δὲ ἄνω
Ἰερουσαλὴμ ἐλευθέρα ἐστίν, ἥτις ἐστὶν μήτηρ ἡμῶν·

The term νομοδιδάσκαλος is almost certainly not used in the
technical sense of Luke 5:17 and Acts 5:34, its only other occurrences in the New Testament. It is applied here to heretical
teachers for the probable purpose of bringing them under the con-
demnation of Paul.[12] Paul in Galatians charges his legalistic

---

[12]M. Dibelius, Die Pastoralbriefe[2] (Tübingen: J. C. B.
Mohr, 1931), p. 13: "Wahrscheinlich will unser Pseudopaulus die
Ketzer dabei mit den Waffen des Paulus schlagen: er nennt sie
Lehrer des νόμος und über solche Leute hatte Paulus ja sein Urteil
gesprochen."

opponents with not properly understanding the Law to which they
wish to adhere.

I Tim. 1:8   Romans A

Οἴδαμεν δὲ ὅτι καλὸς ὁ νόμος ἐάν τις αὐτῷ νομίμως χρῆται.

Rom. 3:19. Οἴδαμεν δὲ ὅτι ὅσα ὁ νόμος λέγει τοῖς ἐν τῷ
νόμῳ λαλεῖ. . . . . 7:7. Τί οὖν ἐροῦμεν; ὁ νόμος ἁμαρτία; μὴ
γένοιτο·. . . . . 12. Ὥστε ὁ μὲν νόμος ἅγιος, καὶ ἡ ἐντολὴ·
ἀγία καὶ δικαία καὶ ἀγαθή. . . . . 16. Εἰ δὲ ὁ οὐ θέλω τοῦτο
ποιῶ, σύνφημι τῷ νόμῳ ὅτι καλός.

Paul and the author of I Timothy both describe the Law as
καλός, and the assertion of the latter seems almost certainly to
be a reminiscence of the former. Paul calls the Law καλός by way
of emphasizing the moral insufficiency of human nature, whereas
I Timothy makes the assertion conditionally, ἐάν τις αὐτῷ νομίμως
χρῆται. Paul's problem is evidently not that of the later Paulinist, but that does not make dependence the less likely. Καλός is
used to describe the Law in the New Testament only in Rom. 7:16
and I Tim. 1:8.

I Tim. 1:9   Galatians C

Εἰδὼς τοῦτο ὅτι δικαίῳ νόμος οὐ κεῖται.

Gal. 5:24. Κατὰ τῶν τοιούτων οὐκ ἔστιν νόμος.

In Gal. 5:23 Paul has enumerated the virtues which he characterizes as ὁ καρπὸς τοῦ πνεύματος. These might, with equal propriety, be asserted as the qualities of the life that Paul would
call δίκαιος. It is with reference to these virtues and the life
that embodies them that Paul makes the assertion of Gal. 5:24.
In the insistence that the Law is inapplicable to the "upright"
the author of I Timothy probably recalls Paul's assertion.

I Tim. 1:12   Philippians C

Χάριν ἔχω τῷ ἐνδυναμώσαντί με Χριστῷ Ἰησοῦ τῷ κυρίῳ ἡμῶν.

Phil. 4:13. Πάντα ἰσχύω ἐν τῷ ἐνδυναμοῦντί με.

I Tim. 1:20   I Corinthians B

Ὧν ἐστὶν Ὑμέναιος καὶ Ἀλέξανδρος, οὓς παρέδωκα τῷ Σατανᾷ ἵνα παιδευθῶσι μὴ βλασφημεῖν.

I Cor. 5:4, 5. Ἤδη κέκρικα ὡς παρὼν τὸν οὕτως τοῦτο κατεργασάμενον ἐν τῷ ὀνόματι τοῦ κυρίου [ἡμῶν] Ἰησοῦ, ... παραδοῦναι τὸν τοιοῦτον τῷ Σατανᾷ εἰς ὄλεθρον τῆς σαρκός, ἵνα τὸ πνεῦμα σωθῇ ἐν τῇ ἡμέρᾳ τοῦ κυρίου.

Paul's παραδοῦναι τὸν τοιοῦτον τῷ Σατανᾷ seems almost to be quoted by the author of I Timothy. In both passages the redemption of the offender is made the purpose of the punishment. Paul does not use the verb παιδεύω here, but in 11:32 he uses it in the sense in which it is used in I Timothy. The only other instance in which Paul uses παιδεύω is II Cor. 6:9.

I Tim. 2:2 I and II Thessalonians C

Παρακαλῶ . . . . ἵνα ἤρεμον καὶ ἡσύχιον βίον διάγωμεν.

I Thess. 4:11. Παρακαλοῦμεν δὲ ὑμᾶς, ἀδελφοί, περισσεύειν μᾶλλον, καὶ φιλοτιμεῖσθαι ἡσυχάζειν καὶ πράσσειν τὰ ἴδια καὶ ἐργάζεσθαι ταῖς χερσίν.

II Thess. 3:12. Παρακαλοῦμεν . . . . ἵνα μετὰ ἡσυχίας ἐργαζόμενοι.

Ἡσυχία is used in the New Testament in Acts 22:2, II Thess. 3:12, and I Tim. 2:11, 12. Ἡσύχιος is used in I Tim. 2:2 and I Pet. 3:4. Ἡσυχάζω is used in Luke-Acts and I Thessalonians. It would seem that I Tim. 2:2 shows acquaintance with the Thessalonian letters.

I Tim. 2:3-6 Ephesians B

Τοῦτο καλὸν καὶ ἀπόδεκτον ἐνώπιον τοῦ σωτῆρος ἡμῶν Θεοῦ ὃς πάντας ἀνθρώπους θέλει σωθῆναι καὶ εἰς ἐπίγνωσιν ἀληθείας ἐλθεῖν. Εἷς γὰρ Θεός, εἷς καὶ μεσίτης Θεοῦ καὶ ἀνθρώπων ἄνθρωπος Χριστὸς Ἰησοῦς, ὁ δοὺς ἑαυτὸν ἀντίλυτρον ὑπὲρ πάντων.

Eph. 4:13. Μέχρι καταντήσωμεν οἱ πάντες εἰς τὴν ἑνότητα τῆς πίστεως καὶ τῆς ἐπιγνώσεως τοῦ υἱοῦ τοῦ Θεοῦ. . . . . 15. Ἀληθεύοντες δὲ ἐν ἀγάπῃ αὐξήσωμεν εἰς αὐτὸν τὰ πάντα. . . . . 1:17. ⌜Δῴη⌝ ὑμῖν πνεῦμα σοφίας . . . . ἐν ἐπιγνώσει αὐτοῦ. . . . . 4:5. Εἷς κύριος . . . . εἷς Θεὸς καὶ πατὴρ πάντων.

There seems to be a basic dependence on Ephesians. Ἐπίγνωσις ἀληθείας is a characterization of Christianity that may well have been suggested by Eph. 4:13, 15. Ἐπίγνωσις occurs in the New Testament only in the Pauline letters, the Pastorals, Hebrews, and II Peter. The occurrence of ἀλήθεια in the New Testament is very rare in the writings that show no acquaintance with Paul's letters. The emphasis on unity in I Timothy does not sound like I Cor. 8:6, where the "one" is contrasted with the "many," but, rather, like Eph. 4:5, 6, where the thought is that, in view of the unity of God, all men should be saved. This latter idea may not have been consciously in the mind of the writer, but, even if he is merely using a formula, it most probably had its origin from Eph. 4:5, 6.[13] The final clause ὁ δοὺς ἑαυτὸν ἀντίλυτρον ὑπὲρ πάντων has an Ephesian emphasis. Ἀντίλυτρον occurs in the New Testament only in I Timothy, but it is the equivalent of ἀπολύτρωσις of Eph. 1:7 (cf. Rom. 3:24).

    Minor points of resemblance which represent possible literary reminiscences are:

I Timothy

4. . . . . Θεοῦ ὅς πάντας ἀνθρώπους θέλει σωθῆναι

Rom. 11:32. Συνέκλεισεν γὰρ ὁ Θεὸς τοὺς πάντας εἰς ἀπειθίαν ἵνα τοὺς πάντας ἐλεήσῃ

5. Εἰς ἐπίγνωσιν ἀληθείας ἐλθεῖν

Col. 1:9. ῞Ινα πληρωθῆτε τὴν ἐπίγνωσιν τοῦ θελήματος αὐτοῦ 2:2. Εἰς ἐπίγνωσιν τοῦ μυστηρίου τοῦ Θεοῦ 3:10. Ἐνδυσάμενοι τὸν νέον τὸν ἀνακαινούμενον εἰς ἐπίγνωσιν

5. Εἷς καὶ μεσίτης (μεσίτης is used in the New Testament only in Galatians, Hebrews, and I Timothy)

Gal. 3:20. Ὁ δὲ μεσίτης ἑνὸς οὐκ ἔστιν, ὁ δὲ Θεὸς εἷς ἐστίν

6. Ὁ δοὺς ἑαυτὸν ἀντίλυτρον ὑπὲρ πάντων

Gal. 1:4. Ἰησοῦ Χριστοῦ τοῦ δόντος ἑαυτὸν ὑπὲρ τῶν ἁμαρτιῶν ἡμῶν 2:20 τοῦ υἱοῦ τοῦ Θεοῦ τοῦ . . . . παραδόντος ἑαυτὸν ὑπὲρ ἐμοῦ

---

[13]Ibid., p. 26.

I Tim. 2:7   I Corinthians B   Ephesians B

Εἰς ὃ ἐτέθην ἐγὼ κῆρυξ καὶ ἀπόστολος, - διδάσκαλος ἐθνῶν ἐν πίστει.

I Cor. 12:28. Καὶ οὓς μεν ἔθετο ὁ Θεὸς ἐν τῇ ἐκκλησίᾳ πρῶτον ἀποστόλους, δεύτερον προφήτας, τρίτον διδασκάλους

Eph. 3:8. Ἐμοὶ . . . . ἐδόθη ἡ χάρις αὕτη — ταῖς ἔθνεσιν εὐαγγελίσασθαι (cf. I Clem. 5:6, Παῦλος . . . . κῆρυξ γενόμενος ἔν τε τῇ ἀνατολῇ καὶ ἐν τῇ δύσει).

Epictetus iii. 22. 69: Τηρῶν δ' ἀπολεῖ τὸν ἄγγελον καὶ κατάσκοπον καὶ κήρυκα τῶν Θεῶν;

In the preceding context I Timothy clearly depends on Ephesians. In Eph. 3:7 the connection with what precedes is very similar to that which is established between I Tim. 2:7 and what precedes. In both, Paul's divine commission to be an apostle to the Gentiles (cf. Rom. 11:13) is stressed. The language, however, is that of I Cor. 12:28, where the threefold ministry is described as ἀπόστολοι, προφηταὶ, and διδάσκαλοι. The use of τίθημι is also very similar. Κῆρυξ occurs in the New Testament in I Tim. 2:7, II Tim. 1:11, and II Pet. 2:5. In I Clem. 5:6 it is used of Paul just as it is used in the Pastorals. Perhaps the "prophet" of an earlier time had, under Stoic influences (cf. Epictetus iii. 22. 69), become a κῆρυξ.

The predication of acquaintance with I Corinthians and Ephesians is warranted here. It is as though Paul was regarded as the embodiment and ideal representative of all phases and types of Christian leadership, and this is what he was for the author of the Pastorals.

I Tim. 2:7   Romans A

Ἀλήθειαν λέγω, οὐ ψεύδομαι.

Rom. 9:1. Ἀλήθειαν λέγω ἐν Χριστῷ, οὐ ψεύδομαι (cf. II Cor. 11:31, ὁ Θεὸς . . . . οἶδεν . . . . ὅτι οὐ ψεύδομαι and Gal. 1:20, ἰδοῦ ἐνώπιον τοῦ Θεοῦ ὅτι οὐ ψεύδομαι).

In three instances in the authentic letters of Paul he says οὐ ψεύδομαι. A pseudo-Paul would hardly have put such an assertion into the apostle's mouth except on the basis of familiarity with the latter's letters. The double form of the affirmation of veracity in Romans is the most probable source of influence.

    I Tim. 2:10   Ephesians C

Δι' ἔργων ἀγαθῶν.

  Eph. 2:10. Κτισθέντες ἐν Χριστῷ 'Ιησοῦ ἐπὶ ἔργοις ἀγαθοῖς.

In the Pastorals "good works" are evidences of genuine Christianity. Paul several times uses the singular in this sense but never the plural. In the plural Paul always uses "good works" as something in conflict with the gospel. The usage of Eph. 2:10 corresponds with that of the Pastorals (cf. Heb. 10:24) and suggests literary relationship.

    I Tim. 2:10-12   I Corinthians A

'Αλλ' ὃ πρέπει γυναιξὶν . . . . Γυνὴ ἐν ἡσυχίᾳ μανθανέτω ἐν πάσῃ ὑποταγῇ· διδάσκειν δὲ γυναικὶ οὐκ ἐπιτρέπω, οὐδὲ αὐθεντεῖν ἀνδρός, ἀλλ' εἶναι ἐν ἡσυχίᾳ. 'Αδὰμ γὰρ πρῶτος ἐπλάσθη, εἶτα Εὔα·

  I Cor. 11:13. Πρέπον ἐστὶν γυναῖκα ἀκατακάλυπτον τῷ θεῷ προσεύχεσθαι; 14:34, 35. Αἱ γυναῖκες ἐν ταῖς ἐκκλησίαις σιγάτωσαν, οὐ γὰρ ἐπιτρέπεται αὐταῖς λαλεῖν· ἀλλὰ ὑποτασσέσθωσαν . . . . αἰσχρὸν γὰρ ἐστιν γυναικὶ λαλεῖν ἐν ἐκκλησίᾳ. 11:8, 9. Οὐ γάρ ἐστιν ἀνὴρ ἐκ γυναικός, ἀλλὰ γυνὴ ἐξ ἀνδρός· καὶ γὰρ οὐκ ἐκτίσθη ἀνὴρ διὰ τὴν γυναῖκα. ἀλλὰ γυνὴ διὰ τὸν ἄνδρα.

  Πρέπω is used in the New Testament in Matt. 3:15; I Cor. 11:13; Eph. 5:3; Heb. 2:10, 7:26; I Tim. 2:10; and Titus 2:1. Only in I Cor. 11:13 and I Tim. 2:10 does it indicate conduct that is appropriate for women. The insistence on silence in church and on submission to men and the validation of the position on the basis of man's priority in creation make it almost certain that I Timothy was influenced by I Corinthians.

    I Tim. 2:14   II Corinthians B

Καὶ 'Αδὰμ οὐκ ἠπατήθη, ἡ δὲ γυνὴ ἐξαπατηθεῖσα ἐν παραβάσει γέγονεν.

  II Cor. 11:3. ῾Ως ὁ ὄφις ἐξηπάτησεν Εὔαν ἐν τῇ πανουργίᾳ αὐτοῦ.

'Εξαπατάω is used in the New Testament only in Paul's letters and in I Tim. 2:14. Only in II Corinthians and I Timothy is it used of the origin of sin and of Eve's temptation. The LXX has ἠπάτησεν.

I Tim. 4:1   II Thessalonians C

Τὸ δὲ πνεῦμα ῥητῶς λέγει ὅτι ἐν ὑστέροις καιραῖς ἀποστή-
σονταί τινες τῆς πίστεως.

There is the probability that I Timothy is here influenced
by the description of eschatological events in II Thess. 2:1-10
(cf. Matt. 24:11, 12; Apoc. Bar. 70:2-6; IV Ezra 9:3, 4). The author of the Pastorals does not give the impression of a real conviction that the end is near. He rather seems merely to recall
that according to Paul false teachings were a primary item in the
eschatological program. Τὸ πνεῦμα λέγει was probably an established
introductory formula.

I Tim. 4:3, 5   Colossians B

Διδασκαλίαις δαιμονίων ἐν ὑποκρίσει ψευδολόγων, κεκαυστηρια-
σμένων τὴν ἰδίαν συνείδησιν, ⌜κωλυόντων γαμεῖν, ἀπέχεσθαι⌝ βρωμάτων
ἃ ὁ Θεὸς ἔκτισεν εἰς μετάλημψιν μετὰ εὐχαριστίας τοῖς πισταῖς καὶ
ἐπεγνωκόσι τὴν ἀγήθειαν. ὅτι πᾶν κτίσμα Θεοῦ καλόν, καὶ οὐδὲν
ἀπόβλητον μετὰ εὐχαριστίας λαμβανόμενον.
           Col. 2:20-23. Εἰ ἀπεθάνετε σὺν Χριστῷ ἀπὸ τῶν στοιχείων
τοῦ κόσμου, τί ὡς ζῶντες ἐν κόσμῳ δογματίζεσθε Μὴ ἅψῃ μηδὲ γεύσῃ
μηδὲ θίγῃς, ἅ ἐστιν πάντα εἰς φθορὰν τῇ ἀποχρήσει, κατὰ τὰ ἐντάλ-
ματα καὶ διδασκαλίας τῶν ἀνθρώπων; ἅτινα ἐστιν λόγον μὲν ἔχοντα
σοφίας ἐν ἐθελοθρησκίᾳ καὶ ταπεινοφροσύνῃ ⌜[καὶ] ἀφειδίᾳ σώματος,
οὐκ ἐν τιμῇ τινὶ πρὸς πλησμονὴν τῆς σαρκός⌝ (cf. I Cor. 10:29, 30;
Rom. 14:14, 20; Mark 7:15).

There is a cult tone in the repudiation of asceticism in
I Timothy that contrasts with the more definitely rational position
of Colossians, but it is highly probable that the thought of the
Pastorals was colored by the Pauline insistence on freedom.

I Tim. 4:12   I Corinthians C
Μηδείς σου τῆς νεότητος καταφρονείτω.
           I Cor. 16:10, 11. Ἐὰν δὲ ἔλθῃ Τιμόθεος, βλέπετε ἵνα
ἀφόβως γένηται πρὸς ὑμᾶς, τὸ γὰρ ἔργον Κυρίου ἐργάζεται ὡς ⌜ἐγώ⌝·
μή τις οὖν αὐτὸν ἐξουθενήσῃ (cf. I Cor. 4:14 and Phil. 2:22).

This defense of Timothy very probably reflects acquaintance with Paul's appeal on his behalf in I Corinthians. Both

insist that Timothy is entitled to respect in view of the cause he
represents and of his devotion to that cause.

        I Tim. 4:12, 13   II Corinthians C

'Αλλὰ τύπος γίνου τῶν πιστῶν ἐν λόγῳ, ἐν ἀναστροφῇ, ἐν
ἀγάπη, ἐν πίστει ἐν ἀγνίᾳ.

        II Cor. 6:4-7. 'Αλλ' ἐν παντὶ συνιστάνοντες ἑαυτοὺς ὡς
θεοῦ διάκονοι· . . . . ἐν ἀγνότητι . . . . ἐν ἀγάπη ἀνυποκρίτῳ,
ἐν λόγῳ ἀληθείας.

In II Corinthians Paul enumerates the credentials by which
he commends his ministry. This enumeration probably suggested the
similar enumeration whereby Timothy is exhorted to "become an example for believers."

        I Tim. 4:13, 14   Romans C

Πρόσεχε τῇ ἀναγνώσει, τῇ παρακλήσει, τῇ διδασκαλίᾳ. μὴ
ἀμέλει τοῦ ἐν σοὶ χαρίσματος, ὃ ἐδόθη σοι διὰ προφητείας . . . .
ταῦτα μελέτα, ἐν τούτοις ἴσθι.

        Rom. 12:6-8. Ἔχοντες δὲ χαρίσματα κατὰ τὴν χάριν τὴν
δοθεῖσαν ἡμῖν διάφορα, εἴτε προφητείαν κατὰ τὴν ἀναλογίαν τῆς πίστεως . . . . εἴτε ὁ διδάσκων ἐν τῇ διδασκαλίᾳ, εἴτε ὁ παρακαλῶν ἐν
τῇ παρακλήσει.

Πρόσεχε τῇ ἀναγνώσει refers to the public reading of the
Scriptures. For the author of the Pastorals this public reading
would probably include Paul's collected letters (cf. Eph. 3:4;
also I Thess. 5:27 and Col. 4:16). There is probably a specific
reference to Paul's letters here, which makes the influence of
some such passage as Rom. 12:6-8 probable.

        I Tim. 5:8   Galatians C

Εἰ δέ τις τῶν ἰδίων καὶ μάλιστα οἰκείων οὐ ⌈προνοεῖ⌉, τὴν
πίστιν ἤρνηται.

        Gal. 6:10. 'Εργαζώμεθα τὸ ἀγαθὸν πρὸς πάντας, μάλιστα δὲ
πρὸς τοὺς οἰκείους τῆς πίστεως.

The only occurrences of οἰκείος in the New Testament are
Gal. 6:10, Eph. 2:19, and I Tim. 5:8. The exhortation of Gala-
tians seems to have been given a rather literal application in I
Timothy.

I Tim. 5:13   II Thessalonians C

Ἅμα δὲ καὶ ἀργαὶ μανθάνουσιν, περιερχόμεναι τὰς οἰκίας,
οὐ μόνον δὲ ἀργαὶ ἀλλὰ καὶ φλύαροι καὶ περίεργοι, λαλοῦσαι τὰ μὴ
δέοντα.

II Thess. 3:11. Ὅτι εἴ τις οὐ θέλει ἐργάζεσθαι μηδὲ ἐσθιέτω. ἀκούομεν γάρ τινας περιπατοῦντας ἐν ὑμῖν ἀτάκτως, μηδὲν
ἐργαζομένους ἀλλὰ περιεργαζομένους·

Περιεργάζομαι occurs in the New Testament in I Thess. 3:11
only. Περίεργος is found in Acts 19:19 and I Tim. 5:13. The meaning of the term in Acts seems to be entirely different from that
in II Thessalonians and I Timothy, which are in agreement. The
author of the Pastorals is probably adapting Paul's advice to a
specific contemporary group.

I Tim. 5:14   I Corinthians C

Βούλομαι οὖν νεωτέρας γαμεῖν, τεκνογονεῖν, οἰκοδεσποτεῖν,
μηδεμίαν ἀφορμὴν διδόναι τῷ ἀντικειμένῳ λοιδορίας χάριν· ἤδη γάρ
τινες ἐξετράπησαν ὀπίσω τοῦ Σατανᾶ.

I Cor. 7:8, 9. Λέγω δὲ . . . . . ταῖς χήραις, ... εἰ
δὲ οὐκ ἐγκρατεύονται, γαμησάτωσαν, κρεῖττον γάρ ἐστιν ⌜γαμεῖν⌝ ἢ
πυροῦσθαι.

The advice to widows in I Timothy is more unqualified than
that of I Corinthians, but the motive is substantially the same.
In each case the interest is in the avoidance of immorality.

I Tim. 5:18   I Corinthians C

Λέγει γὰρ ἡ γραφή βοῦν ἀλοῶντα οὐ φιμώσεις· καὶ Ἄξιος
ὁ ἐργάτης τοῦ μισθοῦ αὐτοῦ.

I Cor. 9:9. Ἐν γὰρ τῷ Μωσέως νόμῳ γέγραπται Οὐ φιμώσεις
βοῦν ἀλοῶντα. μὴ τῶν βοῶν μέλει τῷ θεῷ, ἢ δι' ἡμᾶς πάντως λέγει;
δι' ἡμᾶς γὰρ ἐγράφη, ... 14. Οὕτως καὶ ὁ κύριος διέταξεν
ταῖς τὸ εὐαγγέλιον καταγγέλουσιν ἐκ τοῦ εὐαγγελίου ζῆν.

Both Paul and the author of the Pastorals quote Deut. 25:4
exactly. I Timothy supplements the Old Testament admonition with
what seems to be a quotation of Luke 10:7. I Corinthians seems
also to look to some saying of Jesus. All three writers may be
drawing from the same paranetic tradition, and there may be no

literary dependence in the case of any of them. However, acquaintance with I Corinthians might have suggested the whole reference
in I Timothy, and the latter may merely have made the former's advice more specific by a quotation from the words of Jesus. The
probabilities favor the Old Testament quotation's having been derived from I Corinthians instead of directly from Deuteronomy, because the Pastorals very rarely use the Old Testament.

I Tim. 5:19   II Corinthians C

Κατὰ πρεσβυτέρου κατηγορίαν μὴ παραδέχου, ἐκτὸς εἰ μὴ
ἐπὶ δύο ἢ τριῶν μαρτύρων·

II Cor. 13:1. 'Επὶ στόματος δύο μαρτύρων καὶ τριῶν σταθή-
σεται πᾶν ῥῆμα.

Both writers are discussing the validation of charges
against a Christian leader. Paul plainly quotes Deut. 19:15. The
author of I Timothy also uses an abbreviation of the same Old Testament quotation, but his allusion may as well have been drawn
from II Corinthians as directly from Deuteronomy. In view of the
general usage in the Pastorals with reference to the Old Testament and in view of the fact that Paul applies Deut. 19:15 to
charges brought against a Christian leader, it is very probable
that I Timothy is dependent on II Corinthians.

I Tim. 6:21   Colossians C

'Η χάρις μεθ' ὑμῶν.
Col. 4:18. 'Η χάρις μεθ' ὑμῶν.

Only in Colossians and in I and II Timothy is this brief
benediction used in closing New Testament letters.

II Tim. 1:2   I Corinthians B

Τιμοθέῳ ἀγαπητῷ τέκνῳ.
I Cor. 4:17. "Επεμψα ὑμῖν Τιμόθεον, ὅς ἐστίν μου τέκνον
ἀγαπητόν.

Timothy is designated in this fashion only in the two instances cited. 'Αγαπητός is a term frequently applied by Paul to
his associates. Τέκνον is a characteristic description of the believer's relation to God and the convert's relation to himself.

II Tim. 1:2   Romans C

Χάρις, ἔλεος, εἰρήνη ἀπὸ Θεοῦ πατρὸς καὶ ⌜Χριστοῦ Ἰησοῦ⌝ τοῦ κυρίου ἡμῶν.

Rom. 1:7.   Χάρις ὑμῖν καὶ εἰρήνη ἀπὸ Θεοῦ πατρὸς ἡμῶν καὶ κυρίου Ἰησοῦ Χριστοῦ.

The salutation found in Rom. 1:7 is also found in I and II Corinthians, Galatians, Ephesians, II Thessalonians, and Philemon. It is shortened in Colossians and I Thessalonians.   In Gal. 6:16 is found the combination εἰρήνη . . . . καὶ ἔλεος.   The addition of ἔλεος is the only point of difference between the salutation of II Timothy and that of most of Paul's letters. Because of the very evident influence of Rom. 1:8-12 on II Tim. 1:3-5, it is regarded probable that this influence extends to the salutation.

II Tim. 1:3-5   Romans A

Χάριν ἔχω τῷ Θεῷ . . . . ᾧ λατρεύω . . . . ἐν καθαρᾷ συνειδήσει, ὡς ἀδιάλειπτον ἔχω τὴν περὶ σοῦ μνείαν ἐν ταῖς δεήσεσίν μου, νυκτὸς καὶ ἡμέρας ἐπιποθῶν σε ἰδεῖν . . . . ἵνα χαρᾶς πληρωθῶ ὑπόμνησιν λαβὼν τῆς ἐν σοὶ ἀνυποκρίτου πίστεως.   -

Rom. 1:8.   Εὐχαριστῶ τῷ Θεῷ μου . . . . περὶ πάντων ὑμῶν. . . . . 9.   ⌜Ωι λατρεύω ἐν τῷ πνεύματί μου. . . . . 10.   ῾Ως ἀδιαλείπτως μνείαν ὑμῶν ποιοῦμαι πάντοτε ἐπὶ τῶν προσευχῶν μου πάντοτε . . . . δεόμενος . . . . ἐλθεῖν πρὸς ὑμᾶς.   ἐπιποθῶ γὰρ ἰδεῖν ὑμᾶς. . . . . 12.   Συνπαρακληθῆναι ἐν ὑμῖν διὰ τῆς ἐν ἀλλήλοις πίστεως.

The introductions to ancient letters frequently contained expressions of thanksgiving and the assurance of prayer for those addressed.   This feature was as frequently a stereotyped literary device as an expression of vital piety.

Paul made the letter an instrument for moral and religious instruction and put into the usual forms of greeting a spiritual earnestness and a note of reality that was characteristic of him. II Tim. 1:3-5 is distinctly Pauline in form and tone and expression.   It is almost certainly influenced by Rom. 1:8-12.

II Tim. 1:6, 7   Romans B

Δι' ἣν αἰτίαν ἀναμιμνήσκω σε ἀναζωπυρεῖν τὸ χάρισμα τοῦ Θεοῦ, ὅ ἐστιν ἐν σοὶ διὰ τῆς ἐπιθέσεως τῶν χειρῶν μου· οὐ γὰρ

ἔδωκεν ἡμῖν ὁ Θεὸς πνεῦμα δειλίας, ἀλλὰ δυνάμεως καὶ ἀγάπης καὶ σωφρονισμοῦ.
Rom. 1:11. Ἵνα τι μεταδῶ χάρισμα ὑμῖν πνευματικόν. . . . .
6:23. Τὸ δὲ χάρισμα τοῦ Θεοῦ. . . . . 8:15. Οὐ γὰρ ἐλάβετε πνεῦμα δουλείας πάλιν εἰς φόβον, ἀλλὰ ἐλάβετε πνεῦμα υἱοθεσίας, ἐν ᾧ κράζομεν Ἀββά ὁ πατήρ· 15:13. Ἐν δυνάμει πνεύματος ἁγίου.

Χάρισμα occurs in the New Testament only in Romans, I and II Corinthians, I and II Timothy, and I Peter. Χάρισμα . . . . πνευματικόν in Rom. 1:11 corresponds in meaning with the χάρισμα in II Tim. 1:6, and in both instances it is communicated through Paul. The phrase τὸ χάρισμα τοῦ Θεοῦ occurs in the New Testament only in Rom. 6:23 and II Tim. 1:6. The phrase πνεῦμα δειλίας so closely resembles πνεῦμα δουλείας of Romans in meaning as to leave little doubt of its having been suggested through familiarity with Rom. 8:15. II Tim. 1:7 seems to be practically a recasting of Rom. 8:15.

II Tim. 1:8   Romans B
Μὴ οὖν ἐπαισχυνθῇς τὸ μαρτύριον τοῦ κυρίου ἡμῶν.
Rom. 1:16. Οὐ γὰρ ἐπαισχύνομαι τὸ εὐαγγέλιον.

The fact that the Pastorals are written in Paul's name increases the probability of dependence on Rom. 1:16. Ἐπαισχύνομαι occurs in the New Testament in Mark 8:38; Luke 9:26; Rom. 1:16, 6:21; II Tim. 1:8, 12, 16; Heb. 2:11, 11:16.

II Tim. 1:8   Ephesians C   Philemon C
Μηδὲ ἐμὲ τὸν δέσμιον αὐτοῦ.
Eph. 3:1. Ἐγὼ Παῦλος ὁ δέσμιος τοῦ Χριστοῦ Ἰησοῦ.
4:1. Ἐγὼ ὁ δέσμιος ἐν κυρίῳ.
Philem. 1. Παῦλος δέσμιος Χριστοῦ Ἰησοῦ καὶ Τιμόθεος ὁ ἀδελφός. . . . . 9. Τοιοῦτος ὢν ὡς Παῦλος πρεσβύτης νυνὶ δὲ καὶ δέσμιος Χριστοῦ Ἰησοῦ.
Acts 23:18. Ὁ δέσμιος Παῦλος. 28:17. Δέσμιος ἐξ Ἰεροσολύμων παρεδόθην εἰς τὰς χεῖρας τῶν Ῥωμαίων.

In Acts Paul is known as ὁ δέσμιος, but it is in Ephesians and Philemon that he appears pre-eminently as ὁ δέσμιος τοῦ Χριστοῦ Ἰησοῦ.

II Tim. 1:9   Romans B   Ephesians C

Θεοῦ, τοῦ σώσαντος ἡμᾶς καὶ καλέσαντος κλήσει ἁγίᾳ, οὐ κατὰ τὰ ἔργα ἡμῶν ἀλλὰ κατὰ ἰδίαν πρόθεσιν καὶ χάριν, τὴν δοθεῖσαν ἡμῖν ἐν Χριστῷ Ἰησοῦ πρὸ χρόνων αἰωνίων φανερωθεῖσαν δὲ νῦν.

Rom. 9:11. Ἵνα ἡ κατ' ἐκλογὴν πρόθεσις τοῦ θεοῦ μένῃ, οὐκ ἐξ ἔργων ἀλλ' ἐκ τοῦ καλοῦντος.   8:28. Ταῖς κατὰ πρόθεσιν κλητοῖς οὖσιν. . . . . 12:6. Κατὰ τὴν χάριν τὴν δοθεῖσαν ἡμῖν. . . . . 16:25 f. Κατὰ ἀποκάλυψιν μυστηρίου χρόναις αἰωνίαις σεσιγημένου φανερωθέντος δὲ νῦν.

Eph. 1:4. Καθὼς ἐξελέξατο ἡμᾶς ἐν αὐτῷ πρὸ καταβολῆς κόσμου, εἶναι ἡμᾶς ἁγίους. . . . . 3:5. Ἐν τῷ μυστηρίῳ τοῦ Χριστοῦ ὃ ἑτέραις γενεαῖς οὐκ ἐγνωρίσθη ταῖς υἱοῖς τῶν ἀνθρώπων ὡς νῦν ἀπεκαλύφθη. . . . . 9-11. Καὶ φωτίσαι τίς ἡ οἰκονομία τοῦ μυστηρίου τοῦ ἀποκεκρυμμένου ἀπὸ τῶν αἰώνων ἐν τῷ θεῷ τῷ τὰ πάντα κτίσαντι, ἵνα γνωρισθῇ νῦν . . . . ἡ πολυποίκιλος σοφία τοῦ θεοῦ, κατὰ πρόθεσιν τῶν αἰώνων ἣν ἐποίησεν ἐν τῷ Χριστῷ Ἰησοῦ τῷ κυρίῳ ἡμῶν (cf. I Thess. 4:7).

The conception of salvation or of God's plans concerning it as having been formerly concealed but now revealed is most impressively stated in Ephesians. Πρόθεσις, in the sense in which it is used here, occurs in the New Testament only in Romans, Ephesians, and II Timothy.

II Tim. 1:10   I Corinthians A   II Thessalonians B

Διὰ τῆς ἐπιφανείας τοῦ σωτῆρος ἡμῶν Χριστοῦ Ἰησοῦ καταργήσαντος μὲν τὸν θάνατον φωτίσαντος δὲ ζωὴν καὶ ἀφθαρσίαν διὰ τοῦ εὐαγγελίου.

II Thess. 2:8, 9. Ὃν ὁ κύριος [Ἰησοῦς] . . . . καταργήσει τῇ ἐπιφανείᾳ τῆς παρουσίας αὐτοῦ.

I Cor. 15:24-27. Εἶτα τὸ τέλος, ... ὅταν καταργήσῃ πᾶσαν ἀρχὴν καὶ πᾶσαν ἐξουσίαν καὶ δύναμιν . . . . ἔσχατος ἐχθρὸς καταργεῖται ὁ θάνατος (cf. Phil. 3:20).

Christ is called σωτήρ in the Pauline letters only in Phil. 3:20 and Eph. 5:23. The thought of Philippians is definitely eschatological and in this respect agrees more closely with II Timothy than does Ephesians. Ἐπιφάνεια occurs in the New Testament only in II Thess. 2:8; I Tim. 6:14; II Tim. 1:10, 4:1, 8; and

Titus 2:13; and it regularly describes the Parousia of Jesus. The
Hellenistic character of the terms σωτήρ and ἐπιφάνεια is to be
taken into account. The Pauline use of them and the appropriate-
ness of their use by later Christian writers may be accounted for
in terms of the general influence of Hellenism. However, the sense
in which they are used in II Timothy, when coupled with their contexts, makes the direct literary influence very probably that of
the Pauline letters.

Καταργέω is used in the New Testament once in Luke, twenty-
four times in the Pauline letters, once in II Timothy, and once in
Hebrews. Its use in II Timothy in connection with θάνατος leaves
little doubt of the influence of I Cor. 15:24-27, 54-57. There
may also be a trace of the influence of the very similar use in
II Thess. 2:9.

II Tim. 1:11   I Corinthians B

Εἰς ὃ ἐτέθην ἐγὼ κῆρυξ καὶ ἀπόστολος καὶ διδάσκαλος.

For the very probable reflection of the influence of I Cor.
12:28 in II Tim. 1:11 see the note on I Tim. 2:7.

II Tim. 1:12   Romans A

'Αλλ' οὐκ ἐπαισχύνομαι, οἶδα γὰρ ᾧ πεπίστευκα, καὶ πέπεισμαι ὅτι δυνατός ἐστιν τὴν παραθήκην μου φυλάξαι.
    Rom. 4:21. ῝Ο ἐπήγγελται δυνατός ἐστιν καὶ ποιῆσαι. 11:24.
Δυνατὸς γάρ ἐστιν ὁ Θεός. . . . . 8:38, 39. Πέπεισμαι γὰρ ὅτι
οὔτε θάνατος οὔτε ζωὴ οὔτε ἄγγελοι οὔτε ἀρχαὶ . . . . οὔτε τις
κτίσις ἑτέρα δυνήσεται ἡμᾶς χωρίσαι ἀπὸ τῆς ἀγάπης τοῦ Θεοῦ τῆς ἐν
Χριστῷ 'Ιησοῦ τῷ κυρίῳ ἡμῶν.

For the literary indebtedness represented in the use of
'ἐπαισχύνομαι and πέπεισμαι see the notes on II Tim. 1:5 and 1:8.
The description of God's power and love and of the Christian assurance that these warrant is clearly a use of the ideas and expressions of Romans.

II Tim. 1:14   Romans A

Διὰ πνεύματος ἁγίου τοῦ ἐνοικοῦντος ἐν ἡμῖν.
    Rom. 8:9-11. ῾Υμεῖς δὲ οὐκ ἐστὲ ἐν σαρκὶ ἀλλὰ ἐν πνεύματι,
εἴπερ πνεῦμα Θεοῦ οἰκεῖ ἐν ὑμῖν. . . . . εἰ δὲ τὸ πνεῦμα τοῦ ἐγείραντος τὸν 'Ιησοῦν ἐκ νεκρῶν οἰκεῖ ἐν ὑμῖν, ὁ ἐγείρας ἐκ νεκρῶν

Χριστὸν 'Ιησοῦν ζωοποιήσει [καὶ] τὰ θνητὰ σώματα ὑμῶν διὰ ⌜τοῦ
ἐνοικοῦντος αὐτοῦ πνεύματος⌝ ἐν ὑμῖν.

'Ενοικέω occurs in the New Testament only in Rom. 7:17, 8:
11; II Cor. 6:16 (cf. Lev. 26:11, 12); Col. 3:16; and II Tim. 1:5,
14. Only in Rom. 8:11 and II Tim. 1:14 does it apply to τὸ πνεῦμα.

  II Tim. 1:15   II Corinthians B
  Οἶδας τοῦτο ὅτι ἀπεστράφησαν με πάντες οἱ ἐν τῇ 'Ασίᾳ.
  II Cor. 1:8. Οὐ γὰρ θέλομεν ὑμᾶς ἀγνοιεῖν, ἀδελφοί, ⌜ὑπὲρ⌝
τῆς θλίψεως ἡμῶν τῆς γενομένης ἐν τῇ 'Ασίᾳ, ὅτι καθ' ὑπερβολὴν
ὑπὲρ δύναμιν ἐβαρήθημεν, ὥστε ἐξαπορηθῆναι ἡμᾶς καὶ τοῦ ζῆν (cf.
Acts 19:9).

II Cor. 1:8 is the only specific mention in Paul's letters
of difficulties experienced in "Asia." He does not indicate the
precise nature of the trouble, but the mere mention of such a situation would provide sufficient basis for the allusion in II Timothy.

  II Tim. 2:4-6   I Corinthians C
  Οὐδεὶς στρατευόμενος ἐμπλέκεται ταῖς τοῦ βίου πραγματίαις,
ἵνα τῷ στρατολογήσαντι ἀρέσῃ· ἐὰν δὲ καὶ ἀθλῇ τις, οὐ στεφανοῦ-
ται ἐὰν μὴ νομίμως ἀθλήσῃ τὸν κοπιῶντα γεωργὸν δεῖ πρῶτον τῶν
καρπῶν μεταλαμβάνειν.

The three figures used, but not fully developed, in II
Timothy are familiar in the Cynic-Stoic diatribe. Paul employs
these figures and amplifies their meaning (I Cor. 9:7, 10-14, 24,
25). The author of the Pastorals leaves his point conjectured,
and this may have been done because the implications of the figures are so fully worked out in I Corinthians.

  II Tim. 2:8   Romans A
  Μνημόνευε 'Ιησοῦν Χριστὸν ἐγηγερμένον ἐκ νεκρῶν, ἐκ σπέρματος Δαυείδ, κατὰ τὸ εὐαγγέλιόν μου·
  Rom. 4:24. 'Επὶ τὸν ἐγείραντα 'Ιησοῦν τὸν κύριον ἡμῶν ἐκ
νεκρῶν. . . . . 6:9. Εἰδότες ὅτι Χριστὸς ἐγερθεὶς ἐκ νεκρῶν.
6:11. Οὕτως καὶ ὑμεῖς λογίζεσθε ἑαυτοὺς εἶναι νεκροὺς μὲν τῇ
ἁμαρτίᾳ ζῶντας δὲ τῷ θεῷ ἐν Χριστῷ 'Ιησοῦ.

The Resurrection is one of the significant emphases in

Romans.   In II Timothy the allusion to it is in the language of
Romans.   The Davidic descent of Jesus is also an item of interest
in Rom. 1:3, that being the oldest extant literary allusion to it
and the only specific reference to it in Paul's letters.   The
phrase κατὰ τὸ εὐαγγέλιόν μου is found in Rom. 2:16 and 16:25 (cf.
II Cor. 4:3 and Gal. 1:6, 11, 2:2).

<table>
<tr><td>II Tim. 2:8</td><td>Philippians A</td></tr>
</table>

Τὸ εὐαγγέλιόν μου·   ἐν ᾧ κακοπαθῶ μέχρι δεσμῶν ὡς κακοῦρ-
γος ἀλλὰ ὁ λόγος τοῦ θεοῦ οὐ δέδεται.

Phil. 1:12-14.   Τὰ κατ' ἐμὲ μᾶλλον εἰς προκοπὴν τοῦ εὐαγγελίου ἐλήλυθεν, ὥστε τοὺς δεσμούς μου φανεροὺς ἐν Χριστῷ γενέσθαι
ἐν ὅλῳ τῷ πραιτωρίῳ καὶ ταῖς λοιπαῖς πᾶσιν, καὶ τοὺς πλείονας τῶν
ἀδελφῶν ἐν κυρίῳ πεποιθότας ταῖς δεσμοῖς μου περισσοτέρως τολμᾷν
ἀφόβως τὸν λόγον τοῦ θεοῦ λαλεῖν.

In Philippians, Colossians, and Philemon, Paul refers to
his "bonds."   In Philippians he indicates that his "bonds" have
actually served to popularize the gospel, and this is exactly the
point of II Tim. 2:8.

<table>
<tr><td>II Tim. 2:10</td><td>II Corinthians B</td></tr>
</table>

Διὰ τοῦτο πάντα ὑπομένω διὰ τοὺς ἐκλεκτούς, ἵνα καὶ αὐτοὶ
σωτηρίας τύχωσιν τῆς ἐν Χριστῷ Ἰησοῦ.

II Cor. 1:6.   Εἴτε δὲ θλιβόμεθα, ὑπὲρ τῆς ὑμῶν παρακλήσεως
καὶ σωτηρίας·   εἴτε παρακαλούμεθα, ὑπὲρ τῆς ὑμῶν παρακλήσεως τῆς
ἐνεργουμένης ἐν ὑπομονῇ τῶν αὐτῶν παθημάτων ὧν καὶ ἡμεῖς πάσχομεν
(cf. II Cor. 6:4, 5).

The vicariousness of Paul's sufferings is a theme common
to II Corinthians and II Timothy.   Such an emphasis in II Timothy
would probably have its suggestion in the persecution interest
that is so evident in the Pastorals, and as probably the author
of the Pastorals would adduce the example of Paul as a means of
control.   He very probably found in II Cor. 1:6 the reminiscence
that suggested what he says in II Tim. 2:19.

<table>
<tr><td>II Tim. 2:19, 20</td><td>I Corinthians C</td></tr>
</table>

Ὁ μέντοι στερεὸς θεμέλιος τοῦ θεοῦ ἕστηκεν . . . . ἐν
μεγάλῃ δὲ οἰκίᾳ οὐκ ἔστιν μόνον σκεύη χρυσᾶ καὶ ἀργυρᾶ ἀλλὰ καὶ
ξύλινα καὶ ὀστράκινα, καὶ ἃ μὲν εἰς τιμὴν ἃ δὲ εἰς ἀτιμίαν·

I Cor. 3:10-13. Θεμέλιον ἔθηκα, ... θεμέλιον γὰρ ἄλλον
οὐδεὶς δύναται θεῖναι παρὰ τὸν κείμενον, ὅς ἐστιν Ἰησοῦς Χριστός·
εἰ δέ τις ἐποικοδομεῖ ἐπὶ τὸν θεμέλιον ⌈χρυσίον⌉, ἀργύριον, λίθους,
τιμίους, ξύλα, χόρτον, καλάμην, ἑκάστου τὸ ἔργον φανερὸν γενήσεται.

The emphasis on ὁ μέντοι στερεὸς θεμέλιος and the enumeration of materials χρυσᾶ . . . . ἀργυρᾶ . . . . ξύλινα . . . . ὀστράκινα probably reflect the influence of I Corinthians.

         II Tim. 4:6   Philippians A
ʼΕγὼ γὰρ ἤδη σπένδομαι, καὶ ὁ καιρὸς τῆς ἀναλύσεώς μου
ἐφέστηκεν.
         Phil. 2:17. ʼΑλλὰ εἰ καὶ σπένδομαι ἐπὶ τῇ θυσίᾳ καὶ λει-
τουργίᾳ τῆς πίστεως ὑμῶν. . . . . 1:23. Τὴν ἐπιθυμίαν ἔχων εἰς
τὸ ἀναλῦσαι καὶ σὺν Χριστῷ εἶναι, πολλῷ γὰρ μᾶλλον κρεῖσσον.

Σπένδομαι occurs in the New Testament only in Phil. 2:17
and II Tim. 4:6. ʼΑνάλυσις is found only in II Tim. 4:6, and ἀνα-
λύω only in Luke 12:36 and Phil. 1:23. The connection in which
these terms are used in II Timothy makes it a matter of practical
certainty that the author of the Pastorals knew Philippians.

         II Tim. 4:7, 8   Philippians C
Τὸν καλὸν ἀγῶνα ἠγώνισμαι, τὸν δρόμον τετέλεκα, τὴν πίστιν
τετήρηκα· λοιπὸν ἀπόκειταί μοι ὁ τῆς δικαιοσύνης στέφανος, ὃν
ἀποδώσει μοι ὁ κύριος ἐν ἐκείνῃ τῇ ἡμέρᾳ.
         Phil. 1:30. Τὸν αὐτὸν ἀγῶνα ἔχοντες οἷον εἴδετε ἐν ἐμοὶ
καὶ νῦν ἀκούετε ἐν ἐμοί. . . . . 3:12-14. Οὐχ ὅτι ἤδη ἔλαβον ἢ
ἤδη τετελείωμαι, διώκω δὲ εἰ καὶ καταλάβω, ἐφ᾽ ᾧ καὶ κατελήμφθην
ὑπὸ Χριστοῦ [ʼΙησοῦ]. ἀδελφοί, ἐγὼ ἐμαυτὸν ⌈οὔπω⌉ λογίζομαι κατει-
ληφέναι· ἓν δὲ, τὰ μὲν ὀπίσω ἐπιλανθανόμενος τοῖς δὲ ἔμπροσθεν ἐπεκτεινόμενος, κατὰ σκοπὸν διώκω εἰς τὸ βραβεῖον τῆς ἄνω κλήσεως τοῦ
Θεοῦ ἐν Χριστῷ ʼΙησοῦ.

Paul several times describes his Christian task as a fight
or a race (I Cor. 9:24-27, Gal. 2:2), and he expects to receive a
"wreath" as his reward (I Thess. 2:19, I Cor. 9:25). The clear
acquaintance with Philippians that is reflected in 4:6 and the
marked resemblance of thought and figure that is disclosed make
dependence on Philippians probable.

II Tim. 4:9, 11   Colossians B   Philemon B

Δημᾶς γὰρ με ⌈ἐγκατέλειπεν⌉ . . . . Λουκᾶς ἐστὶν μόνος μετ

ἐμοῦ· Μάρκον ἀναλαβὼν ἄγε μετὰ σεαυτοῦ.

Col. 4:14. Ἀσπάζεται ὑμᾶς Λουκᾶς ὁ ἰατρὸς ὁ ἀγαπητὸς καὶ

Δημᾶς.

Philem. 24. Ἀσπάζεταί σε . . . . Μάρκος, Δημᾶς, Λουκᾶς,

οἱ συνεργοί μου.

This mention of Demas, Luke, and Mark very probably represents the effort of the author of the Pastorals to create an atmosphere of reality.

II Tim. 4:12   Ephesians B   Colossians B

Τύχικον δὲ ἀπέστειλα εἰς Ἔφεσον.

Eph. 6:21, 22. Ἵνα δὲ ⌈εἰδῆτε καὶ ὑμεῖς⌉ τὰ κατ' ἐμέ, τί πράσσω, πάντα γνωρίσει ὑμῖν Τύχικος ὁ ἀγαπητὸς ἀδελφὸς καὶ πιστὸς διάκονος ἐν κυρίῳ, ὃν ἔπεμψα πρὸς ὑμᾶς.

Col. 4:7, 8. Τὰ κατ' ἐμὲ πάντα γνωρίσει ὑμῖν Τύχικος ὁ ἀγαπητὸς ἀδελφὸς καὶ πιστὸς διάκονος καὶ σύνδουλος ἐν κυρίῳ, ὃν ἔπεμψα πρὸς ὑμᾶς.

In Colossians and Ephesians Paul is represented as having sent Tychicus to the recipients of those letters. The author of the Pastorals very probably knew both letters. His specification of Ephesus as the destination of Tychicus may mean that he knew our Ephesians under that title. Moffatt suggests the possibility of Ephesians having received its title as the result of "an editorial combination of 6:21 and II Tim. 4:12."[14]

II Tim. 4:13   II Corinthians C

Τὸν φελόνην, ὃν ⌈ἀπέλειπον⌉ ἐν Τρῳάδι . . . . ἐρχόμενος

φέρε.

II Cor. 2:12, 13. Ἐλθὼν δὲ εἰς τὴν Τρῳάδα . . . . οὐκ ἔσχηκα ἄνεσιν τῷ πνεύματί μου τῷ μὴ εὑρεῖν με Τίτον τὸν ἀδελφόν μου.

Timothy was presumably with Paul on the occasion of the stop at Troas mentioned in II Cor. 2:12, 13. He figured rather

---

[14]James Moffatt, An Introduction to the Literature of the New Testament (New York: Charles Scribner's Sons, 1920), p. 394.

prominently in the Corinthian correspondence (cf. I Cor. 4:17, 16: 10, and II Cor. 1:1, 19).

II Tim. 4:17   Romans C

῍Ινα δι' ἐμοῦ τὸ κήρυγμα πληροφορηθῇ καὶ ἀκούσωσιν πάντα τὰ ἔθνη.

Rom. 10:14. Πῶς οὖν ἐπικαλέσωνται εἰς ὃν οὐκ ἐπίστευσαν; πῶς δὲ πιστεύσωσιν οὗ οὐκ ἤκουσαν; πῶς δὲ ἀκούσωσιν χωρὶς κηρύσσοντος; 16:25. Κατὰ τὸ εὐαγγέλιόν μου καὶ τὸ κήρυγμα ᾿Ιησοῦ Χριστοῦ. 1:5. Δι' οὗ ἐλάβομεν χάριν καὶ ἀποστολὴν εἰς ὑπακοὴν πίστεως ἐν πᾶσιν τοῖς ἔθνεσιν ὑπὲρ τοῦ ὀνόματος αὐτοῦ.

Paul's assertion of his commission "to urge obedience and faith upon all the heathen" probably influenced the representation in II Tim. 4:17.

Titus 1:1   Romans C

Παῦλος δοῦλος Θεοῦ, ἀπόστολος δὲ ᾿Ιησοῦ Χριστοῦ.

Rom. 1:1. Παῦλος δοῦλος ⌐᾿Ιησοῦ Χριστοῦ⌐, κλητὸς ἀπόστολος (cf. Phil. 1:1, δοῦλοι Χριστοῦ ᾿Ιησοῦ).

Titus 1:4   Philippians C

Τίτῳ γνησίῳ τέκνῳ.

For this use of γνήσιος and its possible reflection of the influence of Phil. 4:3 see the note on I Tim. 1:1. Titus figures prominently in Galatians and II Corinthians, but except for these letters he is mentioned in the New Testament only in II Tim. 4:10 and Titus 1:4 (cf. Acts 18:7).

Titus 3:12   Ephesians B   Colossians B

῍Οταν πέμψω ᾿Αρτεμᾶν πρὸς σὲ ἢ Τύχικον.

Eph. 6:22 and Col. 4:8. Τύχικος . . . . ὃν ἔπεμψα πρὸς ὑμᾶς.

See the note on II Tim. 4:12.

<u>Instances of possible literary reminiscence.</u>—I Tim. 1:1; cf. I Cor. 9:16. ᾿Επιταγή is used in the New Testament only in Paul's letters and the Pastorals. The phrase κατ' ἐπιταγήν is used in I Cor. 7:6 and II Cor. 8:8. In Rom. 16:26 there is the expanded phrase κατ' ἐπιταγὴν τοῦ αἰωνίου Θεοῦ. The thought expressed in

I Timothy is in accord with Paul's idea of his mission and is the
equivalent of what he says of himself in I Cor. 9:16, ἐὰν γὰρ
εὐαγγελίζωμαι, οὐκ ἔστιν μοι καύχημα, ἀνάγκη γάρ μοι ἐπίκειται·
In the Pauline letters σωτήρ is applied only to Christ
(see Phil. 3:20 and Eph. 5:23), but in I Cor. 1:21 the conception
of I Timothy is implicit in εὐδόκησεν ὁ Θεὸς . . . . σῶσαι τοὺς
πιστεύοντας.

I Tim. 1:5; cf. Rom. 6:22 and II Cor. 6:7. ᾿Ανυπόκριτος
is used in the New Testament in Rom. 12:9, II Cor. 6:6, Jas. 3:17,
I Pet. 1:22, I Tim. 1:5, and II Tim. 1:5. In I Timothy it is used
with πίστις, but in a series where ἀγάπη is described as τὸ τέλος.

I Tim. 1:11; cf. II Cor. 4:4.

I Tim. 1:12, 13; cf. I Cor. 7:25 and Gal. 1:23. The use
πιστός in I Timothy reminds one strongly of its use in I Cor. 7:
25. This together with the mention of Paul as a persecutor of the
church and of God's mercy toward him suggests dependence on I
Corinthians. The τὸ πρότερον ὄντα . . . . διώκτην is a possible
reminiscence of ὁ διώκων ἡμᾶς ποτέ in Gal. 1:23. The case for
specific literary dependence in each of the possibilities is not
strong. The statement in I Timothy may merely reflect a general
acquaintance with Paul's letters and with the accounts of his
career as a persecutor in Acts.

I Tim. 1:14; cf. II Cor. 4:15 and Rom. 5:20. Πλεονάζω occurs in the New Testament only in the Pauline letters and II Peter.
῾Υπερπλεονάζω is found only in I Tim. 1:14. The type of thought
and expression is thoroughly Pauline.

I Tim. 1:15; cf. Rom. 5:8. The phrase πιστὸς ὁ λόγος occurs in the Pastorals five times: I Tim. 1:15, 3:1, 4:9; II Tim.
2:11; and Titus 3:8 (cf. Apoc. 21:5). It has all the marks of a
formula of citation, and yet it is never possible to be certain
of a specific literary allusion. It may represent a reference to
paranetic tradition, or it may be a device of the writer for asserting his own position as though it were a familiar truth. Conscious allusion to some such written source as Rom. 5:8 is not ex-
cluded, however.

I Tim. 1:15, 16; cf. Eph. 3:2 and I Cor. 15:9. I Tim. 1:
15, 16 is most interesting as indicating the high estimate which
the author of the Pastorals has of Paul: his experience is the

ὑποτύπωσις τῶν μελλόντων πιστεύειν. This opinion of Paul is similar to that held by the author of Ephesians, who felt that Paul
was pre-eminently qualified to interpret the gospel. Paul himself, while humbly saying χάριτι δὲ Θεοῦ εἰμὶ ὅ εἰμι, does not
hesitate to continue (I Cor. 15:10), ἀλλὰ περισσότερον αυτῶν
πάντων ἐκοπίασα. In connection with this assertion of Paul's
greatness in I Corinthians and Ephesians, he is called ἐλάχιστος,
and this very probably is the suggestion of the similar statement
in I Timothy (cf. Barn. 5:9).

I Tim. 1:18, 19; cf. II Cor. 10:3, 4 and Eph. 6:10-18.
The figure of the soldier is most fully developed in the New Testament in Eph. 6:10-18. It is a popular figure in the Pauline
letters (cf. I Thess. 5:8, Rom. 13:12, Phil. 2:25, I Cor. 9:7, II
Cor. 10:3, 4). The noun στρατεία occurs in the New Testament only
in II Cor. 10:4 and I Tim. 1:18, and στρατεύομαι in Luke 3:14, I
Cor. 9:7, II Cor. 10:3, I Tim. 1:18, II Tim. 2:4, Jas. 4:1, and I
Pet. 2:11. The language of I Timothy is closest to that of II Cor.
10:3, 4, and in both instances opponents in the form of rival leaders are being combated. In ἔχων πίστιν καὶ ἀγαθὴν συνείδησιν there
may be a trace of the influence of the description of the Christian
warrior's armor in Eph. 6:10-18.

I Tim. 2:1; cf. Phil. 1:3, 4.

I Tim. 2:2; cf. Rom. 13:1-7. If the author of I Timothy
had a Pauline position in mind as the sanction for his attitude
toward Roman authorities, he would naturally be following Rom. 13:
1-7. Paul does not urge prayer for rulers, but his general attitude would approve it as desirable.

I Tim. 2:5; cf. Phil. 2:7.

I Tim. 2:6; cf. Gal. 6:9.

I Tim. 2:8; cf. Eph. 6:18.

I Tim. 2:8; cf. Phil. 2:14.

I Tim. 3:7; cf. Col. 4:5 and I Thess. 4:12. Οἱ ἔξω is used
of non-Christians several times in the New Testament. Only in I
Thess. 4:12, Col. 4:5, and I Tim. 3:7 are Christians exhorted to
determine their conduct with reference to the opinion of οἱ ἔξω.

I Tim. 3:7; cf. Rom. 15:3. Ὀνειδισμός and παγίς both occur in Romans in quotations from Ps. 69. The one occurs elsewhere
in the New Testament in Hebrews and I Timothy, and the other in
Luke and I and II Timothy.

I Tim. 3:8; cf. Phil. 4:8. Σεμνός is used in the New Testament in Phil. 4:8; I Tim. 3:8, 11; and Titus 2:2. It appears ten times in the LXX.

I Tim. 3:8; cf. Eph. 5:18 and Rom. 14:21. Only in Romans and Ephesians of the Pauline corpus is οἶνος mentioned at all. In Romans the advice against its use is given in view of the obligations of fraternity. The exhortations in Ephesians and I Timothy resemble each other in their negative character and in their counsel against excess.

I Tim. 3:13; cf. II Cor. 3:12.

I Tim. 3:15; cf. Eph. 2:19-22. The figure under which the church is described suggests acquaintance with the description in Ephesians.

I Tim. 3:16; cf. Eph. 5:32. In I Tim. 3:15 the theme was ἡ ἐκκλησία Θεοῦ ζῶντος.

I Tim. 4:3; cf. I Cor. 7:1. Paul advises against, but does not forbid, marriage. The author of I Timothy may be contrasting the mandatory position of heretics with the milder position assumed by Paul.

I Tim. 4:8; cf. I Cor. 9:26, 27. The thought of I Timothy is similar to that of I Corinthians and may have been suggested by the Pauline position. The language and ideas would be as familiar from Stoic teaching, however (cf. Epictetus ii. 18. 27; iii. 3. 14).

I Tim. 4:10; cf. Col. 1:29. The occurrence of κοπιάω and ἀγωνίζομαι in Col. 1:29, together with the emphasis on redemption, suggests the possibility of acquaintance with Colossians on the part of I Timothy.

I Tim. 4:12; cf. I Thess. 1:7.

I Tim. 4:15; cf. Phil. 1:12. Προκοπή occurs in the New Testament only in Phil. 1:12, 25 and I Tim. 4:15.

I Tim. 4:16; cf. Rom. 11:14. Αὐτοῖς in verse 16 refers to ταῦτα and τούτοις, so that it is the equivalent of τὴν διακονίαν of Romans.

I Tim. 5:1; cf. I Thess. 2:12.

I Tim. 5:5; cf. II Cor. 1:10.

I Tim. 5:10; cf. Rom. 12:12, 13.

I Tim. 5:11; cf. Col. 1:10.

I Tim. 5:20; cf. Gal. 2:14. Paul administers a rebuke to

Peter ἔμπροσθεν πάντων, and this may have suggested the procedure advised in I Timothy.

I Tim. 6:6; cf. Phil. 4:11. Αὐτάκεια occurs in the New Testament in II Corinthians and I Timothy. Αὐτάρκης occurs only in Phil. 4:11. The thought of I Timothy and Philippians is more nearly the same than is that of I Timothy and II Corinthians. The saying in I Timothy has more of a Stoic than of a Pauline tone, however.

I Tim. 6:9; cf. Rom. 11:9.

I Tim. 6:10; cf. II Thess. 1:9. ῞Ολεθρος occurs in the New Testament in I Cor. 5:5, I Thess. 5:3, II Thess. 1:9, and I Tim. 6:9. The clearly eschatological connotation of the term in II Thessalonians and I Timothy suggests the possibility of literary dependence.

I Tim. 6:11; cf. Rom. 9:20. Δικαιοσύνη is made the object of διώκω in Rom. 9:30, I Tim. 6:11, and II Tim. 2:22.

I Tim. 6:12; cf. Col. 3:15.

II Tim. 1:2; cf. Gal. 3:21. ᾽Επαγγελία occurs in the New Testament in Luke-Acts, the Pauline letters, the Pastorals, Hebrews, II Peter, and I John. Its most frequent use is in the Pauline letters. The phrase κατ᾽ ἐπαγγελίαν occurs only in II Tim. 1:2 and Gal. 3:21, 29.

II Tim. 1:6; cf. Rom. 8:38. The form of πείθω used in II Tim. 1:6 appears in the New Testament only in Romans and II Timothy. It is found in Rom. 8:38, 14:14, and 15:14.

II Tim. 1:12; cf. II Thess. 1:10.

II Tim. 1:13; cf. Phil. 4:9.

II Tim. 1:13; cf. Rom. 8:39.

II Tim. 2:1; cf. Phil. 4:13. ᾽Ενδυναμόω is used in the New Testament in Acts 9:22, Rom. 4:20, Eph. 6:10, Phil. 4:13, I Tim. 1:12, and II Tim. 2:1 and 4:17.

II Tim. 2:2; cf. Phil. 4:9.

II Tim. 2:3; cf. Eph. 6:10-20.

II Tim. 2:11-13; cf. Rom. 6:8. II Tim. 2:11-13 is almost certainly a stanza from an early Christian hymn. Its language and ideas are Pauline, and the first verse of the stanza is almost verbally from Rom. 6:8. It is difficult to ascribe direct literary dependence on Romans, however, because the hymn seems to have

existed as a part of the general heritage of the author of the
Pastorals (cf. Polyc. 5:2).

II Tim. 2:14; cf. Rom. 1:21, 24.

II Tim. 2:15; cf. Rom. 6:13.

II Tim. 2:15; cf. Eph. 1:13.

II Tim. 2:21; cf. Rom. 9:21.

II Tim. 3:8; cf. Rom. 1:28. The use of ἀδόκιμος in Romans
furnishes the closest parallel for that of II Timothy that is
found in the New Testament. The use of the word is restricted in
the New Testament to the Pauline letters, the Pastorals, and Hebrews.

II Tim. 3:11; cf. II Cor. 11:23-28. The identification of
persecutions experienced by Paul with cities mentioned in Acts,
chapters 13 and 14, clearly indicates an acquaintance with the
Acts accounts of Paul's Galatian ministry. The classical description of Paul's sufferings, however, is found in II Corinthians.

II Tim. 3:12; cf. I Thess. 3:4.

II Tim. 3:16; cf. Rom. 15:4.

II Tim. 4:11; cf. Philem. 11. Εὔχρηστος is found in the
New Testament only in Philem. 11 and II Tim. 2:21, 4:11.

II Tim. 4:14; cf. Rom. 2:6. II Timothy agrees with Romans
in the use of the third person of ἀποδίδωμι. Furthermore, the ma-
jority of Old Testament allusions in the Pastorals are to passages
that are also used in the Pauline letters.

II Tim. 4:18; cf. II Cor. 1:10.

II Tim. 4:19, 20; cf. Rom. 16:3 and I Cor. 16:19. Prisca
and Aquilla are mentioned in Acts 18:2, 18, 26; Rom. 16:3; I Cor.
16:19; and II Tim. 4:19. Erastus is mentioned in Acts 19:22, Rom.
16:23, and II Tim. 4:21. There is the strong probability that the
inclusion of these names among those to whom and from whom greetings are sent in Romans and I Corinthians caused their inclusion
in the closing verses of II Timothy.

II Tim. 4:22; cf. Col. 4:18. These are the only instances
of this brief benediction in the close of New Testament letters.

Titus 1:1; cf. Rom. 8:33. The phrase κατὰ ἐκλεκτῶν Θεοῦ
occurs only in these two instances in the New Testament.

Titus 1:3; cf. Gal. 2:7.

Titus 1:7; cf. I Cor. 4:1.

Titus 1:15; cf. Rom. 14:14.

Titus 2:3; cf. I Thess. 1:3.

Titus 2:14; cf. Eph. 2:10.

Titus 3:3-5; cf. Eph. 2:3-7. The contrast between the former and the redeemed state of Christians in Titus may have been suggested by the similar contrast in Ephesians.

Titus 3:6; cf. Rom. 12:2 and II Cor. 4:16. 'Ανακαίνωσις occurs in the New Testament only in Rom. 12:2 and Titus 3:6. 'Ανακαινόω occurs in II Cor. 4:16 and Col. 3:10.

Titus 3:7; cf. Rom. 3:24.

Titus 3:15; cf. Col. 4:18. See the note on II Tim. 4:22. The benediction of Titus differs from that of II Timothy and Colossians in the addition of πάντων.

The indications of this study are that the author of the Pastorals was acquainted with Paul's letters as a collection and that he knew each of the ten letters that seem to have constituted the corpus. Of the three letters, II Timothy is the fullest of reminiscences, but acquaintance with the older letter collection is evident in I Timothy and Titus. There are no direct and formal quotations from Paul's letters, but the language and ideas of Paul's authentic writings are unmistakably used in many instances.

TABLE OF RESULTS

	A	B	C	Unclassed
Romans..............	6	3	4	26
I Corinthians.......	2	4	6	9
II Corinthians......	.	3	3	9
Galatians...........	.	.	3	6
Ephesians...........	.	4	3	10
Philippians.........	2	1	3	10
Colossians..........	.	4	3	7
I Thessalonians.....	.	.	1	6
II Thessalonians....	.	1	3	2
Philemon............	.	1	1	1